Language and Identity

An Introduction

JOHN EDWARDS

CAMBRIDGE
UNIVERSITY PRESS

CAMBRIDGE UNIVERSITY PRESS
Cambridge, New York, Melbourne, Madrid, Cape Town, Singapore, São Paulo,
Delhi, Tokyo, Mexico City

Cambridge University Press
The Edinburgh Building, Cambridge CB2 8RU, UK

Published in the United States of America by Cambridge University Press, New York

www.cambridge.org
Information on this title: www.cambridge.org/9780521696029

First published 2009
Reprinted 2011

Printed at MPG Books Group, UK

A catalogue record for this publication is available from the British Library

Library of Congress Cataloguing in Publication data
Edwards, John, 1947 Dec. 3–
Language and identity / by John Edwards.
    p. cm.
Includes bibliographical references and index.
ISBN 978-0-521-87381-9 (hardback)
1. Sociolinguistics.   2. Group identity.   3. Language and languages – Political aspects.
4. Identity politics.   5. Nationalism.   I. Title.
P40.5.G76E39   2009
306.44 – dc22   2009022581

ISBN 978-0-521-87381-9 Hardback
ISBN 978-0-521-69602-9 Paperback

To Suzanne

Contents

1 Introduction *1*
1.1 An introductory note *1*
1.2 Chapters and topics *2*
1.3 A concluding note *13*

2 Identity, the individual and the group *15*
2.1 Introduction *15*
2.2 Identity: personal and social *19*
2.3 The construction and maintenance of groupness *25*
2.4 Language and circumstance *27*

3 Identifying ourselves *34*
3.1 Personal names *34*
3.2 Names for groups *36*
3.3 The appropriation of names and narratives *39*
3.4 Cultural voices and scholarly research *42*
3.5 Ethnocentrism and relativism *48*

4 Language, dialect and identity *53*
4.1 Language *53*
4.2 Dialect *63*

5 Dialect and identity: beyond standard and nonstandard *73*
5.1 The 'logic' of dialect *73*
5.2 Ebonics *75*
5.3 Further work on dialect evaluation *82*

6 Language, religion and identity *99*
6.1 Introduction *99*
6.2 Linking language and religion *100*
6.3 God's language – and ours *103*
6.4 Modern times *110*
6.5 Missionaries *118*

7 Language, gender and identity *126*
7.1 Introduction *126*
7.2 Stereotyping sex and gender *127*
7.3 Gender variations in speech *132*
7.4 Concluding remarks *146*

8 Ethnicity and nationalism   *151*
   8.1 Introduction   *151*
   8.2 Ethnic identity   *153*
   8.3 Nationalism   *162*

9 Assessments of nationalism   *175*
   9.1 Civic nationalism   *175*
   9.2 Evaluating nationalism   *185*

10 Language and nationalism   *205*
    10.1 The basic link   *205*
    10.2 Language purism and prescriptivism   *212*

11 Language planning and language ecology   *225*
    11.1 Language planning   *225*
    11.2 The ecology of language   *230*
    11.3 The consequences of Babel   *245*
    11.4 Bilingualism and identity   *247*

    Glossary   *257*
    Notes   *261*
    References   *271*
    Index   *310*

1 Introduction

1.1 AN INTRODUCTORY NOTE

In an earlier book in this series, Spolsky (2004) began by observing that studies of the social life of language are often too 'language-centred'. Any investigation of language that considers only language will be deficient, and inappropriate limitations and restrictions can cripple insights. This is not a problem for this area alone, of course, but it is especially significant in a context where the hope of application fuels much of the effort. Nonetheless, any cursory examination of, say, the language-planning literature or work in the social psychology of language will quickly reveal an undesirable narrowness of perspective. Studies of 'endangered languages' and 'language revival' seem particularly prone to tunnel vision, to the curious notion that these phenomena can be understood and then ameliorated in more or less isolated fashion. Except in the conceits of 'pure' linguistics, no analysis of language can rationally proceed from a 'stand-alone' perspective. Spolsky writes that

> while many scholars are now beginning to recognize the interaction of economic and political and other factors with language, it is easy and tempting to ignore them when we concentrate on language matters. (pp ix–x)

In fact, while one still reads too many disembodied, decontextualised and, therefore, essentially useless studies, the observation here is not quite accurate. For some writers – more nowadays than in the past, I would guess – 'temptation' is not an apt term at all, for the simple reason that a more extensive purview seems simply beyond them. For most of those who do have a sense of the disembodied nature of much of the work, the temptation is of course powerful. It is often reinforced by the intertwined influence of career imperatives of the 'publish or perish' sort, and of the relative ease of committing incomplete theses to print. The best scholarship has *always* paid attention to the bigger social picture, however, and has always resisted the temptation to narrowness.

1

In this book, as in previous work, I have tried to present something of the bigger picture of which language is an important but not unique element. I have tried to make my points and draw my illustrations from what seem the most interesting and compelling settings, and I have not hesitated to stray from the most well-trodden pathways in the sociology of language. The incentive here derives, in part, from Spolsky's cautionary note, but also from the particular thematic thread that underpins all the specific points that I touch upon in this book. The intent throughout is to illustrate the connections between language and identity, and this implies a stronger focus upon the symbolic and 'marking' functions of language than upon the communicative ones. This, in turn, necessitates attention to the social and political settings without which that symbolism, that group 'marking', would be empty. So, in this case at least, contextualisation is not something whose absence would merely be regrettable; rather, its absence would vitiate the whole enterprise.

1.2 CHAPTERS AND TOPICS

Chapter 2 presents a brief discussion of the way in which 'identity' has become a very popular topic; indeed, the currency here has become considerably cheapened. Fashion aside, however, it is clear that identity is at the heart of the person, and the group, and the connective tissue that links them. People need psychosocial 'anchors': it is as simple as that. It is also clear that identities very rarely exist singly: on the contrary, we all possess a number of identities – or facets of one overarching identity, if you prefer – the salience of which can be expected to wax and wane according to circumstance and context. While my emphasis in this book is upon the identity markers and attributes of 'groupness', I begin by arguing that personal and group identities embrace one another. The elements of individual identity are not unique but, rather, are drawn from some common social pool; there is uniqueness at the level of personality, to be sure, but it comes about through the particular combinations and weightings of those broadly shared elements. On the other hand, the social store in which these elements are found is an assembly of personalities. Limitations of time and space prevent further discussion here – of, for instance, the very old notion that the assembly is more than the collection of individuals, that the societal whole is greater than the sum of the personal parts, that there is a sort of *Gestalt* that summarises but goes beyond specific components. This speculation has fuelled discussions of 'crowd psychology', from the Greek golden age, to the reactionary impulses of nineteenth-century commentators worried about revolutionary upheavals in the wake of *Quatre-vingt-neuf*, to contemporary social-psychological investigations.

The second chapter further sets the scene by noting some restrictions on the sort of groups that will receive the greatest attention here: those that, if not always completely involuntary in nature, are of the broadest general significance. More attention, then, to ethnic, national, religious and gender affiliations, and rather less to the linguistic facets of membership in voluntary organisations. It is important to realise from the outset, however, that what appear immutable memberships to some may seem more 'constructed' or 'contingent' to others; equally, some memberships that are more self-consciously or voluntarily acquired may involve linguistic features of great depth and importance. This chapter also illustrates the ease with which groups can be created, how their existence can readily spawn 'in-group' allegiance and solidarity, and how manipulation becomes all too possible. Finally, there is some discussion of the depths and dynamics of language repertoires; the general intent is to show how the multiplicity of identities, or facets of identity, is matched by a range of speech styles and behaviour. It is not only bilinguals who have more than one variety at their disposal: if we are not all bi- or multilingual, many are at least bi- or multi-dialectal – and all of us are bi- or multi-stylistic.

In chapter 3, I turn to naming practices and some of their ramifications. This is not a topic commonly covered in books about the language-and-identity linkage, but the discussion clearly reveals the centrality of names and group labels to the relationship. Names influence our perceptions of others, these perceptions then enter the psychosocial contexts in which we all find ourselves, and these contexts contribute to, and frame, both personal and group identities. Furthermore, the choice of names by which we call ourselves can influence those same contexts. In fact, the socially circular reactions of which names are a part constitute a specific example of Herman's (1961) general observation that language influences our perceptions of the setting, and the setting influences our choice of language. Names are important, as are the 'naming narratives' by which we describe ourselves. Consequently, the misuse or the appropriation of names and stories can be both an insult and an attack on identity. At the same time, an extension of the 'voice appropriation' thesis that has appealed in some quarters – that only like should speak or write about like – leads to some immediate problems. I conclude this part of the discussion by showing how 'popular' treatments of group voice and social description are not unrelated to on-going scholarly debate about dispassionate observation versus committed activism, of sensitivity versus objectivity, and so on. When real identities and real languages are 'at risk', what is the appropriate intellectual posture?

Chapter 3 concludes with a discussion of ethnocentrism and relativism, matters of which naming and 'voice' are elements. Ethnocentrism is surely bad, and the relativism that has acted as a corrective is surely good. And not only good, but often more accurate. How, after all, are we to judge societies as better or worse than one another? What celestial yardstick exists here? And yet, as eminent scholars have argued, a thoroughgoing relativism can lead us into unpleasant cultural byways. Are we seriously to believe, asked Gellner (1968), that a belief in witchcraft is simply an alternative to scientific understandings? Isn't it the case that, given specific matters to consider, we draw non-relativistic conclusions all the time: that, for instance, modern-day Burma is inferior to Denmark in terms of the freedom it allows its citizens? And aren't we right to do so? Gellner also reminds us that societies themselves constantly engage in self-evaluations that involve judgements, not only with other societies, but with themselves at earlier times, times now thankfully in the past. These are deep waters, to be sure, and my conclusion is, simply, that cultural relativism is itself relative. That is, it applies to some things but not to others. A society that believes in witches and practises cannibalism is, I think, worse than one that does not; a society that *used* to believe in witches but no longer does is better than it once was – but why should I also feel obliged to accept that the language of those who eat their enemies is inferior to that spoken by their neighbours, who always turn the other cheek? It is quite possible to argue that, in at least some of their social practices, groups are better or worse than others. It is not possible, as we shall see, to argue that some languages are better or worse than others.

In chapters 2 and 3, then, the discussion is largely concerned with drawing out some of the connections between individual and group identities, considering language and identity at rudimentary levels, pointing out that the general thrust of the book will concentrate more upon the group than the individual and – in the brief notes on relativism – opening the door to the possibility that some aspects of some identities might reasonably be submitted to judgement. In chapter 4, I move more specifically to a discussion of the chief components in this treatment of 'groupness'. My initial emphasis here is upon the distinction between the communicative and symbolic aspects of language. While these generally co-exist in 'mainstream', or majority-group, cultures, they are in fact separable: a language that has lost most or all of its communicative value because of language shift can nevertheless retain something of its symbolic value for a long time. Whether the two facets are joined or not, it is the symbolic charge that language carries that makes it such an important component in individual and group identity. I also pay some attention in this chapter to questions of the relative 'goodness' of languages, and to the related matters of linguistic 'decay' or 'impurity'. *All* languages, it is argued, constitute valid and adequate systems for the needs of their speakers; if these needs change, then languages are more or less infinitely adaptable. But change is not 'decay' and the existence of notions of 'deteriorating' or 'debased' varieties says more about the symbolic and psychological weight with which languages are laden than about communicative loss or lapse.

This fourth chapter also considers dialect, and it is shown that the usual criterion by which dialects are distinguished from languages – that the former are mutually intelligible variants of the latter – is not without its problems. In fact, social and political considerations are important here, reinforcing the aptness of Max Weinreich's famous aphorism that 'a language is a dialect that has an army and navy'. The single most important point of the discussion, however, is that dialects, like languages, cannot be seen in terms of 'better' or 'worse': all dialects are fully formed linguistic vehicles. But the social considerations that intervene at the boundaries of dialect and language have their analogues among dialects too. It is one thing to demonstrate that, on linguistic or aesthetic grounds, no dialect can be seen as superior to another; it would be quite another to expect such a demonstration to have much impact on the street. The power of social convention, attitude and prejudice regularly translates difference into deficiency. Dialect varieties that are simply variants of one another in scholarly eyes – whose description as 'nonstandard' is a non-pejorative acknowledgement of the historical forces that have elevated one section of society and, therefore, its ways of speaking – are popularly viewed as 'substandard', a word that does not exist in the linguist's lexicon. It is completely predictable, then, that those at the top of the social heap are heard to speak most 'correctly'.

It is important to realise that the power of perception creates its own reality, and that dialects broadly viewed as inferior *are*, for all practical intents and purposes, inferior. This is an insight not lost upon those who have found themselves the recipients of unfavourable or prejudicial assessments, and it accounts for a number of possible actions. These can include attempts to alter one's dialect or, conversely, to adjust one's sense of it. The first is obvious: many people throughout history have, with greater or lesser success, moved away from their maternal varieties. The second involves, most notably, reworked evaluations of group pride or self-esteem, evaluations that are typically put in train by changing social circumstances and possibilities. Such reworkings will inevitably include dialect re-assessment: speech forms that were once, largely on the basis of external perceptions, seen as inferior approximations to 'correct' usage may now become the flags of renewed group solidarity. Their speakers may even exaggerate previously scorned features in this process, and the dialect may become attractive to majority 'out-group' members. All of this is clearly relevant for considerations of identity. Regardless, however, of the evaluations – positive, negative, transitional – made by speakers of their own dialect, that variety can always act as a carrier and a portrait of solidarity and belonging. It may be thought of as debased, or incorrect, or slovenly, or vulgar, but it still links people to their group.

The next chapter moves beyond assertions of the basic 'goodness' or 'badness' of dialect varieties, assertions arising reasonably enough by analogy with languages, to consider some of the important evidence bearing upon the matter. The work of William Labov on American Black English is of pivotal significance here, and I follow a discussion of it with an extended treatment of the continuing perceptions of that speech variety, particularly under the heading of 'Ebonics'. Once again, we are confronted with compelling evidence that links linguistic variation to perceptions of identity. Chapter 5 also shows that some further attention to dialect assessment, beyond standard and nonstandard, will flesh out the overall evaluative picture. This part of the discussion begins with the drawing of an important, but often overlooked, distinction between *attitude* and *belief*, particularly as this applies to investigations of dialect. The basic point here is simply that our understanding of respondents' views (of, say, dialect variants) is less comprehensive than it might – and should – be. The bulk of the coverage, however, deals with the social-psychological dimensions that underpin language and dialect evaluations, and with the ramifications of the observation that such evaluations are really about *speakers*; the linguistic samples that we present for assessment in experiments, as well as those that we encounter in ordinary life, are generally triggers for the production of much more inclusive attitudinal or stereotypical judgements.

Chapter 6 discusses the relationships among language, religion and identity. Although there is a reasonably extensive literature on 'religious language' *per se*, there is remarkably little on the interactions between the sociologies of language and religion – even though it is perfectly obvious that both are centrally intertwined in perceptions and postures of identity. As Bill Safran (2008) and others have pointed out, the relative importance of each has waxed and waned with history and circumstance, but neither has ever lost its potency. If discussion of these matters under sociolinguistic headings is rarer than one might like, considerations that take a broad chronological sweep are rarer still. That is why, in the section entitled 'God's language – and ours', I try to show how assertions of linguistic primacy, with all their implications for the possession and importance of group identities, can be traced to the earliest of times. This is supplemented by several contemporary examples of linkages made, and linkages hoped for, between language and 'groupness': here the focus is upon Gaelic and Hebrew.

One of the most fascinating, if often worrying, perspectives on the interaction between language and religion is provided by the work of missionaries. They have often engaged in various social, political, medical and other activities, but these would not exist in the absence of the religious motive. Missionary linguistic practices and perceptions also take shape within a closed system of belief. The other basic element in this picture is that of zeal: the effort and commitment involved in carrying some specific word of some specific god to the unfortunates whose religious choices have hitherto been restricted give a particular energy to all aspects of the enterprise. A sense that one is doing God's work typically galvanises all the ancillary undertakings, so that the missionary attitude towards native languages and cultures is similarly fired with a sense of rightness. Such single-mindedness can obviously create great difficulties for those whose cultures are invaded, especially when they are confronted with different religious interlopers. The zeal with which benighted populations are approached is exceeded only by the fierceness among rival missionaries in the great competition for souls.

Specifically linguistic postures are revealing here, and they have historically taken one of two forms. In some cases, missionaries have taught their own European varieties as a prelude to spreading the celestial word; in others, they have taught themselves local languages and dialects. The desire is the same in both cases, of course, and it is rarely accompanied by a thoroughgoing concern for language *per se*. Missionaries essentially had their own way for a long time, with few at home doubting either their beneficent intentions or the value of their proselytising efforts. But when scholars also moved into the field, when anthropologists and linguists began to formally interest themselves in native languages and cultures, clashes of interest immediately surfaced. In an increasingly secularised world, the religious workers were generally the ones forced to find defensive positions. The activities of the Summer Institute of Linguistics (SIL) – a Protestant missionary organisation – are highlighted here, simply because of the extremely broad scope of its operations in general, and its linguistic activities in particular. The latter have resulted in thousands of publications over the years, most of them resting upon research conducted by highly qualified linguists who are, at the same time, missionaries. A zeal for classification, not unlike the great Mormon genealogical project, has produced the *Ethnologue*, a regularly updated catalogue of the all the world's languages; and, just as non-believers can make use of the Mormon record-keeping that has been occasioned by the argument that the dead must be baptised 'by proxy', so even those who are vehemently opposed to missionaries and evangelism can accept the linguistic fruits of their enterprise. My description of the activities and impulses of the SIL is meant particularly to illuminate the effects of outside linguistic and cultural intervention on the lives, and perforce the identities, of native groups. I believe that the chief sustaining features of 'groupness' are exploited and manipulated for purposes quite alien to people who are both susceptible and vulnerable. This makes for a particularly sad volume in the story of language and identity.

In chapter 7, I present a brief discussion of a burgeoning and many-faceted area: the connections among gender, language and identity. The treatment begins with some general remarks about the persistence and influence of gender stereotypes generally, as a backdrop to some more focused attention on language. Why should there exist differences in the vocabulary items used by men and women in some cultures, and what might these differences tell us about wider social roles and expectations – having to do, for instance, with relative power and subordination, with the nexus of kinship, with sanction and taboo? Relatively recent work in western cultures has revealed that although gender variations may sometimes be more subtle than in other societies, and although they may be adhered to with less regularity or vigour, they too provide a window into gender-role variance. An overall interpretation of findings here suggests that some of the specifics of women's speech reflect a greater desire to 'facilitate' and support others, or to take the edge off assertions that, in the mouths of men, might be phrased more bluntly or directly. The much-discussed differences in polite usage, on the one hand, and swearing and profanity, on the other, are of course implicated in this broad interpretation. While it is all too easy to cast matters in unhelpful and inaccurate dichotomies, there seems little doubt that – as both scholarly and popular works have suggested – habitual differences can hinder effective communication between men and women. The words 'habitual' and 'hinder' are important here, however: these are not practices that are inevitable markers of one gender or another, or cast in stone, or of which speakers must always remain unaware; neither are they of sufficient depth or weight that communications of intent are fatally compromised. And, as is the case with many other settings within the social life of language, the linguistic and paralinguistic variants here are more correctly seen as reflections of underlying variabilities in dominance and social power than as entities having some free-standing or isolated influence.

Chapters 8, 9 and 10 turn to what must really be at the heart of any treatment of language and group identity: ethnonational solidarities. The underpinning of all the specific aspects of the discussion is that the subjective, intangible, non-rational and symbolic pillars of group affiliation are by far the strongest and most enduring. The contribution of particular and more observable markers – most prominently language and religion – can vary widely over time and place, and it is undoubtedly useful for allegiances to have such supports, but none is essential. What *is* essential for the continuation of a sense of groupness is the continuation of a sense of distinctiveness that allows perceptual boundaries to be maintained. As Fredrik Barth (1969) pointed out, the permanence of such borders is much more important than that of any cultural 'stuff' within them. Specific identity markers may come and go, but so long as there exist some affiliative features – objective, subjective or some combination of the two – the frontiers can be delineated. When all belief, of all types, of a boundary between my group and yours has evaporated, then there is only one group. But, as history repeatedly shows, it can take a very long time indeed for this evaporation to be complete.

Discussions of nationalism – and, particularly, of its emergence, its age and its constituents – have increased dramatically in recent years, a fact not unrelated to real-world developments. The interpretation that I defend in this book is that while nationalism as a political force is a more or less modern phenomenon, a cultural arrangement produced and reinforced by radical changes in the old social order, it is not a creation newly sprung from the forehead of political philosophy, not something made of entirely new cloth. On the contrary, it would be better, perhaps, to see it as a 're-arrangement' and amplification of existing elements. Nationalism takes up the ethnic fabric, cutting and trimming it to suit the circumstance, and adding to it the magic elixir of political autonomy. Every nationalist, then, believes that the borders of the *ethnie* – as some entirely natural division of humanity, and also as some sort of nation *in posse* – should coincide with those of the state. The most just arrangement, then, would be a world of nation-states, in the true sense of that term.

Apart from the arguments that swirl around the provenance and antiquity of the nation, considerations of the virtue of nationalism have proved perennially intriguing. Any form of 'groupness' whose most basic foundations are of the 'blood and belonging' variety is obviously one that carries a powerful emotional charge. This in turn can be expected to lead to contact and conflict with others. In fact, of course, if rationality were to be let off the leash here, even the fiercest of nationalists would acknowledge similar zeal on the other side of the frontier – and not merely acknowledge the potency of other national allegiances, but understand and respect them. Sauce for the goose, and all that. But perhaps it is too much to expect that solidarities erected, themselves, on emotion and subjectivity, would be capable of much sensitivity in this regard. History certainly reveals that a great deal of nationalist self-definition and identity maintenance is built upon the denigration of the 'other'. This is entangled with the very general psychological tendency to see individuality and personal variation within one's own group, but only some indistinguishable and monolithic entity across the frontier: a variant, indeed, of the classic 'us and them' formula.

But to see national allegiance resting entirely upon blinkered emotion would be mistaken. As many writers have demonstrated, and as I have already just hinted here, nationalism can be seen as an arrangement, or re-arrangement, arising on the shoulders of necessity. If another generally applicable principle of social existence is that people need affective psychosocial 'anchors', then it stands to reason that where older forms fall away, new ones must be found. Thus, as Gellner (1964) observed, national affiliations do not come about through sentimentality and myth; they emerge because they are required by the social context. It is possible, then, to see how sense and sensibility can come to intertwine as nationalisms emerge, develop and blossom into fully fledged systems. In any event, whatever we may think of the provenance and the value of nationalism, it is very clear that it is a phenomenon that, *pace* some ill-advised predictions, retains a great deal of power in many parts of the world. Indeed, it is possible to argue that nationalism is undergoing something of a resurgence, precisely in those areas where it had begun to weaken. The reasoning here is that large federal political units that tend to swamp earlier and more localised entities may breed, as a sort of reaction, a renewed and more regionally focussed sense of groupness. If a new European Union identity still remains a nebulous or even unappealing proposition, perhaps it will rejuvenate more traditional affiliations; perhaps a reworked and much larger political union can co-exist with much smaller ethnonational allegiances. These are some of the cultural and political matters that exercise the European mind.

Any investigation of contemporary manifestations reveals, too, that nationalists are not at all unaware of the dangers lurking in some unrestrained subjectivity, particularly of course where the power of emotional allegiance is coupled with real social, economic or military clout:

history, once again, shows how easy it can be for an essentially religious fervour on one side to lead to great tragedy on another. It is possible to find more 'enlightened' nationalists, who wish to engender and develop an in-group solidarity without trampling over the ground of others. It is also possible to find nationalists who remain essentially 'unreconstructed' but who are, nevertheless, susceptible to practical (or machiavellian) argument. And it is also possible to find those who think that nationalism itself can be reconstructed and reconstrued, retaining its obvious affiliative appeal while deleting the traditional ethnic exclusiveness. This reworking for a new, more sensitive and more 'inclusive' age is generally called 'civic nationalism'. My argument here involves both semantics and substance. On the one hand, it seems clear enough that what some would now style civic nationalism is really just patriotism renamed, citizenship under a different rubric. I try to show that the cosmopolitanism that often underlies the conception is not at all a new phenomenon; it was at least touched upon by the Greek philosophers, and it was given more specific attention from the dawn of the 'new science' in the seventeenth century.

The most interesting aspect of civic nationalism and, indeed, the very reason why it has emerged with some degree of popular appeal, is that it is supposed to represent the kinder, gentler face of nationalism. We find the rudiments in Kohn's classic (1944) distinction between a good (and western) nationalism – state-based, democratic and rational – and a much less desirable eastern variant that is culturally-based, totalitarian and irrational. In fact, these are more than the rudiments of the present incarnation; they are its continuingly defining principles. Civic nationalism is progressive, democratic and, above all, linked to the political unit of the state; the older form is unpleasantly exclusive and 'ethnic'. I conclude this part of the discussion with reference to some recent developments in *Québécois* nationalism that suggest the hollowness of the civic variety. Sensitive to public opinion and to the obvious historical dark sides of nationalism, provincial 'sovereigntists' claimed that their aims for an independent Quebec were firmly based on the conviction that *all* residents – whether or not they were francophone, whether or not they were of the *vieille souche*, the 'old stock' – were Quebeckers. When the sovereignty campaign failed to win the independence referendum of October 1995, however, the civic mask appeared to slip a little. Thus, Jacques Parizeau said, on referendum night, 'C'est vrai qu'on a été battu. Au fond, par quoi? Par l'argent puis des votes ethniques.'

In chapter 10, I attempt to weave language more specifically into the nationalist tapestry. The argument is essentially that the symbolism of language provides the most central rallying-point while, at the same time, its more ordinary communicative aspects permit a quick enumeration of in-group members. I also argue that it is entirely predictable, once language has been deemed *the* most central and most sacred girder of identity, that strenuous attempts will be made to assert its primacy, to differentiate it from other forms and to protect it. The most basic assertions of primacy are discussed earlier, in chapter 6, where we see the competing linguistic claims for Edenic originality, but it is clear that arguments of all sorts have continued to be made for the unique qualities of one language or another. German, Fichte told us (1807/1968), was superior to the other European varieties because it alone had remained unpenetrated by Latin invasion; French, de Rivarol (1784) famously pointed out, was the pre-eminent language of clarity and rationality. And so on. In this chapter, however, my discussions of linguistic 'purity' and prescriptivism centre upon the scholarly endeavours of academies, councils and individual lexicographers, all essentially charged with the task of ensuring that language remains unsullied and fit to serve as the proudest banner of group identity.

Finally, the discussion of language planning in chapter 11 expands upon the particularity of the purity-prescriptivism issue, to show how selecting and codifying languages, reinforcing and implementing them, and seeing that their development and elaboration keep pace with changing social requirements are all, once again, in the service of group identity. The main point to remember in discussions of these aspects of language planning is that they are never merely technical or instrumental operations. Rather, they are driven by quite particular social and political agendas. Language planning is certainly an exercise calling for considerable linguistic skill, but those who engage in it are better considered as the servants of much larger political agendas than as independent creators. Thus, on the one hand, planners are like management scientists, called in as required to collect, organise and analyse information; their conclusions and their recommendations will be attended to only to the extent that they bolster existing or desired political stances. On the other hand, the literature is full of what are rather disembodied language-planning theses: here, the independence and the creativity of the scholarly researchers and writers are not in doubt, but their efforts typically remain within the academic cloisters, precisely because they have neither the imprimatur nor the attention of those who wield real power and influence.

I also discuss the 'new' ecology in this concluding chapter, with a view to outlining what I believe to be some important misperceptions, flawed reasoning, and less than transparent argument. The basic idea of an 'ecology of language' is of course entirely reasonable and desirable.

Who, after all, would gainsay the value of such a potential corrective to narrow and decontextualised thinking about language in society? In fact, however, the new ecology is driven, above all, by the assertion that linguistic diversity is ever and always a good and valuable thing, and it is therefore devoted to discussions and practices that might maintain and enhance that diversity. 'Endangered' languages, then, are very much to the fore of the new ecological agenda. My initial point here is simply that the meaning of 'ecology' has been co-opted and its required breadth has been reduced. There is not the slightest objection to rallying around languages that seem to be threatened by larger neighbours – although there are grave doubts about the possible outcomes of actions that all too often fall under that 'language-centred' limitation mentioned by Bernard Spolsky – but a fully fleshed ecology must surely go beyond such a posture. With that as a broad and general objection, I then discuss some specific aspects of the 'new' ecology: its romantic perspective, its dubious assertions about the 'co-evolution' of linguistic and biological diversity, its curious and dangerous attitude towards literacy for 'small' languages, its attempt to reinforce what are, in effect, moral and aesthetic positions on diversity with more tangible props, and its much-overstated asseverations about language 'rights'.

The chapter, and the book, conclude with a brief treatment of language–identity linkages in circumstances where more than one language is involved. I merely mention phenomena like translation and 'bridging' varieties – lingua francas, pidgins and creoles – before turning to consider the group sensibilities of those who are bi- or multilingual. Different sorts and different degrees of bilingualism have important consequences for identity, as do the settings and orders in which languages are learned. At the end, however, I return to the central theme of the book: whatever the specifics, whatever the linguistic technicalities, the single most important fact in the social life of language is its relationship to identity.

1.3 A CONCLUDING NOTE

I hope that this survey of the relationships between languages and identities will serve to pull together, if only in a superficial way, most of the central strands in a multi-faceted area. It is an area about which a number of important generalities can, I think, be stated. First, the relationships in question are particularly salient in a world where, for the foreseeable future, social negotiations and re-negotiations will continue to be important. Second, their very existence reminds us of the importance of proper contextualisation. This must, I think, involve historical sensitivity just as much as it necessitates the crossing of narrow disciplinary boundaries. Third, the continuation of large amounts of work within given boundaries not only means that wheels are constantly being re-invented. It also means that the literature – very large already, and getting larger all the time – is one whose height exceeds its depth. Fourth, because of the highly charged nature of the topic, there remains much special pleading, often in the guise of a broad concern for languages and identities seen to be at risk. It is entirely reasonable that in an area that implies a straddling of the frontier between academia and the wider world, scholarship and advocacy should come together. It is also unremarkable that they should co-exist within individuals. But I do think it necessary, in such instances, that people be willing to nail their colours a little more firmly to the mast.

I believe that the chapters to follow are presented in such a way that no concluding or summary statement is needed at the end of the book. They are at once self-contained and elements of a larger picture, one whose caption might simply read 'Defining Ourselves'. In that sense, each segment of the discussion is intended to illuminate a particular area of that canvas. How do we go about labelling ourselves, at both personal and social levels, and how are those levels connected? What *are* languages and dialects – and what are the implications arising from perceptions that have always involved evaluative judgements? If religion, gender and language are among the most central 'markers' of identity, how are they connected? If ethnic and national affiliations are the most obvious examples of identity writ large, what are their most important constituents? These are the broad questions that animate the discussion, and I believe that stimulating further thought about them – preferably in combination – is the single best argument I can make for this book.

2 Identity, the individual and the group

2.1 INTRODUCTION

When I published a book called *Language, Society and Identity* in 1985, the final word in the title was not a particularly common one in the social-scientific literature. There had, of course, existed all sorts of studies of ethnic and national affiliation – largely from political and historical perspectives – but it is only in the last few decades that studies of *identity* have really come into their own. Gleason (1983) argues that this emergence was fuelled in part by the writings of the neo-Freudian Erik Erikson (1968), and it is certainly the case that his writings in the 1950s and 1960s put identity development (and identity 'crisis') in the spotlight. More subtly, Erikson's work situated these *individual* phenomena in their *social* contexts. Besides that, he was a pioneer in what came to be known as psychohistory, with notable biographies of Luther, Gandhi and other important figures. Erikson's work thus provided a psychological addition to earlier studies of 'groupness', an addition that stressed identity in context. It is not surprising, then, that Gleason reports the gradual emergence of entries relating to identity in social science encyclopaedias of the 1960s – from what had been a virtually complete absence a generation earlier.

As Joseph (2004) has noted, the early 1980s saw the appearance of important studies focusing on the linguistic aspects of identity. He mentions Gumperz's (1982) important collection on language and social identity, as well as Le Page and Tabouret-Keller's (1985) monograph on the subject. These were quickly followed by work on a variety of aspects of social identity; some examples are Kroskrity (1993) on language, history and identity, Calhoun (1994) on the politics of identity and Hooson (1994) on geography and identity. These stand at the head of a flood of scholarly work, which has hardly abated. No surprise, then, that many recent commentators – Malešević (2002), Brubaker and Cooper (2000) and Block (2006) among them – have echoed Gleason's observations, with the last of these noting a 'veritable explosion' of interest in identity.

15

Block also makes reference to Zygmunt Bauman's comment (2001: 16) that identity is now 'the most commonly played game in town', but he does not mention that the sub-title of Bauman's book is *Seeking Safety in an Insecure World* – half a dozen words that capture very nicely the perennial underpinnings of identity. If it is true that our age is one in which social stresses and strains are particularly marked, and if we are faced with many sorts of social and political challenges and transitions, then it is entirely understandable that matters of identity – its definition, its negotiation, its re-negotiation – will seem particularly salient. Any cursory historical awareness will reveal that times of transition, whether welcomed or imposed, are always times of renewed self-examination.

Groebner (2004) remarks that identity has become a buzz-word in many areas of cultural studies, useful precisely because of its definitional nuances. 'Identity', he reminds us, can refer to an individual's own subjective sense of self, to personal classification 'markers' that appear as important, both to oneself and to others, and also to those markers that delineate group membership(s). Allied with semantic nuance is an ambiguity that has allowed the concept to be very widely used, or, indeed, misused: Groebner points out that 'identity' is now a very handy word to use in connection with conference proceedings, with applications for research support, with social and political mobilisation of various stripes. We could easily expand his little list to include discussions, both within and without academia, of societal dynamics, of multicultural adaptations, of the rights and claims of minority groups, of ethnonational allegiances, and so on. A word to conjure with, to be sure, and one whose use often implies an alliance with the angels; in an age when politically correct impulses coincide with claims for group 'recognition' and for the pre-eminent importance of 'self-esteem', sins against 'identity' are of the mortal variety.

A collection edited by Hall and du Gay (1996) begins with a discussion of the modern currency of 'identity'; in its labyrinthine treatments of the subject, it demonstrates much of the ambiguity and vagueness that Groebner mentions. Here is a representative passage:

> I use 'identity' to refer to the meeting point, the point of *suture*, between on the one hand the discourses and practices which attempt to 'interpellate', speak to us or hail us into place as the social subjects of particular discourses, and on the other hand, the processes which produce subjectivities, which construct us as subjects which can be 'spoken'. (Hall, 1996: 5–6)

Well, as Abraham Lincoln once noted, people who like this sort of thing will find this the sort of thing they like.

In similar vein, Tusting and Maybin (2007: 576) have argued for a new interdisciplinary approach, 'linguistic ethnography', which is to be part of an emerging reconfiguration 'in the contexts of late modernity and globalisation'. The collection to which their article is an introduction (Rampton *et al.*, 2007) and an earlier piece (Rampton *et al.*, 2004) flesh matters out here; the latter notes (p. 2) that

> linguistic ethnography generally holds that, to a considerable degree, language and the social world are mutually shaping, and that close analysis of situated language use can provide both fundamental and distinctive insights into the mechanisms and dynamics of social and cultural production in everyday activity.

Rampton (2007: 585) goes on to say that linguistic ethnography is best characterised as a 'site of encounter' where various research perspectives can come together; the assumption is that 'the contexts for communication should be investigated rather than assumed'. And Wetherell (2007: 668) suggests that the contributions of linguistic ethnography to our understanding of identity would benefit if we dropped the latter term, replacing it with 'personal order':

> Personal order is derived from social order but is not isomorphic with it. A person... is a site, like institutions or social interaction, where flows of meaning-making practices or semiosis... become organised. Over time particular routines, repetitions, procedures and modes of practice build up to form personal style, psycho-biography and life history, and become a guide for how to go on in the present... In the case of personal order, the relevant practices could be described as 'psycho-discursive'... those which among the sum of social practices constitute a psychology, formulate a mental life and have consequences for the formation and representation of the person.

I apologise for inflicting so much of this on the reader, but it is important to realise (and regret, of course) that this sort of wheel-spinning has come to attract more and more adherents, and that many investigations of identity are now undertaken in such style.

Another collection, edited by Taylor and Spencer (2004), provides a particularly useful overview of the multiplicity of social identities, many of which are held simultaneously. This immediately raises questions of social salience, of the contextual constraints that will elicit one facet of the identity repertoire rather than another, a process similar – if not identical – to the adoption of various social roles or 'masks' according to circumstance (see also Omoniyi, 2006a). Beyond rounding up the usual suspects – class, ethnicity, religion, and so on – contributors to the Taylor and Spencer anthology also touch upon the differences between 'sexual' and 'gender' identities (Hirst; Green) and the sometimes complex relationship between the two; and also upon identity associated with the 'cyberworld' (Rosie) and with various forms of popular culture (Waddington; King).[1] Some of the material presented in the Taylor and Spencer collection represents a sort of updating of Goffman's ideas of social self-presentation (see Goffman, 1959, 1961, 1963). For Goffman's well-known work was of course essentially about identity, its presentation, its negotiation; and, particularly in his treatment of stigmatised or 'spoiled' identities, Goffman discussed the importance of labelling and categorisation.

A discussion by Jenkins (2004: 8) throws a little more light upon the recent salience of identity; he notes that

> 'identity' became one of the unifying themes of social science during the 1990s, and shows no signs of going away. Everybody has *something* to say: anthropologists, geographers, historians, philosophers, political scientists, psychologists, sociologists ... Identity, it seems, is bound up with everything from political asylum to credit card theft. And the talk is about change, too: about new identities, the return of old ones, the transformation of existing ones.

While there obviously exist many actual and potential identities, some have greater importance than others, and Jenkins suggests, for example, that those established early in life may be less 'flexible' than those acquired later on. Indeed, there is a psychological 'primacy effect' which implies that initial experience has greater weight than things that come afterwards – largely because it is, simply, first. So, when Jenkins writes about the importance of the 'formative years', he is only summarising what many theories of personality take to be gospel. But there is also a psychological 'recency effect', whereby later information is more relevant, more up-to-date, and more accessible. And this, too, has been extrapolated to matters of personality, although it has fewer adherents than do variants of the 'childhood is primary' position. The Harvard theorist Gordon Allport (1961: 78) argued that the early stages of life are marked by resiliency and plasticity; the child, he wrote:

> has no concept of himself, no lasting memories, and no firm anchorage of habits. For these reasons we may say that what happens to him in a detailed way ... leave relatively little impress. In a sense the first year is the least important year for personality, assuming that serious injuries to health do not occur.

With this sort of proviso, however, it is surely the case that early experiences often lead to lasting attributes. The view of many post-Freudian psychologists, for example, was the common-sense one that we tend to hang on to existing traits and attributes, for obvious reasons of ease, comfort and familiarity, until new circumstances suggest that alterations need to be made. (At that point, prolonged resistance to change would, in fact, be neurotic.) Jenkins focuses upon two 'primary identifications', one's sense of self and one's gender identity. It is hard to disagree with this, although Jenkins's sociological expertise clearly does not extend very much across the border into psychology; if it did, he would hardly write of *two* identifications here, but of facets of one, and he would certainly have made reference to Erikson's treatment of gender-identity development. Jenkins is on firmer ground when he nominates kinship and ethnicity as the two other fundamental identities – although he believes that they lack the universal applicability of self and gender. Perhaps, but perhaps not.

2.2 IDENTITY: PERSONAL AND SOCIAL

The essence of identity is similarity: things that are identical are the same, after all, and the word stems from the Latin *idem*. And this most basic sense is exactly what underpins the notion of identity as it applies to personality. It signifies the 'sameness' of an individual 'at all times or in all circumstances', as the dictionary tells us, the fact that a person is oneself and not someone else. It signifies a continuity, in other words, that constitutes an unbroken thread running through the long and varied tapestry of one's life. It can even invoke an almost mystical sense of connectedness, particularly when one considers the very real changes that take place in that tapestry. As Orwell observed (1941/1964: 64) in his discussion of the cultural continuity of the English, of the links between the Englands of 1840 and 1940: 'What have you in common with the child of five whose photograph your mother keeps on the mantelpiece? Nothing, except that you happen to be the same person.' We can note at the outset, then – picking up once more on the insights of Erikson and others – that there are obvious and important connections between individual identity and 'groupness', and that the heart of these is continuity. At a personal level, this is what reassures me of my own on-going integrity; at the level of the group, it is a connectivity born in history and carried forward through tradition.

Personal identity – or personality – is essentially the summary statement of all our individual traits, characteristics and dispositions; it defines the uniqueness of each human being. But it is important to realise that individuality does not arise through the possession of psychological components not to be found in anyone else. That would be a strange social world indeed. Rather, it is logical to assume that all personalities are assembled from the same deep and wide pool of human possibilities – logical, and also widely accepted as a philosophical and psychological principle. Most of the sentiments that Montaigne had carved into the ceiling beams of his study emphasised human limitations and frailties, but he did make room for Terence's famous assertion of human solidarity: *homo sum; humani nihil a me alienum puto*, 'I am a human being, and nothing human is foreign to me': the sentiment under-pins all intellectual, scientific and literary enquiries into the human condition.

The uniqueness of the individual comes about, then, through the particular combination or weighting of building blocks drawn from a common human store. To accept this is to accept that no rigid dis-tinction can in fact be made between personality and social identity. Again, this is a view of very long standing: 'no man is an island, entire of itself'. Contemporary social scientists put it rather differently, of course, but their various characterisations essentially reproduce and amplify Donne's seventeenth-century thesis. Our personal characteris-tics derive from our socialisation within the group (or, rather, groups) to which we belong; one's particular social context defines that part of the larger human pool of potential from which a personal identity can be constructed. Thus, individual identities will be both components and reflections of particular social (or cultural) ones, and the latter will always be, to some extent at least, stereotypic in nature because of their necessary generality *across* the individual components.

Identity at one level or another is central to all the 'human' or 'social' sciences, as it also is in philosophical and religious studies, for all these areas of investigation are primarily concerned with the ways in which human beings understand themselves and others. As a many-faceted phenomenon, it would be quite impossible for one short book to deal with identity in anything but a cursory way. Some reasonable restric-tions must be applied, and the delimited range here is that which treats the language–identity relationship. In a way, of course, this is not really much of a restriction, since language itself is such a broad topic and since, as Joseph (2004: 13) has pointed out, language and identity are 'ultimately inseparable'. Indeed, since language is central to the human condition, and since many have argued that it is the most salient distin-guishing characteristic of our species, it seems likely that *any* study of identity must surely include some consideration of it. This is not quite the same thing as using language as our pivotal point of perspective, of course, but we could add here that intelligent investigation from this perspective can inform and feed back into all other disciplinary or topical approaches.

Language can certainly be considered as a 'marker' at the individual level. The detail and nuance of psycholinguistic acquisition patterns, for instance, lead to the formation of the *idiolect* – that particular combination of accent and dialect, that particular assemblage of formal and informal registers, that particular pattern of stress and intonation which, if we were to look closely and cleverly enough, we would find unique to the individual. But, while this microscopic focus upon a single person occasionally possesses some descriptive validity – in clinical or forensic investigations, for example – it is generally *too* nuanced and *too* narrowly individual to be of any other than anecdotal interest or concern. The most common examples of such interest arise within family and friendship circles, where subtle and detailed linguistic portraits are often part of the rich and evolving depictions of those closest to us. And, like other aspects of these portraits, the linguistic ones are often those that highlight, or even caricature, some real or supposed trait. The comic element is often central here, and it is certainly common in literary treatments of those destined to become the best-known and the best-loved 'characters'. To cite only two well-known examples, widely separated in both time and space, we might recall the lexicon and pronunciation of Dickens's Sara Gamp, with her 'when I'm so dispoged' or 'the torters of the Imposition'; or Leo Rosten's immigrant learner of English, Hyman Kaplan, whose contortions of vocabulary and pronunciation nonetheless revealed an astute social observer of his classmates and the New York scene.

Just as a psychological or social distinction between the individual and the collective reflects a division more apparent than real, one could also argue that even idiolectal usage is a social, or group, phenomenon, on the simple grounds that all (well, almost all) language implies someone to talk to, a communicative intent, a linking of the individual to others. But the importance of language as an identity marker at a group level is much more readily evident than that: everyone is used to accent, dialect and language variations that reveal speakers' memberships in particular speech communities, social classes, ethnic and national groups. As well, such variations are obvious when the groupings are based upon gender, or age, or – expanding the linguistic focus to include jargons, registers and styles – occupation, or club or gang membership, or political affiliation, or religious confession, and so on. In the real social world, of course, none of these communities exists except in combination with others, even though the demands of context and circumstance may, at any given time, bring some to the fore and relegate others to the background. In fact, a computation of all the possible combinations and permutations of *group* allegiances and social circumstances would essentially return us to the *personal* level of the idiolect.

In this book I shall be stressing the linguistic aspects of identity 'marking' at more generalised social levels. I shall also pay more attention to those social groupings that, if not always entirely involuntary in nature or if not always highlighted, are of broadly enduring importance, and rather less to those memberships that are acquired: more attention, that is, to ethnic, national and gender groupings; less attention to the linguistic aspects of membership in voluntary organisations. It is of course the case that some of the latter come to assume very great significance in people's lives – particularly, say, if we were to place a life's career or occupation in the 'voluntary' category – and it is equally the case that classifications into which one is born are neither immutable nor always of pivotal importance. But, simply put, my purpose here is to discuss, above all, those linguistic features of identity that are generally the most robust and which, whether through processes of self-ascription or identity assignment by others outside the group, are typically the most salient when thinking about people at a societal level. And what is the rationale for focussing upon this level itself? It is simply that the most important, the most deeply felt, the most life-altering – to say nothing of the most egregious – consequences of the possession of one identity or another have almost always occurred at this level of generalisation. It may be that no strongly logical dividing line can be drawn between the individual and the social, but the most cursory attention reveals that the course of human history, and its implications for every *individual*, is by and large fuelled by perceptions of *groups*.

Smith (1991) provides a 'synoptic view' of group attachment at ethnic and national levels, but he begins by situating these among other identities, many of them held simultaneously, and he concludes with a discussion of 'post-national' possibilities, notably trans-nationalism and cosmopolitanism. He makes a strong case, however, for the continuing force of national allegiances; rumours of their demise have been greatly exaggerated, and Smith observes, simply, that 'of all the collective identities ... national identity is perhaps the most fundamental and inclusive' (p. 143). In a later collection of essays, Smith (1999) considers just *why* national identity continues to have this fundamental appeal; he finds its source in the 'ethno-symbolic' power of myth and memory (see also Leoussi and Grosby, 2007).

It seems clear enough that people need social anchors. If the older and smaller intimacies of family and village are eroded by the urbanising pressures of the modern dystopia, then substitutes will have to be found. When the 'intermediate loyalties' – the affiliations that occupy the space between personal kinship relations, on the one hand, and the impersonality of the overarching state, on the other – have become attenuated, and when the traditional linchpin of religion has become either secondary or nugatory, the 'nation-state is all people have got to shelter them while the gales of international capitalism blow harder and harder' (Mount, 1995). These are exactly the matters that Peter Berger and his colleagues have viewed from a somewhat different perspective. In *The Homeless Mind* (Berger *et al.*, 1973; see also Berger and Neuhaus, 1977), for instance, they write about the crises of belief in a world in which greater freedom often implies bewildering responsibility. Consider, for instance, the vastly enhanced personal mobility that often accompanies – or, in the fullness of time, comes to accompany – technological development, industrialisation, greater literacy, and so on. Given that 'most individuals *do not know how* to construct a universe [of meaning, or of purpose]' (p. 167: original italics), assistance was traditionally provided by institutions, especially the church, that acted as buffers and interpreters. These 'mediating structures' (as Berger styled them) soaked up and rewarded those 'intermediate loyalties' just mentioned. They stood between private lives and the large impersonalities of the state; they maintained a sense of more local community amidst the welter of modern life. But many of these mediating and comforting institutions have themselves lost influence; in many contemporary contexts, for example, religious affiliation is not the pillar it once was. It is part of the job of group activists to promote the familial nature of the loyalties they espouse and offer, precisely as a replacement to what modernity has swept aside. It is a measure of their success that members of 'imagined' ethnonational communities have responded. And the fact that people have been willing to make the greatest of sacrifices for this 'extended family' is an indicator of the strength of commitment.

Brubaker and Cooper (2000) discuss several ways in which 'identity' is used in the literature, along a 'weak–strong' continuum anchored at one end by the idea that identity is a fixed asset and, at the other, by social-constructivist conceptions of identity as a fluctuating, contingent and sometimes quite unstable phenomenon: a process, rather than an entity. It is obviously true that dynamism rather than stasis has always been the fact of human life. The simultaneous possession of many different social roles and masks is uncontroversial, identities are certainly in flux, allegiances vary both diachronically and synchronically – and the language groups of which we are members are very rough approximations to the personal and changeable idiolect. Identity *is* fluid, but the vigorous assertion of impermanence and contingency (and, indeed, the 'unfixedness' of other concepts, like language and

community, that have traditionally been seen as both stable and defin-
able) has become part of the mantra of post-modernism, a development
that can be largely attributed to the dubious insights of dubious intellec-
tuals. Within the broadly linguistic arena, this has become particularly
prominent in 'discourse analysis', an enterprise apparently dedicated
to the idea that there can never be any end, of any sort, in sight. It is
often, like its parent disciplines, an illustration of 'process' gone mad.
This is hardly the place for a fully fleshed critique (see Edwards, in press
a, for some further details); suffice it to say that the preciosities of such
scholarship have had virtually no impact outside the closed circle that
practises and rewards it. Perhaps one of the reasons for this, apart from
the often labyrinthine reasoning on display, is the impenetrability of
the jargon – but, then, discourse analysis is hardly the only language
area whose practitioners are themselves dysfluent. Even those who write
about mundane aspects of language planning and the rights or claims
of minority-language groups are liable to slip when they enter the thick-
ets of hybridity, post-modernism and social constructionism: thus, May
(2001: 39) tells us that 'in line with postmodernism's rejection of total-
ising metanarratives, exponents of hybridity emphasise the contingent,
the complex and the contested aspects of identity formation'.

But we must turn to other quarters for more fully fleshed examples;
here is a representative observation from Bourdieu (1990a: 60):

> the singular habitus of the members of the same [group] ... united in a
> relation of homology, that is, of diversity within homogeneity
> reflecting the diversity within homogeneity characteristic of their
> social conditions of production. Each individual system of dispositions
> is a structural variant of the others, expressing the singularity of its
> own position within the [group] and its trajectory.

(One page earlier, Bourdieu tells us that *habitus* is a 'system of dispositions common to all products of the same conditionings': that certainly
clears things up nicely.) Besides its obscurity, this sort of obfuscation
is interesting in its own right, and the questions of greatest psychological interest have to do with the reasons for its production and, still
more poignant, perhaps, those that account for its positive reception;
the brouhaha surrounding the 'Sokal affair' is instructive here (see Sokal
and Bricmont, 1997).[2] These matters are rendered even more intriguing
when one realises that the perpetrators of these noisome deeds are quite
capable of understandable utterance. Bourdieu himself provides a good
example; 'my work', he says, 'consists in saying that people are located
in a social space, that they aren't just anywhere' (1990b: 47). It would
seem that the choice here is between the opaque and the obvious.

Elsewhere, in a chapter devoted to 'identity and representation', Bourdieu (1991: 221) rightly acknowledges the importance of *perception*; it is the only window on 'reality' that we have, after all. But look how tediously he makes such an obvious point:

> One can understand the particular form of struggle over classifications that is constituted by the struggle over the definition of 'regional' or 'ethnic' identity only if one transcends the opposition that science, in order to break away from the preconceptions of spontaneous sociology [?], must first establish between representation and reality, and only if one includes in reality the representation of reality, or, more precisely, the struggle over representations, in the sense of mental images, but also of social demonstrations whose aim it is to manipulate mental images ... (Bourdieu 1991: 221)

To adapt Orwell very slightly: one has to belong to the intelligentsia to produce or respond favourably to this sort of thing; no ordinary person could be so silly (see Orwell, 1945/1965: 178).[3]

2.3 THE CONSTRUCTION AND MAINTENANCE OF GROUPNESS

Beginning in the 1970s, the social psychologist Henri Tajfel, with his students and colleagues, investigated the formation and maintenance of *minimal groups*. In a series of experimental studies, they demonstrated just how easy it is to divide people into groups on the basis of unimportant criteria (for example, expressing a preference for one of two painters, neither of whom had been heard of before), and how subsequent behaviour (for example, treating another member of your group more handsomely than you do an 'out-group' individual) is affected by this. Indeed, Tajfel pointed out that, in one experiment, the 'height of absurdity was reached ... each subject was explicitly and visibly assigned to one group or the other on the basis of a random toss of a coin' (Brehm *et al.*, 1999: 146). This is probably the most minimal of possible criteria for group formation; yet, even in these circumstances, within-group solidarity and its consequences was demonstrated among those who 'were not long-term rivals, did not have a history of antagonism, were not frustrated, did not compete for a limited resource, and were not even acquainted with each other' (Tajfel, 1978: 33–4).

The idea that, once boundaries have been created – either in the social laboratory or out in the real world – group membership *per se* becomes important, has some obvious relationship to Fredrik Barth's slightly earlier writings about ethnonational borders being somehow more important than the cultural 'stuff' within them; see Barth (1969) on the idea that borders can have a permanence that contrasts with the almost infinite mutability of the culture contained within them. As part of a very succinct overview of the work of Tajfel and his follow-ers, Jenkins (2004) has suggested, however, that there is an important distinction. Whereas Tajfel's work implies that the creation of borders (sometimes a very easy thing to bring about, as we have just noted) leads to a sense of membership and group identity, Barth's view is that bor-ders only arise once a group has already begun to coalesce in some way, typically through individuals' inter-relationships arising from common interests. It is easy to see that there are circular and mutually reinforcing reactions at work here, but it is surely also reasonable to think that some dawning sense of 'groupness' and hence of boundaries must develop very early on in the prosecution of individual negotiations.

For some, the apparent ease and 'minimality' associated with group formation are the interesting matters; the bonding, the solidarity and the rivalries that follow are quite predictable. We all know about group-ness in the field, as it were, and once we learn that it can be grown domestically with little bother, we are not surprised to find that both wild and tame varieties have the same properties. The social psycholo-gists, however, have pushed on a bit here, attempting to better under-stand *what* constitutes the in-group allegiances, and *why* they take the form they do. The results of their work are not particularly breathtak-ing. When you strip away the deposits of jargon, you do unearth the odd nugget of reasonable weight; typically, though, it is something encoun-tered before, in another sort of dig, and is therefore somewhat less original than the prospectors claim. As to *what* in-group allegiance is all about, for instance, the answer is *in-group favouritism*: we favour those with whom we are associated or aligned, our hopes and expectations are often higher for them, we bleed when they bleed, and so on. This can take place very rapidly, once 'us and them' borders have been established, once some social categorisation has occurred. It is not difficult, as well, to understand how the same sense of belonging that creates favouritism can also lead to the formation of stereotypes – blunt characterisations that can be either positive or negative, depending upon which group you are describing – and to the so-called *out-group homogeneity effect* ('my group is made up of many different individuals, but *you* are all alike').

The *why* of this sort of behaviour rests upon the pillars of 'social iden-tity theory' which, like the minimal group paradigm, is also largely associated with Tajfel and his scholarly descendants. Useful overviews may be found in Tajfel (1978, 1982), Turner and Giles (1981), Hogg and Abrams (1988), Abrams and Hogg (1990), Turner (1991), Breakwell (1992) and Robinson (1996); all of these writers have made important contributions to the social psychology of categorisation and identity. The assumption here is that besides our uniquely personal sense of self, we also have social identities based upon the various groups to which we belong. Thus, we can maintain and enhance self-esteem through valued social affiliations, as well as by purely personal activities and achievements. According to the theory, it follows that within-group favouritism is predictable since it reflects and supports the particular 'us and them' boundaries that can heighten feelings of individual worth. A corollary is that in-group solidarity should be expected to strengthen at times when one's sense of worth is threatened or tenuous. Researchers have examined these simple hypotheses under a wide variety of conditions: when self-esteem has been (allegedly) experimentally raised or lowered, in comparisons of people having different degrees of attachment to their group, among groups of different sizes, among group members who differ in status, among those who are more or less prejudiced or bigoted, across various cultures, and so on. Gagnon and Bourhis (1996) asked if inter-group discrimination, the coin that has in-group favouritism on one side, and negative feelings towards out-group members on the other, reflected social identity or self-interest – the whole thrust of this literature, however, is to suggest that the 'or' here is misplaced: social identity *is* self-interest.

2.4 LANGUAGE AND CIRCUMSTANCE

As Llamas (2007) recently observed, there are parallels between the sorts of social-psychological findings just discussed and the approach taken by Le Page and Tabouret-Keller (1985), for whom 'acts of identity' involve attempts at strengthening in-group linguistic connections – via accent or dialect, for example; such efforts, of course, necessarily entail de-emphasising linkages with out-groups. The processes here are fluid and dynamic and may very well operate in 'automatic' or even unconscious ways.

At both informal and empirical levels, there is ample evidence for speech *mobility*, whereby speakers select from their repertoire according to perceptions of situational constraints and demands. This is obvious among people who are bilingual or multilingual, but *all* people possess a range of speaking styles. And, just as bilingualism can range from extremely halting to very proficient, so 'bi-dialectalism' and accent and style variations exist along a continuum. At one extreme, we find those who know only a few words in another dialect, or who can only adopt a rather caricatured non-maternal accent (jokes provide a common illustration here, especially those of the Scotsman-Irishman-Englishman kind). At the other, we find individuals who can assume native-like colouration (some actors are particularly gifted here). However, the most widely available variation for monolingual speakers is at the level of *style*. In a sociolinguistic context, this term refers to speech variations that reflect one's assessment of the social context and of what is or is not 'appropriate'. The most common influence and product is the degree of formality. There is quite a difference, for example, among the statements 'I am extremely fatigued', 'I'm very tired' and 'I'm bloody knackered', yet one speaker might be heard to utter them all, in different settings. This sort of variation is so effortless that we usually do it without much thought, and most members of speech communities adapt all the time. In fact, most are so good at this that we notice the variation only when it seems odd or inappropriate. A doctor who looked over her glasses and said 'Well, it's the high jump for you, squire' would seem frivolous and unfeeling; and a mechanic who reported that 'Your conveyance is, I regret to inform you, in a most sadly dilapidated state' would invite both wonder and laughter. More importantly, each would appear to have stepped out of character, violating our expectations.

Some people are clearly more 'mono-stylistic' than others, less willing or able to alter their speech according to circumstances, or quite unaware of their rigidity. Inflexibility itself clearly has an effect, and perhaps this accounts for the appeal of the exchange between a don and Lawrence of Arabia, recounted by Robert Graves (1929/1960: 246) in his autobiography:

> Professor Edgeworth, of All Souls', avoided conversational English, persistently using words and phrases that one expects to meet only in books. One evening, Lawrence returned from a visit to London, and Edgeworth met him at the gate. 'Was it very caliginous in the Metropolis?' 'Somewhat caliginous, but not altogether inspissated', Lawrence replied gravely.

On the other hand, perhaps this response by Gladstone to a drunken heckler falls more in the 'unaware' category:

> May I request the gentleman who has, not once but repeatedly, interrupted my observations by his interjections, to extend to me that large measure of courtesy which, were I in his place and he in mine, I should most unhesitatingly extend to him. (Russell, 1950: 217)

Russell noted that, in any event, the man was 'sobered by the shock' of Gladstone's eloquence; no doubt the rest of the audience was stunned, too.

A highly readable account of stylistic variation is found in Martin Joos's little book *The Five Clocks* (1967), so titled because the author held there to be five distinct styles of English usage: frozen, formal, consultative, casual and intimate. Although not all would agree that Joos's divisions are the most accurate or have universal applicability, they remain useful, provocative and eminently readable. Joos began in the middle, by discussing the *consultative* style, whose defining characteristics are the provision of necessary background information without which the listener cannot make sense of the message, and the participation of the listener in the conversation. With friends and 'in-group' members we can switch to the *casual* style. We can dispense with contextual grounding and listener participation and, within this format, slang and ellipsis are common. Confusion is common in consultative and casual speech, because we may err in estimating the degree to which an interlocutor actually *does* have the information we possess. Sometimes, then, we outline things that are already known or are unnecessary in the context; at other times, we may leave out information that we incorrectly assume is shared.

In both consultative and casual styles, information is important (even if it need not always be spelled out). In the *intimate* style, however, information and its exchange become much less central; in fact, Joos says that 'an intimate utterance pointedly avoids giving the addressee information from outside of the speaker's skin' (p. 25). If someone simply says 'cold' or 'ready', the meaning can, after all, be quite clear and needs no further amplification. Joos also includes here the use of *jargon* – a permanent in-group code – but he views *slang* as 'ephemeral' and, therefore, something that may be found at casual levels as well. Many professional groups have their own jargon, of course, but an example of a highly restricted and intimate form might be those special 'family' words known and used only under the domestic roof.

To move in the other direction, from consultative to *formal* style, is to delete listener participation. Perhaps the group has grown too large – Joos suggests that consultation is difficult among more than half-a-dozen people – or perhaps the listener is unfamiliar. Formal style is for transmitting information and this is its 'dominating character, something which is necessarily ancillary in consultation, incidental in casual discourse, absent in intimacy' (p. 36). It requires advance planning and is defined by detachment and cohesion. Most university lectures (for instance) are delivered in formal style, and it may also be commonly observed among 'urbane strangers'. The fifth, *frozen* style, is used for declamation and, most commonly, is the form enshrined in print. It lacks participation and intonational clues, and it requires no social exchange between speaker (or writer) and listener (or reader). It necessitates care and planning, for one of its great advantages is that, when written, it can be re-consulted at will. A good frozen style lures us on, and this reminds us that not all written language has the same force, not every attempt to transmit formal knowledge is equally successful. The best frozen language can be equated with timeless literature.

Joos also provides some of the guidelines regulating the use and shifting of the styles. Between strangers, for example, formal usage is largely ceremonial introduction in which no real information is exchanged; it is short-lived and soon displaced by consultation. Formality can return, however, when embarrassment (for example) arises or is imminent, and it may also signal the end of a conversation. While there is generally no requirement to confine oneself to a single style on any given occasion, another rule holds that 'normally only two neighboring styles are used alternately, and it is anti-social to shift two or more steps in a single jump' (p. 19).

I am not suggesting that Joos's work qualifies as a technical, detailed study (and there are other influences on style besides formality) but his basic message is sound: all ordinary speakers have a range of possibilities in their linguistic repertoire, from which they pick and choose according to their sense of the occasion. This is *code-switching*, and its ubiquity and frequency are worth noting, not only because they illustrate a powerful and virtually automatic grasp of linguistic and sociolinguistic subtleties, but also because they link monolingual performances to the more apparent juggling of the bilingual. It is clear enough, from Joos's work, that different levels of style normally correspond to the formality, the seriousness and the intent of an interaction: that is, the situation drives the language to a large extent. We are all perfectly familiar with this; we 'naturally' make different selections from our speech repertoire for conversations with our children, our spouses, the bank manager, our chums in the pub, the vicar, and so on. All of this can be understood as highlighting one or another aspect of identity, and we are again reminded of the work of Goffman on self-presentation.

If context can determine linguistic choice, then, equally, language (or dialect, or accent, or style) choice can affect the social-psychological situation. In a seminal piece of work, Herman (1961) demonstrated that linguistic choices can be an index to our perceptions of the context, and may even change important features of that context. We may wish to put a particular stamp on our conversation; we may want to approach our listener (out of existing or desired intimacy) or we may want to dissociate ourselves (because of dislike, or because we feel the other person is being psychologically invasive). Such desires will have linguistic consequences, whether we explicitly intend these or not. The most thoroughgoing social-scientific investigations of this sort of language *accommodation* are those of Howard Giles and his colleagues (summarised in Giles and Coupland, 1991; Robinson and Giles, 2001). They are not the only perspective, of course, but, as Street and Giles (1982) pointed out, this accommodation model pays the closest attention to the psychological position of listeners as well as speakers, to both subjective and objective speech markers, to broad ranges of speech behaviour, and to both interpersonal and inter-group situations. It is also important to note here that Giles's work on language accommodation has clear linkages to Tajfel's broader conceptions of social categorisation and identity.

In an early formulation, Giles and Powesland (1975) discussed the derivation of speech-accommodation theory from earlier work on similarity-attraction and 'social exchange', work showing that (*mirabile dictu*) personal similarity increases the likelihood of attraction and liking: we like others whom we think are like ourselves. A corollary is that reduction of any dissimilarities may lead to more favourable perceptions. Since the desire for social approval was 'assumed to be at the heart of accommodation' (p. 159), the model initially focussed upon the reduction of linguistic differences as an avenue to these positive perceptions. Accommodation means change, however, and change costs something; findings from the social-exchange literature suggest that accommodation will be initiated only where fruitful 'cost-benefit ratios' seem likely to be achieved. In a nutshell, then, 'accommodation through speech can be regarded as an attempt on the part of the speaker to modify or disguise his persona in order to make it more acceptable to the person addressed' (p. 158).

Three more relevant points were made by Giles and Powesland. First, speakers may not be 'consciously aware' of their accommodative intent. Some strategies may be quite overt, but covert accommodation is also possible, and the listener may not always detect its operation, either. Second, it was quickly realised that a 'desire for approval' need not be the only driving force behind accommodation. It can imply *divergence* as well as *convergence*, linguistic moves away from listeners whose approval is not desired (or who are not liked, and so on). Third, convergent accommodation does not always produce the desired effect, does not invariably lead to social approval. Giles and Powesland cited an example in which an English-speaking European addressed an East African official in Swahili, and where this accommodation was seen to have the condescending implication that the latter was incompetent in English. We also recall here the obvious example of detected flattery.

In terms of the mechanics of accommodation, Giles and Smith (1979) and Giles *et al.* (1977) observed that the most frequent 'intralingual convergences' are in terms of pronunciation (i.e. accent), speech rate and message content; others include utterance length and pausing times, and all can be supplemented by paralinguistic features like smiling (or not), gaze directness and duration, posture, and so on. There is specific acknowledgement here of Tajfel's work on inter-group relations and social change, particularly with regard to *divergence*. Tajfel had proposed that groups in contact make comparisons, and want to see themselves as distinct and 'positively valued entities'. In their attempts to develop a more favourable identity, subordinate-group members have a number of strategies available to them (assuming, of course, that any changes are seen as actually possible). They may move into the other group (assimilation), they may redefine negative qualities as positive (stigmatised features like skin colour or nonstandard dialect, for instance, may be re-assessed in a process of revitalised group pride), or they may create altogether new evaluative dimensions that will favour their group.

Speech accommodations can thus be seen as identity adjustments made to increase group status and favourability, moves towards more favourable psychosocial contexts or attempts to strengthen group distinctions (Barthian boundaries, if you like). There are many further subtleties here. Accommodation can be upward or downward (i.e. towards or away from high-status speech variants); full or partial (in fact, it is probably never completely full: too difficult, too obvious, too self-denigrating) in terms of all the possible points on which convergence/divergence *could* occur; large or moderate (again, too large can be risky: maybe I should shift my accent somewhat towards the manager's, but not aim to clone it); symmetrical or asymmetrical (one or both parties may accommodate: I wish to impress my boss, but he wants to put me more at ease). Running through all these specificities, too, are group–individual distinctions. Is convergence/divergence in the service of facilitating or hindering a purely personal exchange, or is it a component of an interaction in which one (or more) of the participants is acting in some sense as a representative of a group? Neither of these exists in pure form outside the mind of the experimental manipulator, but there certainly is a range of possibilities here.

STUDY QUESTIONS

1. Why is group identity such an important phenomenon, and under what social and political circumstances does it take on particular significance?

2. What are the important links between personal and social identity?
3. How and why do speech and language patterns often reveal accommodation to others?
4. We all have an extensive speech repertoire from which we select according to our perceptions of the social context. What does this suggest about human interaction?

Further reading

Fredrik Barth's (1969) edited book, *Ethnic Groups and Boundaries*, is a classic contribution to our understanding of the maintenance of ethnic identity over time and circumstance.

John Edwards's (1985) *Language, Society and Identity* gives a comprehensive overview of the subject.

John Joseph's (2004) *Language and Identity: National, Ethnic, Religious* is a very good treatment of the most important dimensions of identity.

Anthony Smith's (1991) *National Identity* is a consideration of social and political matters from the pen of one of the leading scholars of nationalism.

3 Identifying ourselves

3.1 PERSONAL NAMES

There is a large literature demonstrating that all manner of individual and group 'markings' can have important consequences for interpersonal judgements. Skin colour, sex/gender and physical attractiveness are immediately obvious here. Social psychological studies have shown, for example, that attractive people may be viewed as less culpable in crime scenarios – unless the alleged crime was one in which attractiveness might have facilitated the offence, in which case judgements may be harsher than those made of less physically appealing individuals. Attractive children may receive more attention and better marks from their teachers. Physical variations often elicit stereotypic perceptions – and we are always sensitive to the perceptions of others, particularly where these have some consistency over time and context. If everyone assumes that, because you are short and fat, you must have certain personality traits, then you may very well come to develop them. In general, there is no shortage of evidence, both anecdotal and formal, that 'involuntary' markers of who we are, what we look like, and what groups we belong to are related to social possibilities and circumstances.[1]

Less 'involuntary' identifiers are also important. Among these are religious affiliations, language-group memberships – and names. Different names have different connotations: some are perceived as much more attractive than others, and those to whom they belong may expect different types of treatment from peers, teachers and bosses. A small example was provided in an honours thesis conducted at my university (MacEachern, 1988). One-page essays, purportedly written by secondary-school students, were presented to student teachers, who were simply asked to provide a mark on the usual 0–100 grading scale. There was only one essay involved, put together by the experimenter, but the students' names that appeared at the top of the page varied. Avoiding rare and bizarre names, relatively popular (Paul, Emily) and less popular

(Albert, Bernice) ones were chosen; decisions here were made on the basis of some previous pilot work. The experimenter drew no particular attention to the names when distributing the essays to the student judges, and the hope was that the little deception – that these were short assignments that had really been written by tenth-grade pupils – would work. It seemed to. Furthermore, statistically significant differences were found: marks given to essays apparently written by students with popular names were higher than those awarded to exactly the same essays when less popular names appeared at the top.

An important variation on this theme links names with gender. Fidell (1975) sent out ten fictitious scholarly resumés to the chairs of almost 150 American psychology departments. The chairs were asked to provide academic rankings to files that sometimes had men's names at the top, sometimes women's. As Eckert and McConnell-Ginet (2003: 94–5) report, 'respondents consistently ranked the same dossiers higher when they believed them to be men's'. And very recently, Nelson and Simmons (2007) have reported on what looks like some onomastic equivalent of Tajfel's minimal-group paradigm. They found that university students whose names began with A or B made better marks than those with names starting with C or D. They invoked what has been called the 'name–letter' effect, another manifestation of which (apparently) is the greater tendency for people called Jack to move to Jacksonville, while Philip goes to Philadelphia and marries Phyllis (see also Pelham *et al.*, 2005). Whether or not some, or all, of these results prove to be robust and replicable, there is no question that they highlight an important and enduring phenomenon. Parents spend a lot of time thinking about names for their children, and it would seem that they are quite right to do so.

The historical, anthropological and linguistic literature reveals that personal names often have powerful religious significance. The names of the dead may be taboo, for instance. Children may be given names that are unpleasant in some way or other, precisely to make them less inviting to evil spirits. In other situations, names with positive spiritual or mundane connotations may be assigned as markers of strength, or as defences against sin or waywardness. 'Faith', 'Felicity', 'Patience' and 'Joy' are modern reminders of Puritan practices in which godly virtues were made into names. 'Increase Mather' was an important figure in seventeenth-century Massachusetts and 'Praisegod Barebone' gave his name to a parliamentary assembly of 1653. Later, of course, came William Makepeace Thackeray. More elaborate naming also occurred along the same lines: more than a few individuals rejoiced in names like 'Fight-the-Good-Fight Jones' and 'Fear-the-Lord Smith'. Readers of

Patrick O'Brian's long series of sea stories will think of Captain Aubrey's steward, the loyal but surly Preserved Killick.

Religious naming practices continue in some contexts. Makoni *et al.* (2007) mention (first) names like Courage, Goodwill, Blessed, Lordwin and Withus in Zimbabwe, for example – and, indeed, the first name of one of the authors is Sinfree. Such names are one of the legacies of colonialism and proselytism in Africa, Asia and elsewhere. Even where an overtly religious intent was not manifest, the replacement of existing names by European ones was very common, something that typically occurred when a child first went to school. Rolihlahla Mandela (1994) thus recounts how, on his first day, the teacher (Miss Mdingane) told him that his new name would be Nelson. It is not surprising, either, to find that indigenous names are often taken up again in post-colonial settings. Makoni *et al.* (2007) give some South African examples: the premier of the Eastern Cape changed his first name from Arnold to Makhenkesi; the defence minister, from Patrick to Mosioua.

3.2 NAMES FOR GROUPS

When we first look at group labels, we discover an interesting connection between the individual and the collectivity. While groups' names for themselves obviously arise in many different ways – variants of 'the people of the river' or 'the mountain-dwellers' are common, for instance – self-descriptions also often suggest that those outside the group are qualitatively different. There is a basic, if rather disturbing, message in Stewart's (1975: 68) observation that 'many tribal names are – at least in primitive stages of culture – not formal designations, but merely equivalents of the pronoun "we"'.[2] This is not unreasonable, perhaps, when groups live in relative isolation from others, when inter-group contact is rare or fleeting, but Stewart goes on to say that 'the appellation may develop into meaning "people", with the implication that those of other tribes are not human in quite the same sense'. He also suggests that this distinction has been heightened still further in some instances, such that a group's name for itself comes to have the connotation of 'outstanding people'. Such names are found in many parts of the world – and Stewart reminds us of some them: Ainu, Bantu, Berber, Chuchi, Inuit, Salish, Washoe (see also Green, 1996; Wilson, 1998). In similar fashion, Pečujlić *et al.* (1982) discuss Latin and South American communities in which self-references typically involve ascriptions like 'the real people', and where the terms applied to those outside the group reveal a powerfully ethnocentric bias. Poser (2006) provides some north-west

American examples: the Beaver people of British Columbia style themselves 'the real people', and the Coast Tsimshian call their language 'the real language'.

A little further research turns up many more examples. The Navajo refer to themselves as *Diné* ('the people'), the Dakota/Lakota self-ascription signifies 'the friends'. The collective name for the groups within the Blackfoot community is *Ni'itsitapi* ('the real people'); and this is also the meaning of the indigenous group name among the Nez Percé (the *Nimi'pu*), the Iroquois (*Ongwhehonwhe*), the Kaluli of New Guinea, the Lapps (the *Sámi*), the 'gypsies' or 'travelling people' of Europe (the *Roma*, where *Rom* means 'man'), the people of the Chiapas highlands of Mexico, the Kannakas of Hawaii (the *Kanaka Maoli*), and many others. Some self-descriptions emphasise the ancestral primacy of the group: the Chippewa and Ojibwe people call themselves *Anishinabe* ('the original people') and the Cherokee are the *Ani-yvwiya* (or *Ani-yunwiya* – 'the human beings', 'the principal people') or the *Ani-kituwah* – Kituwah being a Garden of Eden equivalent (in what is now North Carolina) where God created them. A particularly striking example is found among the Asmat of Irian Jaya: while they are 'the human beings', they classify everyone else as *manowe* – the 'edible ones'. Such ethnic naming conventions are also found, of course, in religiously based groups. Thus, some interpretations within Islam divide the world into those within the sacred 'house' and those without; and, as Castoriadis (1997) reminds us, the Christian Bible echoes with racism, with accounts that describe the 'other' as impure, unclean, idolatrous, evil and depraved.

Biblical examples are hardly the only illustrations of names for 'outgroups' that go some way beyond simply 'not the real people'. As in the Asmat setting that I have just cited, outsiders are often portrayed in unflattering or derogatory ways. While terms like 'Blackfoot' and 'Nez Percé' should not, perhaps, be interpreted as anything more than rough external appellations, some of the Dakota ('the friends') became known as Sioux ('snakes'), an abbreviation of a term bestowed upon them by enemies. Many Inuit consider the earlier term 'Eskimo' to be a derogatory reference to them as eaters of raw meat.[3] While the Welsh call themselves *Cymry* (meaning something like 'fellow countrymen'), the English name for them derives from the Anglo-Saxon *w(e)alh*, via the Germanic *Wälsche* ('stranger', 'foreigner', or even 'barbarian'). The Khoisan speakers of southern Africa call themselves *Khoekhoe* – 'men of men' – but it was the Dutch who called them 'Hottentots' – stutterers. In seventeenth-century Muscovy, foreigners were called *nemtsy* ('mutes'), a Russian labelling now restricted to Germans – 'mute' is *nemoi* (немой), German is *nemets* (немец) and the German language is *nemetskii* (немецкий).

Barbarians and stammerers: the terms are in fact closely associated. The first, signifying all that is brutal, uncouth and tasteless, is derived from a Greek term for the latter (βάρβαρος: an onomatopoeic word), in which rude and uncivilised foreigners are marked by their clumsy and offensive languages; in some instances, the Greeks came close to denying these stammering aliens human status altogether. The Greek word is related to the Latin *balbus* ('stammering'), which, among the Romans, was first applied to foreigners who had neither Latin nor Greek; later, it took on the connotation of primitive and non-Christian. And there is an analogy of sorts here with the Greek *ethnos* (ἔθνος), which signified a nation neither Christian nor Jewish: thus, 'ethnic' meant 'heathen' (which itself could suggest 'pagan' or, in some contexts, 'gentile'). In fact, through mistaken etymology, the Greek term was once supposed to be the source-word for the English 'heathen' – hence the obsolete terms 'heathenic' and 'hethnic' (the latter sounding rather Cockney!). Dr Johnson's eighteenth-century dictionary defined *ethnic* as 'heathen, pagan, not Christian, not Jewish'.

Finally here, to show that naming practices remain a sensitive issue, and to touch upon an illustrative context that I shall return to a little later, we can consider some of the terminology to which the continuing tensions between Quebec and the rest of Canada have given rise. These tensions can be categorised, very roughly, as existing between Quebec nationalists who would like to see their province become an independent state, and federalists, both within and without Quebec, who disagree. First of all, the word 'sovereigntist' quickly came to replace 'separatist' in the Quebec-nationalist lexicon, and words like 'federalist' and 'provincial' took on negative connotations. The perceived divisions between Quebec and the rest of the country became reflected in phrases like *le Québec et le Canada* or *les Québécois et les Canadiens*. The very word *Québécois*, which might logically refer to all people living in the province, came to have the narrower connotation of 'old-stock' francophones, people whose ancestry goes back to the earliest French settlement; thus, a 'real' *Québécois* is a French-speaking sovereigntist (see the illustrative newspaper articles by Gagnon, 1994, 1997a, 1997b).

El Yamani *et al.* (1993) reported the results of an exhaustive trawl through media coverage of majorities and minorities, of 'us' and 'them' in Quebec. The authors turned up about fifty terms used to describe francophones of French-Canadian background, and almost ninety for minority groups. Among the former (not including terms already presented here) we find *Québécois de vieille souche* ('old-stock' Quebeckers), *Québécois pur laine* ('pure-wool' Quebeckers), *Québécois francophones*, *Québécois francophones de vieille souche*, *Québécois francophones du cru* ('vintage' Quebeckers), *majorité canadienne-française* and *Québécois de souche française*. Among the latter are *autres Québécois, compatriotes d'une autre origine, communautés culturelles, membres d'origines ethniques* and *ceux de fraîche date* (new arrivals). The magazine *L'actualité* suggested that the old English élite of Montreal might be thought of as *Montréalais pur tweed*. And the growing presence of black francophones in the province led a Haitian poet to describe that community as *Québécois pur laine crépue* ('pure frizzy-wool' Quebeckers); see *Globe & Mail* (1992–2007).

3.3 THE APPROPRIATION OF NAMES AND NARRATIVES

A powerful manifestation of the importance of names and their historical contexts is the perception of 'voice appropriation', something arising from the resentment felt by many communities that the names by which they are most widely known are not of their own choosing and, relatedly, that their important myths and legends have largely been told by outsiders. This cultural theft is generally seen as a continuation of colonialism. 'Insiders' have always resented the intrusion into the heart of their society, of course: think what it means to have large and powerful neighbours give you the name by which the wider world will know you, tell your stories, reveal your secrets. It is only recently, however, that the resentment has been acknowledged and accepted, a reflection of shifts of attitude on the one hand, and of greater self-assertiveness on the other. The political clout of 'small' speech communities, and the (apparently) greater willingness of larger ones to listen, support and respond, has never been as evident as it is today. Of course, there remains much 'mainstream' hypocrisy, empty posturing and repellent lip-service, but there has been substantive change too, at least in western liberal democracies (for a critical overview, see Williams, 1998; see also the final section in this chapter). The 'indigenous voice' – to cite the title of a collection published some twenty years ago (Moody, 1988) – has never been so united and forceful in its repudiation of what might be seen as a type of 'linguistic imperialism'.

There are examples, once again, from around the globe. Kennedy (1999) discusses the way in which the voices of 'in-group members' have not been sufficiently heard in studies of the fortunes of Scots Gaelic and its speakers, for instance, and writers like Bumsted (1982) and Richards (1982) have commented specifically upon the absence of Highland input. Kennedy's point, however, is that the usual explanations given by such commentators – the inability or the unwillingness of those at ground level to record their own perspectives on important events – are inadequate, in that they fail to realise how overwhelming the English historiographical bias has been. There *are* Gaelic commentaries available, but they have been largely ignored by historians. The result is that, according to Kennedy, we have often been left with a 'formulaic depiction of the Gaelic world as inherently inept' (p. 275). This is casting matters a little too strongly, particularly in the light of the sympathetic – sometimes overly sympathetic, sometimes quite romanticised – treatment of Gaelic culture that 'outsiders' have often provided, but there is certainly something here, particularly since the idealised views of outsiders can be just as damaging as derogatory ones. The larger import of Kennedy's point is surely as a corollary of the familiar dictum that history is written by the winners, and as a specific instance of 'voice appropriation'. If we link the resentment here with our earlier discussion of naming practices – with the fact that, for better or worse, many groups have seen only themselves as '*real* people' – we can see that the wound becomes deeper. To have to put up with unpleasant or unwanted naming and narrative practices from outside the group is one thing; to realise that these have been imposed by people who are, by community definition, not even 'real' is another, and more bitter, one. A further implication here has to do with an erosion of aspects of the age-old sense of group identity. If outsiders who have been traditionally considered as inferior, alien or, indeed, not fully human have come to achieve such obvious social dominance, what does this suggest to the 'insiders' about the validity of their traditional descriptions, about their self-esteem, about the tenuous nature of their cultural continuity?

A further twist to the tale is that in many cultures, particularly in oral societies, the narrative care of the sacred or semi-sacred names, stories and legends was traditionally assigned to certain families or individuals. Many communities, as Sawyer (2001) reminds us, have believed that religious utterances must be repeated ritually and in word-perfect fashion; among other things, this has had the salutary consequence of preserving linguistic forms that might otherwise have been lost in non-literate contexts. Consider the role of the European bards, or the *griots* of West Africa – living libraries, charged with the preservation and transmission of the most central and important group narratives; see Hale's useful treatment (1998) and the more general collections of Henze and Davis (1999) and Kockel and Nic Craith (2007). Not only, then, can outside 'appropriation' be resented at a general level; it can also be construed as a much more focussed assault upon a caste or class of high, sometimes priestly, status.

But I put 'appropriation' in inverted commas because, no matter how much one may sympathise with individuals and cultures who have been badly treated by more powerful societies, the matter is by no means clear-cut. In works of fiction, for instance, 'appropriation' of one sort or another is paramount; as Bakhtin (1981) pointed out in the 1930s, most of one's words are not one's own. More generally, a logical extension of the appropriation argument might lead to the conclusion that no one could ever write about anything beyond one's own immediate experience; only 'insiders' could write about their lives and cultures. Consider, too, that an embargo along these lines, one that would prevent majority-group outsiders from writing about the lives of those in 'small' or culturally 'at-risk' groups, would logically also prevent minority-group members from commenting upon the 'mainstream'. Furthermore: are women never to write about men, blacks never about whites, Germans never about Spaniards? This is clearly nonsensical, an imposition that would have stifled an overwhelmingly huge proportion of the world's literature, and of the knowledge we have of one another as human beings. But at the same time, it is not difficult to understand the grievances that arise when the narrative boundaries that are crossed separate groups of significantly different socioeconomic clout. Sauce for the goose may, logically, be sauce for the gander, but the inequalities that exist between those birds in real life surely mean that some special attention might reasonably be given to the less powerful ones. Dostoevski once said that we could judge the state of a civilisation by seeing how it runs its prisons, and many others have enlarged the point: the way society treats its most needy or vulnerable citizens is a measure of its humanity. And we can surely expand things further still, and say that there must also be a correlation between that humanity and cross-cultural sensitivity. This is why the more thoughtful commentaries on 'voice appropriation' have not stated matters in some either-or fashion but, rather, have argued about the *degree* of cross-border commentary that might be reasonable, the circumstances and contexts in which it ought or ought not to occur, and so on (see Clunie, 2005; Ziff and Rao, 1997).

There are several useful discussions here, including some important Canadian ones involving aboriginal or 'first-nations' groups. Among those who have run into difficulty are Rudy Wiebe, an anglophone Mennonite who has written about the French-speaking Métis (1977), and W. P. Kinsella, who has created many indigenous characters in his fiction (see his 1977 short-story collection, for example). A more recent controversy arose when, in 1987, Welwyn Katz wrote a children's book called *False Face*, in which she drew upon some aspects of Iroquois myth, magic and medicine. Katz was immediately accused of voice appropriation and in 1989 published a response to the charge that she had no right to tell Iroquois stories. As writers typically do, she argued that her story was meant to provide a specific example of a general phenomenon (in this case, prejudice and racism). She also posed rhetorical questions about the sorts of stories that she should or shouldn't write. Her earlier works had touched upon themes as various as primitive European religion, witchcraft, incurable illness and Welsh mythology. Since Katz had no direct experience of any of these matters, would they all be proscribable appropriations?

In 1999, Robert Bringhurst's collection of Haida myths and stories set off another storm, with some praising his polished and poetic versions, others condemning his complicity in a 'theft' that occurred a century earlier. In 1900, an American anthropologist working for the famous Franz Boas had travelled to the Queen Charlotte Islands (*Haida Gwaii* – 'islands of the people') and there took down, in Haida, songs and stories that were apparently 'openly and publicly dictated, and ... paid for' (Abley, 2000: 24). Bringhurst cited these circumstances in his defence. It would seem that, at the time, the Haida elders were not unwilling participants; but now, with the Haida language and culture in a fragile state, the matter has come to be seen in rather a different light.[4]

A celebrated example is found in the engrossing story of 'Grey Owl', the Canadian 'Indian' whose books and articles lauded native life and environmental practices. He toured England in the mid-1930s to great acclaim, including that of the royal family and the young princesses Margaret and Elizabeth. Shortly after his death, however, it was revealed that Grey Owl was really one Archie Belaney, born in Hastings in 1888. His amazing career was the subject of many books – most important are the two by his friend Lovat Dickson (1939, 1973) – and a Richard Attenborough film with Pierce Brosnan in the title role. In fact, two generations on, he continues to be an intriguing figure. Reviled in some quarters as a rank impostor, yet another white man usurping and 'appropriating' a native part, Belaney has retained a favourable celebrity in others; some have maintained that, for all his strangeness, he did after all heighten awareness of the environment and of cultures in harmony with it (see also Donald Smith, 1990).

3.4 CULTURAL VOICES AND SCHOLARLY RESEARCH

Attempting some generalisation in this area, Hurka (1989) outlined three relevant and often-made points: outsiders cannot understand the minority experience, they come to dominate the 'market' or the 'audience' for treatments of this experience, and their actions are essentially cross-cultural theft. As Hurka suggests, these are really all facets of one basic resentment towards external domination. While he rejects the 'grand claim' that it is, in principle, impossible for outsiders to understand others' culture, he does acknowledge the 'realistic claim' that such understanding may be difficult, insensitive, biased or warped (see also Keeshig-Tobias, 1990). Of course, as I have implied in the previous section, each of Hurka's points can be refuted: sensitive outsiders have always been able to both sympathise and empathise with 'foreign' cultures, able presentations by insiders have found both expression and audience, and the idea of cultural theft leads to sterility and narrowness, particularly repugnant perhaps in societies priding themselves on a multicultural heritage (see Skene-Melvin, 1989). The late Sidney Hook (1989: 16) discussed the 'old folk fantasy... that only like can understand like'.

The matter is problematic within research, where all of these concerns exist and where, moreover, they are augmented by the desire to come to grips in substantial ways with 'foreign' cultures, and then to produce scientifically accurate and useful descriptions. The furore over whether or not Margaret Mead deeply misunderstood her anthropological informants is a case in point (Freeman, 1983). Another is Steiner's echo of Roman Jakobson's accusation that much modern linguistic work is vitiated by the fact that 'Chomsky's epigones' typically know only English (1992: 245). And, in 1989, Spolsky suggested that a 'value-free' position may mean lack of concern for the minority language groups under study. This changes the argument slightly – from doubts about the capability of outsiders we move to the idea that a more active commitment to the culture studied may be desirable. One of the strongest supporters of this position is Skutnabb-Kangas (1986) who, making no secret of her own committed position, casts others in the role of so called 'administration' researchers, servants to the cause of an enduring and repressive *status quo*. Or consider Fishman, who approves of researchers coming to the field with a 'deeply unconscious and prescientific' commitment to those communities 'who have not capitulated to the massive blandishments of Western materialism, who experience life and nature in deeply poetic and collectively meaningful ways' (1982: 7–8).

The idea seems to be that, if scholars from within the communities to be studied are unavailable, then the next best thing is for 'outsiders' to become much more than disinterested scientific observers. But there are difficulties here, as well. Cameron *et al.* (1992) present several examples of anthropological fieldwork in which the researchers lived with their informants for considerable periods of time, in which they became 'participant observers'. From this vantage point of something approaching normal friendship relationships, they recorded cultural information – sometimes in unethical ways. While the feelings of those studied towards their new scholarly 'friends' are not always clear, it is obvious that the latter enter into relationships with specific purposes in mind, purposes that have nothing to do with friendship, purposes allied to hopes for augmented professional reputations (see Edwards, 1994d).

Fishman (1997; see also 1993) has continued to praise and encourage the work of 'voices from within'. In his foreword to Fishman's book, Walker Connor rightly acknowledges (1997: xi) that assessments of identity are weak and incomplete if they exclude consideration of the 'emotional, passionate, non-rational dimensions' that inside observers so often emphasise. A thread running throughout the book, and made most explicit in the final summation, is the ignorance and arrogance of the intellectual mainstream, the 'objective' outsiders, the social scientists; these constituencies, Fishman believes, have had the power to impose a cold and clinical rationality upon some of the deepest of human feelings and the most important of group sensitivities. Only in a very few cases does he think that scholars have paid attention to 'the suprarational nature of the ethnonational bond' (p. 143). He asserts that 'mainstream' scholars are unable to understand the love of language found in 'peripheral' groups, and he claims that the 'ethnoculturally tolerant view is still something of an oddity in the scholarly literature' (p. 175), perhaps because 'the recurring critique of ethnicity' has always stressed its irrationality, has always found it factually unsuitable and morally unacceptable for 'sophisticated social theory' (p. 57).

There is a whole army of straw men here, as well as an inaccurate and monolithic assessment of intellectual and scholarly enterprise. It has always been true that majority feelings towards minority groups often reveal heady and unpleasant mixtures of ignorance, intolerance, disdain and fear, and it is clear that scholarship often reflects the mainstream that feeds it. But Fishman is simply wrong to assume that the intellectual community writ large has been unaware of (say) the strength of emotional group solidarity, or the symbolic power of language. It may not, on the whole, have endorsed some of their manifestations, but that is another matter. Similarly, the idea that the alleged irrationality of a phenomenon renders it unsuitable or uninteresting as a scientific study is, again, wrongheaded. Analysis and interpretation are activities that always ought to be subject to methodological standards and rigour, but they can be brought to bear upon anything, rational or not. It is perfectly obvious, for example, that one can mount a scientific study of nationalism or religion, of UFOs or witchcraft.

While not wishing to criticise commitment itself, I do feel that there are very real dangers associated with breathless endorsements of the privileged view of the insider, and it is always worrying to find irrationality praised and rationality rejected. Various types of 'poetic' approaches, for example, have characterised many cultural and linguistic revival movements, and their romantic and unrealistic underpinnings have typically done more harm than good. Hobsbawm (1990: 12–13) took a much stronger line:

> No serious historian of nations and nationalism can be a committed political nationalist, except in the sense in which believers in the literal truth of the Scriptures, while unable to make contributions to evolutionary theory, are not precluded from making contributions to archaeology and Semitic philology. Nationalism requires too much belief in what is patently not so. As Renan said: 'Getting its history wrong is part of being a nation'. Historians are professionally obliged not to get it wrong, or at least to make an effort not to.

In principle, the dual issue of sensitivity/objectivity is not logically resolvable. Minority-group members and apologists clearly have biased positions and particular axes to grind when treating their own (or similar) communities. More culturally removed observers, on the other hand, may lack a necessary awareness; they may also be accused of an unfeeling objectification of matters of immediate and compelling concern. Gans's (1985: 304) view seems reasonable here:

> The domination of ethnic studies by ethnic insiders is harmful, not only because of possible conflicts of interest and intellectual blindness, but also because the greater that domination, the greater the likelihood that outsiders will be ever less welcome. Outsiders have their virtues and vices just as insiders do, and ethnic studies – like all other social research – should therefore be done by both.

Can any general conclusions be reached? Beyond the rather clichéd – but nonetheless sensible – injunctions to pay closer attention to one another, to consider more fully the circumstances and sensitivities of 'the other', it seems to me that there is little point in trying to impose any jurisdictional boundaries beyond the limits already established under the laws and traditions involving slander, libel, misrepresentation, and so on. Little point, and also completely antithetical to democratic conceptions of freedom of expression. Instead, however, of fruitless and potentially disastrous attempts to reduce the input from one side, it would surely be more useful to try and increase it from the other, to facilitate greater and greater participation from those whose voices have been insufficiently heard. As Banks (2000: 87) has pointed out, 'the true story of any form of violence, until it's been said from the point of view of both the victim and the perpetrator, hasn't been told at all'. This is not the place to carry on any fuller discussion of these important matters.

My underlying intent here has been merely to suggest that the whole phenomenon of cultural 'appropriation', of who can speak for whom, and of the intentions and contexts of cultural description, takes much of its force from the powerful connections among naming, narrative and group identity.

There is an ancillary matter that I should like to mention; it is, in a way, a counterpoint to the allegedly unfair, inaccurate, unsuitable and larcenous appropriation of names and narratives. If much of the argument here stems from in-group resentment of depictions that represent both theft and negative stereotype, it is also true that many 'outsider' accounts are stereotyped in the other direction, as it were: romanticised portraits of group life in which the inaccuracy does not stem from portrayals of bleak, cruel, unsophisticated or primitive culture – culture held up to astonishment, ridicule or contempt – but, rather, from what might be called the 'noble savage' fallacy. This is a common phenomenon, observable around the world wherever 'advanced' societies have come into contact with 'underdeveloped' ones. There are suggestions of guilt in most instances, a guilt that stems from the exploitation that has typically accompanied such contact. This guilt is usually of insufficient force, of course, to actually hinder the exploitation, or else it can be conveniently compartmentalised: it is perfectly possible to feel some regret for a massive intervention in a group's way of life while, at the same time, believing that such intervention is necessary, inevitable, in the best long-term interests of all concerned, and so on. As in the Highland context that I cited in the previous section, the net result is often a portrayal in which we can see sentimental conceptions of native nobility, grace and virtue, as yet unsullied by the sophistications of civilisation and 'progress', quite happily co-existing with – or even, indeed, reinforcing – other images: a natural savagery and unreliability, a refusal to enter into the modern age, an uncultured and unlettered peasantry.

It might be argued that, if stereotypes have to exist at all, it is better that they should err on the side of the 'noble savage'.[5] We are finding out more and more, however, that some of the most important ingredients in this picture – natural stewardship of the land, innate respect for all living things, an ecological sensitivity long since lost to mainstream societies – are either false or terribly distorted. This is not only a matter of amendment of the historical record; insofar as that record, as interpreted in idealistic eyes, has influenced contemporary attitudes and reactions to aboriginal lives and aboriginal claims, it is also of some real and immediate concern. As Grove (2001: 14) has noted, 'indigenous claims to land, prior ownership, self-government and ethnic identity are increasingly being made in terms of competence in environmental management'. There may be a logical gap or two here, but the sense is surely correct: people who have been poorly treated and whose traditional ways of life were, at the same time, broadly commendable, may expect to garner more sympathy and thus more tangible assets. (Apologies – sometimes with material compensation – for the sins of the fathers are a relatively recent development here; see Walvin, 2002; Weiner, 2005; and chapter 7.)

Suicide and other social evils are not solely manifestations of modern dystopias, or of poverty-stricken and marginalised aboriginal groups; on the contrary, traditional practices in many indigenous societies in Africa, Asia, Europe and Oceania involved sexual and social abuse, ritual torture, starvation and slavery. Edgerton (1992) shows how indigenous communities deforested much of Europe and the Middle East, and were responsible for the virtual extinction of some animal populations. Krech (1999; see also Bourdon, 2000) paints a similar picture for North America. There, societies inhabited by 'the ecological Indian' were ones of great tumult, of wasteful practices with flora and fauna, and showed the familiar signs of environmental degradation. Profligate ways of life were frequently sanctioned by religion: a belief, commonly held from Alaska to the southern United States, was that over-hunting was impossible, that slaughtered animals returned in new incarnations, that the more meat you ate the more you would have. Obvious causes being rejected, the disappearance of animals from overly exploited areas was seen as a result of lack of 'respect' or because some religious taboo had been broken. In a more focussed study of that most symbolic of American animals, the bison – apparently carefully managed by the Indians, ruthlessly exterminated by the white intruders into the harmonious wilderness – Isenberg (2000) points out that the attitudes and practices of the nomadic inhabitants of the great plains were basically similar to those of the later settlers. The undoubted fact that they were responsible for much less of the slaughter says more about their numbers and their weaponry than it does about any idyllic sense of being at one with nature.

The thesis here is not a popular one in some circles, and it is also true that, as some critics have pointed out, Krech and others have ignored some examples of aboriginal sensitivity to their physical surroundings. But these examples typically, and completely understandably, reflected necessary adaptations, and not some ethereal communication with the land. It is undeniable that the rosy picture that has become popular – of people living an Edenic existence, who then were forced into contact with new arrivals whose interests and desires were entirely different, and entirely rapacious – is inaccurate. Indeed, I think that dispassionate

analysis, informed by some basic psychological and historical understanding of the human condition, suggests that, at basic levels, people
are much more similar than they are different. Whether for better or,
very often, for worse, some quite fundamental human practices appear
remarkably constant across time and space. Even the briefest consideration of indigenous populations in the Americas, Australia and New
Zealand (to name only three of the better documented areas) reveals
conflict, savagery and other inter-group assaults equal to those found
anywhere else. The bitter and bloody struggles among the inhabitants
of the South Pacific, among the Melanesians and the Maori, are a case
in point here, as are the well-known brutalities of the Aztecs and the
Maya – societies exemplified by conquest, atrocity and sacrifice; see
Hassig (1992) and Coe (1992). In my part of the world, Mi'kmaq Indians from the mainland played an important part in the extinction of
the Beothuk of Newfoundland. This is somewhat at odds with a recent
treatment that claimed that pre-colonial Mi'kmaq life represented 'an
egalitarian, almost utopian . . . society at the time of contact . . . [a] Golden
Age' destroyed for ever by the repressions of European civilisation (Nash,
1995: 331). The point here, of course, is not to suggest that indigenous societies were inherently worse than those who came to dominate
them – but it makes no sense to imagine that they were, in any basic
human way, any better either.

3.5 ETHNOCENTRISM AND RELATIVISM

Matters of naming and 'voice' are intrinsically interesting and revealing, but they also illuminate broader matters of ethnocentrism and cultural relativism. For most societies throughout history, ethnocentrism,
hostility and prejudice towards 'out-groups' have been the norm. The
sensitivity that can arise from an attitude of cultural relativism is not
at all common. It may have been evident on occasion at 'theoretical'
levels, however these are to be thought of in times past, but practice on
the ground typically revealed how impotent this was in the face of real
interactions with 'the other'. It is easy to lose sight of this if we confine
our gaze only to contemporary liberal democracies – although even a
cursory consideration will reveal how quickly democracy can unravel in
times of stress and strain – but we don't have to look very far beyond
them to see all too many instances of less enlightened views of our
fellow human beings. Within contemporary debates about the stifling
of the small and the 'authentic' by the blunt actions of 'mainstream'
oppression, it is also easy to lose sight of the fact that it is only modern,

liberal-democratic, 'mainstream' society that has at all criticised itself for being ethnocentric, that has made any serious attempt at cultural relativism. George Steiner (1971: 55) put it quite succinctly a generation ago:

> The very posture of self-indictment, of remorse in which much of educated western sensibility now finds itself, is again a culturally specific phenomenon . . . this reflex of self-scrutiny in the name of ethical absolutes is, once more, a characteristically western, post-Voltairian act.

One must not over-interpret this. As I pointed out earlier, there is much lip-service, and there is more than enough evidence of continuingly unenlightened attitudes and policies. Still, the point remains. One looks in vain for introspective and self-critical consideration of the 'other' in most communities, contemporary or historical.

Cultural relativism has had received status within social science for some time – and a good thing, too, in that a sensitivity to other cultures and an increasing unwillingness to impose one's own standards on them represented a welcome and logical change from the earlier ethnocentrism. To read old anthropological accounts of the 'savage mind', of 'debased lifestyles' and of 'primitive' languages is to recapture something of a once-pervasive scholarly world-view. The contemporary relativistic view is that cultures and languages only *differ* from one another, and implies a realisation that there is no universal yardstick against which all could be measured and ranked. Still, a thoroughgoing relativism, with its blatantly non-judgemental stance, presents obvious problems of its own. Are we to accept such things as rigid caste systems, brutal treatment of women, religious intolerance, cannibalism, slavery and prostitution as merely alternative ways of ordering societies?

The late Ernest Gellner argued (1968: 388) that although cultural relativism cannot be logically refuted, it can certainly be questioned.

> It is worth noting that it is intuitively repellent to pretend that the Zande belief in witchcraft is as valid as our rejection of it, and that to suppose it such is a philosophical affectation which cannot be maintained outside the study.

In a later collection of essays, Gellner (1995) argued once more for the superiority of 'cultures of science', rejecting the relativist stance: cognitive relativism was 'nonsense', moral relativism was 'tragic'. Gellner implied that there *are*, in fact, yardsticks that we could use to compare different cultures: in terms of freedom, for instance, common-sense evaluations show quite clearly that some cultures *are* better than others.[6] Two obvious objections suggest themselves here, although neither is strong. First, can we agree about the meaning of something like 'freedom'? Second, isn't it the case that, if cross-cultural metrics do in fact exist, they are probably only good at differentiating fairly extreme cases, and won't help us very much in close comparisons? As to the first objection, we might bear in mind Gellner's point about 'philosophical affectation'; for most ordinary observers, it is not difficult to apply a few basic tests – are people denied democratic processes, is there social oppression? – whose results will reveal degrees of freedom. For example, as I write these words the Burmese authorities are harshly repressing religious and secular protests in Rangoon; when I factor in these latest developments with what I already know about the longstanding military régime, it is not difficult to believe that Burma is a worse place in which to live than is (say) Denmark. And if, to move on to the second objection, we reflect that this is an easy decision because the two communities are so dissimilar – well, the fact that we have only been able to apply our cross-cultural yardstick in a fairly blatant context does not alter the fact that one clearly exists, that, in a word, not everything need be seen as 'relative'.

For Gellner, the most important argument against relativism was that, while it holds that cultures cannot be judged one with the other, or against themselves at different times, societies have always, in fact, engaged in such evaluation. And this is surely a telling point, one obvious illustration of which is the way in which people vote with their feet: some societies have trouble hanging on to their people, while others are particularly attractive to immigrants. More generally, social evolution involves judgement, repudiation and change, and implicit in progress – however defined, however flawed – is at least the *perception* that change is for the better, that the society of a later time is superior to itself at an earlier one. So, not only are western, 'post-Voltairian' populations the most likely sites in which to find cross-cultural sensitivity, we may now consider that secular and scientific society is in fact socially pre-eminent precisely because of this posture, because (as Gellner would add) it is a dynamic product of social evolution, and because it permits greater individual freedom.

I am not saying, of course, that relativistic sensitivity is necessarily widespread in western secular society, only that it is more frequently encountered there than elsewhere. Similarly, to say that greater individual freedom is permitted in modern scientific communities is clearly not to say that such freedom is ensured. Nonetheless, as I have tried to point out, these are the only societies that regularly criticise themselves for being ethnocentric and that support culturally relativistic views of other cultures. Since many of these other cultures are, themselves, quite closed and intolerant, it is somewhat ironic to consider that were the results of cross-cultural sensitivity to give them greater latitude of action, greater opportunity for self-expression, and so on, there is little reason to think that their own cultural posture would become more liberal. That is why one of the most interesting political debates in liberal-democratic circles today is how tolerance is to be extended to groups who are intolerant, or under what conditions democratic society might be expected to support communities that, if they could, would roll back democracy.

Critical observations on an out-and-out relativism seem to me very well-founded, but they do not apply equally to all features of societies. To cite an example to which I shall return, I would argue that the contemporary rejection of any 'primitive' variety of language or dialect remains a robust one. Cultural relativism is itself a relative matter. Along the lines mentioned above, I take it for granted that a society which condones female circumcision, believes in witchcraft, and eats its enemies is inferior, in these respects at least, to one which does not. I do not see that this constrains me to accept, as well, that the language of that society is inferior to the one spoken next door, even if the neighbours are all feminists, scientists and vegetarians; see also below. (See Patrick Phillips, 2007, for a cogent discussion of relativism; he pays particular attention to the fact that, despite centuries of philosophical criticism, it has never entirely lost its appeal and, indeed, it flourishes particularly well in vague post-modernist musings.)

STUDY QUESTIONS

1. Why are personal and group names such sensitive matters?
2. Many human communities style themselves simply as 'us', or 'the people', or 'the human beings'. What does this reveal about social 'groupness', and what are the implications for inter-group contacts?
3. Discuss the thesis that 'voice appropriation' is indeed a form of colonial oppression.
4. Is cultural relativism itself relative?

Further reading

Deborah Cameron, Elizabeth Frazer, Penelope Harvey, Ben Rampton and Kay Richardson's (1992) book, *Researching Language: Issues of Power and Method*, is a useful collection which illustrates some of the pitfalls associated with becoming closely involved with the subjects of research, generally considered a necessity in many anthropological and ethnographic undertakings.

Ernest Gellner's (1995) *Anthropology and Politics* includes a discussion on the difficulties of relativism.

In Eric Hobsbawm's (1990) book, *Nations and Nationalism Since 1780*, the author deals, as part of this now-classic treatment, with the intertwinings of scholarship and more personal involvement.

Patrick Phillips's (2007) book, *The Challenge of Relativism*, provides a good modern overview of the area.

4 Language, dialect and identity

4.1 LANGUAGE

4.1.1 Language defined

Edward Sapir once stated that 'language is a purely human and non-instinctive method of communicating ideas, emotions, and desires by means of a system of voluntarily produced symbols' (1921: 7). A little later, Morris (1946) described it as an arrangement of arbitrary symbols possessing an agreed-upon significance within a community; furthermore, these symbols can be used and understood independent of immediate contexts, and they are connected in regular ways. First, then, language is a *system*, which implies regularity and rules of order. Second, this system is an arbitrary one inasmuch as its particular units or elements have meaning only because of users' agreement and convention. And third, language is used for communicative purposes by a group of people who constitute the speech or language community. So, a language might be considered as

> a communication system composed of arbitrary elements which possess an agreed upon significance within a community. These elements are connected in rule-governed ways. The existence of *rules* (that is to say, *grammar*) is necessary for comprehension, of course, but it is also essential for the virtually infinite creativity (or productivity) of a system that rests upon a finite number of linguistic gears and axles. [My paraphrase, J.E.]

Implicit here is the idea that languages differ from one another in the ways in which they assign meaning to sounds and symbols. Prescinding entirely from questions about the origins of language itself, and about the evolution of different language communities, I note only that there are numerous language groups in the world, societies whose patterns of communication are not mutually intelligible (although many, of course, are related in language 'families': the Indo-European, the Semitic, the Finno-Ugric, and many others).

There is more to language than communication, however, which means that the description given above is not complete – and which demonstrates the basis of the language–identity linkage. One way to approach the other great attribute of languages is to consider, first of all, the pragmatic advantages that might ensue if there were not so many distinct languages in the world. While there are many 'small' languages hovering on the brink of extinction, thousands of other varieties continue to exist, and this might be seen by some galactic visitor as a bizarre impediment to communication and understanding, particularly in a world that technology has made smaller and smaller. Some have seen the continuation of language diversity as evidence of a wide-spread human desire to stake particular linguistic claims to the world, to create unique perspectives on reality and to protect group distinctiveness: in a word, to protect an important vehicle of culture and tradition. It is with a view to this desire that Steiner (1992: 243) speaks of separate languages enabling groups to keep to themselves the 'inherited, singular springs of their identity'. The vehicle of continuity can also, then, be a vehicle for concealment, secrecy and fiction. This idea is not Steiner's alone. Popper suggested that what is most characteristic of human language is the possibility of storytelling, and Wittgenstein referred to language disguising thought (see Edwards, 1979b). Earlier, Jespersen (1946) had reminded us of Talleyrand's famous observation that language exists to hide one's thoughts, and Kierkegaard's suggestion that language is often used to cover up a complete lack of thought! The idea of language as concealment may seem contrary to the more obvious communicative function, but it should be remembered that communication is a within-group phenomenon, while the 'concealment' is a linguistic attempt to maintain inviolate a particular grasp of the world. The assumption here, of course, is that those who know your language are also members of your group, and this is clearly an assumption that is often incorrect; 'outsiders' can learn your language, or they may gain access to what it contains through translation. But this perhaps only reinforces the urge to conceal and protect, and the historical equation, *traduttore-traditore* ('translation is treason'), quite bluntly suggests an unwillingness to see 'hoarded dreams, patents of life...taken across the frontier' (Steiner, 1992: 244).

There may be some overstatement here, but it seems clear enough that there has always been resistance to the abandoning of a particular language, something that can easily coincide with a desire for a purely 'instrumental' bilingualism in which the original variety is retained. If this pragmatically driven bilingualism involves a language stronger or more dominant than the maternal variety, then the latter may find its own domains of use steadily shrinking. The retreat here may involve an increasing emphasis on the *non*-instrumental functions of the home language, a heightening of the distinction between the *communicative* and *symbolic* functions.

4.1.2 Communication and culture

The essence of the distinction between the communicative and the symbolic functions lies in a differentiation between language in its ordinarily understood sense as an instrumental tool, and language as an emblem of groupness, a symbol, a psychosocial rallying-point. It is a distinction whose salience varies greatly across speech communities. For instance, in any group in which the language of daily use is *also* the ancestral language, intangible symbolic aspects are intertwined with the instrumental function. The symbolic value of language, the historical and cultural associations which it has accumulated and its 'natural semantics of remembrance' (Steiner, 1992: 494) provide a rich underlay for every communicative interaction, a powerful underpinning of shared connotations. It is in this way that we are always 'translating' and 'interpreting' when we speak, and our ability to read between the lines, as it were, depends upon a cultural continuity in which language is embedded, and which is not open to all. (It also depends, of course, upon our more or less instantaneous processing of all sorts of paralinguistic information that accompanies speech itself: body language, intonation, nonverbal cues of many kinds. Studies have shown, in fact, that when it comes to fully understanding a message or determining its truth or relevance, we typically place more emphasis on the nonverbal accompaniments than we do on the actual utterance *per se*. Your mother was right: it's not what someone says, it's how they say it.)

'Outsiders' who have learned a language for practical reasons may develop a highly fluent command, but they may also find that certain deeper levels of communication remain closed to them: the technical capabilities that are more than sufficient for living and working in another speech community may not be so for a full appreciation of that culture's literature or drama. Consider the comic effect of a stage duchess speaking with a cockney accent, an effect that depends upon cultural knowledge that goes well beyond words and their literal meanings. Only those who grow up within a community can, perhaps, participate fully in this sort of 'expanded' interaction, because they alone can make the necessary 'translations'. Steiner (1992: 31) notes, indeed, that 'we possess civilization because we have learnt to translate out of time'.

The complicated interweaving of language and culture that rests upon a fusion of pragmatic linguistic skills and the more intangible associations carried by language is not always immediately apparent to native speakers within a majority-speech community. The indigenous English speaker in England or America, for example, uses the language in all regular domains; it is at once the language of grocery shopping and the language of myth, poetry and literature. However, the two aspects of language *are* separable – the communicative from the symbolic – and it is possible for the latter to remain important in the absence of the former. This is most clearly seen when we examine language use and attitudes in minority groups undergoing (or having undergone) language shift within majority, other-language-speaking populations; or, indeed, in any group where a shift has occurred in the fairly recent past. (The time element is important: we would no longer expect English speakers to attach any significance to Old English or its Germanic precursors.) Ireland provides an example here. A seminal survey (Committee on Irish Language Attitudes Research, 1975) sampled some 3,000 respondents in an investigation of Irish language use, ability and attitudes. Only about 3% of the overall population now use the language in any regular way, there is little interest in Irish restoration, and many are pessimistic about the maintenance of the little Irish still used. Yet, there does remain a value for Irish in the symbolic sense, and it can be argued that Irish continues to occupy some place in the constitution of current Irish identity (see Edwards, 1984a).

The continuing symbolic role of language can also be observed among immigrant groups in the United States. Some years ago Eastman (1984) discussed the notion of what she termed an 'associated' language – one that group members no longer use, or even know, but which continues to be part of their heritage (see also Eastman and Reese, 1981; Edwards, 1984b).[1] Some have suggested that when language operates only at a symbolic or 'associated' level, it is no longer really language. Certainly, the symbolic function of language that co-exists with the communicative is not quite the same thing as symbolism divorced from communication (Irish for most Irish people, Polish for most fourth-generation Polish-Americans, and so on). Still, it should be remembered that language, unlike other purely emblematic markers, is itself a complex system that is at least theoretically capable of regaining an instrumental and communicative status. I simply observe here that, even if they are often joined, the two functions of language are separable, and that ignorance of the distinction between them can lead to lack of clarity and misdirection of action (among linguistic nationalists, for example). There is a further proviso: although the functions are separable, and although the symbolic aspects can long outlast communicative-language shift, these aspects are first given life by a vernacular – not the other way around.

The implication is that the loss or abandonment of a language in its ordinary communicative role must eventually lead to the dilution or, indeed, the disappearance of its symbolic or 'associational' capacity.

4.1.3 Language goodness

Languages are generally considered to be separate and mutually unintelligible: speakers of French cannot understand German. Are some better, more logical or more expressive than others? This has historically proved to be a controversial question, although there are many examples of strong convictions on the matter.

Charles V, the sixteenth-century Holy Roman Emperor, apparently distributed his linguistic fluencies by speaking Spanish to God, Italian to women, French to men and German to horses. Richard Carew, the English poet and antiquary, wrote a little later of the 'excellency' of English compared to other languages:

> The Italian is pleasant, but without sinews, as a still reflecting water; the French delicate, but ever nice as a woman, scarce daring to open her lips for fear of marring her countenance; the Spanish majestical but fulsome, running too much on the o, and terrible like the Devil in a play; the Dutch manlike, but withal very harsh, as one ready at every word to pick a quarrel. (1614: 40)

Carew was essentially providing a picture of foreigners painted by an educated Englishman of the sixteenth century. In the late eighteenth century, Antoine de Rivarol observed that French was synonymous with clarity, and that English, Greek, Latin and Italian were mediums of ambiguity – providing a similar picture as redrawn by a Frenchman (Wardhaugh, 1987: 100). Such 'language' attitudes are, in fact, attitudes towards certain groups of people. As well, they often reflect prescriptivist desires for linguistic 'protection' and 'purity'. I shall return to attitudes and language purism later on.

Many other examples of such sentiments can easily be found (see Edwards, 1995). While it is unsurprising that the 'large' languages of the world have thrown their linguistic weight around in this jingoistic way, exaggerated claims have also been made for 'smaller' or threatened varieties. The movement for the revival of Irish, for example, evoked similar sentiments. Towards the end of the nineteenth century it was extolled for its 'perfection' and 'independence', qualities so pronounced that it must clearly have been one of the first languages spoken on earth; indeed, an earlier scholar-soldier, Charles Vallancey (1772), held that the origins of Irish lay with Carthage, that the language was a 'Punic-Celtic' compound, and that Ireland itself was the 'Thule of the

Ancients'. Irish was also seen as ideally suited for musical expression, and it was claimed that the vocal organs of Irish people were naturally adapted for Gaelic speaking: Irish was already in the heads of non-Irish-speaking Irishmen, so to speak, and teaching it involved a drawing-out rather than a putting-in. At a religious level, Irish was praised as the unique vehicle of Catholicism (see also chapter 3).

While some of the more egregious comparisons have faded away, it is still easy to find references to the greater concision of English (as opposed to French) or the greater aesthetic appeal of Italian (as opposed to German). At less informal levels, however, the question has been more thoughtfully considered where the languages involved are not closely related. Someone who might see little relevance in comparing members of the same language family (French and Italian, say) might nevertheless feel on safer ground in suggesting comparisons between the mother tongues of communities widely separated in terms of 'development' or 'sophistication' (like French and Yup'ik, perhaps). Could there be some correlation between levels of social and linguistic development? The idea has appealed to many in the past and obviously retains considerable contemporary support.

Linguists, anthropologists and others now argue almost unanimously that languages are always sufficient for the needs of their speakers. In fact, formal statements on the matter have existed for a long time; in the sixteenth century, for instance, Joachim du Bellay pointed out that 'all languages are of a like value... to each man his language can competently communicate every doctrine', and he went on to reject the idea that 'diverse tongues are fitted to signify diverse conceptions' (1549 / 1939: 46–7). Even so, and even within the academic community, less enlightened views still surface now and again. Thus, Honey (1983; see also Edwards, 1983b) asked how the language of speakers in 'primitive' groups could cope with higher mathematics, or Wittgenstein, or bio-chemistry; further, if all varieties are adequate for group needs, could we not claim that groups lacking the necessary vocabulary do not need, for example, modern technology or medicine?

There is here a confusion between concepts and words. If a group begins to take an interest in simple arithmetic and, five hundred years later, develops a theory of quantum mechanics, one might expect that vocabulary would also develop. This is, in fact, what happens. There is, incidentally, no need to look at 'primitive' societies here: consider the trajectory of western intellectual and linguistic development. Secondly, and relatedly, it is the lack of the prerequisite conceptual understanding that prevents a group from possessing modern medical procedures (for example). Words themselves are only indicators. The real meaning of scholarly assertions about linguistic adequacy is that language keeps pace with conceptual advancement, which in turn determines the very needs of which speakers can even be aware. While there must obviously be a finite lag between new ideas and new terms, this lag varies inversely with the general importance of the idea. How long did it take for 'astronaut' to enter common usage? And, even while it was waiting to make its entrance, there were all sorts of other descriptive terms to fill the temporary void ('spaceman'). Description, albeit rough, is always possible. While scientists wait for the word 'laser' to appear, they are perfectly able to convey the idea of what the word represents to others; if this were not possible, the new word itself would be empty. All of this rests upon accumulated conceptual advancement, and we have not, so far at least, had an instance of such a gigantic leap forward that description has proved impossible.

It is quite clear, then, that no language can be 'logically' described as better or worse than another. Given that language is an arbitrary system in which communication rests upon community agreement, it follows that the only 'logic' of language is to be found in its grammar (which is a logic of convention). What is grammatical in French (the use of two elements to express verbal negation, for example: 'Je suis heureux' and 'Je ne suis pas heureux') is not in English (where only one is required: 'I am happy' and 'I am not happy'). Who would wish to argue that this reflects upon the relative quality of the two systems? And, if we compare the language of a technologically advanced society with that of a more 'undeveloped' one, we find the same different-but-not deficient relationship. In an influential survey work, Gleitman and Gleitman (1970) noted bluntly that there are no 'primitive' languages, and Lenneberg (1967: 364) put matters this way:

> Could it be that some languages require 'less mature cognition' than others, perhaps because they are still more primitive? In recent years this notion has been thoroughly discredited by virtually all students of language.

Much earlier, Sapir (1921) had observed that

> The lowliest South African Bushman speaks in the forms of a rich symbolic system that is in essence perfectly comparable to the speech of the cultivated Frenchman ... When it comes to linguistic form, Plato walks with the Macedonian swineherd, Confucius with the head-hunting savage of Assam.

Well, the phrasing here is no longer, perhaps, *comme il faut* – and there's more head-hunting now in corporate jungles than in those of Assam – but Sapir's words continue to be endorsed by virtually all linguists.

Languages are best seen as different systems reflecting different varieties of the human condition. Although they may be unequal in complexity at given points, this does not imply that some have greater overall expressive power. To put it another way, we could say that not all varieties have the same capabilities: different social, geographical and other circumstances determine what elements will be needed and, therefore, developed. All are, however, potentially functionally equivalent. Languages differ in lexical, grammatical, phonological and other ways, but questions of overall linguistic 'goodness' are simply wrong-headed (see also the discussion of dialect 'goodness', below).

Environments differ and the things that must be detailed in language must then also differ. The shop-worn example of Inuit using many different words – perhaps as many as 400, in fact – to refer to various types of what English speakers simply term *snow* does not reflect a capability constitutionally denied to non-Inuit. It *does* reflect the fact that different environments evoke, in habitual ways, different linguistic behaviour. English speakers could certainly learn to differentiate among types of snow if they were transplanted to an Arctic setting – or if they become skiers. Incidentally, this illustration is not only tired; it is also inaccurate. In a study at once amusing and enlightening, Pullum (1991) has shown that the Inuit do not, after all, have distinct words for 'snow on the ground', 'fallen snow', 'slushy snow', 'snow drift', and so on. Pointing out that the whole matter would be trivial even if it were true, Pullum acknowledged its popularity and its appeal. And the truth? According to an authoritative Inuit dictionary there are only two relevant lexical roots here: *ganik* (referring to snow in the air) and *aput* (snow on the ground). Many words can then be derived from these, much as the English 'snow' can lead to 'snow-fall', 'snowflake' and 'snowball'.

The particular matter of linguistic adaptation to circumstances – linguistic relativity – was of particular interest to Sapir and his pupil Whorf (see Carroll, 1972). Roughly stated, their hypothesis was that different languages carve up reality in different ways and that, therefore, the language you speak will determine the way you think. If there were, in fact, such a powerful connection between language and cognition, there would be powerful repercussions for cognitive psychology – and powerful incentives for the maintenance of linguistic diversity. After all, one implication would be that language loss would inevitably entail the eradication of a unique window on the world. Such a connection would provide a great deal of ammunition for language nationalists, for all those who believe in an inviolable equation between a particular language and the group identity of its speakers. However, the hypothesis is *not* generally accepted, at least not in this 'strong' version. The single greatest counter-argument is that, while languages obviously differ in important ways, we can obviously translate (if sometimes quite imperfectly) among them, and speakers of one variety whose circumstances change can learn another. The lessons of history are quite clear.

If we find that the Inuit talk and think about snow in a much more fine-grained and engrossing way than do Italians, we should simply understand that important features of their physical, social and psychological environments are quite different. If we found a previously unknown desert community whose colour vocabulary was much more limited than our own, perhaps only ranging over reds and browns, that would be no reason to expect some permanent cognitive inability to perceive and talk about 'green' after they had struck oil and moved to Surrey. The implication here is for a 'weak' Whorfianism, a version of the hypothesis that makes a great deal of sense: language *influences* our *habitual* ways of thinking. This is plausible because it is parsimonious. On the one hand, it would be 'uneconomical' to develop vocabulary and grammar to describe contexts and concepts that are rare or nonexistent in your life; on the other, your particular environment may dictate linguistic nuances that are unnecessary elsewhere. Once such appropriate linguistic evolution has occurred, it is entirely reasonable to think that your maternal variety will tend to differentially 'sensitise' or 'set' you in certain perceptual directions. You will tend to see things in certain ways, and every instance will reinforce the particular linguistic parameters that highlighted it. But none of this implies the development of some unalterable cognitive rigidity.

4.1.4 Language change

If we accept the idea of linguistic 'adequacy', in line with the constraints and circumstances noted, we should also realise that notions of language 'impurity', 'decay' and 'deterioration' are ill-founded. They have always figured in the popular imagination, of course, and at times have also had an appeal in more academic quarters. Indeed, the metaphoric perspective that underlies these ideas – one that sometimes also underpins the use of terms like language *maintenance, shift, decline, death* and *revival* – is an organic one: languages are considered as if they were living things. An early expression was given by Thomas Jones (1688/1972) in his seventeenth-century Welsh–English dictionary:

> To Languages as well as Dominions (with all other things under the Sun) there is an appointed time; they have had their infancy, foundations and beginning, their growth and increase in purity and perfection; as also in spreading and propagation: their state of consistency; and their old age, declinings and decayes.

Franz Bopp, the famous nineteenth-century linguist, apparently enter-
tained similar notions:

> Languages are to be considered organic natural bodies, which are
> formed according to fixed laws, develop as possessing an inner
> principle of life, and gradually die out because they do not understand
> themselves any longer. (see Jespersen, 1922: 65)

The last few words of this quotation are curious, to say the least, but
it is easy to see why the organic metaphor has proved attractive; a
modern variant is the ecological argument that links language diversity
to biodiversity (see chapter 10).

Attractive as these perspectives might continue to be in some quarters,
it is clear that languages themselves obey no organic imperatives. It is
their speakers, their 'carriers' as it were, who must come to grips with
matters of mortality. This was already obvious to clearer heads a long
time ago. Joachim du Bellay (1549/1939: 21) observed:

> Languages are not born of themselves after the fashion of herbs, roots,
> or trees: some infirm and weak in their nature; the others healthy,
> robust, and more fitted to carry the burden of human conception; but
> all their virtue is born in the world of the desire and will of mortals.

The trajectory and span of linguistic existence are granted by human
society and culture rather than by natural laws, and one would be hard
pressed today to find any linguist still believing that languages 'behave
like beans or chrysanthemums', as Aitchison (2000: 208) put it. Different
languages are not intrinsically stronger or weaker in some survival-
of-the-fittest arena, but their fortunes are inexorably bound up with
those of their users. Perhaps we might consider languages as inorganic
parasites on human hosts.

It will come as no surprise to learn that the 'organic' view of language
has most often come to the fore at times of crisis. The Irish nationalist, Padraic Pearse, wrote (1916b) about the nineteenth-century English
educational system in Ireland as a 'murder machine' devoted to the
elimination of indigenous culture and language; and more contemporary writers have also claimed that languages do not 'die natural deaths'
but are, rather, killed by those seeking to destroy a nation. On the other
hand, some observers (Irish among them) have suggested that languages
may commit suicide, and that it may be impossible to eradicate a language which its speakers truly wish to retain. The popular Irish writer
Flann O'Brien believed that 'the present extremity of the Irish language
is due mainly to the fact that the Gaels deliberately flung that instrument of beauty and precision from them' (Ó Conaire, 1973: 125). It is
clear that terms like 'murder' and 'suicide' are highly-charged and likely

to obscure rather than clarify, to overly simplify matters into an 'us versus them' picture in which oppressors and oppressed kindly wear black or white hats, where morality resides exclusively in one camp. But the very existence and use of such words illustrates, again, the potency of language-as-symbol, the degree to which deep psychological and social wells are being tapped, and the obvious conclusion that most discussions of what could be termed 'the social life of language' are, in their essence, not really about language at all. They are about identity.

4.2 DIALECT

Strictly speaking, a dialect is a variety of a language that differs from others along three dimensions: vocabulary, grammar and pronunciation (accent). Because they are forms of the same language, however, dialects are mutually intelligible. So, while French speakers cannot understand Fulfulde speakers, Texans can understand Cockneys. If you *brew* your tea, pronounce it *tay* and say *Come here 'til I pour you a cup*, your friend should know what is happening, even if she *mashes* her tea and would invite you to the table *so that* she can pour you a cup. However, we have all heard some dialects that are almost impossible to understand because of the degree of variation from our own; thus, mutual intelligibility is frequently difficult and sometimes merely theoretical.

Mutual intelligibility as a criterion of dialects (as opposed to languages) falters at another level. For instance, the existence of *dialect continua* may mean that only 'adjacent' forms are mutually understood. Consider four dialects, A, B, C and D. If a speaker of A can easily understand B, 'can just understand C, but cannot really be said to understand D, does a language division come between C and D? But C and D may understand each other quite well' (Petyt, 1980: 14). Such continua are in fact quite common, especially where one language community borders another. There is, for example, the long Spanish–Portuguese frontier in South America, as well as the European chain formed by dialects of German and Dutch. Similar situations exist for varieties of Slovak, Czech, Ukrainian, Polish and Russian, and for western dialects of Italian, French, Catalan, Spanish and Portuguese.

Discussion of dialects soon gives rise to other problems too. If they are different forms that exist under the umbrella of the same language, how finely are we to sieve these differences? Bearing in mind that the logically final distinction here would bring us to the level of the idiolect, convention and convenience generally determine that the analysis stops at some group level, according to need. Petyt (1980: 12) observed that 'sometimes we speak of "Yorkshire dialect", thus implying that the fea-tures shared by all Yorkshire speakers in contrast to outsiders are impor-tant ... at other times we speak of "Dentdale dialect" with the "essential" features being much more detailed'.

Criteria supplementary to the intelligibility notion must be provided, and Petyt and others have focussed upon two. The first has to do with the existence of a written language: if groups who differ in speech patterns share a common written form, they may be said to speak different *dialects*. The second involves matters of political allegiance and national identity (and power: 'A language', as Max Weinreich reported [1945], 'is a dialect that has an army and navy'[2]). Both are involved where Cantonese and Mandarin speakers are concerned. Speakers of these varieties may have considerable difficulty understanding one another but they are nonethe-less considered to speak dialects of Chinese, not only because they use the same written form, but also because of the overarching state of which they are members. On the other hand, while Norwegian and Danish speakers can understand each other well, the demands of national and political identity require that they have different languages. On the basis of intelligibility alone, there are really two Scandinavian languages: a continental variety comprising Norwegian, Danish and Swedish, and an insular language (Icelandic and Faroese). There are other examples, too, of the dominance of political concerns over purely linguistic ones, con-cerns that dictate that Serbian and Croatian, Hindi and Urdu, Flemish and Dutch, and so on, are to be seen as separate languages.

A particularly interesting example was provided by Wolff (1959), who showed how the concept of intelligibility itself may be subject to social pressure. Among the Urhobo dialects of south-western Nigeria, mutual intelligibility was evident and acknowledged, until speakers of Isoko began to claim that their 'language' was different from the rest, a claim coinciding with their demands for increased political autonomy. Another group, speakers of the Okpe dialect that is almost identical to Isoko, were not making such nationalistic claims and, for them, mutual intelligibility remained unaffected (see also Heine, 1979; Maurud, 1976). It is not difficult to see that, given sufficient time, a political desire for linguistic distinctiveness could actually lead to the real loss of mutual intelligibility. This process could be strengthened if, as well, growing feelings of difference led to decreasing group contact. Elements could then be in place like those that contributed to the transition from dialect to language status for French, Italian, Romanian, Portuguese and Span-ish – the Romance languages that began life as dialects of the Latin of the Roman empire. (The word 'romance' comes from the vulgar Latin *romanice* – meaning 'in the local variety, descended from Latin', and contrasted with *latine*, or 'in Latin itself'.)

As with languages, dialects cannot be seen, linguistically, in terms of better or worse. However, while there may be (relatively) few people who would want to argue that French is better than English, the idea that Oxford English is better than Cockney remains a prejudice of broader appeal. 'Dialect' has long been used, of course, to denote a substandard deviation from some prestigious variety or more 'standard' form. Dictionary definitions have supported this view, with even the *Oxford English Dictionary* noting that a dialect is 'one of the subordinate forms or varieties of a language arising from local peculiarities'. In a sense this is correct, but it is incorrect to assume – as the definition would imply to many – that this 'subordinate' status has any inherent linguistic basis. Neither should it be thought, as some have traditionally done (see Wyld, 1934, below), that some varieties simply *sound* better than others or are more aesthetically pleasing. Clearly, we must attend a little more closely to these matters.

If, as we have seen, popular attitudes about the superiority/inferiority of languages are resistant to change despite the weight of linguistic evidence, then those concerning styles, accents and dialects are even more deeply ingrained. 'Ain't', we are instructed, is always wrong; two negatives (in English) make a positive; saying *dese, dat* and *dose* is uneducated (at best); Cockney and Joual depart from both accuracy and propriety; and so on. Vocabulary, pronunciation and grammar that are at variance with a received 'standard' are regularly dismissed, and a great divide is thus perceived between such a standard and all other 'substandard' forms. In fact, however:

> just as there is no linguistic reason for arguing that Gaelic is superior to Chinese, so no English dialect can be claimed to be linguistically superior or inferior to any other ... There is no linguistic evidence whatsoever for suggesting that one dialect is more 'expressive' or 'logical' than any other, or for postulating that there are any 'primitive', 'inadequate' or 'debased' English dialects. (Trudgill, 1975: 26)

By logical extension, Trudgill's point applies to *all* dialects of *all* languages.

4.2.1 Standard and nonstandard dialect

I will have more to say, in the next chapter, about the convincing linguistic evidence for the non-existence of 'substandard' dialects. For the moment, we can proceed on the basis of Trudgill's entirely logical analogy. If, however, there are no inherently deficient or substandard varieties, there are obviously dialects that possess greater status and prestige than others. Thus, in English as in many other languages, *standard* dialects are those that have risen socially with the historical fortunes of their speakers. It follows, then, that all others must necessarily be *non-standard*, but this is not to be understood as any sort of pejorative label, at least not in any formal linguistic sense. Broadly speaking, a standard dialect is the one spoken by educated people, the one chosen in formal contexts, the one enshrined in print. Its power and position derive from political circumstance. If York instead of London had become the centre for the royal court, for example, BBC newsreaders (the earlier ones, at least: there is more tolerance on the airwaves now for regional varieties) might sound different; schools might be promoting another form of 'correct' English in England.

We will see, below, that it is largely investigations of *grammar* that have upheld the rejection of any dialect as being substandard or inferior. There have been attempts made, however, to approach the issue from a different perspective. Some have argued that while dialects may not be better or worse than one another in purely linguistic terms, they differ in aesthetic quality. In the 1930s, for example, two prominent English linguists suggested that Standard English was superior on this dimension. Robert Chapman (1932: 4) praised it as 'one of the most subtle and most beautiful of all expressions of the human spirit' and a little later Henry Wyld (1934: 4) went into further detail:

> If it were possible to compare systematically every vowel sound in RS [Received Standard English] with the corresponding sound in a number of provincial and other dialects, assuming that the comparison could be made, as is only fair, between speakers who possessed equal qualities of voice, and the knowledge how to use it, I believe no unbiased listener would hesitate in preferring RS as the most pleasing and sonorous form, and the best suited to be the medium of poetry and oratory.

I need hardly say that such sentiments are not restricted to those speaking in and for English. Is it possible, however, to test the belief that one dialect is more 'pleasing and sonorous' than another?

Studies by Howard Giles and his colleagues in the 1970s remain the simplest and the most revealing here in their comparisons of an 'inherent value' hypothesis with an 'imposed norm' one. The former suggests – as Wyld and other scholars did, and as many people continue to do today – that aesthetic qualities are intrinsic to language varieties, while the latter implies that they are attached or imposed by listeners. In order to isolate aesthetic qualities from any pre-existing knowledge or stereotype, the listener-judges in the comparison studies were typically ignorant of the variety they were to listen to: their task was simply to say how appealing its sounds were. In one investigation, non-French-speaking Welsh adults listened to European French, educated Canadian French and working-class Canadian French voice samples. Asked to rate the pleasantness and prestige of the voices, the judges were unable to single out any one of the varieties with any regularity: this, in spite of the fact that, in Quebec itself, both formal investigation and a mass of anecdotal evidence had shown a clear 'aesthetic' preference among French speakers for European French accents. In another experiment, British undergraduates who knew no Greek evaluated the aesthetic quality of two Greek dialects, the Athenian and the Cretan. The former is the prestige standard form, while the latter is a nonstandard variant of low social status; within the Greek speech community, the language of the capital is heard as more mellifluous, while the island variety is rougher in quality. As in the first investigation, however, the listener-judges were able to detect no uniform differences between the two dialects. There was, if anything, a tendency to rate the Cretan variety as more pleasant and prestigious than the Athenian (see Giles *et al.*, 1974, 1979).

The compelling element in these demonstrations is the judges' ignorance of the social connotations that the different varieties clearly possess in their own speech communities. The implication is that if one removes (experimentally) the social stereotypes usually associated with given varieties, aesthetic judgements favouring the high-status dialects will not arise. Or, to put it another way, aesthetic assessments of the *sounds* of a variety seem to be heavily influenced by listeners' conceptions of just who is speaking. The 'inherent value' hypothesis fails, and the 'imposed norm' hypothesis is confirmed. Aesthetic standards are constructed by those in the know; the stereotypes that link beauty or harshness to a set of sounds are unavailable to others. Naturally, none of this rules out purely individual preferences: I may think Italian sounds the most attractive, while Gaelic may fall most sweetly on your ear, but we should agree to differ on a matter of subjectivity that seems to admit of no general yardstick.

At about the same time, Peter Trudgill (1975) provided a neat and apposite example of the arbitrary nature of aesthetic and 'status' features in speech. In England, speakers of what Wyld in the 1930s called 'Received Standard English', and what has since come to be better known as RP (Received Pronunciation), do not pronounce the postvocalic 'r' (as in words like *cart* and *mar*). The absence of this feature, then, is associated with high accent prestige. But in New York, exactly the opposite holds: the higher the social status of the speaker, the more likely he or she is to pronounce the postvocalic 'r'. The table 4.1 shows the percentages of possible postvocalic 'r' pronunciations actually used by speakers surveyed in New York and Reading, UK. It simply shows that what is high-status usage in New York is of low prestige in Berkshire and *vice versa*.

Table 4.1 *Percentage of postvocalic 'r' pronunciation in New York and Reading*

	New York	Reading
Upper-middle-class speakers	32	0
Lower-middle-class speakers	20	28
Upper-working-class speakers	12	44
Lower-working-class speakers	10	49

Evaluations of different language varieties are not based upon intrinsic qualities but rest, rather, upon social conventions and preferences. These, in turn, are most obviously related to the prestige and power possessed by speakers of certain 'standard' varieties. Although I have essentially restricted myself to discussing English here, a general rule seems to be that when social stratification is associated with linguistic variation, arguments will be made for the grammatical, lexical or phonological superiority of the variety used by those in power. Social power typically and very easily turns what we now understand to be simple variation into better-and-worse assessments. And since social preferences and prejudices form the foundations of social interactions, with all their ramifications, the net result is that *differences* are regularly translated into *deficiencies*. It is one thing to lay out the rational bases for rejecting inaccurate perceptions – one thing, and a very important thing – but it is quite another to effect real change in these popular evaluations.

There are two exceptions to the rule that equates status with alleged linguistic superiority, and they occur at opposite ends of a prestige continuum. Extremely high-status varieties may seem affected and generally 'over the top': their speakers may move in the highest social circles, but outside those spheres their speech can be something of a joke; see also the remarks on 'poshness', below. Opposite to this is the 'covert prestige' possessed by working-class speech, with its positive associations of masculinity. Research in Britain, for example, has found that both working-class and middle-class males may claim to use nonstandard forms even when they do not customarily do so (Trudgill, 1983; Edwards, 1989). The actual use of such forms, by generally standard-dialect-speaking individuals, is most likely when the speaker wants to appear forceful, direct and unambiguous. Covert prestige rests upon the fact that the direct-ness and the vibrancy of nonstandard speech are perceived as 'macho' qualities and, to the extent that masculinity is viewed favourably, such prestige may be a factor in the use of lower-class variants; see Trudgill's (2000) summary analysis.

Labov (1966, 1977) had earlier commented upon the phenomenon in New York, contrasting its effects with the 'hypercorrect' usage that is a hallmark of nonstandard speakers who may (he suggested) feel linguis-tically insecure about 'stigmatised' features of their dialect and who may (particularly in formal contexts) use higher-status speech forms. In fact, in settings of the greatest formality, Labov reported that his lower-class respondents' use of prestige forms actually surpassed that of upper-middle-class speakers. As well, when asked about their custom-ary linguistic practices, the former tended to exaggerate their use of higher-status forms. The point of interest here, of course, is not the lack of accuracy of such self-reports but, rather, the psychological underpin-nings that give rise to them.

When an American speaker says *kyōō'pon* instead of *kōō'pon*, we have a simple example of hypercorrection; it stems from the (mistaken) belief that, if higher-status speakers say *styōōd'nt* rather than *stōōd'nt*, then an analogous pronunciation must be 'correct' for *coupon*. The further inter-est here is that the more prestigious American pronunciation of *student* is itself a conscious adoption of British usage. Recent work by Boberg (1999) has revealed some pitfalls for unwary speakers here. The Ameri-can 'nativisation' of foreign words spelled with <a> that have entered the lexicon (words like *macho* and *pasta*) has, he suggests, a strong 'aes-thetic' dimension. This favours a rendering of the sound as /aː/ (as in *father*) rather than as /æ/ (as in *fat*). And this 'aesthetic' sense derives from the idea that British usage, in which the /aː/ pronunciation is consid-ered more typical, is prestigious. Ironies arise, Boberg shows, when the American /aː/-based pronunciation of such foreign imports, based upon perceptions of British elegance and 'correctness', in fact diverges from the /æ/ pronunciation given to such borrowings in standard British English; see also Edwards (1999c). Jones (2001) provides some further details in a recent book on American anglophilia (see particularly the chapter entitled 'Gee, I love your accent').

Labov's studies revealed a general tendency for respondents to over-report the use of higher-status pronunciations; Trudgill's results indi-cated that *males*, both working-class and middle-class, often claimed to use nonstandard forms even when they did not customarily do so. The trans-Atlantic variation, it has been argued, might be the result of a weaker assimilation of middle-class norms among members of the

English working class, or of Trudgill's more subtle analyses of sex differences. It does seem clear, however, that working-class nonstandard forms can have an attraction that cuts across class boundaries, one that produces their 'covert prestige'. Since it is based upon associations between nonstandard speech and masculinity, covert prestige is essentially a male phenomenon. Labov (1966) had noted that the positive masculine connotations of nonstandard speech, for men, do not seem to be balanced by similar positive values for women; and, again, the work of Trudgill (1972) in Norwich bears this out. Unlike their male counterparts, the women in his studies there tended to claim more *standard* usage than they actually employed.

The downgrading of personal speech styles that is revealed by hyper-correction efforts does not lead to wholesale abandonment of maternal nonstandard dialects, and it is here that the more latent prestige of those dialects may be seen as a sort of counter-balance. An illustrative example involved a friend of mine, a middle-aged, upper-middle-class American university professor. He was being pressed by two or three male colleagues on an academic matter and, after an inconclusive discussion conducted in the educated dialect appropriate to the region, he finally stopped short, smiled broadly, and said, 'Look fellas, you know they ain't no way I can do it!' This was a signal, immediately understood all round, that the time had come to cut to the chase. Conversation over. All-male social gatherings, as about half the readers will know, often produce such examples. The essence here lies in the perceived contrast between direct and no-nonsense usage, on the one hand, and inflated and often dishonest language, on the other: straight shooting versus humbug – or bullshit, now itself the object of increased scholarly scrutiny; see Frankfurt (2005) and, for more 'popular' treatments, Penny (2005) and Webb (2005). Kiesling (2007: 661), in his discussion of the 'performance' of masculinity, provides one or two other apposite examples. Men's voices are generally lower in pitch than are those of women, but 'when men wish to become "more masculine", they will often lower the pitch of their voice'. He also refers to the work of Bucholtz (1999), who has shown that American (white) men may use features borrowed from African American styles when they wish to signal physical power, directness and other 'macho' qualities.

The masculinity of nonstandard usage that underpins the operation of 'covert prestige' is in some sense the mirror image of the alleged 'poshness' or effeminacy that is associated with 'talking proper' or, indeed, with generally educated usage; see Mugglestone's (1995) insightful treatment, and the earlier study by Blake (1981). There is a sense of affectation at work here, but sometimes more, as well. Bragg and Ellis (1976) reported the Cockney opinion that if children were to speak 'posh', their friends would label them as 'queers'. A generation earlier, Orwell had observed that 'nearly every Englishman of working-class origin considers it effeminate to pronounce foreign words correctly' (1941/1964: 74). Kissau (2006) shows the persistence of these perceptions: Canadian secondary-school boys report that the French classroom is a 'female domain', and not a place for males. One language teacher observed that 'there's still a lot of sexist thinking that a man doesn't learn languages. A man does math or engineering' (p. 415). Equally, Carr and Pauwels (2006) note, in the opening sentence of their introduction, 'from the moment when foreign language study becomes optional, classrooms across the English-dominant communities of the world are inhabited primarily by girls and staffed predominantly by women: boys for the most part disappear' (p. 1). They go on to discuss the 'gendered shape' of language learning at school, embedding their findings in the broader educational context in which boys are gradually becoming the gender of concern because they often seem to be more uninterested, disaffected and disadvantaged than girls; see also Sommers (2000) for a more polemical treatment of this broader context. This is not the place for further discussion of gender differences in foreign-language classrooms: my point is only that a disinclination to become involved in the self-conscious, classroom acquisition of another language is probably not unrelated to a broader disdain for what is seen as 'posh' or 'affected' in one's own.

Allowing for these sorts of exceptions – acknowledging that some forms of upper-crust braying may be very unpleasant to most ears, or that lower-class nonstandard speech may have an attractive, masculine, rough-and-ready quality – the general perceptual linkage between status and standard remains intact and applicable across a wide range of social settings.

STUDY QUESTIONS

1. What is the 'logic' of a language?
2. Dialects, unlike languages, are mutually intelligible varieties. This is true in theory but not always in practice. Discuss.
3. Discuss the seminal work of Labov and Trudgill, in America and Britain, on the relationships between social class and linguistic variables.
4. How do standard and nonstandard dialects arise, and how – and why – are they maintained?

Further reading

Jo Carr and Anne Pauwels, in their (2006) book, *Boys and Foreign Language Learning: Real Boys Don't Do Languages*, present work which provides a fine background to some of the gender-related issues discussed in chapter 4.

John Edwards's (1989) publication *Language and Disadvantage* provides a survey of the relationship between social/educational disadvantage and language.

William Labov's (1994) *Principles of Linguistic Change* is a two-volume contribution to the sociolinguistic and sociology of language literature summarising the many insights of Labov and his colleagues.

Peter Trudgill's (1983) *On Dialect* is an excellent treatment of the social and contextual features of dialect – i.e. those most relevant to understanding the dialect–identity relationship.

5 Dialect and identity: beyond standard and nonstandard

5.1 THE 'LOGIC' OF DIALECT

I noted earlier in this book that the linguistic evidence bearing upon the validity of all dialects was powerful: the term 'substandard' must be consigned to the dustbin, and no variety can be seen as more or less 'correct' than any other. In this chapter, I return to the relevant linguistic scholarship, in connection with the powerful 'test case' provided by Black English in America. I will also point to some further important aspects of dialect – and, hence, identity – evaluation.

Beginning in the 1960s, Labov's investigations of American Black English have remained compelling, and his two-volume overview (1994) provides an admirable summary of work on language variation and change, including replications of some of the early studies reported here. The language of inner-city black speakers was seen to make an excellent illustration of dialect validity in general, since it had for so long been rejected as inadequate by the white middle class, and since its speakers were victims of a prejudice that went well beyond language alone. If it could be shown that Black English were not some incorrect or debased variety, this would make a strong case for the linguistic integrity of all dialects. There were three central strands to Labov's work (for a fuller analysis of which, see Edwards, 1989). First, he justly criticised earlier studies that had elicited samples of Black English speech from youngsters through interview techniques that were both unfamiliar and intimidating, in contexts that were highly unlikely to produce normal, conversational samples. Second, Labov reminded us of what casual observers had known for a very long time: the black community is verbally rich and, like other cultures around the world that emphasise *oral* language, it supports and rewards those who are particularly conversationally adept. Third, and most important, Labov demonstrated the regular, rule-governed nature of Black English. Since rules are the very essence of language, any demonstration that Black English obeyed grammatical regulations would undercut the traditional charges of inaccuracy and sloppiness. A variety of language that follows rules (they need not, of course, be identical to the rules underpinning other varieties) could hardly be dismissed as merely an approximation to 'proper' English.

Here is one of the rules of Black English that Labov and his colleagues illuminated: it is called 'copula deletion'. In sentences like 'She the best student' or 'They in the playground', the words *is* and *are* are not present; they are grammatically required, of course, in other varieties of English, most importantly in standard or educated English. Are the black speakers who produce such utterances unaware of this verb form? The same speakers, however, also say things like 'She was small' or 'They were friends'. Here, the past tense of the verb *to be* does appear, as it would in standard-dialect usages. Why does the copula verb appear in past-tense sentences but not in present-tense ones? Labov's studies revealed a simple regularity governing this linguistic behaviour. In contexts in which Standard English can *contract* the copula verb ('They are going' can become 'They're going', without offending Mrs Grundy), Black English allows *deletion* ('They are going' can become 'They going').[1] There is a rule at work here; it differs from the one obtaining in other dialect varieties, but it is no less 'logical' and is just as rigorously adhered to. The rule is further demonstrated by the fact that, where the rules of Standard English do *not* allow contraction, those of Black English ban deletion. According to standard rules, 'He's as nice as he say he's' is a grammatically incorrect sentence: contraction is not permissible in the final position. Likewise, it is incorrect to say in Black English 'He's as nice as he says he'.

This is just the single best-known example of the grammatical investigations by which Labov showed Black English to be a variety bound, like all others, by rules and regulations. Of course, dialects differ from one another not only in grammar, but also in vocabulary and pronunciation (accent). Vocabulary differences generally prove to raise the fewest hackles among language purists and linguistic bigots: the fact that I *brew* my tea while you *steep* yours may suggest regional variations that can possibly elicit negative stereotypes, but they are unlikely to be used to bolster attacks on speakers' basic linguistic or cognitive capabilities. Indeed, such lexical variation can just as easily give rise to positive evaluations, even if assessments are occasionally tinged with suggestions of quaintness or archaism. As to pronunciation: it is undoubtedly the case that saying 'they' as *dey*, or 'with' as *wif*, or 'something' as *someting*, is likely to attract unfavourable judgements, just as some types of Irish, Newfoundland and Texan accents can conjure up images of unsophisticated bumpkins. But even purists and bigots will realise that there are many dialects of English that sound their 't's as 'd's; and, as we shall see, regional accents can also have some broadly favourable connotations. So, while pronunciation and vocabulary can be important perceptual triggers, it is the grammatical arguments that have always been the strongest underpinnings of assertions of dialect inferiority.

And that is why the linguistic studies of Black English, accompanied by reasonable extrapolations to other varieties, have been so important in demonstrating that there are no substandard dialects. It is also salutary to recall here that, although such studies naturally focus upon differences among varieties, and although these differences have provided the fuel for unenlightened judgements of inferiority, dialects typically have more shared than unique features. Labov (1976: 37) thus pointed out that 'the great majority of the rules of BEV [Black English Vernacular] are the same as rules of other English dialects'. Relatedly, since dialects are, after all, sub-categories of one overarching language, speakers of nonstandard varieties (like Black English) generally understand standard usages, even if they do not habitually employ them. The 'gears and axles of English', as Labov went on to say (p. 64), 'are available to speakers of all dialects.' Black English and other dialects are best thought of as valid systems of English, closely associated in most respects with all other dialects, but also differing in some specifiable and rule-governed ways. And finally here, it is of the greatest importance to realise that demonstrations of dialect regularities not simply do away with ignorant and uninformed assessments of the linguistic inadequacies of certain forms; because of the bridge so often assumed to exist between 'poor' language and 'poor' cognition, such demonstrations *also* undercut suggestions that speakers of certain dialects are both verbally and intellectually deficient. The pedagogical implications here, particularly as they unfolded for black children in America, were both drastic and ill informed: programmes of educational intervention were put in place on the basis of deeply flawed linguistic and psychological understanding. This is not the place for fuller attention to the educational ramifications of faulty thinking, for which see Edwards (1989; in press a).

5.2 EBONICS

The evidence presented by Labov and others for the linguistic validity of Black English and, therefore, for the communicative competence of its speakers, remains strong. It also, and regrettably, remains unavailable to the public in general and poorly understood among teachers in particular. In a recent discussion, for instance, Niedzielski (2005: 259–60) illustrates the continuing problems that can affect black students. She cites work published in 1999 that showed that 'while African-Americans make up approximately 12% of the US population, they make up an astounding 41% of the students in American schools labeled "educably mentally retarded"'. This attribution rests largely on language evalua-tions that continue to see more incorrectness, more impurity and more speech pathology in Black English. Niedzielski also refers to another indi-cation of bias. Although black children are not statistically more likely than their white counterparts to have hearing problems – in fact, there is some evidence that, as a group, there is *less* hearing loss in the black community – they are much more likely to be referred to speech-and-hearing specialists. Data from a professional body of specialists reveal that black children are referred in proportions that are double their actual numbers in the population; see also American Speech-Language Hearing Association (1997).

A study by Edwards (1999a) illuminates both the continuing difficul-ties in teacher's perceptions of nonstandard speech and something of the oral fluency of black children. Among a rural population in Nova Scotia, 9- and 11-year-old black children, white Acadian-French children and white children of English-speaking background were studied. Each child provided three types of speech sample: a set reading passage, a retold story (i.e. the experimenter tells the child a story, who then retells it), and spontaneous speech on any topic of interest to the child. The children were then evaluated by adult judges on standard personality dimensions, the main intent being to see if perceived speaker favoura-bility varied with type of speech sample evaluated. It was found, first, that black children were generally evaluated less favourably than were the other two groups; second, spontaneous speech tended, across the board, to elicit the highest ratings. Of greatest interest here, however, were the interactions found between group and speech type, and here it was found that the black children profited most, so to speak, from the spontaneous speech ratings. To put it another way: the differences in evaluations evoked by black children's reading/story-retelling and spon-taneous speech productions were much more marked than were those pertaining to the other two groups of children. The suggestion is that black children, whose culture is orally strong, will produce the best lin-guistic results ('best', that is, in the perceptions of white listeners) when the context allows them to show evidence of that strength and richness. There are rather obvious implications here, both for further study and for interpreting and reacting to language behaviour in more structured contexts (like classrooms).

Some of the recent developments in the story of Black English have revealed the continuingly potent intertwining of linguistic matters with social, political and even legal ones. Thus, Baugh (2006) demonstrates that the famous *Brown* v. *Board of Education* decision of 1954 – in which educational segregation, even when masked under the 'separate but equal' provisions that had prevailed (or, rather, did not prevail) for half a century – promised a future of real educational equality that has, sadly, not come to pass. Why not? Because other social obstacles to black progress have remained firmly in place and, among these, are the 'tremendous linguistic divisions between those who trace their ancestry to African slaves and those who do not' (p. 91). There are threads, therefore, that connect *Brown* to both of the important cases – in Michigan and California – that I shall touch upon below.

The term *Ebonics* was coined by researchers taking part in a conference in St Louis devoted to the language of black children. As Williams (1975) pointed out, the term (from 'ebony' and 'phonics') arose from the desire to define and describe black language from a black point of view. 'Ebonics' can be generally taken as synonymous with other terms – Black English (BE), Black English Vernacular (BEV) and African American Vernacular English (AAVE), among them – although some have tried to draw distinctions (see Rickford, 2002).

Evolving assessments of nonstandard dialects and, in particular, the awareness that class and regional variation can reveal and flesh out cultural continuities as rich and complex as any available to middle-class 'mainstream' speakers of standard forms, have informed some interesting and useful developments. With regard to BEV, the now-famous 'King decision' is especially noteworthy. Parents of fifteen black children from the Martin Luther King elementary school in Ann Arbor, Michigan, alleged that the school had not properly educated their children. They were doing badly at school and the parents' view was that teachers were unaware of the important sociocultural differences between these children and their white counterparts (80% of the school population), and that language barriers prevented school success. Indeed, the children had been (inaccurately, needless to say) labelled as educationally retarded and learning-disabled, were relegated to speech classes for language deficiency, and were suspended, disciplined and held back. In July 1979, after a month-long trial in which several prominent linguists testified (none for the defendants), a federal court judge ruled that school authorities had failed to act to overcome language barriers, and ordered them to devise curricula to help the children. The schools were required to adapt. Contrary to some reports at the time, the school was not required to teach BEV, nor were teachers required to learn it so as to communicate with their pupils; they already communicated well enough, and the essential problem was with the teaching of reading. The barriers in place here arose because of the negative reactions to BEV, coupled with inaccurate teacher expectations and (to put it bluntly) racist perceptions. The linguistic evidence presented in the case enabled the judge to find that BEV was a valid and distinct English dialect; at the same time, he supported the view that Standard English (some form of Standard American English, perhaps) was a necessary component of success in school and beyond. Indeed, the judge went so far as to say that BEV was not an acceptable method of communication in many contexts.

Naturally, the case received very wide publicity, and much of the press coverage was misinformed and distorted (see Venezky, 1981). As well, general opinion was divided on many aspects. Consequently, a symposium to discuss the elements and implications of the King decision took place in February 1980. The conference itself became a media event with, among others, a BBC film crew and a team from the American National Public Radio organisation in attendance. A book of proceedings soon appeared (Smitherman, 1981a; see also Smitherman, 1981b; Zorn, 1982), and this provides the fullest available account of the whole issue. As one of the linguists testifying at the trial, Labov (1982) also prepared some lengthy notes on the case, with observations on the educational treatment that the black children had received, and that had led to the trial. He also stated that the judge, in invoking federal law directing educational authorities to act against language barriers found to impede pupil progress, did not believe that such law applied only in foreign-language situations. Although this may have been the original thinking in the provision, the judge did *not* class BEV as a separate language. Labov went on to cite the trial as an illustration of linguists' involvement in contemporary, real-life issues; the abstract to his article (p. 165) is worth quoting here:

> Though many linguists have shown a strong concern for social issues, there is an apparent contradiction between the principles of objectivity needed for scientific work and commitment to social action. The Black English trial in Ann Arbor showed one way in which this contradiction could be resolved. The first decade of research on Black English was marked by violent differences between creolists and dialectologists on the structure and origin of the dialect. The possibility of a joint point of view first appeared in the general reaction of linguists against the view that blacks were linguistically and genetically inferior. The entrance of black linguists into the field was a critical factor in the further development of the creole hypothesis and the recognition of the distinctive features of the tense and aspect system. At the trial,

linguists were able to present effective testimony in the form of a unified view on the origins and structural characteristics of the Black English Vernacular and argue for its validity as an alternate to standard English.

As it turned out, the Michigan case was a precursor to a still more widely discussed situation: the 1996 resolution of the Oakland, California, school board declaring Ebonics to be the native *language* of its black students. There are good overviews by Kretzschmar (1998), Baugh (2000), Pandey (2000) and Ramirez *et al.* (2005); my citations from the actual Oakland decisions are taken from the last of these. At the time, Oakland was one of a handful of cities in which a majority of the citizens were African American. Many of their children were doing very poorly at school (Baugh, 2004). Among the most contentious sections were the two opening paragraphs, which noted that 'validated scholarly studies ... have also demonstrated that African Language Systems are genetically-based [*sic*] and not a dialect of English', and the ensuing implication that, as speakers of 'limited English proficiency', black pupils were entitled to financial dispensations under the provisions of the federal programme of bilingual education. Both the statements and the implications drew immediate criticism, with the result that the Oakland board soon issued a 'clarification'. Because of 'misconceptions in the resulting press stories', the board now claimed that its intent had been misunderstood. Specifically, it denied that it meant to 'teach Ebonics in place of English', or to 'classify Ebonics (i.e. 'Black English') speaking pupils as bilingual', or to condone 'the use of slang'. The first and last of these points are no doubt accurate, but the second is at least debatable.

While some of the phrasing was less than clear, the intent was obvious: Ebonics is an independent system, with a 'genesis' unrelated to English. It soon became obvious that further changes would be necessary and, early in 1997, an amended resolution was passed. The initial phrase now read: '... demonstrated that African Language Systems have origins in West and Niger-Congo languages and are not *merely* dialects of English' (my italics). Even in its revised form, the Oakland school board's declaration was not without ambiguities and infelicities: it was clearly not a document produced by professional linguists. This reality, together with the intense reaction to its activities, led the board to delete references to Ebonics entirely (Baugh, 2004). The whole matter, however, remains instructive in a number of ways.

While both scholarly and official determinations have argued that Ebonics is a form of nonstandard English, we are still left with an informative chapter in the sociology of language. Some aspects have been briefly but usefully summarised by Wolfram (2005), who points to the public conceptions and misconceptions triggered by the Oakland affair. The school board resolutions suggested, first, that Ebonics was a separate language *tout court*; second, that Ebonics was an *African* language; third, with the unfortunate term, 'genetically based', that African Americans were 'biologically predisposed' to Ebonics; fourth, that speakers of Ebonics were as eligible as (say) Hispanic Americans for federal bilingual-education funding; fifth, that pupils were to be taught in Ebonics by suitably prepared teachers. And a final important summary point is provided by Baugh (2004: 316): 'the Ebonics debate that began in Oakland was never fully resolved; in the wake of a hostile public reception, it was simply abandoned'. Among the chorus of voices, many were hostile (as we shall see, below), and even the more enlightened ones were critical and cautious. And so an important issue was left hanging, while 'far too many African American students continue to attend underfunded and overcrowded schools' (p. 316), a situation that, in combination with other social and political issues, ensures on-going educational underachievement.

The language–dialect debate is of particular interest here. It is clear that classifying Ebonics as a separate language is not generally endorsed by linguists (see Baugh, 2002, 2004), although this need not imply any diminished concern for the speakers of Ebonics-as-dialect. Baugh (2006: 97) reminds us that a good case can be made for 'educational policies targeted to the needs of nonstandard dialect speakers'. Those who have argued for Ebonics-as-language, however, have sometimes accepted the broadly held (but, as we have seen, quite mistaken) belief that 'dialect' *does* signify a language form that is inferior, incomplete or inaccurate, and they have typically been motivated by well-intentioned concerns for the status of Black English. Hence the impulse behind the label of 'language', and hence the inference that proponents of that label are not language scholars. As Steigerwald (2004: 12) points out, the claims of those who argue for Ebonics-as-language arise from 'the intersection of nationalist [sic] politics and sketchy linguistic science'. Not being a linguist hardly means that one must forfeit one's opinion, but arguing from conviction is not the same as arguing from evidence. As we know very well from many debates in many arenas of life, the co-existence of the two perspectives can easily lead to misunderstanding and conflict, difficulties arising from lack of awareness or, more worryingly, from wilful neglect or ignorance. Wolfram's (1998) report that he has often been asked if he 'believed' in Ebonics is telling in this connection.

What about some specific examples of reactions to Ebonics? Wright (2005) has assembled a bibliography of about one hundred 'scholarly references' and fifty-five newspaper articles (listed chronologically, from December 1996 to September 2003; see also Todd, 1997). A number of prominent black scholars rejected the Oakland approach, while at the same time endorsing the underlying motivation. Henry Louis Gates, for instance, said that the original declaration was 'obviously stupid and ridiculous', but also that it was the 'sheer desperation of public schools in the inner city', the 'grave national crisis', that pushed the 'panicked Oakland board' to move as it did. Gates was also taken aback by the intensity of the reaction and the 'national fixation' on Ebonics. 'As an African American', he said, 'I'm desperate for solutions to illiteracy . . . I'd be open to any smart solution, but the Oakland school board didn't come up with one.' Yet it was the board's 'non-solution' that attracted all the attention, rather than the underlying problems (see Rich, 1997). The reverend Jesse Jackson initially decried the Oakland declaration: to say that black students did not speak English was 'foolish and insult-ing . . . this is an unacceptable surrender, bordering on disgrace . . . it's teaching down to our children'. He apparently changed his mind, how-ever, after meeting with the Oakland school board and some linguists (Todd, 1997: 15). Other prominent black Americans, from Maya Angelou to Bill Cosby, were also critical of the Oakland approach (see also Lippi-Green, 1997). The reaction of one black journalist, Brent Staples of *The New York Times*, was such that it prompted Baugh (2000) to accept a com-mission to write about the Ebonics controversy. Staples (1997) joined the anti-Oakland brigade, claiming that the school board deserved the scorn that greeted its assertion that 'broken, inner-city English [is] a distinct "genetically based" language system'.

One could agree or disagree with the attitudes of black commenta-tors who are not linguistic scholars, with Bill Cosby (1997), for example, who said that 'legitimizing the street in the classroom is backwards. We should be working hard to legitimize the classroom – and English – in the street.' After all, these are not silly sentiments; indeed, they could be interpreted in the light of earlier discussions about the way in which linguistic *difference* is translated into linguistic *deficit* through the power of social pressure. But these earlier arguments *also* pointed out that the difference-into-deficit transformation was based upon an invalid assess-ment of nonstandard dialect: it may be pervasive, but it is inaccurate, and ought therefore to be contested wherever possible. It is clear that the black critics of Ebonics do generally see it as a deficient variety, a point of view that demonstrates their lack of linguistic awareness, and for which they may fairly be criticised. They cannot be criticised, however, for their genuine concern for black children, nor, obviously, can they be accused of rejecting BEV on racially prejudiced principles; this is an accusation that can be levelled at many of the 'popular' reactions to the Ebonics debate, reactions that are merely specific manifestations of long-held stereotypes and prejudicial opinions.

In a recent study of attitudes towards Ebonics among a large sample of university students (roughly evenly divided between black and white, male and female), Barnes (2003: 252) found that none was 'overwhelmingly in agreement about Ebonics as a communicative and teaching tool'. More specifically (p. 258):

> it is clear that knowledge about the Oakland School Board resolution tended to negatively affect the viewpoints of many sample members. Awareness about the controversy reduced positive opinions about Ebonics and reinforced more negative views . . . This finding confirms the influential role played by the media in shaping public opinion.

Barnes's results are not quite as straightforward as she presents them, but they demonstrate, at the least, considerable ambivalence about the status and possible role of Ebonics. It also seems likely that this ambivalence was in many instances pre-existing, but then became further reinforced by the popular press in all its forms. And, since that medium was generally negative – either downright prejudiced or, in the case of some black commentators and 'celebrities' of one sort or another, cautious and/or dismayed – it is also reasonable to suppose that ambivalence tended to be 'shaped' towards the unfavourable end of the attitudinal scale.

5.3 FURTHER WORK ON DIALECT EVALUATION [2]

If we (rightly) reject linguistic and aesthetic arguments for dialect superiority, we have, in a sense, only cleared away some annoying underbrush. It is very useful to know that the real bases for language evaluation rest upon social convention, a product of the historical vagaries of sociopolitical dynamics, but we must not forget that scholarly brush-clearing has not had much effect upon the wider community. We may hear (and see) more diversity in the media nowadays, and the more reasonable workings of political correctness have had some influence upon the public expressions of prejudice, linguistic and otherwise, but any informal survey of the people on Main Street, or on the Clapham omnibus, or on the Bondi tram, will show that strong expressions of linguistic preference remain very common indeed. 'Substandard' and its synonyms may no longer be heard in academic groves, but they continue to thrive elsewhere. If experts and the laity disagree about judgements of 'correctness', however, they can agree on the existence of further evaluative dimensions within the ranks of nonstandard varieties.

Bloomfield (1944) published what must be one of the first attempts by a linguist to come to grips with 'conventional popular statements about language and of certain characteristic reactions called forth when these are brought into question' (p. 45). He touched upon the folk wisdom that argued for the Elizabethan 'purity' of some American dialects, believed Basque and Malayalam to be mutually intelligible, and knew that the languages of some 'savage tribes' comprised only a few hundred words. Bloomfield goes on to discuss various folk etymologies, the systems produced by naïve lexicographers that offer full Chinese fluency with only two months work – and, above all, the popular rejection of the overly liberal attitudes of linguists in matters of grammar and 'correctness'. It is interesting to think that people who would never dream of offering a lay opinion on, say, nuclear physics or cell biology have no such compunctions when language is involved. Of course, it is much more difficult to set up as an expert in something with which everyone is quite familiar. Many linguists are engaged in undertakings far removed from the messy reality of breathing speakers, but the scholarly inaccessibility that reinforces their 'expert' status is hard to maintain for their more applied colleagues – and it virtually disappears when the latter enter the public arena. (See also my brief return to this topic in chapter 9.)

There is a large literature dealing with language and dialect attitudes (for a recent succcinct overview, see Giles and Edwards, in press), but before considering its general import, a cautionary note is needed. The concept of attitude, a cornerstone of traditional social psychology, is not one about which there has been universal agreement. At a general level, however, attitude may be understood as a disposition to react favourably or unfavourably to a class of objects. This disposition is comprised of three components: feelings (the affective element), thoughts (cognitive element) and, following upon these, predispositions to act in a certain way (behavioural element). That is, one knows or believes something, has some emotional reaction to it and, therefore, may be assumed to act on this basis. Two points are important here. The first is that there often exist inconsistencies between assessed attitudes and the actions presumably related to them. In a 'classic' study (LaPiere, 1934), a Chinese couple (accompanied by the experimenter) toured the United States in the early 1930s. Visiting some 250 hotels and restaurants, they were refused service only once. Afterwards, when LaPiere wrote to the places they had visited, more than 90% of his respondents said they would not serve Chinese people. Although not without some methodological problems, this study clearly demonstrated that what people think and feel may not always be reflected in what they do. There are, of course, a great many reasons why this should be so, ranging from immediate self-interest, to the desire to avoid embarrassment, to a difference between views of an abstraction (members of a given ethnic group, for example) and of concrete instances.

The second point is that there is often confusion between *belief* and *attitude*, and this is particularly so in the realm of language studies, often showing up on questionnaires and interviews. Since, as I have just indicated, belief is one of the three components of attitude, a mother's response to the query, 'Is a knowledge of French important for your children, yes or no?' indicates a belief. To gauge her *attitude*, one would require further probing into the feelings that are associated with her statement. It would be a mistake, after all, to simply equate a 'yes' answer to the question above with a favourable attitude towards French. The mother might think – might *know* – that a knowledge of French will be important for her children's career success, but she might heartily dislike everything she has heard about the language and its speakers. Many 'attitude' questionnaires are really 'belief' questionnaires.

More illumination would clearly be useful here. Consider, for example, a case in which speaker A sounds more intelligent to judges than does speaker B. Might it not be valuable to probe further, to attempt to find out something of the reasons for the choice, to try and add the *affective* element to the *belief* component already assessed? Research along these lines would not be wholly original; it could profitably draw upon earlier work. For example, the view that nonstandard varieties evoke less favourable reactions has typically been discussed in terms of speakers' differential status or prestige. It would be useful to confirm this, from the *judges'* point of view, by asking them the bases for their evaluations; see also Edwards (1999c).

Further evidence for the utility of fuller probing of answers given lies in the fact that, as most researchers will know, 'subjects' or 'informants' are often extremely willing to go along with the tasks they are asked to perform. This is at least partly related to a general desire to be helpful, and to follow through on an initial agreement to participate, particularly if the researcher is seen as a socially or scientifically prestigious person. The notorious examples of Milgram's 'shock experiments' or Zimbardo's mock-prison study are ample demonstrations of how easy it can be to get 'subjects' to behave in apparently egregious ways. Other work has shown that participants in experiments can equally easily be induced to spend long periods of time working away at boring, repetitive or downright nonsensical tasks: the real point of many such studies, in fact, is precisely to demonstrate human malleability. At the more mundane levels of survey research, too, there are clear indications of suggestibility and the desire to please. Subjects almost always comply with requests to fill in all the scales provided, even though they clearly feel that some are less appropriate than others. We know this because many respondents express various sorts of doubts during or after the procedures – in which, nevertheless, they almost always continue to participate. A generation ago, Choy and Dodd (1976) asked teachers to evaluate children who spoke either standard or nonstandard English. As expected, standard-dialect-speaking children were consistently favoured in the ratings: they were judged to be more confident, better at school, and less 'disruptive' in the classroom. Now, some of the scales with which the the teacher-judges were provided were plausible enough; even on the basis of a very short sample of children's speech, it is perhaps not impossible to say something useful about oral fluency, to comment upon pronunciation and grammar, even to venture an opinion about style and confidence. But the teachers were also asked to say what they thought about the children's success in life after school, about the strength and depth of their relationships with others, about the happiness of the marriages to come. The silliness in providing such rating dimensions is exceeded only by the willingness of the judges to fill in the scales; as far as I know, not one teacher demurred. And Choy and Dodd's work is merely an extreme example of a very wide-ranging phenomenon (see Williams, 1974; Edwards, 1979c).

The more general problem here lies not only with ratings given in areas about which evaluators know nothing at all; it affects every 'bald' judgement made, recorded and subsequently analysed. Consider two questionnaire items that you are to respond to in the absence of any contextualising information or any opportunity to amplify or qualify your response. You are simply to indicate 'yes' or 'no', or to make a tick-mark somewhere along a 7-point scale or on a line anchored by 'completely agree' at one end and by 'completely disagree' at the other. Consider, in other words, an absolutely standard survey instrument. Consider, third, that the first item touches upon a topic that has been near to your heart and mind for a very long time, while the other brings to your attention something to which you have never given a moment's thought. As a good subject you will, in each case, dutifully make your mark – and each mark will then be weighted exactly the same in the investigator's analysis. But one of your answers means a lot more than the other, and any reasonable interpretation of the two opinions you have recorded on the questionnaire sheet would take that into account. Of course, that doesn't happen.

Faced with that sort of issue, acknowledging that raters' evaluations may not be entirely adequately expressed by checking a single point on some semantic-differential scale, Williams (1974, 1976) introduced a 'latitude of attitude acceptance' measure. His judge-listeners made the usual single ratings, but then gave him a sense of the perceived precision of those evaluations. This was done by indicating other rating possibilities that would be generally acceptable, as well as those definitely rejected. Here is a sample item involving a typical 7-point semantic-differential scale:

This child seems: Passive $\underline{|+|*|+||-|-|-|}$ **Active**

Here the judge has indicated that his or her 'latitude of acceptance' covers the three rating possibilities at the 'passive' end of the scale, with the single best estimate (the starred one) in the second-from-the-left position. The blank in the middle denotes indecision or neutrality, while the three minus-signs indicate possibilities definitely rejected. Since the mean of the latitude of acceptance is likely to represent the judge's single best estimate, the addition to our knowledge here is the information we now have about the deviation around this mean.

A little later, in a study of my own (Edwards, 1979c), I carried on in the Williams vein, attempting to measure the judges' *confidence* in their ratings. The introduction of the 'latitude of acceptance' measure had been seen by Williams to extend his understanding of the evaluations made by his subjects; in similar fashion, I considered that measures of judges' confidence in their own ratings could suggest how wide implicit latitudes of acceptance might be, if in fact they existed at all. To this end, speech samples were gathered from two groups of 10-year-old Dublin children, drawn from lower-class and middle-class populations. These were recorded and presented to the male and female teachers-in-training who constituted the listener-judges. Seventeen semantic-differential scales were provided, probing for assessments of attributes like fluency, intelligence and enthusiasm; in addition, accompanying each of these 17 scales was another, on which the judges indicated the degree of confidence they had in the substantive rating just made.

Considering only the confidence-scale data here, it was found that the middle-class youngsters were generally assessed with greater (assumed) certainty than were their less well-off counterparts. Perhaps this was due to the middle-class backgrounds of the teacher-judges. But the more interesting results here had to do with, first, the relationships found between the 'substantive' and the confidence ratings and, second, with the gender of the judges. Some of the 17 substantive scales were rated with greater certainty than were some others. Judges tended to be more confident when asked to rate aspects that might plausibly be revealed in the brief speech samples they heard (perceived fluency, reading ability, pronunciation and the like); they were less comfortable in dealing with scales relating to such things as the happiness of the child, or overall school standing, or, indeed, general intelligence level. The import here is that, if given an opportunity, respondents can and will provide useful information about the *reasons* for choices made. The other intriguing finding was that, while the male raters were found to give higher overall ratings on the substantive scales than were female judges, the reverse was the case for the indications of confidence. In general, the male teacher-judges made more positive ratings, but were less sure of them; their female counterparts were more confident about their somewhat less favourable substantive ratings. Two implications suggest themselves. The finding reinforces our belief (and our hope) that rating-scale exercises do not elicit simple and general response tendencies for one gender to make higher or lower marks on a scale – any scale – than the other. As well, males may have *over*-committed themselves in their 'substantive' ratings and then taken the opportunity provided by the confidence scales to 'soften' their judgements, as it were. Females, having been more circumspect from the start, may not have found this necessary. This in turn suggests some further attention to gender variations – not only because scales and surveys are so common in social-scientific research, but also because we may be looking at an illustration of more general gender-differentiated response tendencies.

As we shall see below, social-psychological insights and methodologies have produced a sizeable body of evidence bearing upon perceptions, stereotypes, and language 'attitudes'. We can now predict with some confidence what sorts of reactions will be elicited when people hear varieties of Black English, Newfoundland English, Cockney, 'Received Pronunciation', Boston English and many others. We can also make predictions about listeners' evaluations of those varieties produced by non-native speakers of English that show the influence of their first language. We understand, at a general level, how such assessments come about – via a sort of linguistic 'triggering' in which reactions to speech are, in reality, reactions to speakers – and how they reflect something of the listeners' stereotypical attitudes or beliefs. Investigators have not, however, gone very much beyond fairly gross explanations; that is, they have typically not related speech evaluations to particular speech attributes.

Thus, while hundreds of experiments have revealed negative reactions towards Black English, we have virtually no information relating specific linguistic features of that variety to such reactions, features that might include, for example, pronunciation patterns, particular grammatical constructions, the use of dialect-specific lexical items, or (most likely, of course) various combinations of these. It is true that social psychology has interested itself from time to time in *non*-linguistic features that may stimulate or influence evaluative reactions: such matters as context, topic and salience, as well as degrees of emotionality, humour and abstraction, have figured in many studies. Perhaps the closest approaches to the investigation of linguistic 'triggers', however, are found in work on levels of speech formality/informality. There have been calls for more concerted efforts in this regard. For example, Giles and Ryan (1982: 210; see also Edwards, 1999c) pointed to the value of 'more detailed linguistic and acoustic descriptions of the stimulus voices' in examinations of 'the relative evaluative salience of these particulars for different types of listeners'. In general, though, social psychologists have done little in the way of isolating 'linguistic and acoustic' variables and relating them to evaluative judgements. This is hardly surprising, for such work is simply not their métier.

It is to linguistic research that we turn if we are interested in descriptions of features that characterise and differentiate language varieties. In recent years, a considerable amount of work has been done here, work that focusses on those very social-class and ethnic varieties of particular social-psychological concern. Thus, linguists (including Laver and Trudgill, 1979, in a book on 'social markers' that remains a useful reference) have pointed out such phenomena as:

> the nasality habitually associated with some (RP, for example) varieties of English; the wide dialectal variations in consonant pronunciation: thus, RP speakers pronounce lock and *loch* more or less identically, with a final /k/, but (some) Scottish pronunciations involve final /x/; also recall here the information about /r/ pronunciation in New York and Norwich; grammatical variations (like the copula deletion in American Black English); lexical differences (some English speakers *brew* their tea, some *mash* it, some let it *steep,* some let it *set,* and so on).

If, however, linguists have been the ones to describe such variation, they have either been relatively uninterested in its relation to differences in social ratings or have simply assumed that the more obvious and salient linguistic markers are the triggers for differential ratings. Like social psychologists, they too – with some notable exceptions (Labov and Trudgill, for instance; see also Milroy and Preston, 1999) – have stuck to their lasts. Overall, then, we would clearly benefit from efforts to bridge the work of psychology and linguistics in this regard; the effect would be to refine and particularise our knowledge of how *specific* aspects of speech elicit *specific* types of evaluative reactions; see also Jenkins (2007).

A basic problem in investigating two or more dialects was touched upon in the extract (above) from Wyld's 1934 monograph, and it was exemplified in the studies investigating the 'imposed norm' and 'inherent value' hypotheses. For example, if I wish to compare two speech varieties along some dimension or other, and if I then record a native speaker of each and have the voices judged by listeners, how do I know if any differential ratings are actually due to features of the dialects themselves? Might they not be, at least in part, reactions to quite individual qualities of voice: tone, pitch, rhythm, pace, and other idiosyncratic variations? A way around this difficulty was devised in the 1960s by Wallace Lambert and his colleagues in Montreal, whose methodological initiative provoked a great deal of work over the following decade or so, work whose illuminative value remains undimmed today.

Lambert *et al.* (1960) introduced the 'matched-guise' technique as a method of investigating reactions to speech variants. Judges evaluate a recorded speaker's personality, along any dimension of interest, after hearing him or her read the same passasge in each of two or more languages, dialects or accents. The fact that the speaker is, for all 'guises', the same person is not revealed to the assessors (who typically do not guess this). Since potentially confounding individual variables will of course be constant across the 'guises', the ratings given are considered to more accurately reflect stereotypic reactions to the language variety *per se* than would be the case if separate speakers of each linguistic variant were used. In the matched-guise methodology, it is assumed that speech samples serve as convenient identifiers, facilitating the evoking of those stereotypes which, in turn, lead to judges' evaluations. It is the speakers who are really being assessed in these exercises. The matched-guise technique has been criticised, most importantly for its alleged artificiality. That is, judges hear a series of disembodied voices all speaking the same words and are asked to rate the speakers on various personality scales. Do the judges, who generally comply with requests to assess speakers in this way, nevertheless feel that it is a pointless task? How would the judgements stand up in the light of more information about the speakers? It seems, overall, that the technique has provided useful and robust information; employed in many different contexts, it makes an addition to, rather than a distortion of, our understanding of speaker evaluation (see Edwards, 1989 for further details here).

In Lambert's initial study, French- and English-speaking students were asked to provide their assessments of French and English voices on a number of semantic-differential scales. On most of the dimensions (including 'ambition', 'intelligence' and 'sense of humour'), English-speaking judges reacted more favourably to English guises. Of greater interest, however, were the ratings given by the French-speaking judge-listeners, for not only did they too evaluate the English guises more positively than they did the French ones, they *also* gave less favourable responses to the *French* guises than did their English-speaking counterparts. That is, the findings not only revealed favourable reactions from members of the high-status group towards their own speech, but also that these reactions had been adopted by members of the lower-status group. The investigators interpreted these findings as evidence of what they termed a 'minority-group reaction': the French-speaking student judges, perceiving themselves as subordinate in some ways to the English-speaking population, apparently adopted the stereotyped values of the more dominant group. The 'minority-group reaction' seems to be a testament to the power and scope of social stereotypes in general, illustrating how they may be adopted by those who are themselves the object of unfavourable evaluation. Early matched-guise work in Britain lent some support here: Cheyne (1970), for instance, later found that *both* Scottish and English judges tended to rate Scottish speakers as lower in status than their English counterparts.

Further confirmation of this 'minority-group' effect (*not* using a matched-guise in this instance) was provided by d'Anglejan and Tucker (1973) in their study of French dialects. First, French-Canadian students, teachers and factory workers (more than 200 in total) were asked their opinions of Quebec, European and Parisian French. They rejected the idea that Quebec French was inferior to the other two, or that Parisian French was the 'best' form of the language. Nevertheless, when presented with the taped voices of upper-class and lower-class French-Canadian speakers, and European French speakers, the respondents downgraded both Canadian styles along dimensions such as 'ambition' and 'intelligence'; even in terms of perceived 'likeability', the European speech style evoked more favourable responses. In 1975, Carranza and Ryan asked 64 Mexican-American and Anglo-American students (of Spanish) to judge speakers of English and Spanish; sixteen such speakers were presented, on tape, talking about simple domestic or school events. The personality characteristics to be evaluated broadly reflected either prestige (status) or what the researchers termed *solidarity* (involving traits like 'friendliness', 'kindness' and 'trustworthiness'). Over all judges, English was viewed more favourably when the speaker's topic was school-related, Spanish when it dealt with domestic matters. Further, English was reacted to more favourably on both status-related and 'solidarity' traits. One implication is that a low-prestige language variety may have more positive connotations in terms of qualities like 'integrity', 'social attractiveness' and 'friendliness' than it does when perceptions of 'intelligence', 'ambition', 'industriousness' and 'competence' are at issue – and that this relationship seems to obtain both for members of the low-prestige group and for more middle-class speakers. In related work, Ryan and Carranza (1975) found similar results when considering the evaluations of Standard English and Mexican-accented English made by Mexican-American, black and 'anglo' speakers: the former were assessed as higher in status than the latter. And, in a further refinement, Ryan *et al.* (1977) found that the *degree* of dialect nonstandardness influenced judges' evaluations: ratings of Spanish–English bilinguals reading an English passage showed that favourability of impressions decreased as degree of Spanish accentedness increased. Studies from the same period involving black American speakers are also suggestive. Tucker and Lambert (1969), for example, presented a number of different American English dialect varieties to northern white, southern white and southern black groups of university students, finding that all groups evaluated Standard English speakers most favourably.

Since these early investigations, some consistency has been found, in the form of broad groupings of individual rating-scale assessments. Some dimensions ('intelligence' and 'industriousness', for example) are seen to reflect a speaker's *competence*, some ('helpfulness', 'trustworthiness' and other such traits) reflect *personal integrity*, and some ('friendliness', 'sense of humour', and so on) underlie *social attractiveness*. The interesting thing about these broader evaluations is that speakers of high-status varieties do not fare equally well on all of them. In fact, although standard accents and dialects connote greater prestige and competence, some nonstandard regional accents may evoke a greater sense of integrity or social attractiveness. Perhaps the speech patterns of nonstandard speakers are seen as quaint or down-to-earth, but we have already noted the 'covert prestige' phenomenon as well. Besides, it is not difficult to appreciate that those whose speech suggests competence, intelligence and status may not necessarily be those with whom we will most readily identify, trust, or generally get on with. However, since personal competence is a factor of some importance, one might consider that the nonstandard speaker, with a regional or class speech style, comes out somewhat the worse in the exchange, particularly in vital areas of life like school and employment. This matter becomes even more interesting when we recall that 'minority group reaction', when we realise the general tendency for nonstandard-dialect speakers to accept the often negative stereotypes of their own variants.

A further relevant factor at this point in the discussion is that, among those languages having standard forms (not all do), there may in fact be more than one. *Regional* standards are quite common, for example: an urban Texan variety of English and an old Bostonian one may each be the vernacular of educated standard-bearers and, at the same time, be viewed as nonstandard from a broader or national perspective. A Canadian study investigated the matter a bit more formally. English speakers from mainland Nova Scotia, Cape Breton Island, Newfoundland and Massachusetts were evaluated by listeners on the three dimensions of 'competence', 'integrity' and 'attractiveness' (this was not a matched-guise study; different speakers provided the speech samples). The mainland variety was associated with the greatest competence, but no important differences were detected in evaluations made of the four varieties on the other two personality dimensions. This suggests that the mainland Nova Scotia speakers were seen to possess a *regional* standard status, inasmuch as they evoked the prestige and competence associated with standard dialects *and* – because of their local character – did not lose ground, as it were, to the others on the two dimensions typically related to nonstandardness (Edwards and Jacobsen, 1987).

While the recurring groupings of competence, integrity and attractiveness had been remarked upon by the 1970s, more recent attempts have also been made at codification; see Edwards (1995). For example, an 'organisational framework' has been suggested in which there are two broad determinants of language perceptions: *standardisation* and *vitality*. While a standard variety is typically associated with dominant social groups, 'vitality' refers to the number and importance of the functions served by any given variety. It is obviously bolstered by the status that standards possess, but it can also be a feature of nonstandard varieties, given sufficient numbers of speakers and community support. The framework also suggests two main evaluative dimensions, *social status* and *solidarity*, the latter including dimensions ('integrity' and 'attractiveness') already discussed here. Finally, refinements in measurement techniques have been suggested, involving direct and indirect assessment, as well as content analysis. The first usually means questionnaire or interview methods, the 'matched-guise' approach is a good example of the second, and the third implies historical and sociological observation, together with ethnographic studies. This hardly exhausts the recent developments in the area, but it is abundantly clear that, for almost half a century, researchers have continued to find important language judgements involving speakers' competence, prestige and status, on the one hand, and their warmth, integrity and attractiveness, on the other.

The relevant literature here confirms what has been well understood at a popular level for a long time. The speech patterns of regional speakers, of ethnic minority-group members, of lower- or working-class populations – categories that frequently overlap, of course – elicit negative evaluations in terms of perceived status, prestige and levels of skill and education. The stereotypic patterns seem to hold whether or not listeners are themselves standard-dialect speakers. Some of the earliest studies, undertaken before the more recent emergence of black or Hispanic 'Pride', do reveal hints of linguistic and psychological developments to come. Flores and Hopper (1975), for instance, found slight preferences on the part of Mexican-American judges for the speech styles of *compañeros* who referred to themselves as 'Chicano'. But it would be naive to assume that negative language stereotypes are generally on the wane. Indeed, there is every reason to think that undesirably prejudicial evaluations are still very much with us. As implied already, one of the most poignant aspects here is the widely reported tendency (within and without academia) for nonstandard-dialect speakers to accept and agree with unfavourable stereotypes of their speech styles. Labov (1976) found, for instance, that those whose speech includes nonstandard or stigmatised forms are typically their own harshest critics, a clear demonstration of Lambert's 'minority-group reaction'. This is, of course, a linguistic manifestation of social dominance/subordination and, some would argue, of more blatant social control. We should note here, however, that social relationships are dynamic, and that the linguistic aspects of them can often provide a useful perspective on change.

For example, the black respondents to whom Labov spoke in the 1970s are not the same as those interviewed by Ogbu (1999) a generation later. Their linguistic attitudes have become more complex: they continue to accept that 'white talk' is somehow better than their own speech, but there is a pride in their vernacular that was either not felt or not given voice in earlier investigations. Ogbu (1999) describes how black people in West Oakland (California) consider that, while 'proper' English is white English, Black English is poor slang or 'just plain talkin''. On further investigation, it becomes clear that BEV is seen as the ordinary vernacular, the 'low' variant in a diglossic situation. And Ogbu also found that (although they did not articulate the notion) his respondents felt caught: the BEV that represents home, familiarity and group identity is threatened by the mastery of 'proper' English, a mastery that is seen as necessary for school and work success. They believe, in other words, in a sort of 'subtractive bi-dialectalism'. It is ironic, of course, because a more or less stable bi-dialectalism is the norm in many contexts; it is regularly practised, indeed, by large numbers of black Americans. The 'dialect dilemma' in which Ogbu's informants find themselves is the belief that the necessary acquisition of Standard English tends to erode the vernacular. Furthermore, there is a belief in some quarters that this process is part of the assimilatory intent of 'mainstream' school and society. Ogbu notes that black professionals, advocates, educators and communities endorse the learning of Standard English, but then condemn its acquisition on the grounds that it threatens 'Black English identity and racial solidarity' (p. 180). But they, too, live bi-dialectally, even if they don't acknowledge it. Is there, then, any real 'dialect dilemma' here? It is possible, but it is just as possible – particularly given the scope of black American culture and its current pervasiveness, well beyond the boundaries of the black community itself – that a BEV-'proper' English diglossia will prevail for some time to come.

But there are some further complexities. Ogbu's informants told him, for instance, that when a black person 'is talking proper, he or she is *puttin' on* [italics added] or pretending to be white or to talk like white people' (pp. 171–2). They told him that it is 'insane to pretend to be white', and that speaking Standard English is a pretence, a fake. They don't actually speak of some 'betrayal' of the group but the implication is plain; see also the *vendido/vendu* phenomenon discussed below. Ogbu's 'dialect dilemma' is the same phenomenon that Smitherman (2006) discusses under the heading of 'linguistic push-pull', a contradiction whereby black speakers simultaneously embrace Black English and hate it. 'On the one hand', Smitherman says (p. 129), 'Blacks have believed that the price of the ticket for Black education and survival and success in White America is eradication of Black Talk. On the other hand, Blacks also recognize that language is bound up with Black identity and culture.'

'Push-pull' dialect dilemmas obviously affect many nonstandard-language speakers in many settings (although they will often be more severe where differences between groups are 'marked' in more than linguistic terms). The solution, a theoretically plausible bi-dialectalism – eating your linguistic cake while still having it – is sometimes not so easy to maintain. If negative reactions to speech typically reflect broader social or racial attitudes, it follows that, for a black person, or any other member of a 'visible minority' group, learning and using a standard dialect may not necessarily alter things very much. Indeed, there is some suggestion in the literature that black speakers who sound 'white' may elicit *more* negative attitudes. Some early work by Giles and Bourhis (1975) demonstrated this among West Indians in Cardiff; similar observations have been made in Canada and the United States (see Edwards, 1989).

The feeling that one's own speech is not 'good' is a common phenomenon, for reasons that are as clear as they are unfair. It is a particularly disturbing one, however, when we consider how easily the belief may be exacerbated by those who might be expected to know better: teachers immediately come to mind here. As Halliday (1968: 165) once observed:

> A speaker who is made ashamed of his own language habits suffers a basic injury as a human being; to make anyone, especially a child, feel so ashamed is as indefensible as to make him feel ashamed of the colour of his skin.

Some have debated the depth of the injury here; no enlightened opinion, however, doubts the indefensibility, the unfairness, of the process.

The reliable comic tradition of having that stage duchess speak with a Cockney accent has its more banal counterparts as well. The perceived incongruities that produce comedy on the stage and elsewhere would not be effective without an audience fully alive to the powerful social connotations of linguistic variants. Given that people are aware of negative stereotypes of their own speech styles and, indeed, that they themselves have often accepted them, we might ask why low-status speech varieties continue to exist. After all, it would seem that a realisation of the potential limitations, in practical terms, of some varieties might lead to their eradication or, at least, to the expansion of the linguistic repertoire, to the development of bi-dialectal capability. We know that this is not, in principle, a difficult accomplishment. It is very common among actors, for example; and, at more mundane levels with which we are all familiar, the process of selecting from a linguistic pool of possibilities according to perceptions of the setting is even more common. It can hardly be alleged, either, that speakers of nonstandard dialects are without adequate models for repertoire expansion. Teachers once comprised the traditional pool here, but today their still powerful influence has been magnified and enhanced by the pervasive intrusions of the public media into all corners of society. The result is that virtually all nonstandard-dialect speakers have at least passive access to standard forms. Nevertheless, the levelling of local speech styles and, more pointedly, the gradual disappearance of low-status variants – predicted in some quarters as an inevitable consequence of the spread of the broadcast media – seem not to have occurred.

Pride in one's culture often means pride and affection for the language of that culture. Linguistic pride and self-confidence can be resurgent when groups previously oppressed, discriminated against and thought to be inferior rediscover a broader social strength and assertion: this can be as true for cultural sub-groups and dialects as it is for larger populations and languages. Thus, Carranza and Ryan (1975) discussed the 'solidarity' function of language in contemporary American black and Chicano contexts. A language or dialect, though it may be lacking in general social prestige, may nevertheless function as a powerful bonding agent, providing a sense of identity. Indeed, it is a social and linguistic fact that *any* variety can be the voice of group identity, a central element in the revitalised 'consciousness' of nonstandard-dialect speakers. A language variety may lack social prestige but it is still *ours*. The 'identity function' is carried as much by Cockney as it is by Oxfordese, as much by Quebec *joual* as Parisian French. Ryan's (1979) brief article on the persistence of low-prestige dialects remains instructive here, and a recent piece by Abd-el-Jawad (2006) discusses the persistence of minority *languages*: where the ordinary communicative functions have been largely or entirely replaced by a 'larger' language, the smaller may yet persist because of the strong symbolic value it retains for group members. We have already seen, of course, how a language no longer widely spoken may remain the repository of a group's tradition, literature and so on.

The solidarity function of language – its symbolic role, that is to say, in the articulation of group identity – is clearly not restricted to situations in which earlier self-denigration has now given way to admiration and allegiance. For we also observe a disinclination to alter speech styles on the part of groups who have not experienced any sudden upsurge in group pride, and who continue to adhere to the larger society's unfavourable stereotypes of their speech patterns: speakers of low-status dialects of urban British English are examples here. Can we put this down to a more generally liberal attitude towards speech variants *per se*? It is true that views are not as rigid as they once were; the linguistic variety to be found now in the mainstream media is an indication here, and an even more interesting development is the aping of non-mainstream behaviour, attitudes and speech style by certain middle-class constituencies (notably young people; recall also the discussion of 'covert prestige'). But prejudicial views obviously persist, even if their force has lessened in some quarters, and even if their overt expression is less forceful than once it was.

Group identity is a known and 'safe' quantity, even if its linguistic vehicle lacks prestige. On the other hand, attempts to alter one's speech style, to jettison a low-status variant, or even to add another dialectal string to the bow, are risky undertakings. Failure may lead to a sense of marginality, a sense of not being a full (and fully accepted) member of *any* social group. The Mexican American who abandoned Spanish for the socioeconomic rewards of English sometimes risked being labelled a *vendido* – a 'sell-out', a linguistic quisling; his francophone counterpart in Quebec might attract the label of *vendu*, 'sold'. And the individual who wishes to add, and not to replace, may also fall between stools: the maintenance of Spanish (language and culture) may exist uneasily alongside the acquisition of English in settings where bilingualism is often a way-station on the road to a new monolingualism (see Edwards, 1995).

Finally here, it is not invariably the case that lower-class speakers consider their own language patterns to be inferior variants. I have already mentioned how altered social circumstances – a reawakening of group 'pride' or 'consciousness', for instance – can lead to altered self-perceptions, including linguistic ones. This process is underlined by the increasingly common tendency to exaggerate or heighten, consciously, speech styles that were previously disapproved of. What was once an 'inferior' variety goes beyond mere equivalence with erstwhile 'better' forms, and comes to be seen as superior to them: more direct, more pithy, more animated. In this way, nonstandard speech comes to possess a new status for its speakers and, indeed, for others. In a recent analysis of the language habits and attitudes of black secondary-school students, Fordham (1999: 272) reported that BEV is now the 'norm against which all other speech practices are evaluated'. Standard English is no longer privileged; indeed, 'it is "dissed" (disrespected) and is only "leased" by the students on a daily basis from nine to three'. Black English has come to possess quite evident attractions for some middle-class and more or less standard-dialect-speaking adolescents. For them, there is a sort of 'street prestige' here. Even more interesting, perhaps, is the way in which such status can more subtly reveal itself in bigger arenas: hence the phenomenon of 'covert prestige'.

STUDY QUESTIONS

1. Why has the investigation of Black English proved so important to our wider understanding of dialect variation?
2. What were – and are – the central elements in the controversy surrounding Ebonics?
3. There are three main strands to the evaluations made of different dialects, and they could be termed the aesthetic, the logical (or grammatical) and the social. Discuss the structure and the force of each.
4. Outline the differences between attitudes and beliefs, and go on to discuss the implications of the distinctions here.

Further reading

John Baugh's (2004) 'Ebonics and its controversy' in Edward Finegan and
    John Rickford's edited book, *Language in the USA: Themes for the Twenty-first
    Century*, is a fine consideration of the many facets of Ebonics, and the
    controversies surrounding it, by one of the foremost scholars in the
    area.

Nikolas Coupland and Hywel Bishop's (2007) article, 'Ideologised values for
    British accents', provides an up-to-date assessment of the study of atti-
    tudes to British varieties.

Howard Giles and Andrew Billings's (2004) chapter, 'Assessing language atti-
    tudes', in Alan Davies and Catherine Elder's *The Handbook of Applied
    Linguistics* is another good contemporary overview of attitudes.

William Labov's (1976) *Language in the Inner City* is a collection of early
    work which includes his now-famous article, 'The logic of nonstandard
    English', the most thoroughgoing and fair-minded assessment of Black
    English in America of its time; the central features of Labov's argument
    remain central today.

6   Language, religion and identity

There are lots of possible choices for the source of the greatest evil and misery, but many have singled out religion. The late Milton Himmelfarb, however, thought that this was but 'a feeble joke'. He cited ethnonational affiliations, racial and class differences, and linguistic and ideological compartmentalisation for persecution, hatred and conflict. Or, indeed, 'simple bloody-mindedness' (see Berger, 2007). The last seems rather weak in the company of those other, more powerful motivations, but if we consider the historical propensity that human beings have shown for letting small matters spiral into large ones, or the dynamic potential of Freud's 'narcissism of minor differences', or the dubious contributions made over the centuries by conceptions of 'honour', then perhaps we should acknowledge Himmelfarb's point.

Still, ethnocentrism and relativism have always had religious counterparts. The holy books of most religions emphasise love, tolerance, justice, truth, and just about every other positive human characteristic. It is disappointing, then, that the history of religion contains so many dark and unpleasant chapters – disappointing but not very surprising, perhaps, given the strain of outfitting other-worldly ideals in mundane clothing. This is in fact the argument usually made when religious practices are criticised and seen to fall short of divine writ: the ideas are pure and good but, alas, they are interpreted on earth by misguided, or narrow, or evil, or corrupt officers. Well, whether the faults lie with us or our stars, it is sad to think that systems which ought, overall, to have generally benign tendencies, to contextualise human frailties and to curb excesses and pretensions of all kinds, have created so much division and discord. Perhaps it is as Jonathan Swift suggested: 'We have just enough religion to make us hate, but not enough to make us love one another.'

6.2 LINKING LANGUAGE AND RELIGION

Safran (2008) has recently noted that language and religion have been the two most important markers of ethnonational identity: sometimes linked, sometimes at odds. He argues that religion was historically more often the bedrock of identity, and that its replacement by language is a more contemporary phenomenon: 'religion had the upper hand until the Renaissance, and language from then until the present' (p. 178). This may be a little too neatly drawn, but the relative emphasis is right. Furthermore, Safran makes the familiar point that nationalism is, in fact, a religion itself. It may be a 'secularised' one, but, at both ideological and mundane levels, it seems quite clear that nationalists are a sect of the faithful.

Nonetheless, it can reasonably be argued that insufficient attention has been given to the important relationships between language and religion. Spolsky (2003) points to the paucity of material here, and Schiffman's (1996) chapter on the interrelated topics of language, religion, myth and purism was an unusual one. There is quite a large literature on 'religious language', and there is at least one recent encyclopaedia devoted to language and religion (Sawyer and Simpson, 2001), but the former is not directly concerned with sociolinguistic or sociology-of-language matters, nor are these the focus of the latter (as Spolsky observes). Further interest does now seem to be developing, however; there is, for instance, a useful collection edited by Omoniyi and Fishman (2006) and, although most of the chapters are devoted to quite specific contexts, individual chapters by each of the two editors provide some overall perspective.

Of course, history reveals that, in many parts of the world at many different times, powerful and consequential connections have existed between particular languages and particular religions. With fewer than half the citizens in revolutionary France actually French-speaking, many regional varieties were seen by the new political masters as mediums of religious fanaticism. Bertrand Barère – the *de facto* propaganda minister – argued that superstition spoke Breton and fanaticism spoke Basque (Wardhaugh, 1987). Later, in nineteenth-century Russia, 'polonisation' in Lithuania was associated with Catholicism, a threat to the official Orthodox church. Vandenbussche *et al.* (2005: 51) write about the 'almost evangelical discourse' of anti-French sentiment in nineteenth-century Flanders, and about the ways in which language activism was – for some ultramontane Catholics – merely a feature of larger religious motivations. They discuss the ways in which Flemish was seen a barrier against godlessness, and they refer to a specific argument against the 'heathen and devilish' influences of German pronunciation on Dutch, an argument that traced them back to Luther, 'the German antichrist' (p. 55).

It is curious that, at one point, Vandenbussche *et al.* suggest that religious impulses are only 'rarely observed' in discussions of language 'protection' (see Edwards, 2007a; Githens-Mazer, 2008). In fact, the evangelism of language activists can be seen as a particular instance of a general and wide-spread principle that I shall return to later on. It is that 'language' movements are energised by the symbolic and identity-carrying aspects of language, and very rarely by the language *per se*. It is true that actual linguistic matters, sometimes very fine-grained, can be zealously taken up but, again, these are invariably related to group boundary marking. At a conference I attended in Santiago about fifteen years ago, an argument over one small point in Galician orthography brought one of the debaters to tears; the underlying issue had to do with competition between Spanish and Portuguese templates. If one accepts that ethnic and national affiliations have many 'religious' constituents – that they are often, in fact, 'secular religions' – then almost all discussions of language and group identity necessarily touch upon sacred matters.

There are many important social and psychological points of connection between language and religion, some having to do with their complementarity as markers of groupness, some dealing with the language *of* religion, some involving the work of missionaries. In all cases, clear and important links to identity can be illustrated. First, and most obviously, the spread of religions has often been accompanied by that of languages (see Cooper, 1982, particularly the chapter by Ferguson; see also Mühleisen, 2007). With the spectacular expansion of Islam in the seventh and eighth centuries, and the establishment of an empire stretching from Asia to the Atlantic, Arabic became a world language. With the fourth-century conversion of the Emperor Constantine, Latin became the lingua franca of Christianity and the old principle of *cuius regio, eius religio* – the religion of the ruler is the religion of his domains – was strongly reinforced. In the Holy Roman Empire of the sixteenth century, the principle was re-affirmed, in the interests of international harmony.

In his important study of translation, George Steiner (1992:300) referred to the power and appeal of linguistic 'enclosure and willed opaqueness', a phenomenon seen nowhere more clearly than in attitudes towards sacred texts. The Buddhist Sutras, the Hindu Vedas, the Christian Bible, the Holy Qu'rān and the Hadith, the Torah and the Talmud, and many other religious works are all sacred in and of themselves, to varying degrees. Some, for instance, are not to be translated at all, while particular versions of others – the King James Bible, for example – have achieved iconic status (see Sawyer, 2001; Spolsky, 2003; Mühleisen, 2007). Catholic missionaries were willing to produce catechisms in vernacular languages, but generally resisted bible translation, a posture intended to reinforce priestly control; Protestant ministries, as we shall see, generally felt otherwise. The idea of the holiness of 'the word' – of a linkage between words and things, of divine creation, even of the creator itself – predates both the Christian era and the Greek Golden Age. Some time during the twenty-fifth Egyptian dynasty (that is, between about 750 and 650 BC), an already existing theological discussion was inscribed on a stone, now in the British Museum. In this 'Memphite Theology', we read that the god Ptah, having first *thought* the world, created it by saying the name of all its elements. Thus, in the Egyptian mythology, as in later ones, names and things coincided, the former perfectly capturing the essence of the latter.

In the Christian tradition there is, from earliest times, the mystical association of the 'word' – *logos*, the Greek λόγος, with its many related meanings of word, thought, pervading principle, reason and logic – with the all-pervasive and divine spirit. We read this at the opening of St John's gospel in the most forthright way:

> In the beginning was the Word, and the Word was with God, and the Word was God . . . and the Word was made flesh, and dwelt among us.

The Word, the scriptures, were divinely incarnate in Christ: Jesus *is* the *logos*, and 'the word' in biblical usage typically means 'Christian belief'. We know, from *Genesis* (I: 3), that God created light by *saying* 'let there be light'. The holy connection here has never been broken: God created things by naming them, and thus calling them into being; things were commanded into existence through speaking. *Opera dei sunt verba eius* – 'the works of God are his word'. God's creative power involves a 'sort of language through which he calls things out of nothing', and his 'omnipotence lay in the primordial identity of speech and action, of thought, language, and being' (Stam, 1976: 204–5); see also the words of St Paul (*Romans* IV: 17). The view was most recently summarised in April 2005, when Joseph Ratzinger (later to be Pope Benedict) said that 'from the beginning, Christianity has understood itself as the religion of the Logos, as the religion according to reason' (see Ratzinger, 2005a, 2005b).

It follows that any tampering with 'the word' is of the utmost gravity. Indeed, there are clear demonstrations – in Judaism and Christianity, to give but two examples – that translation is blasphemy. He who has 'been in Christ' must not (or, perhaps, cannot) repeat the *arcana verba* in mortal words (II *Corinthians* XII: 4). And Jewish writings from the first century record the belief that the translation of the holy law into Greek led to three days of darkness (Steiner, 1992: 252). There are groups who believe that the name of God is never to be uttered, others who reserve this honour for the priestly caste, and still others who argue that *no* language at all is adequate for religious purposes; Sawyer (2001: 263) reminds us here of the 'Quaker predilection for silent worship'. Levy (1993), Marsh (1998) and Cabantous (1998) all provide good overviews of blasphemy, of the act of speaking evil of that which is sacred.

6.3 GOD'S LANGUAGE – AND OURS

From the general notion of the sacred status of language, of 'the word', there quickly arose more specific assertions about particular languages. These were based upon speculations about the language of Eden. *Genesis* (II: 19) tells us that God formed all the birds and beasts, 'and brought them unto Adam to see what he would call them: and whatsoever Adam called every living creature, that was the name thereof'. Once, then, there was an original and ideal language and, unlike all natural languages since, there was a mystical but perfect correspondence between words and the things that they named. What *was* this first, divine language that God implanted in the first man? How is this matter relevant in discussions of identity?

From the earliest times, the question of the first language was a question of the first importance. As Rubin (1998) has pointed out, those who speak that language, or whose ancestors did, may claim a special, intimate and 'chosen' relationship with divinity: as she observes (p. 308):

> It is the language itself, not the message or revelation conveyed by it, that decides this question, the winner claiming first and foremost linguistic and cultural superiority over all other languages and cultures.

Little wonder, then, that claim and counter-claim were so important. Conceptions of social and political group identity would be immeasurably (quite literally) strengthened if their linguistic, cultural and religious components were fashioned by God himself.

From about the second century BC, Jewish literature described Hebrew as the first language; it was the medium of revelation, the language in which God spoke to Adam, the variety used by all creatures until the fall, and by all people until Babel. Rubin makes clear that the assertion of Hebrew's primordial status coincided with its place as the expression of Jewish identity. She notes succinctly that 'national identity and language were so closely linked that 'Nation and Language' – *umma velashon* – became a hendiadys meaning "nation"' (p. 314). Hebrew had the support of most of the Christian community too. Virtually all of the Greek, Latin and (later) Byzantine patriarchs supported its primary status; so, too, did most of the Arabic-speaking Christian theologians. Among other things, this support was itself a buttress of the Christian claim to be the 'new Israel'. Still, Hebrew did not have it all its own way. A pagan hellenistic response argued that it was a construction that had only come into being with the exodus from Egypt; it could hardly, then, be the language of creation. And Aramaic, a variety widely spoken throughout the middle east generally, and within the Jewish community specifically, was a rival for top honours.

The primacy of Aramaic was proclaimed (unsurprisingly) by the Syriac church fathers, and part of their reasoning was etymological. The Greek and Latin fathers (Augustine is a good example here) had said that, at the time of the confusion of tongues, only the people of Heber were free of the sin of Babel, and only their language survived. This primitive variety was called after Heber (or 'Eber), the grandson of Shem, and thus the great-grandson of Noah (see *Genesis* X: 21). But the Syriac patriarchs suggested that this derivation of 'Hebrew' was incorrect, highlighting instead the Syriac word *hebra* (meaning 'crossing'). And Rubin explains the significance of this, in connection with Abraham, the prepotent patriarch for Jews, Christians and Muslims:

> Abraham, having originated in Mesopotamia, must have spoken the local tongue, i.e. Syriac or Aramaic, which was the primordial language. It was only after he had 'crossed the river' [the Euphrates] that the Hebrew language was formed. (p. 324)

Thus, 'Abram the Hebrew' (in *Genesis* XIV: 13) was rendered in the (Greek) Septuagint as 'Abram, the one who crossed over'. So, *'ibrî* or *'ivri* (Hebrew) may derive from the verb *'ābar* ('to cross'). The fact that the scriptures were in Hebrew did not prove inconvenient, since they were given to the Jews and would naturally, of course, have been written in their language. It turns out that, like Hebrew for the Jews, Aramaic was the language in which a specific Syriac group identity was to be expressed, an identity that it was felt necessary to defend from the powerful influence of the Greeks. Rubin also cites an interesting, if somewhat atypical, example of Arabic Christian support for Syriac in these celestial stakes. Proud of its particular Aramaic dialect, a Melkite community in Palestine held to a belief that Noah and his family had visited the Garden of Eden, collecting there 'holy books written by Adam in Syriac-Palestinian writing, that is the language in which the Lord conversed, and the language of his speech' (p. 330). As might be expected, there were also heated arguments about the particular Aramaic/Syriac *dialect* that was the medium of Eden.

Among early Muslim scholars, the claims of Hebrew and Aramaic were both seen to be strong ones – with the latter predominating. In fact, given the seemingly powerful claims of Aramaic, an interesting accommodation was made: Adam's language was Arabic; he spoke Syriac after his expulsion from the garden – but, upon repenting, he returned to speaking Arabic (Kister, 1993). It was perhaps inevitable, given the all-important linguistic buttressing of group identity, that primacy for Arabic, the language of the *Qur'ān*, would be claimed. As Kister describes the argument, 'Adam descended from Paradise speaking Arabic because Arabic was the language of God, of the angels, and the people of Paradise' (p. 140). Furthermore, in distinction to the Syriac argument just noted, Adam was the first poet – and his verses were of course in Arabic. It should also be noted, however, that there was a linguistically pluralistic tradition among Arab scholars, as there was among some Hebrew theologians; thus, some argued, for example, that God had given Adam many, perhaps all, languages.

These ancient arguments are not only of historical interest; they are also early reflections of a continuing language-and-identity discourse whose most basic elements have remained remarkably constant. Also continuing well into the seventeenth and eighteenth centuries was a related question: did the first language survive in some form or other? Was it contemporary Hebrew? Was it the apparently nonsensical utterings, the *glossolalia*, of Pentecost?[1] Could we recapture it, either literally or by analogy – by inventing, perhaps, a new language whose symbols, unlike the words of existing languages, actually depict in some logical fashion the things they represent? These were some of the questions that intrigued the pioneers of language making (see Cornelius, 1965). Many argued that Hebrew was the original *lingua humana* and that certain of Noah's descendants had continued to use this divine tongue, even after the great confusion of Babel (the second great human 'fall', after the expulsion from Eden). Of course, it was obvious that, even if Hebrew *were* the Adamic language, its contemporary varieties must have lost that essential 'character' that allowed a perfect fit between words and things. Referring to the fact that no specific biblical claim is made for Hebrew as the Edenic language, John Wilkins (1668: 11) pointed out:

> Though the Scripture doth not mention anything concerning the invention of these [characters] . . . yet 'tis most generally agreed, that *Adam* . . . did first invent the ancient *Hebrew Character*: whether that which we now call the *Hebrew* . . . is a question much debated.

Wilkins wisely declined to enquire further into the question. Like many others who assumed that some 'primitive' Hebrew *was* the Adamic language, Wilkins's view was that searching for that variety was a pointless task. It followed that no attempt to reconstitute the *lingua humana* as a new universal medium could possibly succeed. A little earlier, Thomas Hobbes (1651: 12) had expressed the same reservations: while 'the first author of Speech was *God* himself, that instructed *Adam* how to name such creatures as he presented to his sight', the scriptural record 'goeth no further in this matter'. Besides, Hobbes added (p. 13), whatever *may* have been the situation in the Garden of Eden, all of Adam's linguistic invention was 'lost at the tower of *Babel*, when by the hand of God, every man was stricken for his rebellion, with an oblivion of his former language'.

But if the strongest minds felt that no real traction could be gained here, others were not deterred from making heroic efforts. Cornelius (1965) and Katz (1981) remind us of the work of Jan van Gorp (Joannes Goropius Becanus), whose linguistic study (published in 1569) convinced him that Flemish was a direct descendant of the divine language. Many of his contemporaries laughed Goropius to scorn: in his famous *Pilgrimage* (1613: 46), Samuel Purchas observed:

> *Goropius* by a few Dutch Etymologies grew into conceit, and would haue the world beleeue him that Dutch was the first language . . . but his euidence is too weake, his authoritie too new.

In *Hudibras* (1663), Samuel Butler mocked the idea; a little later, in *The Alchemist* (1612), Ben Jonson did the same. As might be imagined, however, Goropius did find some disciples, particularly in the low countries. Richard Verstegan (1605) not only endorsed the idea himself, but also implied that the great Ortelius – Abraham Ortels, the cartographer who produced the first modern atlas – was also a believer. At more or less the same time, Abraham van der Myl (1612) and Adriaen van Schrieck (1614) published etymological works supporting the Dutch/Flemish theory.

Van Schrieck (1614), along with Samuel Bochart (1646), Pierre Borel (1655) and others, also took another tack: focussing upon Celtic languages, they suggested that modern varieties may have derived from Hebrew. Scholars such as these were not cranks, and they did not attract the scorn that Goropius did; Bochart, for example, was a widely respected intellectual, a man of multilingual capacities, a theologian whose scriptural researches were both broad and deep. A century on, Vallancey (1772) was still arguing that Irish was really a 'Punic-Celtic' compound, and that Ireland was the Thule of the ancients; see also Titley (2000: 6) for the story of how the Irish language was constructed from the bits and pieces of the 72 tongues that had existed before Babel (so, it was clearly 'the very essence and distillation of the first tongue of the earth'). The celebrated eighteenth-century Gaelic poet, Alasdair Mac Mhaighstir Alasdair (Alastair Mac Dhonuill, 1751), explained that Adam and Eve spoke Gaelic in Eden. Perhaps the poet's tongue was in his cheek, but after yet another century, Canon Bourke (1875: 107) was speculating that Irish was an 'Aryan' language, and that

> the primaeval language of man, called amongst the learned of the present day – the *Aryan*, of which Keltic is a dialect, brings us back to the period before the human family had emigrated from the first home wherein they had settled.

Similar arguments were made about the antiquity and the chronological primacy of Welsh. Thus, Morgan (1983: 67) relates the seventeenth-century idea that Welsh was 'somehow linked with Hebrew... [and] that the Welsh could be traced back to one of the grandsons of Noah'. He goes on to describe the activities of William Owen (Pughe) – 'the greatest and most effective of the language mythologists' (p. 72) – who proclaimed Welsh to be 'the language of heaven', the medium of the patriarchs.

There were many other conjectures. In 1636, the physician and antiquary, Ole Worm (Wormius) suggested that Danish was the original language, for example; and there were supporters of Swedish, Polish, Basque, Hungarian, Breton, German and Chinese as the 'primitive' language (see Katz, 1981; Gera, 2003). Eco (1993) reminds us that these bizarre suggestions were not unrelated to political developments and aspirations. A case in point is found in a treatise by Louis le Laboureur (1667), whose explicit aim was to proclaim the superiority of French: he cited the view that God spoke Spanish to Adam, the Devil spoke Italian, and Adam and Eve subsequently apologised to God in French. Müller (1862) reported that some Persian scholars felt that Adam and Eve spoke their language, that the snake spoke Arabic, and that Gabriel spoke Turkish. All of this was satirised by 'Simon Simplex' (Anders Kempe, 1688); he ridiculed the many attempts to claim one language or another for the Adamic original, by suggesting that God spoke Swedish, Adam spoke Danish, and Eve was seduced by a snake speaking in French. A little earlier, Richard Simon (1678) made the same point: the urges of identity politics underpinned the many ludicrous claims made on behalf of different languages. Father Simon, however, ran afoul of the hierarchy because he also doubted that Hebrew was the language of heaven; he was forced to admit that Hebrew *might* be the Edenic variety, after all.

As I have noted, such wild surmises were derided by important thinkers of the time. Vico (1725: 430), for instance, wrote of 'opinions so uncertain, inept, frivolous, pretentious or ridiculous, and so numerous, that we need not relate them'. Eco (1993:100) discusses Vico's 'acid' comments, and also cites a letter written by Leibniz in 1699 in which he too ridicules those wishing to 'draw out everything from their own language', and in which he observes that if the Turks and Tartars became as learned as Europeans, they would argue that *their* languages were the mother tongues of all (see also Müller, 1862). Eco also mentions, however, that Leibniz himself was not above making a nationalistic language claim, supporting a 'Celto-Scythian' hypothesis that would embrace German (see also Walker, 1972). Perhaps Leibniz was influenced by Gerard Meier, who wrote to him:

> There is nothing in our Saxon language that is random or confused, so that it is clear that none of the confusion of the tower of Babel has clung to it . . . I am often struck with admiration that in our language there is not one word which naturally and properly denotes any vice or moral defect; which is a proof that our language was founded at the time of those first men and is the very ancient tongue they spoke. (Leibniz, 1717: 239, 245)

Leibniz rejected some of the more extreme claims that Meier made, but he corresponded with him (in Latin – rather surprisingly, given both native fluencies and the context) and published his (Meier's) observations in his own *Collectanea*. Similarly, while Leibniz was certainly among those who ridiculed the excesses of Goropius, even coining the verb *goropiser* to indicate etymologically unsound activity, the latter's conjectures on behalf of Germanic languages accorded with Leibniz's own views. Given his intellectual breadth, in fact, it is curious perhaps that Leibniz's nationalistic sentiments were so pronounced:

> the German nation has priority over all Christian peoples . . . we Germans have a peculiar touchstone for thoughts, which is unknown to others; and, when [others] are eager to know something about this, I tell them that it is our very language; for what can be said in it intelligbly without loaned or unusual words is really something solid; but empty words, with nothing at the back of them, which are only the light froth of idle thoughts, these the pure German language will not accept. (Leibniz, 1838, I: 449, 452–3)

With even the more sober minds at least entertaining these thoughts, it is hardly surprising that language-origin theories were both numerous and popular. And, while they are of great interest in illustrating the perceived links among religion, language and identity, they were also theoretically obstructive. Thus, Müller (1862) pointed out that the most common opinion – that Hebrew was the original language – seriously retarded the progress of linguistic science. The emphatic beliefs of the church fathers were, as we have seen, transmitted up to and beyond the seventeenth century. Consequently, when scholars began to think about linguistic classification, they were essentially concerned to show how Hebrew had produced so many offspring, and how one might trace matters, through them, back to Hebrew. 'It is astonishing', Müller wrote, 'what an amount of real learning and ingenuity was wasted on this question during the seventeenth and eighteenth centuries' (p. 129).

In 1786, William ('Oriental') Jones gave the famous address to the Asiatick Society of Bengal (published in 1798) in which he suggested affinities among Sanskrit, Greek and Latin; his suggestion strongly reinforced existing but incomplete ideas about an Indo-European family of languages. (Olender [1994: 8] says that while Jones 'did not invent the idea of an "Indo-European" language . . . he signed its academic identity card'.) The antiquity and dominance of Sanskrit in such a family had the effect of finally displacing Hebrew as any reasonable contender for the *lingua humana* – although, as Olender (1989) points out, it did not go without a struggle, and nineteenth-century disquisitions on the place of the 'Aryan' family and the newly-styled 'Semitic' varieties continued for some time. A common accommodation held that the two could have been 'twins at the origin of civilization . . . in the same or neighboring cradles' (pp. 15, 152).

In his preface to Pellerey's book on *le lingue perfette*, Umberto Eco (1992) situates the growth of interest in a 'perfect language' in a Europe in which the influence of the *ecumene imperiale* was beginning to wane, and where Latin was beginning to give way to the new 'vulgar' tongues. Here we find, he says, the various quests for a perfect language. Many of these involved schemes for a new 'universal' or 'philosophical' language, a variety that would become the international lingua franca. Before the appearance of the *volgari europei*, Eco continues, there had of course been some attention given to earlier languages, but largely as carriers of wisdom that might be usefully recaptured. But when European languages were themselves burgeoning, the story of Babel, the *confusio linguarum* and all its consequences really came to the fore. Soon there were searches both backwards and forwards: backwards, in the hope of regaining *l'ebraico adamico* or some other variety in which words and things were in harmony; or forwards, with the construction of some new language, a human contrivance to replicate the pre-Babel universality.

Most of the efforts to investigate the language of Eden, or to stake a claim for one modern variety or another as the primary descendant of that sacred variety, now seem very odd indeed. And it is also true that, even at the time they were being made, some of the leading intellectual lights were quite aware of the insurmountable methodological diffi-culties involved, to say nothing of the flimsy theoretical foundations upon which these quasi-linguistic undertakings rested. But we would be very wrong to dismiss them out of hand, for they remain of consid-erable social-psychological value. I call them 'quasi-linguistic' because, like most enquiries into various aspects of the 'social life of language', they were essentially about group identity. Indeed, we could be more specific and say that they were essentially about ethnonational identity: the arguments that Adam spoke Hebrew rather than Aramaic or, per-haps, French rather than Flemish, were arguments about an important cornerstone of that identity, about the establishment of group distinc-tiveness and group boundaries. Since they occurred at a time when biblical affiliations and divisions were of the utmost significance, the tight intertwining of linguistic and religious elements seems very nat-ural indeed. Finally here, it is surely very clear that this intertwining is still extremely powerful in many parts of the world. Not all of them are far away, either: there are many millions of evangelical Christians, for instance, who continue to believe that the bible is the *literal* word of God, for whom the ancient connotations of the *logos* still hold good.

6.4 MODERN TIMES

6.4.1 Hebrew in Israel

Religion remains an important factor in many contemporary language-and-identity settings. One inevitably thinks of Hebrew here, the rejuve-nation of which is the archetypal success story among language revival efforts; indeed, Nahir (1977) counts them all as failures, with this sole exception.[2] What accounts for the success of Hebrew?

Without a real communicative need, linguistic revival movements must rely upon other and often less urgent motivations. With the incorporation of a linguistically heterogeneous population, such a need clearly existed in Israel – it was not unique to that country, of course, but there *also* existed here an old language with a powerful religious claim on the population. This combination of circumstances suggests the uniqueness of the Israeli case while, at the same time, demonstrating that the rejuvenation of Hebrew is not quite the miracle it has occasion-ally been made out to be. A generation ago, Fellman pointed out that Hebrew was never a dead language (indeed, he argued there is *no* attested historical case in which a truly dead variety has been revived; see Fell-man, 1973a, 1973b, 1976). Hebrew was a living community language in

Palestine until about AD 200, although it had been abandoned by Jews outside the homeland several centuries before. However, it continued as a religious language – within which limits many Jewish men remained competent – and also, in some communities, as a secular one for certain purposes: Cooper (1989) mentions legal, scientific and philosophical texts here. Among European Jews in the middle ages there were many who were literate *only* in Hebrew. By the nineteenth century, Hebrew was indeed dormant for most Jews in western and central Europe, but it still existed in a diglossic situation for eastern European Jews.

So, when Eliezer Ben-Yehuda first advocated the use of Hebrew as the national tongue in Palestine, in the late 1870s, there still existed a linguistic base, leading Fellman (1976: 17; original italics) to note:

> through eastern European Jewry, in particular, then, the revival of Hebrew could – and did – proceed apace, *without any overriding or insurmountable difficulties.*

Not everyone concurs completely with Fellman, but it is fair to say that the difficulties surrounding the Hebrew revival had more to do with sociopolitical issues – including the claims made in some quarters for Yiddish to become the Israeli lingua franca (see Berdichevsky, 2003) – than with breathing entirely new life into a dead entity. It is arguable, in fact, that the particular circumstances surrounding Hebrew revival efforts suggested likely success from an early stage, quite apart from the pioneering work of Ben-Yehuda. This is to take nothing away from the 'father of modern Hebrew' who, after arriving in Palestine in 1881, established the first Hebrew-speaking home (his own) in our times, and whose son (the writer and journalist Itamar Ben-Avi) was the first maternally Hebrew-speaking child in the modern era; see also Fellman (1997) and Safran (2005).

It is the particular context in which a communicative need coincided with an existing *langue intime* – and one with quintessentially religious connotations – that distinguishes the Hebrew revival from others. Without it, such rapid and pervasive results would simply not have come about; with it, the success or failure of *particular* aspects of the language-planning exercises put in place by Ben-Yehuda (and many others) becomes of secondary, technical interest. In fact, the Hebrew case demonstrates that the power of self-conscious or formal language planning – a topic to which I shall return – tends very much to depend upon existing social forces, and that in most cases such planning involves the 'tidying up' (often a substantial task, of course) of processes put in train or made possible by larger forces. If one were to read only the language-planning literature, it would be easy to lose sight of the fact that, as

Kedourie (1960: 125) once put it, 'it is absurd to think that professors of linguistics . . . can do the work of statesmen and soldiers'. Planning and policy-making are directed by those who possess some variety of power and who, at least in democracies, respond to and elaborate upon sociopolitical needs and requirements. The particularity of the Hebrew 'case' is that the religious factor was central – and in two ways: first, during the long period when the language almost ceased to exist as a 'normal' vernacular, religion provided a sheltering home for it; second, the development and maintenance of a *Jewish* state obviously implied powerful intertwinings between belief and language.

6.4.2 Gaelic in Ireland and Scotland

There are other modern instances of the close connections among language, religion and identity that are as interesting, if not always as dramatic, as those linking Hebrew with Jewish religion and culture. Chief among them, perhaps, are the situations of the Celtic languages, because we can observe interplays between the strongest of languages (English, except for French *vis-à-vis* Breton) and the strongest of religions (Protestantism and Catholicism). A common feature here is that of a powerful cultural element (religion) bolstering a frailer one (an 'at risk' language); another is the use of a language by those whose aim is proselytism, the gradual uncoupling of the two elements and, ultimately, the decline of both.

If religion is a central pillar in the identity and culture of a group whose language is at risk, it makes sense to exploit its strength and to suggest that it is uniquely expressible through the threatened tongue. This posture is generally the political component, activated at need, of an underlying belief that the language has always been inextricably intertwined with the religion. In their study of Nova Scotia Scots, Campbell and MacLean (1974: 178) reproduced the sentiment that

> the one who is taught the Gaelic acquires knowledge of wisdom and an understanding of truth and honour which will guide his steps along the paths of righteousness, and will stay with him for the rest of his life. The Gaelic is a powerful, spiritual language; and Gaels who are indifferent to it are slighting their forefathers and kinsmen.

This is a broad expression of the spirituality inherent in one's most intimate language. Others have been rather more pointed. In the battle with English – and the modernity it represented, so disliked by leaders of the movement to support Irish – the secularisation and 'sordid soullessness' of that language were frequently stressed. Irish, on the other hand, was 'the casket which encloses the highest and purest religion that any country could boast of since the time of the twelve apostles' (Fullerton, 1916: 6); it was 'the instrument and expression of a purely Catholic culture' (O'Donoghue, 1947: 24).

These Catholic sentiments were hardly the only expressions, in Ireland, of linkages between language and religion. Formal attempts had been made, beginning in the last years of Elizabeth I's reign, to use Irish as a tool of Protestant proselytism, an activity which of course did little to increase the popularity of the language amongst the mass of the population. These efforts continued, picking up greater force again in the nineteenth century. Thus, Dewar (1812: 143) noted that supporting Irish would actually hasten its decline, since suitably instructed people would obviously come to see the advantages of English; at the same time, Irish could be invaluable in converting the peasantry from the 'errors of popery'. Anderson (1818: 59) bluntly stated:

> the great object ... of teaching the reading of Irish, etc. is not to make those who are to be the subjects of that instruction a learned, or what may be called a reading people ... but almost exclusively to bring them acquainted with ... Christianity [Protestantism].

Henry Monck Mason (1846: 9), in his history of the Irish Society, a Protestant mission to the native Irish established in 1818, reinforced the point:

> the primary object was not proselytism from any particular sect; yet, as it was foreseen, that the sure result of the study of divine truth would be the abandonment of human error ... it was resolved, that this Institution should be brought into close connection with the established [church] of Ireland [Protestantism].

While several Tudor edicts, particularly during the time of Henry VIII, promoted English and proscribed Irish, the most formalised anti-Catholic efforts were the Penal Laws of the sixteenth and seventeenth centuries, laws for 'the suppression of Popery'. By and large these statutes affected the Irish language only indirectly, as the maternal variety of those whose legal and religious rights across a broad spectrum were systematically restricted. In one or two instances, however, Irish is mentioned specifically. In 1695, an Act of William III suggested that the toleration of Catholics as teachers meant that many of the natives were kept ignorant of 'true religion', neglected the 'laws and statutes of this realm' and did not use 'the English habit and language'. Consequently, the legislation directed that 'no person whatsoever of the popish religion shall publickly teach school'. The following section of the Act reaffirmed an edict of Henry VIII, to the effect that every Irish parish was to maintain 'a school to learn English'. The intent of Henry's law (enacted in 1520) having been frustrated over the years 'by reason of ... Irish popish schools being too much connived at', it was now time to renew its application.[3]

Just as Irish, as the language of popery, had been proscribed under the Tudors, then used to facilitate religious conversion, then indirectly proscribed again, so its religious associations were later exploited by revivalists. (For a general discussion of the narrow cultural and religious nationalism of the zealots – those who advocated a self-imposed isolation, a walled society – see O'Leary, 1994; and also the entries in Edwards, 1983a.) As implied above, it was thought that the strength of Catholicism could be used to halt, shore up and perhaps even reverse the decline of Irish. In fact, as I have suggested elsewhere (Edwards, 1985, 1995), the strength of Catholicism in Ireland may have actually *facilitated* the decline of the language; as an obvious and potent component of Irish identity, the continuity afforded by adherence to the church may have diluted the urge to protect the linguistic component. This has often been the fatal flaw in what is otherwise the clever and obvious strategy of having a weaker constituent of identity (language, in this case) 'carried' by a stronger one (religion): if the weaker one remains weak, despite best efforts, a certain resigned acceptance may set in, bolstered by the conviction that, after all, group identity is still on firm ground. And what, if mundane push comes to shove, could possibly be stronger than whole-hearted, sincere and unstinting religious commitment? Something for which people are willing to make the final sacrifice is clearly a powerful pillar of identity.

In any event, as attempts were made to bolster Irish through its religious associations, so English was simultaneously condemned on the grounds of *its* association with a materialistic and godless culture. In a pamphlet aimed at Irish women, Butler (1901: 2) wrote of a war between 'Irish ideals and British sordid soullessness'; and Forde (1901) pointed out that, since modern materialism had made England turn away from God, anglicisation was evil. It was, in any event, a Protestant medium and therefore unsuitable for Ireland.[4] (I have already cited the remarks of the reverend Mr Fullerton.) A few years later, it was still possible for the argument to be made: Irish revival would at once strengthen Catholicism and counter foreign (i.e. English) materialism (Clery, 1927). The reverend Edward Cahill (1930), one of the more temperate religious commentators, pointed out that the Catholic and Irish-language heritage of the *Gaeltacht* (the remaining Irish-speaking areas) constituted an important barrier against the corrupting influences of the anglophone world. And later still, as we have seen, O'Donoghue was re-making the case.

There is a type of religious Whorfianism in all this, but the arguments, however bizarre, do reflect a powerful possibility. If, after all, it had proved possible to convince the Irish people – a population almost entirely Catholic – that there was a necessary and indissoluble link between their strongly held faith and the Irish language, the fortunes of the latter might have shown a dramatic improvement.

The role of religion in the unfolding story of Gaelic in Scotland is also a complex one. Although circumstances there were far from identical to those in Ireland, there is little doubt that, as in that country under the British, the hierarchy and many of the local ministers endorsed English. Where they did make room for Gaelic, this was generally in the service of more efficient proselytism. Desires to root out popery and to bring enlightenment and 'progress' were always foremost in the minds of Protestant churchmen and educators. But a related motivation was a purely pragmatic desire to reach accommodation with the temporal authority. This has often been the posture adopted by organised religion: one power structure respecting another, perhaps, but also a reflection of the idea that saving souls must ultimately take precedence over other matters, even important cultural ones. The most obvious example of this in the Irish context was the unwillingness of the Catholic church (until conveniently late in the day) to support Irish. In Scotland, with the Protestant sweep through the Highlands and Islands, we find ministers rather than priests most often taken to task under this heading.

With fuller notes on the Scottish context available elsewhere (Edwards, in press b), I largely restrict myself here to one instructive snapshot. In his *Gloomy Memories of the Highlands* (1841), Donald M'Leod (Macleod) reported on evictions in Sutherland and the contribution made by the local ministers to the suppression of dissent. His account is a famous and a passionate one, full of family misery and genuine grievance. The social upheaval in Sutherland, Macleod claimed, was solely the result of the cruel tyranny of the landlords and factors, whose actions were materially assisted by the clergy, who neglected their sacred duty to 'denounce the oppressors and aid the oppressed' (p. 7). Instead, Macleod tells us that they

> found their account in abetting the wrong-doers, exhorting the people to quiet submission, helping to stifle their cries, telling them that all their sufferings came from the hand of God, and was [sic] a just punishment for their sins ... the clergy, factors and magistrates were cool and apparently unconcerned spectators ... no spiritual, temporal or medical aid was afforded ... the clergy, indeed, in their sermons, maintained that the whole was a merciful interposition of Providence to bring them to repentance, rather than to send them all to hell, as

they so richly deserved ... the clergy of the Established Church (none
other were tolerated in Sutherland), all but Mr Sage, were consenting
parties to the expulsion of the inhabitants, and had substantial reasons
for their readiness to accept woolly and hairy animals ... in place of
their human flocks. (pp. 7, 31, 36–7)

The ministers' pastures were generally held in common with those of
the crofters, and these, Macleod notes, were inviolate, thus:

had the ministers maintained those rights, they would have placed in
many cases an effectual bar to the oppressive proceedings of the
factors ... but no! anxious to please the 'powers that be', and no less
anxious to drive advantageous bargains with them, these reverend
gentlemen found means to get their lines laid 'in pleasant places' and
to secure good and convenient portions of the pasture lands enclosed
for themselves ... new manses and offices were built for them, and
roads made specially for their accommodation ... they were the bosom
friends of the factors and new tenants ... they were always employed to
explain and interpret to the assembled people the orders and designs
of the factors; and they did not spare their college paint on these
occasions ... they did not scruple to introduce the name of the Deity;
representing Him as the author and abetter of all the foul and cruel
proceedings carried on. (pp. 37–8)

In these circumstances, Macleod argued, religion began to lose its hold
on the minds of the cottars; 'who can wonder at it? – when they saw these
holy men closely leagued with their oppressors' (p. 39). He concluded by
noting the persistent efforts of the lairds, 'their favourites and retain-
ers, and their ever-subservient auxiliaries, the parochial clergy' to stifle
any formal enquiry into their activities. Obviously, Macleod wrote, they
can hardly be expected to 'expose themselves', since their claim is that
Highland destitution is to be attributed to the 'indolent, improvident
and intractable' peasantry (p. 75).

Several things are clear from MacLeod's narrative. First, while his own
sufferings clearly galvanised him to action, other evidence from other
quarters gives no reason to doubt that the evictions he described were as
violent and unfeeling as he claimed. Second, the one group that might
have been expected to assist the tenantry largely abdicated their duty.
But, as with the proselytising efforts observed elsewhere, one is forced
to consider just how the clergy conceived that duty. In Scotland, it is
quite clear that many ministers were motivated by greed, but some of
them – together with many important social and political figures – also
felt that the clearances were an essential, and essentially desirable, part
of a progressive economy; it was entirely possible to decry the brutality
of methods while endorsing the basic undertaking. In these terms, the

language shift from Gaelic to English was inevitable. And what is more, 'there is no evidence, unfortunately, that if the Clearances had never happened Gaelic would have been, therefore, spared' (MacInnes, 1992: 126).

In 1845 *The Times* became aware of Macleod's writings, and reported – as Samuel Johnson had, two generations earlier – that the people were beaten down, mere shadows of their former selves. The violence of the clearances began to make an impact upon the wider British public and a formal enquiry into the conditions of crofters and cottars was established. The report that followed (Napier Commission, 1884) made many recommendations concerning increased security of tenure for subsistence farmers, thus contributing to the passage, in 1886, of Gladstone's Crofting Act. But it also considered other aspects of Highland life, including religious and linguistic ones. With existing provisions making little or no place for Gaelic in state-approved schools, the Napier Commission argued that, while all children should be taught English, their education should make use 'of the only language the [Gaelic-speaking] child understands' (p. 78); the Commissioners went on to observe:

> We are further of opinion that the Gaelic language, in virtue alike of its being the vernacular tongue of so considerable a population and of its now recognised place among ancient languages, is entitled to something more than permissive recognition . . . a due acquaintance with it ought to be encouraged rather than despised. We think it very desirable that all children whose mother-tongue is Gaelic should be taught to read that language; and the rule of the Society for Propagating Christian Knowledge, that Gaelic should be taught first and English afterwards, seems founded on reason . . . We think that the discouragement and neglect of the native language in the education of Gaelic-speaking children, which have hitherto so largely influenced the system practised in the Highlands, ought to cease, and that a knowledge of that language ought to be considered one of the primary qualifications of every person engaged in the carrying out of the national system of education in Gaelic-speaking districts.[5] (p. 81)

Returning more directly to religious matters, we find that MacKenzie (1883:22) argued that 'the professed ministers of religion sanctioned the iniquity [of the clearances] and prostituted their sacred office and high calling'. He is citing Macleod here, half a century on. And, after yet another fifty years, Scott-Moncrieff (1932: 71) made exactly the same point: 'at the time of the incredibly brutal Clearances, the ministers (unlike the priests both in Scotland and Ireland), with hardly an exception, turned traitor to their people'. Richards (1973: 41) suggests that this quisling reputation is too blunt, but he acknowledges that the church has often been blamed for 'preaching a fatalistic acceptance of landlordism'. In a new treatment, based upon surveys of Presbyterian parishes in Sutherland and Ross, Paton (2006) attempts a more nuanced consideration of the role of the clergy, suggesting that what he terms the 'materialist' view of their actions is insufficiently subtle. Higher religious motives, he implies, must ultimately trump the mundane. Well, this may be true for some clerics, but it is of little comfort to many of their flock. Besides, some of the citations that Paton makes demonstrate that materialism *was* in fact the operative factor in most of these actions, although the clerics would no doubt have seen it as a necessary way-station on the road to more celestial matters. That is, in Scotland – as in Ireland – the clergy had become used to making accommodations with English authority, their rationale being that, in order to save souls, other things must be sacrificed (see above); going along with the civil powers was necessary for the continuing ministry. In Scotland, clergy who were largely dependent upon conservative Lowlanders were unlikely to mount very much opposition to the latter's sense of the rights of private property in the Highlands. As Thomas Devine (1974) observed (cited by Paton), there was also the idea that violence was inherently wrong, as was any attempt to relieve suffering by acting against the public order. And Richards (1973) implies that that 'fatalistic acceptance of landlordism' meant that clergy probably saved lives and prevented futile resistance. Handy points of view, to be sure – with not a whiff of any nineteenth-century liberation theology.

This little Scottish vignette is not meant to lead to any broad conclusions. I include it here only as an illustration of some of the important intertwinings among language and religion, particularly at the level of education, particularly where children are concerned – and of particular significance, therefore, for matters of identity. To conclude this section, let me just cite a piece by Meek (2000). He mentions the assessment of a contemporary Presbyterian minister who believes that – whatever may have been the case in the past – God is now quite clearly ill-disposed towards Gaelic. Given that there are no Gaelic-speaking candidates for the ministry, the reverend gentleman states that 'since the Lord is not sending out Gaelic-speaking labourers to toil in His harvest, I must draw the conclusion that it is not His will that Gaelic survive as a language' (p. 44).

6.5 MISSIONARIES

There may be few Gaelic-speaking labourers now at work in the fields of the Lord, but in other parts of the world – now, and for several centuries past – missionary activity has been closely entwined with linguistic matters. There is not the slightest doubt that a great deal of extremely useful linguistic work has been accomplished by missionaries, and not all of it was undertaken merely in the service of expediting conversions. As Müller (1862: 135) pointed out:

> after it had once been recognised as a desideratum to bring together a complete *Herbarium* of the languages of mankind, missionaries and travellers felt it their duty to collect lists of words, and draw up grammars wherever they came in contact with a new race.

More recently, Grenoble and Whaley (2006: 196–7) have argued that missionaries can play 'an important role in language documentation and other forms of language preservation' at the same time as they are acting as agents of 'culture change'. Some might see this as rather a difficult double act, and Grenoble and Whaley themselves acknowledge that 'there is an inherent tension here'. While we should not 'romanticize the relationship' between missionaries and local people, neither should we 'demonize the missionary-linguist, who can readily become the scapegoat for problems facing local cultures today'. All this is in the best traditions of academic balance, but I feel that the authors are being a little too balanced here: it is really impossible to act simultaneously for both cultural change and cultural preservation, and missionaries have more often been bellwethers than scapegoats.

As Ferguson (1987: 233) reminds us in his study of nineteenth-century Lutheran evangelism among the aboriginal peoples of Australia, missionaries may have a real interest and fluency in local cultures and languages, but they have generally been 'uncompromisingly opposed to many aspects of the traditional religion'. Similarly, the informants cited by Martí *et al.* (2005: 195) believe that

> the use of the local language in religious acts, rites and practices always has the ultimate object of continuing acculturation or leading them [local people] away from their own original beliefs, cultures and languages.

This is the most basic argument against missionaries and their work: they may claim to hold out spiritual and cultural 'alternatives' but the usual result is social upheaval and destruction. As Makoni and Meinhof (2004: 94) point out, native peoples around the world have acquired Christianity in a 'package' with literacy: 'they are offered no choice' (see also Makoni and Pennycook, 2007). Errington (2001, 2008) has written generally about 'colonial linguistics', providing an excellent historical overview that is both intrinsically interesting and a basis from which to understand the missionary operations of contemporary proselytising organisations. I can delve no further here into this topic at a broad level, but I can note some of the better recent treatments (most of which are critical of both missionary aims and tactics): see, for example, Read (1980), Moody (1988), Martin (1990), Mühlhäusler (1996), Moran (2001), Barros (1994), Pompa (2003), Pennycook and Coutand-Marin (2003), Pennycook and Makoni (2005) and Menezes de Souza (2007).

Missionary work has often involved great rivalries. Different religious groups have jockeyed for souls in many parts of the world, and – while feverishly notching more tallies on their religious score-cards – have often created serious and longstanding rifts among local populations. Some of these have developed from denominational divisions established, like Tajfel's 'minimal groups', where none had previously existed. Others have developed more indirectly. For instance, Catholic missionaries – who formed the majority before the eighteenth century – were willing to prepare catechisms in local languages, but bible translation was not approved. On the other hand, such translation was often a priority for their Protestant colleagues. Different orthodoxies were at work here and, in particular, different assessments of the sort of connections 'ordinary' people ought to have with God. The consequences for the breadth and depth of literacy development are not hard to imagine. Samuels (2006) gives a fascinating account of the work of some *two dozen* different Christian denominations at work among the Apache of Arizona. And Stoll (1990) discusses the more general case of Catholic–Protestant clashes in South and Central America. Concerned with the development of Protestant activities – largely under the auspices of the Summer Institute of Linguistics (see below) – the 1983 conference of Latin American bishops, in Haiti, had a particularly compelling item on their agenda:

> the spread of fundamental Protestantism. In November 1984, the Vatican's apostolic delegate in Mexico declared that Latin American governments should move against the Summer Institute of Linguistics and other Protestant groups preying on Latin Americans. Shortly thereafter, the Brazilian bishops sent the Vatican a report suggesting that behind sectarian infiltration in Latin America stood the Central Intelligence Agency. (p. 32)

There is a certain pot-and-kettle flavour to this, of course, and the suggestion of CIA involvement is a lovely piece of dirty-work – but the statement is nevertheless a demonstration of the scope of activities here.

6.5.1 Local languages and proselytism

Sixteenth-century Jesuit missionaries like José de Acosta reported that a diversity of tongues frustrated their activities: even where an indigenous lingua franca existed, 'its primitive vocabulary was quite inadequate for explaining the *mysteria fidei*' (Knox, 1990:127). In the seventeenth century, the preface to George Dalgarno's *Ars Signorum* (1661) – a scheme for a 'universal language' – advertised the work's contribution to

> the matter of Communication and Intercourse between People of different Languages, and consequently a proper and effectual Means, for advancing all the parts of Real and Useful Knowledge, Civilizing barbarous Nations, Propagating the Gospel, and encreasing Traffique and Commerce. (p. 128)

This little excerpt also illustrates how, from the earliest times, religious motives accompanied less celestial ones. Charles V of Spain, for instance, received reports from the missions, but he was also told by his merchant adventurers in the Americas that linguistic confusion interfered with the discovery and exploitation of gold, silver and other valuable resources.

The use of *gesture* for exploration, proselytism and plunder was of course common, and several schemes were on offer. John Bulwer's *Chirologia* (1644) was a 'naturall language of the hand'. It was based upon the principle that gesture is the

> onely speech that is naturall to Man ... [it] speakes all languages, and as an *universall character of Reason*, is generally understood and knowne by all Nations, among the formall differences of their Tongue. (I: 3)

The engraved frontispiece to another language project of the day, Cave Beck's *Universal Character* (1657), shows a European gentlemen holding a paper upon which are seen some of the 'characters'. He is seated at a table with men from the Orient and Africa; a representative of the New World stands near, one hand holding an arrow, the other lifted in a pacific gesture.

But gesture was limited. While Dalgarno, Beck and other language 'projectors' were suggesting gestural accompaniments for their new characters, the great Czech educator Johann Comenius (Jan Komenský) displayed another sort of missionary zeal in his quest for broad linguistic harmony. Lacking the apostolic gift of tongues (i.e. *glossolalia*) or the capacity to work miracles, it might prove useful to approach certain groups in their own vernaculars. 'Let some of our own people', Comenius noted, 'through intercourse with the barbarians learn their languages.' This is a course of action that has since been widely followed. The Victorian missionaries in Africa found it expedient to learn local languages, and so do the current members of the Summer Institute of Linguistics (see below). Some may object today (although many still do not) but, at the height of European missionary interventions, very few indeed would have questioned the idea of proselytism. Comenius went further:

> if those peoples [the barbarians] are under our control, let us take some of their children, and in as large a number as possible . . . teach them our language and the harmonies of things . . . [then] send them back to be apostles to their own people. (1668/1938: 226–7)

A rather more dubious approach but, again, one that has been widely practised; many children in many parts of the world have routinely been removed from their homes and placed in residential schools. The ostensible reason has always been to better educate them in the ways of modernity and, therefore, to improve their prospects; more subtly, however, the aim was often to interrupt older traditions, cultures and languages that were seen, at best, as passively primitive and, at worst, as actively opposed to the dictates of a conquering or a dominant power.

Comenius's final statements on the civilising influences carried by certain languages involve the very opposite of intervention in barbarian lives. He suggests that an alternative would be to ignore 'smaller' languages altogether, and focus only upon those groups whose languages 'have a more general currency and are accepted by most nations' (p. 227); he specifically mentions Latin and Arabic. These, then, would be the conduits through which further transmission to the 'small' varieties would take place. And this, once more, has its modern counterparts. Who has not come across the argument, made either directly or implicitly, that people will be attracted to English because of its obvious global dominance and, therefore, its very wide usefulness? 'They' will come to 'us' if they know what's good for them; 'they' will make the linguistic moves necessary to connect their communities to ours. So, if speakers of 'big' languages shy away from the arrogance of imposing them upon others, there is always this *de haut en bas* position on which to fall back.

Predictable trouble arose when missionaries met anthropologists, when the linguistic and cultural machinations of the religious met the social-scientific investigations of the secular. Each side was extremely wary of the other, sensing (quite correctly) that their aims and methods were incompatible. A collection edited by Franklin (1987) and an article by Headland (1996) exemplify the attempts that have occasionally been made to put some sort of a truce in place, usually on the grounds that God and scholarship should be able to work together – if not in tandem, then at least in parallel – but cease-fires are hard to sustain while battles are still raging. Some general observations may be found in Benthall (1995), who writes about 'missionaries and human rights', following a session on the topic at the previous year's conference of the American

Anthropological Association; in a piece by Pickering (1992), the editor of a special journal issue devoted to the interplay between anthropologists and missionaries; and in a special issue of *América Indígena* (1984; see particularly the articles by Rappaport and Stoll). The most comprehensive and sustained criticism of the missionary position is that of Hvalkof and Aaby (1981); more recent critical statements are made by Dobrin and Good (2007), Epps (2007) and Epps and Ladley (2007). The last take a very strong line indeed, arguing that the goals of academic linguists and those of missionaries are entirely incompatible, that the religous workers are duplicitous and destructive, and that any existing partnerships should be terminated.

6.5.2 The Summer Institute of Linguistics

One contemporary organisation, the Summer Institute of Linguistics (SIL), has attracted the lion's share of attention, largely because of its very broad scope: thousands of workers, in virtually every part of the world, are underwritten by huge amounts of money (Epps and Ladley, 2007). Its linguistic activities have resulted in a great many publications, including *Ethnologue*, a comprehensive catalogue of all the world's languages; it is updated regularly and the current edition is the fifteenth (Gordon, 2005). Established in the 1930s and now based in Texas, SIL is the more secular face of its partner, the Wycliffe Bible Translators (WBT). In fact, it likes to assert that the relationship is much looser than it really is, and mention of religious activities is very much downplayed. On its website, for example, it fleetingly acknowledges that it is a 'faith-based organization', but goes on to emphasise its concern for 'small' languages, community development, cultural preservation and the like. Mühlhäusler (1996; 166) cites a SIL pamphlet which describes the group as

> a philanthropic, non-governmental organization committed to linguistic research, language development, literacy, and other projects of practical, social and spiritual value to the lesser known cultural communities of the world.

Only one word here suggests anything other than normal academic procedure. Very similarly, Kindell (1997: 279) writes that

> the purpose of the Summer Institute of Linguistics (SIL) is to serve the ethnic communities of the world in meeting their deepest needs through seeking to assist them in all areas of language development.

Putting aside the rather infelicitous phrasing, only 'their deepest needs' implies spiritual designs; see also Edwards (1999b). The tactics here are quite traditional ones, in fact: the descriptions given are disingenuous, the sins are ones of omission.

Crowley (1989) has described SIL as 'two-faced', and Menezes de Souza (2007: 141) notes that its tactics include 'downplaying and masquerading [sic] its essentially missionary role'. Stoll (1990: 17–18) shows that, in order to 'avoid Catholic and anticlerical opposition', the overtly biblical arm of the Texas institution called itself SIL, 'primarily a scientific research organization'; in Mexico it had for years 'obfuscated its evangelical goals by claiming to be concentrating on linguistic research'. A wonderful argument was made by William Townsend, the founder of SIL/WBT, in reply to the charge that his organisation was dishonest in its self-presentation. He said that, just as Jesus 'came out of Nazareth disguised very effectively as a carpenter, Wycliffe missionaries go into the field as linguists . . . was it honest for the son of God to come down to earth and live among men without revealing who he was?' (Lewis, 1988: 106). Perhaps this metaphysical 'ends justify the means' assertion reveals that Townsend had something of a God complex; it certainly reveals more about his organisation than most of his minions have cared to let on. Kenneth Pike, the linguist and SIL activist, also suggested something a little surreptitious (1962). Christianity should enter a new society 'quietly' so as not to create chaos in existing cultures – which, after all, are also sanctified forms of life – and then act carefully to transform the moral institutions of those cultures. This certainly acknowledges the evangelical intent, but it does so in a rather illogical way: why should native cultures, 'blessed of God', stand in need of transformation at all?

Diamond (1989) characterises SIL as a 'conservative and pro-capitalist' body that has historically had a close relationship with American officialdom; in fact, she writes that SIL missionaries have been seen as 'assets' of the CIA. Errington (2008: 157) notes that, during the Cold War, SIL members had access to areas that were off limits to others, and SIL was able to enlarge its operations, 'often in parallel with expanding American military, political and economic interests'; see also Stoll (1982), Colby and Dennett (1995) and Pennycook and Coutand-Marin (2003). It is beyond my present purpose here to do more than point the reader towards important further discussion: broad critical overviews include those of Colby and Dennett (1995), Hvalkof and Aaby (1981), Diamond (1989), Martin (1990), Epps (2007), Menezes de Souza (2007), Perkins (2004) and Stoll (1982, 1990).

Some SIL members have discussed their organisation and its work, and their writings, while generally accurate, are most notable for what they typically omit: the author's affiliation, and the evangelical underpinning of SIL (see, for instance, Kindell, 1997; Bendor-Samuel, 1999;

Lewis, 2001; Olson, 2007). Headland (1996), however – while making the case for amicable relations between academics and evangelists – does get to the heart of the controversy. The real reason for the ever-present tensions here has less to do with the documented instances in which missionaries have created cultural and linguistic problems where none need have arisen, and much more to do with the clash of ideologies: secular liberalism versus conservative fundamentalism. As if scoring a point for the missionary team, Headland adds that many anthropologists and other scholars have shrugged off their own earlier Judaeo-Christian backgrounds.

STUDY QUESTIONS

1. What are the typical historical linkages between particular languages and particular religions?
2. Why were the fierce debates about the 'first' human language so important in terms of religion and identity?
3. Does Hebrew in Israel constitute a unique instance of language revival?
4. Did the continuing strength of Roman Catholicism actually contribute to the rapidity of the decline of the Irish language?

Further reading

Umberto Eco's (1993) *Ricerca della lingua perfetta nella cultura europea* is a discussion of the longstanding historical interest in the 'first' or the 'perfect' language which reveals the powerful connections between national identity and religion.

Joseph Errington's (2008) *Linguistics in a Colonial World: A Story of Language, Meaning and Power* ably demonstrates that any attention to language contact in colonial settings very soon brings religious matters to the fore.

Milka Rubin's (1998) article, 'The language of creation or the primordial language: A case of cultural polemics in antiquity', provides an historical perspective, an excellent complement to Eco's more general study.

William Safran's (2008) article, 'Language, ethnicity and religion: A complex and persistent linkage', is a very recent treatment of the theme, whose brevity does not compromise utility.

7 Language, gender and identity

7.1 INTRODUCTION

In obsolete usage, 'gender' could refer to types or sorts. 'Diseases of this gender are for the most part incurable,' wrote a seventeenth-century physician. As a verb, it once indicated copulation: 'elephants never gender but in private, out of sight', said Ambroise Paré in his *Chirurgie* (1564). A little later we find the related sense of the getting of offspring: William Wilkie thus wrote in his *Epigoniad* of 1757 that 'from tigers tigers spring; pards gender pards'. But, from at least the fourteenth century, 'gender' was essentially a grammatical term.

Words may refer to males or females, or to things that have become associated with these categories. In English, therefore, we find 'he' and 'she', 'actor' and 'actress', as well as some less obvious ascriptions – that designate ships as feminine, for instance. Other languages also have a 'neuter' gender (and, in English, 'it' is a neuter pronoun). It can be difficult to understand some gender allocations: in German, for instance, 'knife' (*messer*), 'fork' (*gabel*) and 'spoon' (*löffel*) are, respectively, neuter, feminine and masculine. In French, *pénis* is masculine – but so is *vagin*. Italian sopranos are masculine, but the sentries are feminine. In both French and Italian, the moon (*lune, luna*) is feminine, and the sun (*sole, soleil*) is masculine; in German, however, the moon (*mond*) is masculine and the sun (*sonne*) is feminine. *Und so weiter*. And so on. *Et ainsi de suite. E così via.*

There are some early usages of the noun 'gender' that approach contemporary non-grammatical ones, although they are generally of a facetious nature. Lady Montagu, the eighteenth-century feminist whose letters are her chief literary legacy, wrote to a woman friend:

> of the fair sex . . . my only consolation for being of that gender has been the assurance it gave me of never being married to any one among them. (Montagu, 1709/1965: I: 135)

The current sense of 'gender' as an indication of the masculine or feminine behaviour of men and women dates only from about 1960. It is usually, and usefully, distinguished from 'sex': biological characteristics define the latter, while gender, although built upon biological categorisation, is a social construction. Here, maleness or femaleness is seen to exist along a continuum of elaborations, manipulations or, indeed, rejections of sexual inheritance. This seems a necessary refinement in a world in which traditional dichotomies are giving way to more nuanced appreciations, to 'trans-gendered' possibilities of various kinds. The idea of intermediate or 'third' sexes is not, of course, new. Eunuchs have been in existence, after all, for a very long time: the Greek origin of the word signifies 'bed-keeper', an apt designation for the role eunuchs were meant to play in the harem. Just like the 'third' sexes of India (the *hijara*) or of North America (the *berdache*, the 'two-spirit people' of the western prairies), eunuchs may or may not have undergone surgical alteration: the important and the obvious features are social and behavioural.

7.2 STEREOTYPING SEX AND GENDER

A good place to begin here is with the folk 'wisdom' reflected in proverbs, sayings and quotations: these bear some relationship to the laws and mores of a society, and they can tell us something of social attitudes. Many of them encapsulate views of men and women and, beyond the enlightened cloisters of academe – and often, it must be said, within them – the sentiments they convey are often remarkably constant. Consider these well-known observations:

> Frailty, thy name is woman.
> *Varium et mutabile semper femina.* (women are ever fickle)
> Do you not know I am a woman? When I think, I must speak
> The female of the species is more deadly than the male.
> Your daughter and the Moor are making the beast with two backs.

or

> Home is the hunter.
> Men were deceivers ever.
> The more I see of men, the more I like dogs.
> The silk stockings and white bosoms of your actresses excite my amorous propensities.
> In seduction, the rapist bothers to buy a bottle of wine.

The first set reveals the (stereotypic) eternal woman: weak, changeable and unreliable, endlessly talkative – but also dangerous, and dangerously sexual. The second gives us the eternal male: the strong hunter who provides for the home, but a predatory and untrustworthy character, particularly in sexual matters. This is, of course, a very small sampling from a very wide field, but it is incomplete rather than unrepresentative. It is appropriate to point out here, and in any discussion of sex, gender and their differentiation, that most of our proverbial assessments of men and women have biological sexuality at their heart. This suggests, I think, that the modern scholarly distinctions between sex and gender, valuable as they are, have not moved very far beyond those scholarly cloisters. (Many academic insights, of course, never leave those limited intellectual grounds.) This in turn suggests why so much popular usage is quite rightly called 'sexist' and not 'genderist'.

Any consideration of apophthegmatic expressions relating to perceptions of biological sexuality very soon comes to Freud's famous observation that 'anatomy is destiny'. Much less well known – but much more pointed (and, no doubt, much more offensive in many quarters) – was the statement by Rudolf Virchow, an eminent nineteenth-century physician and pathologist: 'woman', he said, 'is a pair of ovaries with a human being attached; whereas man is a human being furnished with a pair of testes' (Dally, 1991: 84). These sorts of statements suggest an interesting difference in perceptions of men and women beyond the immediate and obvious one. The character of woman has traditionally been seen as more superficial, and as possessing less moral depth, than that of man: *la donna è mobile*, after all. Women who seemed competent in matters of morals and intellect were generally regarded as anomalies, and their achievements were likely to be belittled. On 31 July 1763, Dr Johnson pointed out to Boswell (1791/1958) that 'a woman's preaching is like a dog's walking on his hinder legs. It is not done well; but you are surprised to find it done at all.' A century later, Francis Galton (1883: 39), that pioneer in the study of individual differences, was still clinging to the view that the intellectual capacity of women was limited, that their powers of discrimination were feeble, and that

> coyness and caprice have in consequence become a heritage of the sex, together with a cohort of allied weaknesses and petty deceits, that men have come to think venial and even amiable in women, but which they would not tolerate among themselves.

Galton was ever the courteous Victorian gentleman, but, as Buss (1976) reports, he was puzzled at the entrance of women into the world of work. Indeed, several women working in his biometrics laboratory were dismayed to learn of his membership of an anti-suffrage society.

Women's lives have often been seen as grounded more deeply than those of men in the essentials of biological life; Sherry Ortner's (1996) interesting assertion that culture and construction are essentially male, while women are somehow more 'natural', is also relevant here. The intellectual superiority of men, and their greater capacity for practical application – largely views of men *by* men, of course[1] – pale somewhat at this level: unlike the biological comportment of his female counterpart, man is now seen as superficial, flighty and inconstant. Even if we were to believe, however, that there were some basic truths operating here, we could not logically assume that all individuals could be neatly categorised in these regards. Even accepting the strength of various biological imperatives, it is obvious that we can 'rise above' them in various ways. But it may be that, for most human beings, there exists a deeper and more stable intertwining of sex and gender than some modern (and post-modern) accounts would have us imagine. Relatedly, arguments that aim to refute assertions of the anatomy-is-destiny variety – typically replacing them with accounts of historically different patterns of socialisation for men and women – must surely come to grips with the obvious further question: what lies behind those very socialisation patterns?

7.2.1 The early appearance of stereotypes

It is certain, of course, that the force of socialisation patterns typically begins very early in life, has a great deal of strength across many domains, and receives more or less constant reinforcement from many quarters. From a large literature, a few examples will make the point. Best *et al.* (1977) found that, among 5- and 8-year-old children in the United States, Ireland and England, knowledge of traditional sex-trait stereotypes was already well developed. The children were presented with a number of 'pictures', in each of which were two black silhouette figures; no features were shown, but male and female were identified in a manner similar to that used on the doors of public toilets. The experimenters read a short descriptive vignette to the child, one accompanying each pair of silhouettes. Each of these little 'stories' encapsulated one aspect of male–female stereotypes, and the child was simply asked to point to the silhouette he or she thought the vignette applied to. Thus: 'one of these people is always pushing other people around and getting into fights. Which person gets into fights?'; or, 'one of these people cries when something good happens, as well as when everything goes wrong. Which one cries a lot?' In all, 32 pictures-plus-vignettes were presented. While many interesting nuances appeared when the results were analysed, the general patterns were quite clear: children in each country knew, from the earliest age, that women were gentle, affectionate and emotional, and that men were strong, aggressive and dominant. Not all the familiar stereotypes were in place among the 5-year-olds – many more had been learned by the older children – but the broad strokes were evident (see also Williams *et al.*, 1977). Indeed, other work (by Williams *et al.*, 1975; Widen and Russell, 2002) suggests that children as young as 3 years have some non-trivial degree of awareness of adult-defined sex stereotypes.

Edwards and Williams (1980) extended the generality of these results when they demonstrated that Canadian children were very much like their American and European counterparts. Their conclusions summarise this whole line of research:

> The implications of the present findings revolve around the continued existence of perceptions that are increasingly being challenged in western society. At a time when discriminatory treatment of men and women is seen, more and more, as unacceptable and, indeed, without justification, these data suggest that the more traditional views still permeate society. The distortions and exaggerations inherent in any stereotype tend to obscure the variability found among individuals. To the extent that they accurately reflect one set of stereotypes, these findings indicate a continuing problem in the psychological definition of male and female characteristics and roles, and a disinclination to view individuals in terms of their unique patterns of abilities and interests. (pp. 218–9)

Since I was the one who conducted the Irish and Canadian segments of these studies, I had ample opportunity to talk to teachers and others about the findings, and to assess their reactions. This proved very easy to do: virtually everyone was dismayed to find that the pervasive nature of sex-trait stereotypes had shown itself among young children, even before they first went to school. Female teachers, in particular, were upset and annoyed to think that – by the time they first received children into their classrooms – blunt and often prejudicial attitudes had already appeared among their charges. In general terms, of course, the findings here are not to be wondered at. They reflect continuing trends in the larger society. In advertisements – merely to take one very obvious example – gender-role allocations have remained quite constant, reinforcing the insights of Goffman's (1976) investigation in which, in hundreds of illustrations, he found overwhelming evidence of the depiction of 'conventional' roles for men, women and children.

If these sorts of investigations show just how early sex stereotypes appear, another Irish study of about the same vintage reveals something of their influence upon children's speech. More specifically, I tested some of the implications of language perceptions and prestige in a group of prepubertal children (Edwards, 1979a). Physiological sex differences relating to speech production are of course not very marked in such children, but earlier work had confirmed what common sense knows: judges can guess the sex of young children (on the basis of speech samples) with a high degree of accuracy (typically on the order of 75–80%). It is children's early adherence to social norms concerning male and female speech that allows such accuracy in sex-identification. In this study, voice samples of 20 working-class and 20 middle-class 10-year-olds were presented to 14 adult judges (Irish trainee teachers) whose task was, simply, to identify the sex of each speaker. As well, five other judges were asked to rate all the voices on four dimensions related to masculinity/femininity.

Among both girls and boys, the voices of working-class children were perceived as rougher and more masculine than those of their middle-class counterparts. The major finding, however, was that – although the high overall degree of accuracy in sex-identification found in earlier work was confirmed (it was about 84%, in fact) the errors made were not randomly distributed. First, female judges were more accurate than the male assessors in identifying children's sex. This accords with observations, both within and without the literature, of females' greater sensitivity in interpersonal relationships in general, and in verbal interactions in particular. Second, beyond the differential accuracy of male and female judges, a significant interaction was found, in terms of errors made, between social class and the sex of the child. That is, among the working-class children, few boys were mistaken as girls, but errors made about girls were considerably greater; for the middle-class children, the pattern was reversed, and more errors were made with the boys than with the girls.

It appears as if the general masculinity of working-class speech caused girls to be mis-identified as boys by the middle-class judges. Middle-class speech, relatively more feminine, allowed the operation of what we might term the 'boys sound like girls' principle, one that reflects the fact that, at puberty, it is boys' speech that changes most markedly in assuming adult characteristics. So: different social conventions operate for working-class and middle-class speech, young children are aware of these, and this awareness is exemplified, in their own speech patterns, by adherence to the appropriate norms. Differential accuracy in the identification of children's sex can then be seen as a reflection of these social processes.

This Irish study supports the earlier ones on sex-trait stereotypes in its suggestion of their pervasiveness, their strength and their early appearance. The last piece of evidence I shall touch upon here is provided by the classic study of Condry and Condry (1976). About 200 male and female subjects were shown a film of an infant confronting various stimulus objects; half were told that the baby was a boy, the others that it was a girl. Allowing for some variation attributable to judges' experience with infants, the results showed that different emotions, and different *levels* of emotion, were reported, and that these differences rested upon the sex of the judge and, more importantly, on the sex attributed to the baby. For example, when the child was described to them as being a boy, judges were more likely to see its reaction to a jack-in-the-box as being more angry and less fearful. Condry and Condry termed this the 'eye of the beholder' effect. A little later (1983), working with Pogatshnik, they demonstrated a (roughly) analogous 'ear of the beholder' one. Here, judges heard a baby waking up and, again, some were told it was a boy, others that it was a girl. While men responded quite slowly, regardless of the alleged sex of the infant, women responded more quickly to 'girls' than to 'boys'. The fact that questionnaire data showed that neither male nor female judges agreed with the opinion that girls are frailer creatures than are boys makes the results here less crystal-clear; nonetheless, it was again demonstrated that considerations of sex are likely to affect our perceptions, our assessments and our responses.

All of this should be seen as the general field of which more specific *language* issues are but one aspect. If we turn now to some of these specifics, we will have an opportunity to compare stereotypes and assumptions, on the one hand, and actual behaviour, on the other.

7.3 GENDER VARIATIONS IN SPEECH

7.3.1 Some general observations

The greatest variation, of course, would be found in a speech community in which men and women spoke different languages. This may seem unlikely, to say the least, but a famous instance was reported three hundred years ago by Europeans in contact with the Carib Indians of the new world. How could this come about? The Indians themselves provided this explanation (Trudgill, 2000: 66):

> When the Caribs came to occupy the islands these were inhabited by an Arawak tribe which they exterminated completely, with the exception of the women, whom they married in order to populate the country ... [thus] there is some similarity between the speech of the continental Arawaks and that of the Carib women.

A more considered analysis, however, indicated that:

> The men have a great many expressions peculiar to them, which the women understand but never pronounce themselves. On the other hand the women have words and phrases which the men never use, or they would be laughed to scorn. Thus it happens that in their conversations it often *seems* as if the women had another language than the men. [my italics]

It would indeed be odd to find men and women unable to understand each other's language, but there are situations in which women customarily speak language A and men language B, and where the two sexes are bilingual. One such is found among Amazonian Indians living along the Vaupés river (Holmes, 1992). The language of the longhouse is Tuyuka, which is used by all the men, and between women and children. However, since men must marry outside their tribe, the first language of the wives is not Tuyuka; thus, a woman might be a native speaker of Desano and continue to use it with her husband – who answers her in Tuyuka. More common is the Carib scenario, in which certain features of men's and women's speech differ. Typical here are variations in pronunciation or morphology. Among the Gros Ventre of Montana, for example, the women say *kyatsa* for 'bread', while the men's form is *jatsa*. In Yana, another North American variety, the words of men and women differ because the former typically add a suffix: the word for 'deer' is *ba* (for women) and *ba-na* (for men), and 'person' is *yaa* or *yaa-na* (Holmes, 1992).

Beyond this, there are many examples of vocabulary differences between the sexes, although these seem never to be very extensive. In the 1930s a classic study was undertaken of Koasati, a language of Louisiana, which revealed sex differences with verb forms (Haas, 1944; see also Trudgill, 2000). In the phrase 'You are building a fire', men used the term *osch* while women said *ost*; in 'I am saying', the male variant was *kahal*, the female *kahas*; and so on. Vocabulary differences are seen in Japanese too, where women say *ohiya*, *onaka* and *taberu* for 'water', 'stomach' and 'eat', while men say *mizu*, *hara* and *kuu* (Holmes, 1992). Or consider Chiquito, a Bolivian language: here a woman says *ichibausi* to mean 'my brother' where a man would say *tsaruki*; 'my father' is *ishupu* for females, but *ijai* for males. Many of these variations say more, of course, about an elaborate system of kinship designation than about sex differences *per se*. After all, the relationship of a sister to her brother is not the same as that of brother to brother, and there is no reason why sisters and brothers should refer to other brothers with the same word.

There are languages in which the sex of the *listener* rather than that of the speaker determines the variant used, and there are others in which the sex of *both* speaker and listener is influential. In Kūrux, a Dravidian language of India, a man speaking to either a man or a woman, and a woman speaking to a man, would say *bardan* ('I come'); a woman speaking to another woman, however, says *bar?en* (i.e. with a glottal stop). Speaking to a man, either sex says *barday* ('you come'), but speaking to a woman, a man would say *bardi* and another woman would use the form *bardin* (Ekka, 1972).

Why do such differences exist? In some cases, social and religious taboos can have linguistic consequences. In others, women's forms appear to be older than the men's: changes have occurred in men's speech which the women have yet to adopt. It is a common observation that women's linguistic patterns tend, overall, to be more conservative than those of men. Related to this, and supporting the maintenance of distinctions, is the view – expressed more in some cultures than in others – that the older forms are *better*.

The variations just considered are of the 'sex (or gender)-exclusive' variety (Bodine, 1975). But 'gender-*preferential*' features will be more recognisable to most readers of this book: linguistic practices and markers which are more *common* to one sex than to the other. The most general observation is the one I have just mentioned: women's speech tends to be more conservative, more 'standard' and more 'polite' than men's speech. In a much-quoted study, Fischer (1958) found, among young children in New England, that girls were much more likely than boys to use *-ing* rather than *-in'* for the ending of the present participle. Although the degree of differentiation varies, this has proved a robust finding in other contexts. While American research has predictably shown that the use of multiple negation ('I don't want none') is much more common among working-class speakers than among upper-class ones, it also reveals that women use it (and other similar grammatical variants) much less frequently than do men.

Findings within a speech community reveal that women's speech tends to be more standard than that of their male colleagues. An apparently contradictory finding is that, where a more prestigious variety is threatening a 'smaller' one, and where language shift to the former is underway, women tend to be early 'shifters' (see Scherer and Giles, 1979). But this seeming contradiction is resolved when we consider just why women's speech should be more standard than men's. Most explanations centre upon women's allegedly greater status-consciousness (Trudgill, 1983). If women are less socially secure than men, for example, they may wish to gain status through the use of more standard forms. It has also been suggested that, with women traditionally less likely to be defined by markers of occupation and income, they may make their speech a sort of surrogate status marker; see also Trudgill (1972; 2000). They may also, in their maternal role, be more conscious of the importance of their children's acquisition of prestigious speech variants and thus, consciously or otherwise, see part of this role as linguistic model. Beyond this, there is also the already noted association between working-class speech and masculinity which, for males of *all* classes, can constitute so-called 'covert prestige' (see below). Research here has shown that males often *claim* to use more nonstandard forms than they actually do while females are more likely to over-report *standard* usage.

If women's and men's speech differs because the status (and hence, status-consciousness) of the genders differs, then it is clear that large social issues of power and subordination are involved. If women are expected to use 'better' forms than men, if they are supposed to be more 'polite', if their use of profanity and obscenity is more severely sanctioned, then we might conclude that they are a subordinate group whose linguistic (and other) behaviour has limits placed upon it. It is an irony, of course, that the forms this limiting takes are often velvet-lined: isn't it good to be polite and to avoid swearing? The fact remains, however, that if women are on some sort of linguistic pedestal in these regards, they have been *placed* there – and pedestals offer little room for movement.

A subordinate social role implies less freedom of movement, greater insecurity, uncertainty and lack of confidence. It is exactly these features that were elucidated by Robin Lakoff (1973, 1975, 1990) in her much-cited studies of women's language. These include:

(a) lexical 'hedges' or 'fillers' (*you know, sort of, you see*);
(b) tag questions (*she's very nice, isn't she*);
(c) emotional, expressive but often 'empty' adjectives (*divine, charming*);
(d) precise colour terms (*magenta, taupe, mauve*);
(e) intensifiers (*I like him <u>so</u> much*);
(f) excessive politeness, avoidance of commitment and indirect requests;
(g) euphemisms and avoidance of swearing;
(h) emphatic stress (*it was a <u>brilliant</u> performance*);
(i) use of diminutive forms;
(j) collaborative rather than competitive conversational style;
(k) greater use of gesture and intonation (i.e. nonverbal or paralinguistic accompaniments);
(l) 'breathier' voice quality;
(m) imprecision in diction.

There were several difficulties with Lakoff's work. Her methodology was questionable and her analysis was imprecise; her lists of features were hardly comprehensive; and she implicitly adopted a 'male-as-norm' perspective. Nonetheless, her attempts to at least begin a classification of recurring gender differences in speech have been widely recognised and applauded (see the appreciation by Crawford, 1995; Colley, 2005). The most interesting features are those involving either overstatement or understatement, because either of these can suggest nervousness, insecurity, desire to mollify, and avoidance of unpleasantness. And these, in turn, are related to gender differences in communication: men dominate conversations, men interrupt women more than women do men, women provide more conversational feedback then men – that is, they make more encouraging and facilitating remarks during exchanges – and so on. This, at least, has been the received wisdom.

It would be easy to see all of this as evidence of clear-cut differences in which comparisons are not generally favourable to women. These speech variants fit very nicely into the broader gender-trait stereotypes that I have already touched upon: in language as in social behaviour generally, women are timid, dainty, 'nice' and eager to please. The areas in which they are acknowledged to be more accomplished than men – presumably *because* they are 'women's work' – are themselves less 'serious', and certainly less rewarding in terms of the usual coins of society. Could there be, after all, any possible doubt about the relative importance of an extensive and fine-grained colour vocabulary, or an expanded capacity to endlessly discuss and dissect 'relationships', when compared to the discourse of engineers, surgeons, philosophers and other traditionally male groupings?

But what is easy is not always what is correct, and one or two points should be made. The speech characteristics traditionally associated with women are not, after all, exclusively theirs. The features do not always signify the same thing. And a dominant–subordinate dichotomy is clearly an inadequate explanation for gender variations. As an example, consider 'tag questions', one of the most widely discussed features of women's speech. Must they *always* imply uncertainty, do they *always* invite the listener to make a correction or at least expand upon a dubious utterance? Some clearly do ('*It's a wonderful painting, isn't it?*') but others are better understood as 'facilitative', giving the listener a comfortable conversational entry ('*You've just changed jobs, haven't you?*'), and others still may work to soften a criticism ('*That was a bit silly, wasn't it?*'). Readers will immediately see that these usages are frequently employed by both men and women. Tags can also be confrontational ('*You see what I'm telling you here, don't you?*'); in this sort of case, readers may be right to believe that men are the more frequent users. In fact, Holmes (1992) analysed these and other features, plotting their gender distribution in a large corpus of speech. She found that most women's tag-question use (about 60%) was facilitative, another third expressed uncertainty, and only about 6% had a mollifying function. Men's use was clearly less facilitative (about 25%) – but about *twice as likely* to be used to 'soften' or to express uncertainty. These findings seem to turn stereotypes on their heads. Can men's language really involve more mollification of other speakers and listeners? Can men really be more uncertain in their opinions than women? And if they are more apt to 'soften' their views, why are they not more 'facilitative': wouldn't these tend to go together? Well, yes and no. As with the data concerning confidence and certainty of judgement (see chapter 5), it may be that men are more linguistically aggressive than are women, and hence feel a more frequent need to moderate their expressions; similarly, they may forge ahead with ill-informed points of view, only to have to back-pedal somewhat later. None of this need touch upon the 'facilitation' function that, indeed, seems to be taken more seriously by women.

Very recently, Cameron (2006, 2007) has shown, too, that women can be as conversationally aggressive as men in terms of turn-taking and interruption. Many of the 'classic' features identified by Lakoff do not, after all, discriminate particularly well between men and women. And it is noteworthy that some of the commentaries in the revised edition of Lakoff's classic work (2004) are now suggesting that it was always more about ideology and power than about this or that specific linguistic feature.

More fine-grained analyses of gender differences in speech reveal that 'women's' features, greater female politeness, increased use of standard variants and so on may all imply more about genuine facilitative and supportive desires than they do about insecurity and lack of confidence. The broader point, of course, is that men and women may use language for different social purposes, having been socialised in different ways from earliest childhood. Alleged differences in men's and women's 'gossip' are instructive here. The latter is traditionally seen to focus on personal relationships, experiences and problems, in a generally supportive atmosphere in which 'networking' is key. The former is more concerned with factual information, often in a competitive or combative format; of course, the tradition for men avoids the word 'gossip' altogether. Leet-Pellegrini (1980) succinctly remarked that men typically ask themselves if they have won in conversational exchanges, while women ponder whether or not they have been sufficiently helpful.

7.3.2 Verbosity and silence

If we return for a moment to proverbial aphorism, the most general proposition is that speech may be silver, but silence is golden. It is better to remain silent and be thought a fool, said Abraham Lincoln, than to open one's mouth and remove all doubt. The picture here contrasts the garrulous ass with the strong, silent type, and there is the further suggestion that, with wisdom, one expects taciturnity. The German proverbial assertion about silver and gold (*Reden ist Silber, Schweigen ist Gold*) is amplified by the further note that talking is natural (and common), while silence is wise (and rarer): thus, *Reden kommt von Natur, Schweigen vom Verstande.* No prizes are awarded for deducing the gender linkages that have suggested themselves here. Woman, the more 'natural' of the sexes or genders (see above) is inevitably also more 'common'; wisdom thus comes less frequently to her than it does to man. Besides, lacking the physicality of men, women find that *la langue est leur épée,* and it is a sword that they will not let rust. This, despite the fact that they are so often reminded about that golden silence that not only reflects sagacity but also – and even more importantly – obedience and submission. Silence may be the best ornament of a woman, but it is one she all too seldom wears.

In fact, however, there is abundant evidence that men talk more than women. The most recent demonstration of this is revealed in a meta-analysis of 150 studies involving thousands of informants conducted by Leaper and Ayres (2007). While the overall differences were slight (but significant), the authors found that nuances of speech *context* and *type* were more indicative of gender variations: women's speech, for instance, was more 'affiliative', men's more 'assertive'. These and other effects, however, can be substantially moderated or mitigated by specific setting variables (the gender of conversational participants, the topics being discussed, status and age variations, and so on). A recent book by Cameron (2007) criticises the received wisdom that there are, in fact, substantial differences between men's and women's language, paying particular attention to the 'verbosity' myth; see also below.[2] In the same way, there is abundant evidence that silence can be used in different ways. In one interpretation, silence can be an 'affiliative' device (hence, a 'feminine' one) that allows another participant an entry into the conversation. There is, of course, only a short interpretative step here between perceptions of polite consideration and of subordinate status (inferiors speak only when spoken to, otherwise remaining silent). In another interpretation, silence can be a reflection of male power. Sattel (1983) provides an excerpt from Erica Jong's *Fear of Flying,* in which the man's lack of response to the woman is an exercise in dominance. In his commentary on this, Kiesling (2007) also makes the important point that social views and, more importantly, preconceptions are operative here: if a man is silent, this may well be seen to confirm his authority and potency; if a woman is silent, this may be taken as a confirmation of her weakness or timidity; see also Mills (2006) for a recent discussion of women as a silenced or 'muted' group.

7.3.3 Miscommunication between women and men

Coates (2004) provides some very useful general commentary here, much of which builds upon the familiar belief that while women's questions are used for conversational facilitation and maintenance or, more importantly, to invite discussion, men typically interpret them as they would their own – as requests for information *tout court*. This then leads to cross-purposes across the breakfast table. Cameron (1995, 2006, 2007) reminds us again, however, of the large overlap in the way men and women speak, and she is particularly critical of some of the 'popular' literature that has reinforced our sense of gender miscommunication. Commenting on the well-known work of Deborah Tannen (1986 and 1990, for instance), Cameron notes that problems arise, not because of linguistic gender differences, but because of variations in power. When the man says to his wife, 'Is there any ketchup?', the message is really 'Bring it to me.' If the daughter asks the same question, it is much more likely that the mother will respond by telling her that it is in the cupboard. Cameron (1995) is particularly insightful when she writes that the underlying theme in 'popular' books is that there are both real differences between men's and women's language, and useful ways of dealing with them. The 'strategies' here are essentially directed to women. These are self-help books, part of what Cameron (1995) styles the 'you and your relationship' genre, obviously meant for women. The problem, then, is that they really only deal with adaptation and tolerance; they do not come to grips with the reasons for either the behaviour or the stereotypes, and no contribution is thus made to any possible change.

Other 'advice' has suggested that women should speak more like men if they want to be taken seriously, to do well in the corporate world, and so on. Perhaps, on the other hand, women ought to be reassured that it is all right to be 'different'. But the first tack has sometimes contributed to the stereotype of the business woman who has surrendered her femininity, while the second may simply perpetuate older stereotypes; see Romaine (1997). It is instructive to learn that advocacy organisations for women in business, like *Catalyst* in the United States and Canada's

Women's Executive Network, continue to point to some very familiar problems. Pamela Jeffery, the current president of the Canadian body, has (Immen, 2008a) noted that – besides male prejudice and continuing difficulties in reconciling work and family life – women remain hampered by certain perceptions of language and style. There is the 'femininity' issue: successful women are seen to be abrasive and domineering, traits that attract much less negative comment in men. As well, Jeffery notes that female executives continue to find that assertiveness and social control, typically seen to be necessary for effective management, are hard to reconcile with other qualities – she mentions compassion and empathy – traditionally more evident among women. Immen (2008b) has recently reported that when *Vogue* offered her a place in the magazine, accompanied by photographs to be taken by Annie Liebowitz, Hillary Clinton declined on the grounds that appearing in that context would make her appear 'too feminine'. For further documentation of the most recent trends here, see Immen (2008a) and Rosenzweig (2008). Finally here, Immen (2008b) cites recent survey work suggesting that, in fact, some combination of 'male' and 'female' characteristics may be the most effective for women in executive positions:

> female managers who blend the traditional direct and authoritative style of leadership with a more nurturing and inclusive feminine style consistently achieve greater success than women who act strictly like men.[3]

7.3.4 Names and words

Coates (2004) refers to some of my own work on disadvantage (see Edwards, 1989), correctly pointing out that my treatment does not make clear that women constitute a disadvantaged social group in their own right. My discussion involved immigrants, ethnic-minority groups and working-class populations, and my particular focus was upon the social and linguistic difficulties encountered by children at school. But, as this chapter has already demonstrated, the traditional subordinate status of women is clearly marked in terms of language usage, attitudes and stereotypes. Some of these earlier and more egregious examples (cited by Smith, 1985) are no longer so apparent, perhaps:

> Barrister and woman found dead. (newspaper headline)

> QE-II 'wife free' fares across the Atlantic.
> They add to the pleasure but not the price. (Cunard advertisement)

> Drivers: belt the wife and kids – and keep them safe. (Road-safety poster)

> If it were a lady, it would get its bottom pinched. (Fiat advertisement)

However, as Hellinger and Pauwels (2007) have recently demonstrated, the days of sexist language – usage that is insulting or trivialising to women – are far from over. References like 'mankind', 'lady philosopher' and 'delegates and their wives' still slip under the radar, despite current attention, omnipresent writers' guidelines, and so on. (Romaine [1999] writes of being the only 'lady professor' at Merton College.) The most interesting questions, which go well beyond my purposes here, have to do with the appropriate response to sexist, inaccurate and unfair language.

Romaine (1999: 291) summarises things: language both reflects and constructs woman's status; it often casts her in an inferior or unfavourable light. So what to do? Ought we try and change society, secure in the knowledge that language change will follow? Should we make attempts at language reform, as a way of speeding the happy day? Is it language as symptom, or is it language as cause? Cameron (1992b) deals with this point, too. Her view is that suggesting changes to sexist language pays attention to words rather than to the meanings that underlie them (see also Spender, 1980). On the other hand, it is surely possible that attempts to change language, to change symptoms, could be useful. I am reminded here of anti-segregation moves in the American south. For instance, legislation banning the practice of consigning blacks to the back of the bus was considered by some to be dangerously ahead of prevailing (white) attitudes – pushing the envelope, to use a phrase not then in use. But the counter-argument was that action taken a little in advance, as it were, of attitudes could actually expedite changes in them. And so it proved in this case. The distance between attitude and action in these matters is crucial, of course.

Many would point to the apparently rapid adoption of the title 'Ms', although Romaine suggests that our applause should be a bit restrained. 'Ms' was meant, of course, to replace both 'Mrs' and 'Miss', to be analogous to the use of 'Mr', regardless of a man's marital status. As Romaine suggests, however, it is often now a third option alongside the two terms it was to replace, or else is used as a replacement for 'Miss' alone. A Canadian study found that 'Mrs' was retained for married women, 'Miss' for unmarried ones, and 'Ms' for those who had divorced. For some, 'Ms' apparently suggests a woman who is trying to hide her marital status. Romaine provides an interesting note from a study by Ehrlich and King (1994): state authorities in Pennsylvania told their information officers that, if they recorded 'Ms' for a female, they should then put either 'Miss' or 'Mrs' in brackets immediately afterwards.

In a discussion less dated than his presentation of headlines and advertisements, Smith (1985) referred to the fact that words associated with masculinity are more likely to be associated with prestige; conversely, 'feminine' words with negative connotations are more frequent than 'negative' men's words. Some caution is needed here, however, since prestige was defined as involving either skill or power over others. More elaborate investigations by Williams and Best (1982, 1990), however, involving adults and children in thirty countries, have shown that the affective components of trait descriptions can indeed vary significantly along evaluative dimensions. Adjectives seen to be associated with men score higher in terms of perceived strength and activity, for example, although no marked differences between the sexes/genders were found in terms of 'favourability'.

Personal names and their implications have been usefully discussed by Gibbon (1999) and Cameron (1990, 1992b); the latter has particularly relevant treatments of 'naming and representation', and within the 1990 collection there is a valuable study by Schulz on the 'semantic derogation of woman'. Spender (1980) also remains instructive reading here. Much of the discussion has become quite familiar now. Thus, sexual terms associated with males ('macho', 'stud' – even 'ladies' man') are often positive or, at least, reflect a sly admiration, while those for women tend to be demeaning or pejorative ('slut', 'tart'). Animal names applied to men and women ('dogs' and 'bitches') also differ in their force and direction. 'Bulls' are not merely male 'cows', and 'bachelor' is not merely a male equivalent of 'spinster'. Beyond these rather shopworn illustrations are some less familiar onomastic notes. We know that names that can apply to either gender are sometimes spelled differently (Lesley/Leslie), but it is apparently the case that, once a name is used for girls, it loses its popularity for boys (Beverley, Evelyn). Boys' names are often shorter, and end with a firm, consonantal stop. Girls' names are longer, often derivative of boys' names (Roberta, Patricia), and often end in a 'softer' vowel. Many female names mean something nice: virtues (Patience or Faith) or precious stones (Ruby, Emerald) or flowers (Violet).

7.3.5 Swearing, politeness and standard usage

As I have already noted, standard middle-class usage has typically been more attractive as a status marker to women than to men. This is related to the common perception that women's speech is 'politer' and more 'correct', and that they are less prone to profane and obscene language. A greater linguistic insecurity among women has been seen as important here, an insecurity that may rest upon a more pronounced status-consciousness, coupled with a traditional lack of social, occupational and other markers of place – markers that operate for men, beyond the front gate, but that have been less available for those whose role keeps them nearer home and hearth. These are the familiar explanations that will be found in sociolinguistics texts. They are undoubtedly valid, but they hardly do justice to the great historical sweep that has created gender roles and stereotypes in all societies. Women in western society, for example, may use fewer 'four-letter words' than do men, and this may indeed reflect a less solid social footing, real or perceived. But it is surely also the residue of a very long period during which linguistic sanctions of all sorts have become so thoroughly ingrained in the essence of 'femaleness' that they can be expected to retain something of their force long after status differentials have begun to shrink. Many attributes and practices survive the passing of the conditions which initially gave rise to them.

I chose this example on purpose, however, because – as most readers can readily attest – women do seem to swear more often nowadays. (Also noteworthy is the increased likelihood of *men* swearing when women are present.) It is also the case that shifts in usage here are more marked in some contexts than in others. I have been in factories, for example, in which powerfully obscene language was the norm for both men and women. Montagu (1967: 87) cited a war-time aircraft factory setting in America in which signs directed at the (female) workers read 'No swearing. There may be gentlemen about.' Hughes (2002) reports on the extensive use of expletives among working-class women in Salford. These are perhaps the contemporary descendants of the Billingsgate fishmongers, particularly fishwives (see Hughes, 2006). Occupational and educational levels, then, are important variables here – as is age: the four-letter words I regularly hear used by female undergraduates in the corridors are not nearly so frequent in the mouths of their women instructors, even when the latter are relaxing after work, even when (so I am reliably informed) they are in same-sex venues.[4] Finally here, studies have shown that, even in this linguistically permissive age, there are still some words (fewer than once was the case, of course) that women tend not to use. There is swearing and swearing. Among others, Coates (2004), Jay (1992) and Hughes (2006: 195) note, for example, that, while women may actually swear *more* than men in some contexts, they still 'lag significantly behind men in using terms for the genitalia' (it is debatable, of course, whether 'lagging behind' is entirely apt here). My point in all this is that any argument that holds men to be less polite and more profane than women is entirely too simplistic. Hughes's (2006) long essay on women's swearing, in his wonderful encyclopaedia, provides an excellent brief overview, all the way from the earliest European written records to the language of female characters in *The Sopranos*.

The better analyses have always recognised the nuances here, going back at least to the work of Brown and Levinson (1987), and most recent overviews have appropriately expanded the arena of enquiry, first by embedding the discussion in broader perspectives on gender variations in language and, second, by treating both genders under the one roof. Coates thus accompanied her initial book on women's language with one on men's talk (1996, 2003) and her most recent discussion brings them together (2004). Crawford (1995), Holmes (1995) and Mills (2003) provide valuable discussions of 'politeness' and 'nonstandardness' in the dynamic context of power and its negotiation. Salkie pointed out (2004: 29) that 'politeness is what in the language field we call a Whelk (What every linguist knows)'. Perhaps swearing is another. It is certainly the case that studies in politeness and swearing – and, more broadly, in the whole standard–nonstandard continuum – have increased dramatically in the last two decades.

There are many interesting modern works dealing with obscenity and profanity. A useful place to begin is McArthur's (1996) brief discussion of offensive words; it concludes with a six-page chronology (from 1300 to 1900) that outlines swearing in print. All the important milestones are here: Chaucer, Shakespeare, Grose's famous dictionary of 'the vulgar tongue', the activities of Thomas Bowdler, the *Lady Chatterley's Lover* case, and so on. McArthur also draws our attention to the periodic attempts to ban or regulate offensive usage; she mentions the nineteenth-century American Comstock Law and the twentieth-century attempts to give some legal definition to 'obscenity'. Interesting here is the *Act for the More Effectual Suppressing [of] Profane Cursing and Swearing*. McArthur records a date here of 1694, and implies an English origin, although Benjamin Franklin printed off copies of this title in 1746. There were probably many such acts, on both sides of the Atlantic, with the same or similar title. Trevelyan (1949–1952) notes the various moves against swearing, drunkenness, indecency and Sunday trading in early eighteenth-century England. A tract entitled *Kind Cautions Against Swearing* was distributed among the coachmen of London; another was *Kind Cautions to Watermen*. Trevelyan also reproduces (III: 36), in its entirety, a broadsheet headed *A Short Warning, or Reproof, to all Desperate and Prophane Swearers, Cursers, Damners, etc.*, distributed for one 'Philaretus' (the name means 'lover of virtue').

There are many accounts of swearing, from many theoretical perspectives; the psychoanalytic literature is particularly rich. On a more eclectic note, Jay (1992, 2000) provides comprehensive overviews of 'cursing' in many settings. His work is notable for its combination of experimental findings (on usage and attitude) and theoretical underpinnings: what is swearing, why and when does it occur and so on. Most relevant for our purposes here are his relatively brief remarks on gender. The most general observations are that, over time, the 'swearing gap' between men and women has narrowed, but that men still swear more frequently than do women, and that they remain more likely to use what are broadly judged to be the most offensive words of all. Long ago, Robert Graves, in his *Lars Porsena* (1927/1972), advanced the theory that swearing increases at times of stress. He began with the observation:

> Of recent years in England there has been a noticeable decline of swearing and foul language, and this, except at centres of industrial depression, shows every sign of continuing until a new shock to our national nervous system, a European war on a large scale or widespread revolutionary disturbances at home, may (or may not) revive the habit of swearing, simultaneously with that of praying. (p. 1)

Of course, Graves's little book is essentially a literary excursion, not a sociological one, but this does not make it without interest – even today – nor should the reader be put off by the rather weaselly 'may or may not' phrase. This interest need not extend to acceptance of the author's thesis; his sense that offensive language was in decline in the late 1920s probably reflects the restricted circles in which he moved, and the great alterations in his life since his years of familiarity with army profanity during the First World War (see Graves, 1929/1960). In his foreword to the later edition of *Lars Porsena* (1972), Graves slips again:

> Swearing has now virtually ended in Britain, except for words like 'bloody' and 'fucking', still commonly used as intensives. This is because the age of sexual permissiveness initiated by the Pill makes pornography no longer either legally punishable or morally shocking; because the almost total decay of religious faith has taken all the punch out of mere blasphemy.

There is an interesting theory lurking in this, but it is of course an incorrect one. What would Graves have made of modern politicos who wear their religion on their sleeves, of the rise of the evangelical right in America, of Islamic fundamentalism, of the many shades of political correctness?

Montagu's (1967/2001) classic study gave only two pages (out of almost 400) to what he styled 'the sexual factor in swearing', and these were largely devoted to the idea that while swearing is generally a way of 'letting off steam' for men, the women's traditional equivalent has been weeping. This remains, he argued, a 'dependable outlet' for frustration and anger, and one to which a woman can resort without social penalty. Montagu reinforced his point by noting that those women (he mentions prostitutes) who *do* swear rarely cry; his point of reference here is Hamlet's reference to whores, drabs and scullions. A corollary is that 'if women wept less they would swear more' (p. 87) and that the modern woman has indeed made a transition here.

Holmes (1995) reminds us that politeness is a good thing, a social lubricant that can make people feel safer and more comfortable; it is an obviously central aspect in any form of 'facilitative' speech. As with swearing, Mills (2003) and others remind us that the frequency, form and function of polite usage are important matters. As with swearing, it would be incorrect to simply say that women are more polite than men. As with swearing, social-class variables may be more generally predictive of politeness than those of gender. In some ways, politeness is to swearing as the masculine directness attributed to working-class speech is to the more 'feminised' middle-class usage (recall here my 1979 study, described above). Politeness that is seen as excessive or insincere is often associated with subordination and deference – which can, in turn, reinforce its 'feminine' connotations. On the other hand, when we consider the regularity with which we hear empty suggestions ('Have a nice day'), or have someone tell us who they are, for obviously venal reasons ('Hi! I'm Chuck, and I'll be your waiter this evening') or are inappropriately reassured ('Hey! No problem'), and when all such noxious utterances blithely cross every conceivable divide of age and sex, it is possible to imagine that the entire currency has become so incredibly cheapened that it would be stupid to try and attach any gender nuances to its use.

7.4 CONCLUDING REMARKS

Although the chapter title here singled out neither men nor women, I seem to have written mostly about the latter. There are good reasons for doing so, and they have been implicit throughout the discussion. It can be more instructive, in linguistic terms, to study Spanish rather than English language policies in the United States; it may be more revealing, in racial terms, to consider the social situation of blacks rather than whites there, too. Likewise, it may be more appropriate to focus upon women than upon men. The general point here has to do with Dostoevski's argument that understanding the treatment of subaltern populations provides the single best perspective on a society.

Kiesling (2007) notes that women are more attended to than men in this literature, because the latter have been, and continue to be, the benchmark; they are the 'unmarked variant', dominant and taken for granted. This is why, when men *have* been the object of linguistic study, it is gay men, or black men, or male members of some other 'marked' community who have attracted attention. Kiesling (p. 654) also points to what he calls the two main 'schools' in the area of language and gender: dominance and difference. He notes:

> the dominance view supposedly saw the root of (almost) all gender differences in language as being related to male dominance and female subordination, while the difference perspective viewed these differences as arising from the different 'cultures' that girls and boys inhabit when they are young.

At first blush, these seem analogous to the more familiar dichotomies of nature and nurture, or heredity and environment. It is apparent, however, that both dominance and difference could be ascribed to environmental influences; just as easily, however, both could be laid at the feet of hereditary ones. Consequently, they are unsatisfactory and essentially false theoretical positions. From a feminist point of view – or, indeed, from any other that would like to see some alteration in male–female interactions, linguistic or otherwise – aetiologies are less important than some might wish to claim. If, on the one hand, environmental or cultural variation contributes the most to differences between men and women, then there is always the possibility of change: man (woman) is both proposer and disposer. If biological imperatives form the foundation of behaviour, on the other hand – well, there is no reason that we cannot rise above them: God's (nature's) ability to dispose can be trumped by our own.

Since the work of Kramarae (1981), at least, the best treatments have attended to both men and women (e.g. Coates, 2003, 2004; Cameron, 2007; Holmes, 1995; Johnson and Meinhof, 1997). These all make the point, for example, that assessments of women's politeness, or swearing, or use of tag-questions, are often built upon unexamined assumptions about the men's speech from which women's is seen to depart. Most of them are well aware, too, that any bald comparison between men and women *tout court* is likely to be of extremely limited interest; in fact, such comparisons are usually only possible within sterile experimental settings. Almost everything here depends upon context and circumstance; the assertive father can be a timid office worker; the polite little woman can prove to be as forceful and profane as the burly soldier; David Hockney probably knows more colour terms than does Nigella Lawson; female roller-derby skaters are more personally competitive than are male baseball players; men gossip more about the trivialities of sport than women do about shopping; Joan Rivers interrupts people more often than her husband does – but only in public; and so on.

Eckert and McConnell-Ginet (2003) provide an excellent discussion of the vagaries and vicissitudes of 'networking' and its organisation, in which it appears that much of women's activity is driven by practical necessity, and much of men's gossip is intensely personal. Folk-wisdom is turned on its head. If one were to put together a corpus of women's exchanges about child-rearing, and compare it to a similar assemblage of men's talk about work or sports – just to remain in traditional arenas here – the inconsequentiality of the latter would likely be in stark contrast to the practicality and applied value of the former. Here, women discuss tangible matters of immediate and obvious relevance, while men natter on about who said what, who cheated, who was strong and who was weak. Any thoroughgoing and fair-minded investigation must always take on board various social divisions, all of which interact in important ways. Central here, of course, are the many possible interactions involving gender variables themselves: all women, all men, men and women together, younger men and older women, young women among older men, low-status workers with bosses, and so on.

Hannah and Murachver (2007) have demonstrated – or re-demonstrated, to be more accurate – the presence of some of the 'classic' gender differences; they have done so, however, in a way that illustrates the interactive nuances just mentioned. Both men and women, in conversation with more or less 'facilitative' partners, for instance, showed systematic adaptations to them. Over time, though, they tended to shift towards more 'gendered patterns': men began to talk more than women, to make longer utterances, to become less facilitative; women began to speak less, and to ask more questions. The authors note that while these differences seem robust enough, the fact that they emerge most markedly *after* an initial period in which the speech style of one participant has had time to affect that of another suggests the importance of considering the 'interrelatedness' of conversational exchanges. Gender variations do not occur independently of contextual constraints (see also Crawford, 1995; Tannen, 1994), and it is thus an error to consider them in some disembodied manner. Kramarae (1981) was one of the earliest writers to attend to gender-in-interaction, and subsequent authors have emphasised it more and more; other early studies of note include Tannen's more 'popular' treatments (1986, 1990); see also her edited collection (1993) and the recent Tannen *et al.* (2007), in which discourse among parents and children is examined. Finally here, the rise of the internet has led to some interesting work on gender differences in a context devoid of the usual conversational cues. Fox *et al.* (2007) have shown that while 'instant messaging' practices are broadly similar across male and female users, the latter are more expressive in their use of emphasis, adjectives and number of topics. They also used more 'emoticons' (the use of characters or symbols, like ☺, to insert emotion into a message); see also Provine *et al.* (2007).

Throughout, however, the point that men and women use language, at least some of the time, for different purposes is surely reasonable; and there is ample evidence that this is generalisable across cultures (Bull and Swan, 1992). Despite considerable recent advances in both information and sensitivity, we must continue to be alert to the danger of seeing the speech of one gender (need I say which?) as the norm from which that of the other differs or deviates. Why say women are more polite than men, or swear less, or are more conversationally facilitative, or hedge their linguistic bets? Why not ask, rather, why men are ruder, more confrontational and more unreasonably assertive? An answer is provided by Frank and Anshen (1983: 46):

> If it were shown that men speak more surely than women, hesitating less, this would certainly be greeted as another sign of masculine superiority. The halting speech of women would be seen as evidence of their tentative, feminine nature. Yet, when Jespersen found just the opposite phenomenon, that men hesitate more than women when speaking, he naturally attributed this fact to a greater desire for accuracy and clarity among male speakers, which leads them to search for just the right word.

This is a variant of the familiar 'heads I win tails you lose' perspective, the same sort of agreement that Freud made with himself, but only with himself: if some symbolic entity resists all attempts to fit it into an emerging psychoanalytic picture, then it can be assigned an altogether new value. And this is the same Jespersen who, standing at the head of a long line of later authors, both male and female, felt obliged to include in his *Language* (1922) a chapter on women but none on men. An analysis of tag-questions that built upon Holmes's insights had as its title 'Not gender difference, but the difference gender makes' (Cameron, 1992a) – and this apt phrase is relevant to all investigations in the area.[5]

STUDY QUESTIONS

1. On what (linguistic) grounds might miscommunication between women and men be expected?
2. Why should the language of men and women continue to show – if, in some circumstances, in somewhat attenuated form – differences in both politeness and profanity?

3. Studies suggest that children learn and reproduce gender-trait stereotypes at a very early age. Is this worrisome? What, if anything, might be done to intervene here?
4. How might society better combat sexist language?

Further reading

Deborah Cameron's (2007) *The Myth of Mars and Venus: Do Men and Women Really Speak Different Languages?* is a very insightful commentary on the topic, one that pays particular attention to different practices that may not, in fact, be as different as both popular perceptions and academic insights have made them out to be.

Marlis Hellinger and Anne Pauwels (2007), in their chapter 'Language and sexism', give a good overview of the area.

Scott Kiesling's article (2007) 'Men, masculinities and language' is useful. Common-sense suggests that men's language may require some attention too, as several recent authors have argued; Kiesling's brief overview brings the most important findings up to date here.

Robin Lakoff's (2004) *Language and Woman's Place: Text and Commentaries* is a revised and updated presentation of her classic 1975 monograph, here supplemented by a number of scholarly commentaries on her work.

8 Ethnicity and nationalism

'Identity' can be more or less of a fixed quantity. Some of the possible variation here depends upon the *type* of identity that is under discussion: a sexual identity that rests upon biology, for example, is generally more stable than a gender identity that can owe more to environmental influences. But, as we shall see, there are arguments about degrees of 'fixedness' even within the same identity category. Is ethnicity, for instance, an immutable identity, or is it better seen as a social construction, more malleable and more subject to the vagaries of social relationships? Anne Phillips (2007) has investigated the claim that to consider ethnicity as a real or fixed entity is to fall into the same error that once divided human beings into different races. Just as 'race' is now broadly understood to be a political construct rather than a scientific one, so we would do better to think of ethnic identity as something more plastic than solid. Its emergence as a 'real' category may owe more, then, to the manipulative desires of political organisations and activists than it does to any grass-roots insistence. Phillips's argument coincides with that of Brubaker (2004: 8). In a treatment of 'ethnicity without groups', he points to a mistake made in discussions of 'groupism'. It is an error, Brubaker writes, to consider ethnic collectivities as 'basic constituents of social life, chief protagonists of social conflicts, and fundamental units of social analysis'; or to think that they are 'substantial entities to which interests and agency can be attributed'; or to 'reify' them, 'as if they were internally homogeneous, externally bounded groups'; or to 'represent the social and cultural world as a multichrome mosaic of monochrome ethnic, racial, or cultural blocks'. All this is not so much a reworking of social-constructivist arguments about the *nature* of the reality of ethnic 'groupness' as it is an enquiry into that reality itself.

Phillips is worried that, in perspectives that stress the power and agency of the collectivity, individual concerns are pushed aside or ignored. Her focal point is a feminist one: among the individuals who may suffer because of an overemphasis upon the group, women are often particularly vulnerable. This is certainly a valid point, one brought to the fore in an important collection of articles edited by Cohen *et al.* (1999), and in a number of works since then (the most recent of which is McKerl, 2007) – all of which question whether or not policies of multiculturalism erected upon certain assumptions about 'groupness' are in fact detrimental to women's interests. This is a variant of the more general comment made by Brubaker (above) about the presumed homogeneity prevailing within ethnic groups. A similarly general observation was made by Appiah (2005: 135), in noting that cultural survival, as conceived in some quarters, 'can't always be squared with ethical individualism'. He too mentions women, but also points out that 'parents sometimes want their children to persist in some practice that those children resist'. And, in the broadest extrapolation of the point, he notes the difficulties that may arise when 'a whole generation of one group wishes to impose a form of life on the next generation'. There are many philosophical subtleties connected to these sorts of arguments, and Will Kymlicka is among the most prominent of those philosophers to have engaged with them (e.g. Kymlicka, 1989, 1995a, 1995b, 2007), essentially arguing for a variety of liberalism that will pay some attention to *groups* as well as to *individuals*.[1]

An excellent example arose in the recent Canadian political arena. In the early 1990s, the anguished deliberations about the relationship of Quebec to the rest of Canada, the arguments about that province's so-called 'distinct' status within the federation, necessarily came to involve all the other important social players. Chief among these were the aboriginal populations, the 'First Nations'. They were quick to point out that, if any sort of 'distinct' status were on the table, their own claims ought not to go unheeded. Their point of view was favourably received by most Canadians, on two grounds. First, there was very broad acknowledgement that the indigenous peoples had indeed suffered at the hands of European settlers and that, therefore, it was only right that greater attention should be paid to them; this response can be seen as a specific example of the posture of apology and redress that has become common in many countries in recent times.[2] Second, the opposition of many aboriginal groups to some of the demands made by Quebec nationalists coincided with majority anglophone opinion. Because of this, considerable support arose for greater aboriginal autonomy within Canada; a so-called 'third level' of government was even mooted. Such autonomy would be granted, of course, on the basis of aboriginal ethnicity. However, as discussions were unfolding, some native *women's* organisations introduced serious objections. They were unhappy with the possibility of increased autonomy on collectivist principles because they felt that this would further strengthen elements of a traditional system that had proved historically disadvantageous for them, and which they were unwilling to see perpetuated. A little later, the president of the Native Women's Association of Canada pointed out that 'it is fine and dandy to have self-government...but one must make sure that all rights – including male and female, and especially our children [sic] – are protected' (Anderssen, 1999).[3] At a stroke, then, these women recognised the dangers inherent in presumptions of internal group homogeneity. They reminded us, very forcefully, that groups are not monolithic or 'monochrome' entities, and that attention paid to groups *qua* groups may act against the best interests of individuals within them. For their part, the women argued for treatment in line with the usual and prevailing liberal-democratic practices. Fuller details of this interesting episode, and of the larger political machinations in which it figured, can be found in Edwards (1994a, 1997a).

8.2 ETHNIC IDENTITY

Walker Connor's contributions to our understanding of ethnicity, nationalism and their ramifications have been many and varied, and one of the recurring themes in his work is a concern for terminological accuracy. He has noted (1978: 386), for example, that

> authorities have had difficulty agreeing on a term to describe the loyalty of segments of a state's population to their particular nation. Ethnicity, primordialism, pluralism, tribalism, regionalism, communalism, and parochialism are among the most commonly encountered. This varied vocabulary further impedes an understanding of nationalism by creating the impression that each is describing a separate phenomenon.

Later, Connor found it necessary to begin a new work (*Ethnonationalism*) with the suggestion that there is a continuing need to repudiate Humpty-Dumpty usage; specifically, he warned that 'slipshod use of the key terms, nation and nationalism, is more the rule than the exception, even in works purportedly dealing with nationalism' (1994: xi). In a more careful world, in which it were generally agreed that nationalism necessarily implies ethnic connectivities, the word *ethnonationalism* would be a prolix and redundant extension of *nationalism*. The fact that Connor felt obliged to use it in his title demonstrates that, even in the scholarly literature, confusion continues to exist between *state* and *nation*, and between nationalist allegiances and state loyalties; I shall return briefly to terminological matters a little further on.

Concern with terminology need not be a narrow exercise smelling strongly of the lamp. In areas that engage powerful emotions, and in settings of contact and conflict, varying descriptions of reality are of the greatest importance. It is salutary to remind ourselves periodically that the most pervasive theme in modern social psychology is the importance of *perception*. We do not react to the world on the basis of sensory input alone but, rather, in terms of what we perceive that input to mean. This is the foundation of all our social constructions, of all our individual and group relationships, and it is a foundation that reflects in an ongoing fashion our accumulated social knowledge. Perception is the filter through which sensory data are strained, and it is obvious that the establishment and maintenance of this filter are culturally specific and – within social groupings – personalised to a greater or lesser extent. For example, because every individual has accumulated a unique set of experiences, each set of perceptual spectacles is itself special to some extent. At the same time, however, there are many social perceptions that group members hold in common; at one level, we can think of these as *stereotypes*, at another as *culture* itself.

Terminological differences and disputes are often symptomatic of variations in perception, and this is nowhere more clearly and obviously seen than in the group narratives that we construct to describe ourselves and others. Connor has always been particularly sensitive to the importance of the subjectivity of group attachments and, as a reviewer has pointed out, he has consistently stressed that 'what ultimately matters is not what is, but what people believe is' (Allcock, 1994). Issues of the accuracy and acceptability of disciplinary terminology are inextricably linked with the emotionally charged nature of the topic. Furthermore, semantic variability and linguistic ambiguity are at the heart of many nationalist manifestations. It was Ernest Renan (1882/1947) who wrote that while a sense of national identity obviously rests upon feelings of shared heritage, it also rests upon things that have been conveniently and collectively forgotten – *perception*, again. And it was Karl Marx who observed that

> men make their own history, but they do not make it just as they please; they do not make it under circumstances chosen by themselves, but under circumstances directly encountered, given and transmitted from the past. (1852/1963: 15)

This was aptly adapted by Jenkins (1997: 142), who wrote that 'actors may make their own identities, but they do not do so in circumstances of their own choosing'. But this adaptation did not extend to reflect Marx's further note:

> Just when [men] seem engaged in revolutionizing themselves... precisely in such periods of revolutionary crisis they anxiously conjure up the spirits of the past to their service and borrow from them names, battle cries and costumes in order to present the new scene of world history in this time-honoured disguise and this borrowed language. (p. 15)

The fuller citation reveals Marx's belief that the glories of the past are made to serve the revolutionary purposes of the present, and it requires no great effort to see that this sort of process undergirds many attempts at language, literary and cultural revival – all, themselves, in the service of group identity.[4]

Perception, subjectivity and symbolism: these are powerfully important words in any discussion of ethnicity and nationalism. Drawing substantially upon Brubaker (1999), Dieckhoff (2005: 65) has suggested that 'if ethnicity is interpreted strictly as common descent, ethnic nationalism is indeed a very narrow category'. But, on the other hand, if ethnicity were to be considered more broadly, 'as synonymous with cultural belonging', then virtually all nationalisms would be 'coded as ethnic', because they all resort to ideas of culture in their self-definitions. Dieckhoff illustrates his points by noting, correctly enough (see Edwards, 2007a), that leaders of ethnic movements often come from outside the group and are therefore ethnic only by adoption, as it were. This, together with the altogether looser criterion of 'cultural belonging', suggests to him that the descent criterion cannot be crucial. But what of the masses who are to be galvanised by these powerful outside agitators? And, is it not both possible and meaningful to accept that merely asserting a sense of belonging is not enough to make group membership a reality? Finally, is it not also sensible to accept that, whatever the historical or ancestral realities may have been, such an assertion has just the same force as blood connections if it rests upon an honestly held belief? Things are not so arbitrary, after all. Once we admit the power of psychosocial perception, and rely upon the honesty of personal and group conviction, it remains eminently reasonable to contend that ethnicity *does* centrally rely upon descent criteria.

Even allowing for various levels and types of confusion, there is clearly a close relationship between ethnicity and nationalism. (Rather surprisingly, perhaps, scholarship on the two has not been very well coordinated; see Jenkins, 1997, and Eriksen, 2002.) The latter has, in fact, been seen as a more formal and more organised extension of ethnocultural solidarity. Some modern suggestions that ethnicity is a sort of incomplete nationalism, a nationalism that is not completely 'self-aware', rest upon Max Weber's (1922/1968) observation that the presence of ethnic solidarity is insufficient to constitute a sense of 'nation'. Connor has thus written of 'pre-national' groups or 'potential nations', endorsing the much earlier view of Barker (1927): a nation is essentially a self-aware ethnic group. So, Connor (1978: 388) suggests that 'while an ethnic group *may* . . . be other-defined, the nation *must* be self-defined'. But what are the necessary and sufficient conditions for ethnic or 'pre-national' groups, and how important is the question of self- versus other-definition? At a very simple level, I once defined ethnicity as a 'sense of group identity deriving from real or perceived common bonds such as language, race or religion' (Edwards, 1977: 254). But, although true, this definition invites more questions than it answers. What, for example, are the most important common bonds? Are some more central than others? Are some essential? And why might some phrase like 'real or perceived' be necessary?

Malešević (2004) has provided an overview of several of the most prominent sociological approaches to ethnicity, from the materialist emphases of Marxism and 'rational-choice' theory to the more subjective assessments of social constructivism. It is unnecessary here to delve too deeply into competing nuances, but it is worth mentioning one or two of the larger matters under debate. Some theoretical approaches stress the individual within the group – more of a psychological thrust, really – while others consider ethnicity as essentially a collectivist phenomenon; some stress material and tangible features, others believe in the greater motive force of subjective and symbolic attachment. From some perspectives, both ethnicity and nationalism are seen as longstanding historical constants, while other views hold them to be more malleable and, above all, much more situationally determined. While the connections here are neither rigid nor logically necessary, it is nevertheless true that the latter approach tends to put ethnonational attachments on a par with other identities that exist in the human repertoire, becoming more or less salient as the context seems to suggest.[5] The former, on the other hand, often considers such attachments as deeper and more profound constituents of identity, existing as a more or less permanent psychosocial backdrop to more evanescent components of our multiple-identity universe.

In a sort of meta-analysis that remains very useful for our restricted purposes here, Isajiw (1980; see also 1990) examined sixty-five studies of ethnicity and found that fifty-two of them gave no explicit definition of ethnicity at all. He also considered theoretical treatments of the subject, assessing more than two dozen definitions. Although there was a great deal of variation, several themes recurred, and an examination of these will assist in a more satisfactory definition of ethnic identity.

First, an equation is frequently made between *ethnic* group and *minority* group. This is particularly likely when immigrant populations are under discussion, accounting for the tendency of many authors to write about ethnic groups as social sub-groups. A little thought will confirm, of course, that *all* people are members of some ethnic group or other, that many have a foot in more than one ethnic camp and that, therefore, there can be no unique association between *ethnic* and *minority*. In this regard, however, as in many others, the politics of power and dominance can turn convention into reality: thus, 'dominant groups rarely define themselves as ethnics' (Royce, 1982: 3). But this *is* only conventional thinking among the socially dominant. Besides underpinning all within-society groups, majority as well as minority, ethnicity may also cross sociopolitical boundaries, as contemporary and historical 'pan' groupings indicate.

A second factor in any discussion of ethnic identity is the amount of importance to be accorded to group *boundaries* or group *content*. Barth (1969) was the most influential among contemporary scholars who have stressed that the essential focal point is the boundary between groups. The reasoning here is that the cultures enclosed within boundaries may change – indeed, we should stress that they *do* change, since all groups are dynamic – but the continuation of boundaries themselves is more longstanding. This emphasis has the attraction of illuminating group maintenance across generations; for example, third- and fourth generation immigrants in the United States are generally quite unlike their first-generation forebears, yet, to the extent to which they recognise links here (and, of course, differences from other groups), the concept and utility of group boundaries will continue to be significant.

Jenkins (1997, 2004) is quite right to point out that Barth's insights have been rather too easily shunted aside in many quarters. Sometimes, indeed, they have been rather misinterpreted. For instance, Hutchinson (1994) – otherwise a most careful commentator – suggested that the views of Barth and of Anthony Smith are very different. Smith's position is (as we shall see) that nationalism makes use of pre-existing ethnicities, drawing particularly upon what he came to call 'ethnosymbolism', but it is incorrect to imagine, as Hutchinson apparently does, that a Barthian perspective rules this out. It is true that the ethnic 'stuff' within the group boundaries is malleable – and, as I have just implied, fourth-generation Germans in the United States seem not very much like their forebears who stepped off the ship at Ellis Island – but the malleability is better understood as a gradual, temporal evolution of cultural 'markers'. This sense of a connecting thread is surely more accurate than Hutchinson's suggestion that 'there is no necessary relationship to earlier ethnic loyalties', with the implication that symbols are merely gatekeepers or border guards, instrumental factotums with 'little ideological content and, by extension, little formative power' (p. 27).

A third major feature of ethnic identity has to do with *objective* versus *subjective* indicators of group membership. On the one hand, there are many definitions of ethnicity that stress objective characteristics (linguistic, racial, geographical, religious, ancestral, and so on). From such a perspective, ethnicity is a 'given', an immutable historical inheritance: while allowing for alterations, it emphasises shared practices of culture and developmental socialisation. Conceiving of ethnic-group membership as 'involuntary' in this way permits an easy differentiation from other forms of association, like clubs and societies; membership of these is not involuntary and does not depend upon common socialisation patterns (although these could of course develop, where organisations persist over generations).

To this point, then, we could understand ethnic-group membership as an involuntary phenomenon in which all are participants, in which members share common cultural characteristics, and in which a continuing 'us-and-them' differentiation means that a sense of membership boundaries can long outlast any particular social manifestation or practice within them. Such an objective approach has some serious shortcomings, however, as evidenced by the fact that Isajiw's survey found only one definition that made single-minded reference to it. The main difficulty here is that any definition of ethnicity that relies solely upon objective markers will provide only an inadequate explanation of its persistence across generations within rapidly changing social contexts. The North American immigrant experience is, again, relevant here. If the continuation of perceived group boundaries can co-exist with radical changes of the cultural 'stuff' within them, if a psychologically real sense of 'groupness' can remain long after visible or tangible links with earlier generations have disappeared, how are we to more fully understand ethnic allegiances?

It is clear that something more than objective indicators is needed. Shibutani and Kwan (1965: 40–1) had suggested that 'an ethnic group consists of people who conceive of themselves as being of a kind ... united by emotional bonds'. They did not, of course, deny the power of a shared ancestry, but 'far more important ... is their *belief* that they are of common descent' (my italics). This is more or less directly

taken from Max Weber's contention (1922 /1968: 389) that ethnic collectivities are

> those human groups that entertain a subjective belief in their common
> descent . . . it does not matter whether or not an objective blood
> relationship exists. Ethnic membership . . . differs from the kinship
> group precisely by being a *presumed* identity. [my italics]

With words like 'belief' and 'presumed', as well as with Weber's blunt
assertion about the unimportance of blood relationships, we have clearly
left objective markers behind. Isajiw's (1980) survey turned up many
references to phenomena as broad and undifferentiated as a 'sense of
peoplehood', and his overall gloss was that the (usually implicit) definition of ethnicity typically involved some statement as loose as 'any
group of people who identify themselves or are in any way identified as
Italians, Germans, Indians, Ukrainians, etc.' (p. 14). Unless the exercise is
to dissolve entirely into more Humpty-Dumpty usage, however ('If I say
I'm Armenian, then I *am* Armenian'), it is important to understand that
the subjectivities of ethnicity are not entirely arbitrary. As Jenkins (1997:
169) has rightly pointed out, ethnic identity 'is not infinitely variable,
malleable or negotiable . . . there are limits to the plasticity of ethnicity'.
There must be *some* linkage, however much groups and individuals have
changed, between past and present.

Steinberg (2001) considered the American interest in ethnicity that
re-emerged in the 1970s (the 'new ethnicity', as some termed it) as representing the dying gasp of ethnic vitality. He argued that economic
and social-class factors are now far more explanatory in understanding
groups and group behaviour than is ethnic-group membership, and he
noted that ethnic boundaries are increasingly easily disregarded when
socioeconomic advantage beckons. Contemporary attempts – by elements within the scholarly community, or by ethnic 'revivalists' and
enthusiasts of various stripes – to bolster the shrinking relevance of
ethnic-group membership are thus seen as misguided and doomed to
failure. Others, too, have seen modern emphases on ethnicity as retrogressive. Patterson (1977), for instance, saw current manifestations of
ethnicity as chauvinistic impulses, as longings for boundaries now very
much out of place and, indeed, destructive. Earlier still, and from a
Canadian perspective, Porter (1975) and Vallee (1981) discussed 'ethnicity as atavism' and 'ethnicity as anachronism'. (I shall return to these
criticisms in the next chapter.)

The great failure of arguments that would consign ethnicity to the
historical dustbin, and the great difficulty involved in seeing ethnic-
group membership as a reflection of anachronistic, meaningless or

unworthy longings, are revealed by the simple continuing presence of ethnic allegiance. All around the world today it remains a real force, genuinely felt, and capable of rousing strong emotions for good or ill. Any attempt to understand the continuation of boundaries, particularly among groups whose cultural 'content' has altered dramatically over generations, highlights the importance of subjective and psychological aspects of the phenomenon. The contribution of so-called 'symbolic ethnicity' (as coined by Gans in 1979) is central here. Gans began his argument by acknowledging that the 'new ethnicity' did not imply any tangible ethnic revival (in the United States – but we could expand the scope to other new-world 'receiving' societies whose modern fortunes have been built upon immigration). Rather, assimilation and acculturation had continued. Nevertheless, he suggested that there had developed a 'new kind of ethnic involvement ... which emphasizes concern with identity' (p. 1). Any apparent paradox is resolved, Gans claimed, when one understands that this new involvement is a minimal one and does not require traditional ethnic culture or context. It rests, instead, upon symbolic pillars. Such a 'symbolic ethnicity' is clearly less fully fleshed than earlier manifestations; it is less culturally 'complete' than the societies from which immigrants came; see Breton's seminal work (1964) on the significance of 'institutional completeness'. The objective markers of identity, including language, clothing and cuisine, once coincided seamlessly with the more intangible attributes of group membership in settings where boundaries between groups were of long standing and were not subject to the osmotic pressures that the new-world experience would produce. In that sense, symbolic aspects of ethnicity are weaker links in the chain of identity: Gans himself called symbolic ethnicity 'an ethnicity of the last resort' (p. 1).

But there can be strength in weakness, and what is intangible and subjective can survive longer than more visible marks of difference, marks that may impede or may be judged to impede desirable social advance. This is particularly true for immigrant populations, for whom success in the new setting is, after all, what will make the painful, difficult and sometimes dangerous act of emigration worthwhile. As a latent attribute, symbolic ethnicity can persist for a long time without penalty. Indeed, if the times become propitious, some visible ethnic manifestations may become possible again, although these typically do not occur until they have become diluted, almost culturally neutered. Gans himself pointed out (p. 10) that, although 'films and television programs with ethnic characters are on the increase', these characters do not engage in very 'ethnic' behaviour and 'may only have ethnic names'; thus, 'they are not very different from the ethnic audiences who watch them'. And

I am thinking, too, of the Oktoberfests that are open to everyone, not just Germans; as long as you can hold a stein or wear leather shorts, it doesn't matter if your name is O'Hara or Matsumoto. Similarly, St Patrick's Day has become a holiday for all. Where I live in Nova Scotia, there are many Gael-for-a-day possibilities that attract the Matsumotos and the Müllers to the Highland Games and to the *ceilidhs* that are so much a part of the tourism thrust. A television programme about the annual 'Grandfather Mountain Highland Games' in North Carolina – described by the narrator as a 'Highland Disneyland' – depicted what must be the ultimate extension of this democratic tendency. Whatever their own ancestry, passers-by were told that, for a few dollars, they could join *any* clan (or, indeed, more than one). One southern-accented Scot breathlessly proclaimed, 'If you love it, that's enough' (see Edwards, in press b). There is perhaps an air of new world freedom in the thought that anyone can be a Campell, even if their surname is Bronowski, or that someone called García can win the Highland 'heavy' event, but there are surely lessons here, too, about the strange contortions of ethnic continuity in changing circumstances.

Fishman (1966) once remarked upon the 'secret' that ethnicity had learned in America: to maintain any sort of meaningful existence, it had essentially to make a strategic retreat into the shadows. Precisely because they have become largely symbolic, ethnic attachments can remain as psychologically important anchors; the weight of these anchors is infinitely adjustable. In such a form, they do not stigmatise or 'mark' group members, and can easily co-exist with the more patent characteristics that are increasingly shared among all. Of course, things can emerge from the shadows; latent attachments can be made manifest again. It is interesting to consider that, in line with the 'democratising' tendencies I alluded to in the previous paragraph, contemporary manifestations of ethnicity become more and more likely when they have become cheapened, vulgarised and opened up to commercialisations that welcome all customers. In this way, even the most public of ethnic demonstrations is still only symbolic.

It is now perhaps possible to attempt a somewhat fuller definition of ethnic identity. It must take into account the fact that ethnicity is not a synonym for minority-group allegiance, that perceived group boundaries can be maintained across generations whose usual cultural practices may have undergone quite radical alterations, and that objective trait descriptions do not fully encompass the phenomenon. On the basis of his analyses, Isajiw (1980: 24) wrote that 'ethnicity refers to an involuntary group of people who share the same culture or to descendants of such people who identify themselves and/or are identified by others as belonging to the same involuntary group'. This is unexceptionable as a minimal statement, but it does rather define by excluding non-essential or non-contributory aspects. A fuller version might be something like the following:

> Ethnic identity is allegiance to a group – large or small, socially dominant or subordinate – with which one has ancestral links. There is no necessity for a continuation, over generations, of the same socialisation or cultural patterns, but some sense of a group boundary must persist. This can be sustained by shared objective characteristics (language, religion, etc.), or by more subjective contributions to a sense of 'groupness', or by some combination of both. Symbolic or subjective attachments must relate, at however distant a remove, to an observably real past.

History suggests that we must also make room here for the ascription of ethnic-group membership by others, by 'outsiders'. There have been many instances in which people have been placed in groups regardless of their own sensibilities or desires. In some cases this has been done with evil intent and with tragic consequences; see Müller-Hill's (1988) study of the wartime 'selection' of Jews, Slavs, Gypsies and others, to cite only the most egregious instance. In others, there is at least confusion, upset and resentment. In Singapore, for example, there are four official languages – Tamil, Malay, Mandarin and English – and all citizens are placed in one of these groupings; they all have 'mother tongues' bureaucratically assigned, as it were. Difficulties arise when, for example, Singaporean Indians who speak Malayalam or Gujerati are officially designated as Tamil speakers. Similarly, while most Singaporean Chinese speak Hokkien, Teochew or Cantonese, Mandarin is officially 'their' variety. An interesting case was reported of a civil servant whose 'real' mother tongue was Malay and who was refused permission to sit an examination in Malay. Why? As an ethnic Chinese, this government employee was irrevocably in the Mandarin-language category; see Edwards (1995).

8.3 NATIONALISM

Most would acknowledge a connection between ethnicity and nationalism – nationalism as 'self-aware' ethnicity, or ethnicity as a state of 'pre-nationalism', or nationalism as 'organised ethnocultural solidarity', and so on. Because of this connection, some of the preceding notes on ethnic identity will apply *mutatis mutandis* to the national variety. Nationalism and ethnicity share, above all, that sense of 'groupness' or 'peoplehood' that defines and differentiates. While they are obviously not identical phenomena, I want to say at the outset that the greatest difference between them is one of scale and not one of principle. Nationalism is broadly understandable as an extension of ethnicity inasmuch as it adds to the belief in shared ancestry and characteristics the desire for political autonomy, the feeling that the 'only legitimate type of government is national self-government' (Kedourie, 1960: 9).

This opening paragraph skates rather too rapidly, however, over a large literature. One of the aspects of that literature most relevant for matters of ethnicity and nationalism has to do with the age and modernity of the latter. Some have claimed, for example, that nationalism is a relatively new phenomenon: if so, perhaps it has little to do with ancient ethnic connections. In any event, the discussions of the antiquity (or not) of nationalism that have occupied recent scholarship provide an obvious context for further comment upon the ethnicity–nationalism relationship. They represent, then – if sometimes indirectly – a sort of remedy for that underdeveloped investigation mentioned by Jenkins and Eriksen (above).

A common scholarly position is that nationalism, at least as we think of it today, is a product of the French Revolution and the growth of romanticism (especially in Germany): thus, 'cultural nationalism, as explicit ideology, is a German invention under French influence, and now a bit more than two hundred years old' (O'Brien, 1988a: 192). But elsewhere (1988b), he pointed to some foreshadowings, mentioning Dante, Machiavelli and others. Since a strictly 'modern' view cannot, perhaps, take on board what some have seen as an essential 'prenational' period, nationalism can then be considered to have developed out of existing ethnicities, important arguments here can be found in Connor (1990), Anthony Smith (1990), Hutchinson (1994) and Armstrong (1982). On the language aspects of nationalism, specifically, there has again been debate. While some have felt that the markers of *ethnies* that evolved into nationalisms must naturally have included linguistic ones, others have wanted to make a rather stronger and more specific 'modernist' case for language. Smith (1971: 182) observed bluntly that 'nationalism as a linguistic movement derives from Herder's influence' (that is to say, from the late eighteenth century).

Herder is certainly an important figure in the literature, and nationalist sympathisers have often depicted him in a positive light. Fishman, for example, referred approvingly to the 'Herderian glorification of diversity', applauding him as one of those who have 'altruistically dedicated themselves to the advancement of marked [i.e. minority-group] languages and cultures' (1989: 445–6). However, Herder was entirely capable of nationalist prejudice. He told Germans, for instance, to 'spew out the ugly slime of the Seine' (Edwards, 1985: 24), and his followers, notably Fichte, were even more vitriolic. That one of the high priests of cultural and linguistic nationalism was prone to lapses of taste and sensitivity is indicative of the dark side of the phenomenon. Some of the most useful recent notes on Herder are found in Craig (1990), who sees in this 'difficult', 'thin-skinned' and often rather sour individual someone who possessed a genuine enjoyment of other languages and cultures, but whose writings also contributed to the decline of enlight- enment thinking. Herder's romanticism stemmed in large and specific part from his dislike of the French, and it made him, according to Craig, 'singularly ill-equipped' to discuss (much less influence) intercultural relations; I shall return to Herder in chapter 9.

While logic does not require that fellow feeling be accompanied by disdain for 'out-groups', a sense of groupness has typically had just such accompaniment. Connor (2007) devotes a section of his treatment of 'loyalty' to ethnonational affiliations, pointing out that central to this is an emotional sense of belonging which typically requires the presence of an 'other': 'the causes to which the individual is loyal must be balanced by alternative causes to which the person could be loyal... it is not necessary that this prospect be a viable one, merely that it is present' (p. 80) – or, we might add, that it is believed to be present. It is worth remembering, too, that the word 'loyalty' derives from the Latin root that also leads to 'legal'; indeed, there are some older English senses in which the two terms are synonymous, the implication being that a concept like 'national loyalty' may be seen to have greater force than (for example) the loyalty that sports fans show to 'their' football team.

8.3.1 Nationalism, ethnicity and modernity

A relationship between nationalism and ethnicity – one that I empha- sise myself – has not been self-evident to all commentators. May (2001) has referred to Hobsbawm's apparent argument, for instance, that the two phenomena are not essentially related at all. If we look at Hobsbawm (1990) himself, however, we find that the main argument is that nationalism comes before nations do, that their emergence is a product of industrialisation, and that while any specific 'proto-national' bonds are not *necessary* for a national consciousness, it is clear that lan- guage, religion and kinship (the usual suspects) commonly act as such bonds. Thus, in his attempt to avoid a 'vulgar materialism', Hobsbawm seems to re-admit ethnicity into the discussion; see Grosby (1991, 2001) for critical reviews here, and see also the interesting arguments made by Breuilly (1993) in this connection. Of course, nationalism is primarily a political principle, and many have argued that it is a consequence of relatively recent historical and social development. But this hardly rules out the place of ethnic attachment as the 'stuff' that constitutes its content (see also Jenkins, 1997).[6]

The late Ernest Gellner wrote extensively about the modernity of nationalism, suggesting that it has only 'shallow roots' in the human psyche, and that it was the development of industrialisation that spawned nationalists and nations; the order here is important. This is a variant of Marxist perspectives on nationalism that typically invoke reactions against the depredations of capitalism (see Nairn, 1977, for example). In broader Marxist perspective, nationalism is both a good and a bad thing: good inasmuch as it can sap capitalism; bad if it continues on past its best-by date, interfering with the triumph of class consciousness and solidarity. As Lessnoff (2002) has pointed out, Gellner's position *vis-à-vis* Marxism is one of agreement about the primary importance of economic factors, but disagreement over the quarter from which change can be expected to arise – an emphasis, that is to say, upon nationalist activists rather than the working class. The fact that Gellner's ideas about the birth of the nationalist impulse rested upon materialist bases and, therefore, economic pressures, has led to some dispute. It is quite possible, for instance, to acknowledge the stimulus that modernity and industrialisation provided for the nationalist impulse, without accepting that the components of ethnonational consciousness are wholly economic or materialist. Even Perry Anderson (1992), for example, has argued that Gellner and his fellow-travellers (historical materialists from both the left and the right; see Nairn, 2003) discounted the most relevant element, which is identity. And, in his famous treatment of 'imagined communities', the other Anderson brother, Benedict (1991), has argued that the print revolution created the cultural wherewithal for the rise of nationalism, long before wide-spread industrialisation.

The old agrarian certainties that existed for an illiterate peasantry – for whom 'culture' was a highly localised and immobile quantity – became replaced by new technologies, new occupations, new social niches. Industrialisation represented a great break in conditions of life and orders of solidarity that had obtained for a long time. New allegiances and attachments were required to provide that 'groupness' that is so central to human life; more specifically, the literacy and the broadening of social perspectives demanded by technological progress provided a basis for a new and less localised sense of common culture. And so activists – nationalists – arose. It is interesting to consider, as Lessnoff (2002) points out in his commentary on Gellner, that behind *both* modern industrialisation *and* nationalism lies the rationalism of the

Enlightenment. It is only fleetingly paradoxical to consider that such a powerful stimulus should engender both its own continuation and, at the same time, strong reactionary impulses. Indeed, it would be interesting to delve further into the intertwined dynamics of rationalist 'progress' and the coincident romanticisations of nationalism. (There are, in any event, one or two further problems with the industrialisation thesis. For instance, nineteenth-century nationalist fervour in Germany preceded industrialisation, 'swept through the Balkans when there wasn't a factory to be seen', and largely avoided Britain and the United States, pioneers of industrialisation; see Mount, 1995, and Smith, 1998.)

Gellner's most relevant point for our purposes here was that nationalists did not somehow organise and galvanise existing ethnic collectivities. That is, they were not the 'midwives' that they themselves typically thought themselves to be (see Lessnoff, 2002); similarly, Minogue's comment on Gellner (2001: 109) suggests that 'what nationalists are doing is actually different from what they think they are doing'. Nationalists will of course *say* that they merely highlight existing ethnocultural bonds and boundaries; it is in their clear interest to engender a sense of antiquity; see also note 5 to this chapter. In fact – to summon up an image of my own here – they are really so many Frankensteins, with much more creative roles to play. Of course, even Dr Frankenstein had to have pre-existing material to work with, and Gellner himself acknowledged a certain selective rummaging around in cultural cupboards. But this is not at all the same, he argued, as bringing some sort of 'nationalism in waiting' into the light of day. Writing very shortly afterwards, however, Smith (1986; see also 2001c, 2007; Armstrong, 1982) argued that this 'pre-existing' material *was* in fact the ethnic community, the *ethnie* that has existed virtually forever. This, then, is the crux of the matter: the nature of the materials that nationalists and nationalisms have had to work with.[7]

Primordialism is the name for the view that ethnies and nations are fundamental elements in human social life, that they are 'emotional givens' dating to earliest times. There is a sense of continuity here, from antiquity to the present, that is not necessarily present in *perennialism*: this also looks to the past, claiming that nations *per se* have always existed. On the other hand, *instrumentalism* (or *social constructivism*) sees ethnonational boundaries as social constructions, and ethnicity itself as a dependent variable that can be reconfigured at need; one inevitably thinks here of the evocatively titled *Invention of Tradition*, edited by Hobsbawm and Ranger (1983). *Modernism* considers that the nation is a more or less recent product of literacy, or industrialisation, or uneven waves of socioeconomic development – at any rate, of some historically modern evolution. 'Primordialists' are also, of course, 'perennialists', and 'instrumentalists' tend to be 'modernists', but there are many potential and actual permutations. As McGarry (2001: 129) usefully points out, 'no modern social scientist dissents from the view that identities are constructed and contingent'; the question, he says, is rather one of *relative malleability*. I would put it somewhat differently, and say that the question is whether there may be some bedrock of identity – upon which, of course, many sorts of marker manipulation may be possible – or whether the post-modernists are to have their way completely, asserting that everything is constructed, that it makes little sense at all to talk about any bedrock of identity at all. Further discussion of this matter can be found in Conversi (2002, 2007), Smith (1998, 2001b), Uzelac (2002), Grosby (2005), Roshwald (2006), Özkırımlı (2000, 2005) and Özkırımlı and Grosby (2007); the number of recent references indicates something of the timeliness of the topic.[8]

An interesting take on the 'age' issue is that of Greenfeld (2006: 167), who suggests that, while nations are modern – 'as an historical form of social organization' – the greater significance is that modernity is nationalistic, that the contemporary world has been 'defined and shaped by nationalism'. On similar lines, Keating (2001) notes that some see nationalism as anti-modern, a laudable attempt to turn back the clock, a championing of the individual in a world of numbers and machines, a return to kindlier, gentler collectivities; others see it as one of the unpleasant faces of modernity itself, a retrogressive step, a phenomenon that stifles individualism in the name of the community. Keating's own rather non-committal view is that the 'ambiguities and contradictions' inherent in these descriptions demonstrate the complex nature that nationalism can be expected to have in the modern world.

In his classic treatment, Kohn (1944/2005) traced the progress of 'nation' and 'nationalism' in considerable detail and, if nothing else, it is clear that early uses of the term *nation* do not accord with contemporary views. Specifically, it is a fairly recent perspective that associates *nation* with common sympathies, sentiments, aims and will, a perspective dating to the beginning of the nineteenth century. Thus, Kedourie (1960) described nationalism as a European doctrine, invented at that time, that is undergirded by three basic assumptions: there is a natural division of humanity into nations, these nations have identifiable characteristics, and national and political boundaries should coincide. As to national characteristics, Kedourie argued that language was the central delineating feature, although, personally, he felt that possession of the same language ought *not* to entitle people to governmental autonomy. More generally, political matters should not be based upon cultural criteria. And, more generally still, Kedourie believed that nationalism was generally a pernicious doctrine,

Smith has criticised some aspects of Kedourie's analysis of nationalism, partly on the grounds of an over-emphasis upon language. There are instances, Smith argues, in which language is not as important as other markers for the development and maintenance of nationalistic attachment. He believes that in Africa, for example, national identity is rarely associated with language *per se* since this could lead to excessive 'balkanisation'; and, in countries as varied as Greece, Burma and Pakistan, religion and not language has been the pre-eminent 'self-definer'. In general, Smith (1971: 18–19) argued that 'the linguistic criterion has been of sociological importance only in Europe and the Middle East (to some extent)'. Language aside, however – an aspect of nationalism to which I shall return – Smith broadly endorsed Kedourie's view of nationalism, with its three basic assumptions. He focussed particularly upon the idea that, when freedom and self-realisation are held to rest upon a whole-hearted identification with the nation, and when national loyalty overrides all other allegiances, there arises quite naturally the belief that the nation and the state must coincide. This is what he styled the 'core nationalist doctrine', and there is here an obvious conceptual link between ethnicity and nationalism. The essence of this core doctrine does not, after all, specify the characteristics of perceived nationhood; rather, some supporting theoretical framework is required. This is precisely the point at which we can insert, as it were, our previous description of ethnicity. Nationalism can then, indeed, be seen as ethnicity writ large, ethnicity expanded by a desire for total or partial self-government. Just as ethnicity does not inevitably require language (or any other specific feature) as a component, neither does nationalism.

Considerations of links between ethnicity and nationalism, of emerging ideas of the desirability or, indeed, the necessity to have one's nation also be one's political state, suggest a little further attention to the historical lineage of nationalism. I have already mentioned Kohn's contention that the idea of a *nation* being erected upon common sympathies and aims is a modern one. Before the nineteenth century, in feudal and other societies in which social mobility was usually restricted and often impossible, the idea of a common consciousness can hardly be said to have characterised even those groups sharing certain sociocultural traits. This is the underlying reason why many writers have linked modernisation with nationalistic feeling. In particular, the French Revolution, with its ideals of a popular sovereignty, and the growth of romanticism (especially in Germany: see below) are seen as major contributors to the emergence of national consciousness. Kohn's much quoted statement is that 'before the [French] Revolution there had been states and govern-ments, after it there emerged nations and peoples' (1944/2005: 573); it was an idea that he followed up in a later work called *Prelude to Nation-States* (1967). We might simply remember here the old admonition that *ex nihilo nihil fit* – or, as Lear famously says to Cordelia, 'nothing will come of nothing' – and ask ourselves about 'prelude' conditions. It is clear, after all, that such a potent and emotionally charged phenomenon as nationalism did not spring, fully formed and independent, from either the social philosopher's mind or from some radically altered social context.

There have been many other revolutionary upheavals, and other peri-ods in which emotion has reigned over enlightenment, but few have contributed in any substantial or enduring way to nationalistic con-sciousness. On the other hand, late eighteenth-century revolution and nineteenth-century romantic reactions to rationalism are firmly embed-ded in an historical context in which the emergence of such conscious-ness became almost uniquely possible. In this sense, Kedourie's descrip-tion of nationalism as an 'invented' doctrine may have led some into the mistaken notion of a rather sudden eruption; his own subsequent dis-cussion of revolution, reaction and romanticism underlines the unfor-tunate nature of his choice of the word. Smith's (1971) analysis of a gradual evolution from a 'pre-modern age' to a 'post-revolutionary' one is more accurate. Or, as Orridge (1981) put it, nationalism, like other political phenomena, is an emergent process whose roots go deep. He suggests that the 'first and most influential kind of nationalism has been that of the nation-states of Western Europe ... the prototypes of modern nationalism'. Political entities like England, France and Den-mark may have never been (and are not now) 'complete' nation-states (see below) but their histories do reveal the development of increasingly homogeneous entities: 'at their core', Orridge continues, 'lay a sizeable population with a degree of initial cultural similarity that increased as time went on' (p. 42).

As we have already seen, Connor (1978) has argued that communities possessing ethnic solidarity but lacking the final feature – the desire for some degree of autonomy – can be thought of as *pre-national* groups or *potential* nations. If we return to Barker (1927) here, we find an acknowl-edgement that, while national self-consciousness emerged strongly in the nineteenth century, and while, in this sense, the nation could indeed be seen as modern, 'nations were already there; they had indeed been there for centuries'. He added that 'a nation must be an idea as well as a fact before it can become a dynamic force' (p. 173). Any apparent paradox is resolved if we acknowledge that pre-nineteenth century 'nations' were waiting, as it were, for that galvanic spark of consciousness. This does not mean (as Nairn, 2003, has pointed out) that neat little entities were hanging about in history, waiting to clothe themselves in autonomy; rather, the ethnic *elements* were there, the necessary ingredients for further developments. Perhaps, however, it would be somewhat more accurate to think of 'potential' nations (i.e. ethnic groups) *becoming* nations, rather than to speak of the nation as a group first lacking, and then acquiring, some vital spark. That is, while we can accept that nations do not materialise suddenly (and, in that sense, are hardly 'inventions'), they are not actually *nations* before the 'idea' has occurred. The transition is thus from ethnic group to nation, something made possible by the self-conscious desire for autonomy, and the 'idea' here has to do with the imagined possibilities of that autonomy. So we can essentially agree with Connor's analysis, although his assertion (1978: 388) that 'while an ethnic group *may* . . . be other-defined, the nation *must* be self-defined' seems not entirely accurate. *Both* ethnic group *and* nation are self-defined: the essential difference between them has much less to do with the provenance of labels, and much more to do with the nation's possession of that additional 'idea', that conscious wish for some degree of meaningful autonomy, that is absent or incompletely formed at the level of the *ethnie*. It is in *this* sense that both Gellner (1964), when he spoke of nationalism inventing nations, and Anderson (1991) – with his well-known definition of the nation as an *imagined* political community – are surely correct.

There is little reason to delve further here into the historical forces bearing upon nationalism and the very extensive literature devoted to them. Many useful treatments may be found, including older coverage that has retained its relevance (Kohn, 1944/2005, 1967; Kedourie, 1960) as well as some excellent contemporary assessments (Smith, 2001c; Conversi, 2002; Leoussi and Grosby, 2007). But we can say that it was in the rhetoric surrounding 1789 that nationalism, national loyalty, the notion of the 'fatherland' and, above all, the belief in unity and autonomy first found forceful and enduring expression in the modern age. It was in German romanticism that the notion of a *volk* and the almost mystical connection between nation and language were expounded so fervently in modern times. Thus, Fichte stressed the absolute centrality of the linguistic criterion of nationhood in his famous *Addresses to the German Nation*. More pointedly, in coupling an emphasis upon the importance of his own language with a virulent deprecation of others, Fichte foreshadowed much of the negative rhetoric of nationalism that was soon to arise. At one juncture, for example, he pointed out that 'the German speaks a language which has been alive ever since it first issued from the force of nature, whereas the other Teutonic races speak a language which has movement on the surface only but is dead at the root' (1807/1968: 58-9). From a linguistic standpoint the sentiment is of course absurd, but its psychological and social implications are quite revealing: it illustrates the essentially irrational (or, to be less pejorative, non-rational) power and appeal of linguistic nationalism.

8.3.2 Terminological confusion

It is necessary to return briefly to the terminological matters that I touched upon earlier. As a word, 'nationalism' seems first to have appeared around the end of the eighteenth century, although it did not find a permanent place in dictionaries until almost a century later; the related term, 'nationality', apparently received *its* contemporary launching from Lord Acton in 1862. Many important commentaries soon appeared, and issues concerning the 'corporate will' of peoples were addressed in the highest quarters: Disraeli, John Stuart Mill, Lord Acton, Ernest Renan, were among the earliest luminaries to make important contributions.

It is in the relationship between nation and state that confusion often occurs. 'Nation', after all, is frequently and incorrectly used to refer to countries, political units that may or may not be ethnically homogeneous, that may contain substantial populations of different national allegiance, and that are more properly termed *states*. While states are easily defined, nations are more elusive. Nationalism and ethnicity have both objective and subjective aspects, for instance. This implies that the former can take many shapes, with no single essential element – except, I would argue, some ethnic 'prelude'; and, as we have seen, psychological bonds and a sense of solidarity built upon affective ties are the common and necessary components of ethnic identity. The state, then, is a political and territorial unit, while the nation is, at base, a subjective or 'imagined' community in Anderson's sense: 'imagined', inasmuch as it depends at root upon an 'image of communion'. Much earlier, Weber had argued that 'nation' and 'nationalism' were essentially terms within the 'sphere of values' (1910/1961: 172), and the general point has been made by many scholars, from Renan to Seton-Watson to Gellner. The most important matter, of course, is the *nature* of the national ethos, and the most compelling argument is that nationalism represents an extension of ethnic attachment. Thus, Weber understood ethnicity to be 'a *presumed* identity' (1922/1968: 389; my italics), an assessment that draws tight the connection with Anderson's 'imagined' national bond.

Connor (1978) suggested that, while the very earliest uses of the term 'nationalism' did not confuse nation and state, or ethnic and political allegiance, it has increasingly been used to indicate state loyalties as well. Indeed, we commonly refer to the 'nations of the world' and the 'United Nations', even though such usages are clearly incorrect. Of course, loyalties can interact and overlap: allegiance to a nation can coincide with state affiliations, but only when the unit in question is a true *nation-state*, a political entity comprising a homogeneous national group. This arrangement is quite a rare bird. Surveying the 132 states existing in 1971, Connor (1978) found that only 12 were nation-states; another 50 contained a major ethnic group comprising more than three-quarters of the total population. Among the remaining 70 states, 31 had a majority ethnic group accounting for half to three-quarters of the population, and in the other 39 the largest single ethnic community formed less than half of the total population. So, while in many countries there is a large and often numerically dominant ethnic group, there are few indeed for whom we could assume that national and state loyalties coincide; see also Anthias and Yuval-Davis (1992) on this point. Ignorance of these distinctions or, at least, inattention to detail is easily found. Patterson (1977), for instance, correctly noted that Great Britain, the United States and Canada are not nation-states, but went on to claim that Ireland, France and most other European states are. A case might be made for Ireland, but most continental countries are clearly not nation-states, containing as they do many groups; in France, for example, one finds continuing regional allegiances among Alsatians, Basques, Bretons, Corsicans, and others. Even Royce (1982: 107), in her continuingly useful work on ethnic identity, confused nation and state, and muddied the relationship between ethnicity and nationalism: 'one does not have to give up allegiances based on primary ties such as ethnic group membership', she wrote, 'in order to function within a unit such as a nation, which operates on the basis of civil ties'. Of course, 'civil ties' are not absent in nations, but Royce seems to refer here to what should more properly be called a state.

A useful recent summary is found in Smith's (2001a) entry in an encyclopaedia of nationalism. He acknowledges the confusions and, indeed, points to modern usages (see Giddens, 1985 and Guibernau, 2001, for instance) that see 'nation-state' as an acceptable term for entities in which the second word denotes the dominant force. But, agreeing with Connor, Anthias and Yuval-Davis, among others, Smith writes that few 'contemporary polities can be characterized as "nation-states" in the strict sense of the term' (p. 286). Perhaps, he notes, it might be more accurate to refer to most of these polities as 'national states', where this term suggests an *aspiration* towards a congruence between country and culture. I am reminded here of d'Azeglio's famous pronouncement following mid nineteenth-century Italian unification: 'we have made Italy, now we must make Italians' (Maturi, 1962). Even those who would allow some less rigid sense of nation-state – one that would include, for instance, most European polities over the last couple of centuries – often acknowledge, if only indirectly, that a sense of *direction* may be more important than current reality: 'once the most powerful regions of the world *had organized themselves as nation-states at home* ... the nation-state became the accepted objective of political movements' (Breuilly, 2001: 791; my italics). In my view, the idea of *aspiration*, coupled with retention of the more *limited* sense of 'nation-state', is of particular importance; it maintains useful distinctions while, at the same time, it helps us come to grips with polities (like the new-world 'receiving' countries of America, Canada and Australia) that are not nation-states but may, in the fullness of time, become so. Accuracy here could then reflect the dynamism of social and political evolution.

The crux of the matter goes beyond mere accuracy, although this is always a desirable thing, and care in small matters promotes confidence in weightier ones. There is simply no need to use the term 'nation-state' in place of the terser and correct 'state' or 'country' – unless, of course, one is referring to rare arrangements like Portugal or Iceland or Monaco; the idea of the nation-state, strictly considered, 'is a fiction virtually everywhere' (Yuval-Davis, 2001: 298). And even in the Monacos and Icelands of the world, we can be sure that there is no perfect alignment between nation and state; we are talking, rather, of some mono-ethnic preponderance. Some, of course, take a different view. Keating (2001: 5–6) observes, for instance, that 'most nations ... comprise several different ethnic groups'. The United States, he adds, 'is no less a nation because within it citizens recognize and organize themselves into rival [*sic*] ethnic groups'. For him, ethnonationalism is but one 'mode of nation building ... civic nationalism is a different mode'. (I turn to 'civic nationalism' below.) It may be that an overly strict sense of what constitutes a nation-state is not always called for, and it is certainly the case that the social dynamics that create unity out of heterogeneity – or, indeed, the reverse – continue their operations. Nation-states have not always been more or less homogeneous entities, after all; and, even assuming that we could agree on some of them, eternal homogeneity is unlikely. If, for instance, we acknowledged Japan as a nation-state, we could profitably pay attention to the Ainu and Korean populations there; if we acknowledged Ireland as one, we might agree that the sizeable communities of eastern Europeans and Africans are something to be reckoned with. Equally, states that are currently composed of several substantial ethnic groups may be in the historical process of forging a new nation: the 'melting-pot' of the new-world immigrant-receiving countries has already produced remarkable homogeneity in the United States, for example.

STUDY QUESTIONS

1. What are the essential similarities and differences between ethnicity and nationalism?
2. Discuss the place of language within ethnonational identity.
3. Why is there so much discussion about the *age* and the historical development of nationalism?
4. Does the rise of cosmopolitan modernity spell the end of national allegiances?

Further reading

Thomas Hylland Eriksen's (2002) *Ethnicity and Nationalism* is one of the best treatments to bring ethnicity and nationalism under the same academic roof.

Elie Kedourie's (1960) *Nationalism* is a classic study, succinct and powerfully argued.

Hans Kohn's (1944/2005) *The Idea of Nationalism: A Study in its Origins and Background* is another classic, now supplemented by an excellent lengthy preface by Craig Calhoun.

Anthony Smith's (2007) chapter, 'The power of ethnic traditions in the modern world', is a brief but very fluently presented overview.

9   Assessments of nationalism

The argument that the term 'nation-state' is widely misused, that it has a focussed and specific meaning that should be retained, and that it ought not to be blithely employed as a synonym for 'country' or 'state', has been rejected in some quarters as narrowly pedantic, and in others as an illustration of a static mentality that fails to take into account changing sociopolitical circumstances. The first assertion need not trouble us greatly, especially given the sesquipedalian tendencies of those who prefer 'nation-state' to 'country'. The second is more interesting, because it leads us towards a modern position that holds that there are two basic *types* of nationalism and that 'nation-state' can thus be a perfectly acceptable description, even of countries lacking any significant ethnic homogeneity. Implicit in this distinction, furthermore, is a sense that one type of nationalism is more advanced, more inclusive and less problematic than the other – which is why it is appropriate to discuss the matter under the general rubric of 'assessment'. I turn here, then, to the concept of 'civic nationalism'.

9.1 CIVIC NATIONALISM

Whereas 'ethnic nationalism' (or 'ethnonationalism') stresses the idea of a unity based upon ethnic attachments and a desire for the coincidence of national-group and political-group boundaries, 'civic nationalism' suggests another possibility. Anthony Smith (2007: 325) refers to a 'cosmopolitan vision', a perspective that some have come to see as superseding older and darker arrangements. Civic nations are, Smith notes:

> based on the voluntary association of individual citizens who agree to live according to common values and laws which are essentially utilitarian and instrumental, and whose relationship to the state is direct and unmediated. Uniformity of laws, equality before the law, and universal reciprocity of rights and duties, are the guiding

175

principles of a 'civic' conception of nationhood. The nation itself is
seen as an autonomous legal-political community, defined by common
territory, shared civic history and common laws, its members united
by a common public culture.

In the civic nation, individual identity becomes a political phenomenon
and not something based on foundation myths, ancestral ties, blood relationships and the other appurtenances of the ethnic bond. This philosophical reworking of 'the nation' also derives some of its appeal from
the possibilities that seem open to such civic arrangements but often
closed to ethnic ones. Most notable here are cross-state connections –
the European Union is the obvious example – that might, in time, transform and enlarge identity yet again; there is a burgeoning literature,
indeed, on the emergence (or non-emergence) of a 'European identity';
some useful recent treatments include Smith (1992), Ammon et al. (1995),
Breakwell and Lyons (1996), Cinnirella (1997), Florack and Piontkowski
(2000) and Baycroft (2004). And, as Smith notes, in a shrinking world
where economic and other forms of interdependence take on more and
more importance, the 'cosmopolitan vision' can look forward to a virtually global identity. He notes the 'ideal of the world as "one place", a
truly universal city' (2007: 326).

   The idea of some new and improved 'universal city' is, in fact, a very
old one, and Smith might have gone on to connect modern cosmopolitan ideals with the social and scientific dynamism of the early seventeenth century. We find, for instance, Tommaso Campanella (1602/1623)
describing the famous *Civitas Solis* – his 'city of the sun' – just after
the turn of that century, and Johann Andreä (1619) writing of another
utopia, *Christianopolis*. A little later, and most famously of all, comes
Francis Bacon's *New Atlantis* (1626); here he describes a fictional island
(Bensalem) in which progress and development rest upon a firm basis
of science and rationality. What links these utopian speculations with
more contemporary yearnings is the desire to move beyond narrow
and restrictive tribalisms. In the age of Bacon's 'new science', these
impediments to social and scientific advancement were superstition
and 'immoderate' religious zeal (as Bacon had pointed out a little
earlier: 1620). In the modern era, the civic attachments that some
believe could lead to ever-widening political unifications are hindered
by the very ethnic affiliations that they are seen to be a significant
advance upon. In each case, then, the new development is seen to represent the triumph of rationality over emotion.

   In his examination of violent eruptions of nationalism, Ignatieff
(1993) concluded by espousing civic nationalism, with its ideals of an

equal citizenry, and rejecting the ethnic variety, with its unpleasant and volatile emphasis upon primordial linkages and group exclusivity. As Smith has implied, Ignatieff sees this as a cosmopolitan impulse that rises above the old narrowness, extolling and encouraging multicultural and pan-ethnic sensitivities. He admits, however, that cosmopolitanism is a post-national posture, generally available only to those who have few immediate or personal concerns about their social position; ironically, their security typically rests upon membership in the very sort of community that they would like to see superseded. Well, I suppose even cosmopolitans have to hang their hats somewhere.

There are some difficulties with the idea of civic nationalism. Some, like the currently limited social scope of the underlying cosmopolitanism, are of a relatively mundane nature. The chief implication of these is that while civic nationalism is obviously the next important stage in large-scale social arrangements, its eventual triumph over more primitive ethnic attachments has yet to arrive in any substantial or concerted way. However, the relationships among ethnic attachments, civic ties and social transition constitute an essentially unexplored field. Some writers, for instance, have argued that ethnic solidarities are *passé* (or ought to be), and that some societies are, even now, in the process of becoming cosmopolitan and 'post-ethnic'. Conversi (2001), Resnick (2005), Delanty (2006) and others have provided good surveys of 'post-national' cosmopolitanism; importantly, they also demonstrate that the cosmopolitan idea is a very old one, whose appeal has waxed and waned since the time of Socrates; see Appiah (2005, 2006) for recent treatments. Modern conceptions of cosmopolitanism, then, are better seen as a re-emergence than as something new, something arising from the ashes of earlier and more tribal affiliations. Hollinger (1995, 2006) has written about this in terms of the American experience and Igartua (2006) has suggested that, Quebec aside, Canada has quite quickly abandoned its ethnic attachments to Britain, and has become a 'civic nation'.

Here is an obvious point of entry, as it were, for civic loyalties. But it may be that such apparently 'de-ethnicising' societies are not stable entities at all, and that they will come to be seen as transitional. Old ethnicities stream into one another in the American melting-pot, let us assume, and this suggests to some the development of a new entity, an essentially 'civic' entity, a post-ethnic America. A new *ethnic* mixture, a new framework of blood-and-belonging attachments, however, may be in formation: perhaps the transition is not from a multi-ethnic collectivity to a post-ethnic polity but, rather, to a new national homogeneity (a nation-state?). Transitions between heterogeneity and (relative) homogeneity are, after all, common enough if one is willing to consider *la longue durée.* So 'civic nationalism' might be merely a way-station on the road to a new version of its more full-blooded counterpart. And 'full-blooded' may indeed be the proper term here, since one counter-argument to civic nationalism is that it can never rival the deepest levels of attachment that ultimately spring from family and the ethnonational extensions of 'family', the 'imagined' (but not imaginary) community. If conceived of as patriotism by another name, civic nationalism can co-exist (if sometimes uneasily) with ethnonational solidarity, but it cannot replace it. As Calhoun (2005: xxxi) phrases it, can 'belonging' be based upon adherence to an abstract 'idea' of political community? The route away from the evils of ethnic nationalism that is preferred by those he calls 'extreme cosmopolitans' is not an easy one.

There is also the suggestion that the the 'globalisation' of human soci-ety, with its culturally levelling and homogenising features may actually strengthen more local bonds. Smith (1990) has thus suggested that cul-tural 'globalisation' is not likely to diminish nationalist fervour and, indeed, may stimulate it. Trends towards 'cosmopolitanism' may evoke or re-awaken more particular allegiances, solidarities that can nourish the parts that other attachments cannot reach. As Ernst Schumacher (1973: 54) pointed out in his famous study of the beauty of smallness, all men may be brothers, but our relationships are usually limited to a relative few, 'and we are called upon to show more brotherliness to them than we could possibly show to the whole of mankind'.

There are deeper waters here, too. There is, for instance, the higher moral ground that civic nationalism is seen to hold: it is inclusive and good, while ethnic nationalism is exclusive and bad. We could go back at least to Kohn's (1944/2005) classic treatment here, in which there is clearly a desirable nationalism (state-based, democratic, rational, and essentially western) and an unpleasant one (culturally based, undemo-cratic, irrational – and eastern). As Calhoun (2005: ix) has pointed out, Kohn's *magnum opus* is the source of 'both the opposition of civic to eth-nic nationalism and of its association with a parallel opposition between Western and Eastern versions of modernity'. The dichotomy continues to gain strength. In a representative discussion, Igartua (2006: 3) notes that, because it is seen as more compatible with liberalism, civic nationalism becomes the 'morally superior' variant. It is entirely understandable, then, that many modern nationalist movements make strong claims that theirs is a civic variety (I turn, below, to a revealing example from Quebec). We can also ask, quite simply, whether or not the concept of civic nationalism has any logical force or any unique features. Perhaps it is a disingenuous *succédané* for 'citizenship' or 'patriotism'. If there *is* a civic nationalism, possessing the characteristics noted previously here, even if it is only a re-labelling of earlier terms, why has it become so popular a conception, how does it constitute a more attractive label than (say) patriotism? Is it, perhaps, that it suggests democratic social inclusivity without entirely jettisoning more basic sorts of attachment? Is it nationalism without tears?

This is not the place for a fuller philosophical exploration, but it is worth noting that the matter reminds us of the attention that Walker Connor and others have given to the use and misuse of important terms. Since I almost always agree with Connor's analyses, I can endorse here his strong conviction that 'all nationalism is ethnically predicated, and those who employ the term nationalism to refer to a civic identity or civic loyalty are confusing *patriotism* with nationalism' (Conversi, 2002: 3; see also Viroli's very useful discussion, 1995). There is, in any event, a growing literature on civic nationalism: see, for example, the discussions to be found in Beiner (1999), Brown (2000), Brubaker (1996, 2004), Couture *et al.* (1998), Dieckhoff and Jaffrelot (2005), Greenfeld (1992), Keating (2001), Kymlicka (1999, 2000), McCrone (1998), Nairn (1997), Nielsen (1996), Smith (1998) and Yack (1999a). Again, the extent of the recent literature reveals the importance of the topic. Civic nationalism is, on the one hand, seen as a sort of salvation for a more basic phenomenon that has become sullied; on the other, it is seen as, at best, an unnecessary neologism and, at worst, as some sort of academic sleight-of-hand.

I should also point out here that, while the concept now occupies a place in the general literature, it has received particular attention in francophone circles; see Balthazar (1995), Breton (1988), Cahen (1994), Touraine (1997) and, especially, Schnapper (1994).[1] This is because, from revolutionary times, the French have struggled to reconcile the requirements and the desires of a centralised state with the obvious ethnic heterogeneity within *l'hexagone* (France). A new and more 'rational' form of nationalism has thus suggested a scenario in which cakes can be both had and eaten. In Schnapper's view, for example, the nation *may* have been one thing or another in the past, but now – the subtitle of her book is *l'idée moderne de nation* – it has evolved into a political unit, a 'community of citizens' whose membership in the nation revokes earlier ethnic attachments. Ethnonational groups may aspire to nation status, but Schnapper suggests that they will not attain it without abandoning the very affiliations that currently bind them together. These will be replaced with something better, however, a national spirit that owes nothing to earlier allegiances of blood and myth, but whose distinctiveness arises precisely from its particular and unifying *projet de société*. It will perhaps come as no surprise that France, with *its* national project being the liberty-equality-brotherhood triumvirate, is depicted as the leading light in this new democracy of nationalism, the country in which national integration has worked the best. One is tempted here to think of the old assimilating colonial undertaking, the *mission civilisatrice*, by which some of the lucky, or intelligent, or well-placed inhabitants might hope to become *évolués* – to evolve, that is, into fully formed human beings under the kindly tutelage of their masters. Well, everyone knows how all that turned out in Africa and Asia. And, in France itself, the immigrant explosions in the *banlieus* in 2005 have also tended to put something of a mark on integrative policies. See Yack (1999a, 1999b) for some critical comments on Schnapper's thesis in particular, and on conceptions of civic nationalism in general.

9.1.1 An illustration: nationalism in Quebec

As I mentioned above, it is entirely unsurprising that contemporary nationalist movements would seek to downplay older ethnic associations, and to emphasise instead a new 'civic' social inclusiveness. Thus, it has always been an article of faith among modern Quebec separatists that they are democratic in their actions and their intentions, and that their aspirations for an independent country are built upon the firm conviction that *all* residents of the province, francophones or not, are Quebeckers. In early 1995, Premier Jacques Parizeau reiterated his commitment to the protection of minority rights, and to civic inclusivity. Of course, the primary motivation of his 'sovereigntist' *Parti Québécois* had always been – and continues to be – the protection of francophone culture in a North American anglophone sea that is fifty times greater in size; and their ultimate goal is the holy grail of nationalists: the alignment of national with state boundaries. Consequently, in the run-up to the 1995 referendum on Quebec independence, and in the anticipation of a close outcome, there was a revival of an old and nagging fear in some nationalist quarters: it would surely be manifestly unjust if the destiny of largely francophone Quebec came to hinge upon the votes of anglophones and 'allophones' (a term used in the Canadian context to indicate those immigrants whose first language is neither English nor French).

In public, 'separatists get very indignant when others suggest that there is a xenophobic streak in Quebec nationalism' (as a leader in the *Globe & Mail* put it, 1 March 1995). Nationalist sentiments of an 'ethnic' sort did crop up now and again, however. In 1993, Premier Parizeau himself had said that Quebec sovereignty could be achieved 'even if for the most part those who vote for it are almost exclusively Quebeckers of old stock'; see El Yamani *et al.* (1993) for fuller details. And, at the beginning of the referendum campaign, he made reference to 'we' and 'our' more than 150 times, in a speech lasting less than five minutes (see Gray, 1996). The *Globe & Mail* editorial itself was able to report that a member of the *Bloc Québécois* (the separatist party that carries the torch of provincial independence in the *federal* parliament in Ottawa) had asked why, 'just for once', the referendum couldn't be decided solely by those 'old-stock' Quebeckers (*Québécois de vieille souche*, or *Québécois pure laine*). Indeed, a number of the more fervent nationalists argued amongst themselves that voting ought to be restricted to French speakers. Others suggested that citizenship itself might be similarly restricted or, at least, that immigrants should sign a contract promising to 'live and prosper in French' (see Picard, 1994, 1998; Aubin, 1996).

The old question of defining the Quebec 'family' came to the fore most pointedly on referendum night, the last day of October 1995. The vote for sovereignty failed by a margin of only 1.2% (49.4% to 50.6%), and a deeply upset provincial leader could not hide his feelings. 'It's true we have been defeated, but basically by what?', said Parizeau. 'By money and the ethnic vote'. He went on to speak ominously of the 'temptation for revenge' and promised to 'exact revenge' for the referendum loss by building a francophone nation in Quebec. Bernard Landry, Parizeau's second-in-command at the time – but a future leader of the *Parti Québécois* and provincial premier – noted that 'the country we want we will have soon'. He also reportedly told a Montreal hotel clerk that 'you immigrants' were to blame for the loss (*Globe & Mail* leader, 30 January 1996). The day after the referendum, Parizeau remained unapologetic: 'I used words that were strong last night', he said, 'but they underline a reality that exists.' A month later, Pierre Bourgault, a long-time separatist and former advisor to Parizeau, supported the premier: 'It's the Jews, the Italians and the Greeks who vote in an ethnic block. They're the racists, not us.' Bourgault also said that those groups 'don't think of themselves as Quebeckers, but as Jews, Italians, Greeks'.

The reaction to these remarks can be imagined: disgust, mingled with not a little satisfaction on the part of federalists. Sovereigntist discourse also provoked some predictably vehement rejoinders. A *Globe & Mail* leader (1 November 1995) suggested that Parizeau's references to the 'the ethnic vote', and to 'revenge', were no mere slips of the tongue:

> the Premier did not misspeak himself. In fact, he was artlessly honest and exquisitely consistent. In singling out immigrants, the English and business – all of whom largely voted no – he shouted his atavistic tribalism.

Responding to Parizeau's grudging acknowledgement that his words may have been 'badly chosen', the leader writer noted that, though unpleasant, Parizeau's statements were hardly surprising. 'If it is any consolation to him', the editorial stated, 'they were warmly endorsed by that tribune of tolerance, Jean Marie Le Pen.'

In a response to an article I wrote about Quebec nationalism (Edwards, 2002b), an anonymous critic wrote that Parizeau's 'despicable statement' on referendum night led to his resignation, the implication being that his vehemence reflected only a minority point of view within the ranks of Quebec nationalists. It is indeed true that Parizeau was replaced as party leader almost immediately after the vote. My critic also asserted that virtually all the luminaries in the sovereigntist movement have always publicly underlined their determination to achieve a 'civic-inclusive form of nationhood'. Of course, I agree with the proviso that a little underlining is necessary in the assertion itself, under the word 'publicly'. As I have already mentioned here, what nationalists *say* is not always what their actions suggest they *mean*. And sometimes, as with Parizeau's referendum-night comments, even the public mask slips a little.

In any event, such critical comments would have more force if, after his universally rejected remarks about 'ethnic voters', Parizeau had been cast into the outer darkness. In fact, he remained a potent force; even today, he crops up now and again as an *éminence grise*, as a living reproof to the current lassitude in the independence movement. While demonised in many anglophone eyes, Parizeau continued to represent a no-nonsense approach applauded by many hard-line sovereigntists. In a letter to *Le Devoir* in early November 1996, Parizeau returned to an arguably ethnocentric conception of Quebec society, in which the 'real' Quebeckers, the francophones, have had their hopes frustrated by 'the others' (Gray, 1996). In a speech in Alberta a year later, an apparently unrepentant Parizeau pointed out:

> I've repeatedly said ... that the Jewish Congress of Canada [Quebec section], the Greek Congress of Canada and the Italian Congress make a very good fight against sovereignty. And when I said to them, 'You've been very efficient,' they say, 'You can't say that.' (Stevenson, 1997)

Among the many responses to this, the most perspicacious came from Stephen Scheinberg (of B'nai Brith), who noted that Parizeau was now referring to ethnic *organisations* (not ethnic *voters*, as on referendum night), and was 'conjuring up some kind of illusion of ethnic power in these congresses ... [which] have very little power over their memberships and have very little money' (Stevenson, 1997).

It might be objected that Parizeau's continuing media presence said more about sensational newspaper copy than about real representativeness or influence. However, in January 1999, the *Bloc Québécois* hired the former premier as an adviser on Quebec sovereignty. His stiffening influence on the *Bloc* leadership soon became apparent, and his arguments for re-igniting the sovereignty issue became increasingly popular, pushing the new Quebec premier to highlight his own unwavering desire for independence. In May 2000, Lucien Bouchard told his *Parti Québécois* colleagues that 'our objective, our obsession, is Quebec sovereignty as soon as possible' (Séguin, 2000).

I think the evidence is very clear. A considerable part (at least) of the Quebec sovereigntist movement is an ethnic and not a civic phenomenon. I find this both understandable and unsurprising. Equally predictable, I suppose, are the continuing arguments that the independence movement is *not* an ethnically specific and non-inclusive enterprise, arguments that persist in spite of the obvious belief that the aspirations of the 'real' Quebeckers, the old-stock francophones, are thwarted by the presence and the votes of 'the others'. The delineation of 'us and them' interests and voting patterns is, of course, quite accurate: virtually all non-francophones in Quebec are opposed to sovereignty; and this illustrates perfectly the corner in which nationalists so often find themselves nowadays. In contemporary Canadian society, and in the modern world at large, it is simply not on to 'divide people up into mere Quebeckers and full *Québécois*' (*Globe & Mail*, 1 December 1997), whereas, in fact, such divisions are precisely what motivate the nationalist project, precisely what represent the democratic fly in the sovereigntist ointment. In September 1998, Bernard Landry (then Quebec's deputy premier) said, in reference to the idea that any successful vote for sovereignty ought to involve more than a simple majority: 'everyone knows well that if we put the bar too high it's like giving a right of veto to our compatriots, brothers and sisters from the cultural communities, on our national project. That can't be done' (Ha and Séguin, 1998). What could be easier here than deconstructing 'we', 'our compatriots' and 'our national project'?

Despite the separatists' claimed adherence to a civic nationalism, the Quebec variety is, after all, an ethnic phenomenon. The powerful elements in the Quebec context have re-opened, in a sense, the debate over the very existence of 'civic nationalism'. This context is clearly only one among many in which arguments about 'ethnic' versus 'civic' attachments – and, therefore, group identity – have occurred. But the Quebec setting is a particularly instructive one, not least because sovereigntists themselves, much more sophisticated than their nationalist *confrères* in less subtle parts of the world, beat the civic drum particularly loudly. In a piece that appeared about a month before the October referendum, Stark (1995) cited the views of Louis Balthazar, a prominent academic, who suggested that the Quebec 'collective identity' was based on 'aesthetic and ethical choice' rather than upon language and culture, that it was aiming for a 'non-nationalist approach to sovereignty'. Four weeks later, Parizeau was thundering about the iniquities of the 'ethnic vote' that had upset the great nationalist *projet de société*.

The strength of the Quebec sovereignty movement reached a point in 1995 which it has yet to regain, but it would be quite inaccurate to say that it has disappeared from the political map. The Quebec 'issue' is not something to be solved once and for all; it is, rather, part and parcel of the on-going Canadian fabric. Indications of continuing desires for greater regional autonomy can be expected to surface from time to time. The very latest of these (in October 2007) involves the *Parti Québécois* proposal that provincial citizenship should be dependent upon immigrants having 'an appropriate knowledge' of French, pledging to be 'loyal to the people of Quebec' and developing an adherence to 'Quebec values'. Now, it is true that language competence (generally fairly rudimentary) often figures in citizenship requirements: this is the case in the United Kingdom, for example, as well as in the United States (where 'basic English' is called for) and Canada (French or English sufficient to conduct a 'simple conversation'). But Quebec is not (yet) an independent state, and the predictable argument against the *Parti Québécois* private member's Bill (which failed to find its way into law, in the Liberal-dominated Quebec government) is that it would create two classes of citizenship in the province: one could be a Canadian citizen, but not a Quebec one. Since the bill would have made some forms of political participation available to citizens only, some felt that this was an attempt to bring about 'sovereignty through the back door' (see *Globe & Mail*, 2007, leaders of 20 October and 24 October; Séguin, 2007a). It is certainly reminiscent of earlier separatist laments about francophones not being in charge of their own 'destiny'.

Seven years before the Quebec referendum, Breton (1988) had suggested that civic nationalism was replacing earlier ethnic affiliations in an increasingly multicultural Canada and, more specifically, in Quebec. Four years after the 1995 vote, Poole noted (1999: 42) that 'the grounds for being authentically *Québécois* have changed in recent years from being ethnically French to a preparedness to assimilate to *Québécois* culture'. Both now seem to have been a bit 'previous' in their assessments. With hindsight, we can see the possibility of a double error here. First, it is by no means clear that, in their heart of hearts, Quebec nationalists see any other than francophones as 'authentic' Quebeckers. Second, if the most recent news is anything to go by, some see 'preparedness' as a quantity that needs to be forced along a bit.

Even within the ranks of francophones, there are continuing difficulties. Dieckhoff (2005:65) has argued that, in latter years, Quebec nationalism has become 'secularised', has come to have 'a purely linguistic basis ... it is perfectly feasible for a new immigrant to master French and, thus, to be part of the *Québécois* people'. Feasible, yes, but not always easy. A mastery of French obviously cannot confer 'old-stock' status, something that continues to matter in some circles. And, too, there is the issue of skin colour, 'otherness' and racism. Given the combination of considerable control over immigration policies, and concern about *la survivance*, Quebec has actively encouraged francophone immigrants. And they have come in large numbers – but not all of them have white faces. New francophone arrivals from Haiti, Zaire or Congo may be a welcome addition to the language statistics, but, as the provincial Minister of Immigration and Cultural Communities (the use of the term 'cultural communities' is, itself, not without interest) has acknowledged, they often face considerable obstacles. Many are victims of 'attitudes ou comportements discriminatoires' (Thériault, 2005: ii). The most recent development here is that Quebec hopes to be attracting 55,000 immigrants annually by 2010 (the current rate is about ten thousand fewer); as expected, French speakers will predominate, with roughly equal numbers to come from each of Africa, Asia, Europe and the Americas (see Séguin, 2007b). And, in early 2007, Quebec established a travelling comission whose remit it was to gather opinions about immigration and immigrants in the province, with a particular focus upon 'reasonable' religious and cultural accommodations. It is under the joint chairmanship of two prominent academics, Charles Taylor and Gérard Bouchard. As Peritz (2007) has pointed out, testimony from various quarters has revealed unpleasant strains of xenophobia and intolerance; see also *Globe & Mail* (2007, leader of 3 November) and Yakabuski (2007).

9.2 EVALUATING NATIONALISM

My argument to this point is that nationalism can indeed be thought of as 'organised ethnocultural solidarity', where the organising has to do with a desire for political autonomy, and where ethnic attachments form the main underpinnings. Both ethnicity and nationalism rest upon a sense of community that can have many different tangible manifestations, none of which is indispensable for the continuation of the sense itself. The visible 'content' of both ethnicity and nationalism is eminently mutable; what is immutable is the feeling of 'groupness'. When *this* disappears, the essential boundaries are gone. While analyses of nationalism that concentrate solely upon objective characteristics miss the essential point, it must be remembered that the subjective fidelity that is so important is not itself arbitrary; it must rest upon real or honestly perceived communalities, however diluted or altered over time. The continuing power of ethnicity and nationalism resides exactly in that intangible bond which, by definition, can survive the loss of visible markers of group distinctiveness. Its invisibility and its apparent weakness often constitute its strength, and account for its persistence over long periods of time.

If specific objective criteria are important but non-essential in the formation and continuation of national consciousness, and if its ultimate strength lies in subjective and emotional bonds, an implication is that nationalism is largely a non-rational phenomenon. Many, of course, have seen it as frankly irrational. Benn (1967: 445) suggested that the symbolism of 'blood and soil' nationalism really removes it from the field of serious study: 'enormously important as it is for the historian and sociologist, it would be absurd to treat it as if it invited serious rational criticism'. This is a profoundly mistaken point of view. Historical and sociological analyses do not lie beyond the bounds of rational criticism. As well, the fact that a topic is steeped in subjectivity and emotion does not mean that it cannot be studied in a formal – indeed, in a scientific – way; there is no methodological barrier to scholarly investigation of phenomena as varied as witchcraft, religion and beliefs in inter-galactic visitors. And further, if the bases of nationalism are largely affective in nature, it need not follow that all elements of the nationalist 'superstructure' are. If, however, Benn's view is mistaken, it does reflect something of the common prejudice that the careful study of concepts as illogical as nationalism is unlikely to make much headway. When we further consider that there are a great many examples showing that the illogicality is often pernicious, it is easy to understand why nationalism has often had a very bad press indeed.[2]

I have already alluded to the idea that deep feelings of solidarity with one's own group might logically co-exist with acknowledgement and respect for the claims, attributes and aspirations of others. Indeed, one could go further and argue that a heightened awareness of 'in-group' traditions, and heightened desires to protect and maintain them, should obviously suggest that 'out-group' members will have similar feelings and wishes. One could go still further, and suggest that such cross-group sensitivity will be positively correlated with perceptions of in-group fragility: the more difficult one's own nationalist struggles, the more keenly one should understand those of others. The fact that what is both theoretically possible and socially desirable so rarely occurs is in itself a comment upon the nature of nationalism. Most students of the subject would agree that nationalism is always something to be carefully monitored. Smith, for example, who by no means views nationalism as bad *tout court*, has argued for the need to 'damp down the fires' (1990: 24), and other writers well known to social science have gone further. Chomsky referred to nationalism as 'a very horrifying thing' (Wojtas, 1990), Steiner (1967: 132) described it as 'the venom of our age' and Orwell (1945/1965) considered it to be hunger for power mixed with self-deception. (He went on to attempt a distinction between the power-hunger of nationalism and the more benign attachments of patriotism; see also below.) In his discussion of the 'new' nationalism, Snyder (1968) summarised in one paragraph the frequently cited evils of nationalism: an outmoded and anachronistic doctrine, a deep-seated disease generated by egotism, an invidious boundary-marker between 'us' and 'them', a division into 'squabbling states', an allegiance that takes precedence over moral and ethical considerations, a belief system that over-emphasises one's own group while simultaneously denigrating others, a kind of religion that easily slips into oppression and imperialism. And the upshot of all this negativity is largely to breed further 'reactive' nationalisms.

More subtly, and more aptly, Smith (1990) describes nationalism as both progressive and reactionary. Nationalistic movements clearly want something to change, but they also include a nostalgic romanticism that often manifests itself as a desire for stasis once old wrongs have been redressed, 'melted' groups unmelted, territorial integrity and autonomy restored or established, and so on. Relatedly, we should expect that such movements will have both liberal-democratic and conservative-authoritarian impulses. The first set arise in the struggles to deal with those old injustices; the second in support of the development and maintenance of some new regime. This is simply to say that the desire to replace one species of domination with another is a common mark of the zealot.

All of the better characterisations are nuanced. For instance, Weber (1910/1961: 172) noted that the concept of 'nation' belongs in 'the sphere of values'. This does not remove it from the possibility of scholarly enquiry, but it does suggest a particular starting point for investigation. Further, Weber observed that 'the fervor [of nationalism] does not, in the main, have an economic origin' but, rather, 'is based upon sentiments of prestige' (p. 171). This merely pushes matters back a level, of course, since we will now wish to know just how 'prestige' originates and is assessed. Gramsci (1978, 1985) felt that economics was the major influence on culture, but he also argued that culture can itself activate emotions and sentiments which are, thus, only indirectly related to economic well-springs. And, in a paper discussing the shaping of nationalism and its priorities, Trevor-Roper and Urban (1989: 11) seemed to agree:

> When the chips are down, national sentiment, the call of tradition, feuds and irredentism – that is to say, irrational, visceral factors – tend to determine the amount of peace we can have among nations... Left to themselves, nations seem to have a curious order of priorities: independence first, prosperity second, internal freedom and democracy only third.

To complete this circle, consider Gellner's (1964: 160) view that 'men do not in general become nationalists from sentiment or sentimentality, atavistic or not, well-based or myth-founded: they become nationalists through genuine, objective, practical necessity, however obscurely recognised'.

A possible gloss here might be that nationalism is based upon practicalities, or, at least, upon perceived practicalities – recall the disruptions of industrialisation – but, as it blossoms into a fully fleshed solidarity, it displays more and more of its emotional undergirding. Another might be that economic and pragmatic concerns remain central but become increasingly filtered through non-rational strata. In any event, is is surely clear enough that, within certain epistemological boundaries, many elements of nationalism appear rational, logical and, indeed, irrefutable. To better appreciate this, consider the 'closed' nature of belief systems, either political or religious. The in-group solidarity that they provide rests upon shared myths, beliefs and faiths which, when accepted, constitute a foundation for all future action and practice. It is in light of this implied social contract that religious and nationalist practices make sense. Outside the psychosocial universe of which they are a part, they may seem very strange. They may appear selfish, insensitive and racist, and they may lead to hardship and conflict by solidifying inter-group borders. From within the perimeter, however, the perspective is naturally quite different. And this perspective need not be confined solely to those considerations of belief and value that initially produced it. It may – indeed, we can say that it will – come to involve mundane concerns having to do with economic and material issues.[3]

9.2.1 Some basic perspectives

The first modern, well-argued criticism of nationalism was that of Lord Acton in 1862. He claimed that liberty and prosperity became victims of the quest for self-determination, which ultimately leads to material and moral ruin. This argument, which has clear contemporary descendants, is based upon the potential danger that nationalism, as a *group* phenomenon, poses for *individual* freedom. Many have felt that, having escaped the shackles of feudalism and oppressive aristocracy, it was ironic and disappointing that human beings should almost immediately wish to lock themselves again within the confines of a group mentality (or that they should be led into this by others). A little earlier – in 1849, writing in the *Westminster Review*, which he had co-founded with Bentham – John Stuart Mill had also drawn attention to the negative aspects of nationalism; he saw it as anti-social and barbarously indifferent to all those in what we would now term the 'out-group' (see Quirk, 1982: 70).

But then, in his famous essay on representative government, published at the same time as Acton's discussion of 'nationality', Mill (1861/1964: 361–6) revealed his awareness of the powerful appeal of national self-consciousness and its bonding function. Indeed, Mill is sometimes taken as a champion of the cause, given these words that so exactly focus upon the deepest political aspirations of nationalist sentiment:

> Free institutions are next to impossible in a country made up of different nationalities. Among a people without fellow-feeling, especially if they read and speak different languages, the united public opinion, necessary to the working of representative government, cannot exist...It is in general a necessary condition of free institutions that the boundaries of governments should coincide in the main with those of nationalities.

Mill's praise was hardly unqualified. Within the excerpt just presented here, he also observed that it was advantageous for 'inferior and more backward' groups to be absorbed by others:

> When proper allowance has been made for geographical exigencies, another more purely moral and social consideration offers itself. Experience proves that it is possible for one nationality to merge and be absorbed in another: and when it was originally an inferior and more backward portion of the human race the absorption is greatly to its advantage. Nobody can suppose that it is not more beneficial to a Breton, or a Basque of French Navarre, to be brought into the current of the ideas and feelings of a highly civilised and cultivated people – to be a member of the French nationality, admitted on equal terms to all

the privileges of French citizenship, sharing the advantages of French protection, and the dignity and prestige of French power – than to sulk on his own rocks, the half-savage relic of past times, revolving in his own little mental orbit, without participation or interest in the general movement of the world. The same remark applies to the Welshman or the Scottish Highlander as members of the British nation.

We see, then, that Mill goes beyond a cautionary stance on nationalism, to one which some (the Basques, Bretons, Scots and Welsh, for starters) would see as distinctly hostile. Is Mill's point of view paradoxical? Some modern commentaries have felt it so, reinforced perhaps by his blunt assertions about civilisation and savagery. In fact, however, like all enlightened liberal thinkers, Mill was at once pulled towards more modern conceptions of democracy, equality and, indeed, the bonds of ethnic attachment ('fellow feeling'), while at the same time remaining strongly convinced of powerful qualitative social differences that we now either deny, under the banner of cultural relativism, or refuse to publicly acknowledge. In a useful study of Mill's views, Semmel (1984) clarified some of the contradictions within his liberalism, and discussed the struggle between romanticism and utilitarianism so often found among thinkers of the time.

A third nineteenth-century commentator on nationalism was Ernest Renan (1882/1947). Like Mill, he has sometimes been taken as a fellow traveller in the nationalist cause but, as with Mill, this assessment must be qualified. In fact, a close reading of Renan's famous *Qu'est-ce qu'une nation?* reveals a balanced and by no means overly enthusiastic consideration of nationalism. Renan agreed that specific characteristics – he discusses language, religion, common interests, geography and race (clearly rejecting, incidentally, the idea of 'pure' races) – do not capture the deepest well-springs of nationalism. Above all, he said, 'une nation est une âme, un principe spirituel...la possession en commun d'un riche legs de souvenirs... le désir de vivre ensemble' ['a nation is a spiritual principle...the shared possession of a rich store of memories...the wish to live together'] (p. 903). Neither language nor broad similarity of interests is essential. For, as to the first, 'il y a dans l'homme quelque chose de supérieur à la langue; c'est la volonté' ['there is something more important for human beings than language; it is *will*']; and, as to the second, Renan pithily reminds us that 'un *Zollverein* n'est pas une patrie' ['a customs union doesn't make a homeland'] (pp. 899, 902). Above all, there is Renan's famous observation that the potency of national feeling rests not only upon a sense of a shared cultural inheritance, of important things held in common, but also upon a useful capacity to *forget* or to blur certain things from the past.

In their public pronouncements, at least, most nationalists believe that, once ancient wrongs have been righted, once old injustices have been rectified, their nation will enter into a long golden age. Renan, on the other hand, argued that nations do not live forever, and he predicted that a European confederation would no doubt eventually replace contemporary groupings. His most central point was that while nations were for the moment both good and necessary, they represented a stage on the road towards some much more desirable universality. For Renan, then, the ultimate contribution of nations was their own demise in a 'grand concert de l'humanité' (p. 905). This was the human condition foreshadowed by the great figures of the renaissance, citizens of the global community *avant la lettre*. If individuals possessed the characteristics of nations, Renan went on, they would be unpleasant, vainglorious, jealous, egotistical and troublesome. But, taking nations themselves as elements in a universal collectivity, 'toutes ces dissonances de détail disparaissent dans l'ensemble' (p. 905). This is a broad view rarely found among nationalists.

An important extension of these nineteenth-century cautionary notes on nationalism is found in the work of the late Elie Kedourie (1960). He endorsed the view of Lord Acton in particular. Nationalism substitutes one set of shackles for another and, in the nationalist quest for redress for past injury and injustice, more is generally created: 'no balance is ever struck in the grisly account of cruelty and violence' (p. 139). The modern history of Europe, according to Kedourie, has shown clearly the disastrous possibilities of nationalism: 'it has created new conflicts, exacerbated tensions, and brought catastrophe to numberless people innocent of all politics' (p. 138). Because nationalism seeks to reinterpret history and hopes to improve present conditions for its supporters, it is inward-looking and contemptuous of things as they are. This 'ultimately becomes a rejection of life, and a love of death' (p. 87); here, Kedourie cites the philosophy of the German romantic tradition which, indeed, can be seen as a sort of stagnant wistfulness for the unattainable. Similar views were expressed a little earlier by Sean O'Faolain (1951: 48, 53), the Irish writer and stringent critic of narrow nationalism: 'sooner or later, it ossifies the mind . . . the ultimate evil of nationalism (and most other *isms*) is this threat to the creative individual by the tyranny arising from the idolisation of an abstraction'.

The common association of contemporary nationalism with nineteenth-century German romanticism is the point on which Smith (1971) criticised Kedourie. Smith's belief was that, since the essential nationalist doctrine need not embrace the views of the romantics, Kedourie has misrepresented the case by castigating the former for the

sins of the latter. We ought not to forget, Smith writes, the 'advantages
and blessings' of nationalism, which has inspired all sorts of cultural
activities, historical research, and so on. Anderson (1991) also reminded
us of the love that nationalism can inspire, even going as far (too far,
I should say) as to suggest that it has promoted little hatred of others. Fishman (1977) has seen the Acton–Kedourie line as a road-block in
our understanding of nationalism and ethnicity. They are not inherently
negative phenomena, he argues, and ought not be decried as 'despoiler[s]
of civility and modernity'. We should not confuse the 'exploitation' of
such attachments with the attachments themselves. From his first major
work on the subject (1972) to his later writings (e.g. 1997), Fishman has
continuously extolled the virtues of nationalism. The overall implication
of these sorts of comments is that, while nationalism has had its dubious
moments, it is unfair to consider only these.[4] The claims of nationalists
themselves are often overblown and ought not to be taken at anything
like face value; Smith (1971: 14) wrote that Kedourie and others tend to
take nationalist assertions too seriously, thus obscuring 'the real message behind the florid appeals'. We might want to probe further into
this 'real message', however, and we might want some guidance about
the exact degree of seriousness we should accord to nationalist 'florid
appeals'. It is of course true that there are positive aspects of nationalism, but these seem almost inevitably to accompany negative ones. As
noted, while it is theoretically possible for nationalism to operate without a disdain for the claims of others, there is not much evidence for this
in practice. Kedourie does not specifically reject nationalism's potential
for good, and he may have overstated the bleaker aspects, but his attention to what Quirk (1982: 70) has called 'the darker side of nationalism'
seems, unfortunately, to be justified.

Marxism constitutes another important perspective on nationalism,
which it has generally seen as an anomalous form of bourgeois romanticism long past its best-by date. Traditional Marxist–Leninist philosophy
was not opposed, of course, to the struggles that often animate nationalism, but it considered such struggles to be subordinate to those waged
on class lines. This means that nationalism within capitalist societies is
good, because it loosens the hold of the bourgeoisie; under socialism,
however, continuing nationalism is unnecessary and, indeed, constitutes a reactionary undermining of socialist unity. The weapon against
this is proletarian *internationalism*, as the famous slogan in the Commu-
nist Manifesto indicates (see also Lenin's famous remarks, 1951, on the
'national question').

The Marxist interpretation of nationalism as anachronistic when it
conflicts with socialist class principles has a counterpart in capitalist

philosophy. With characteristic bluntness, Toynbee (1956: 508) referred to the 'spirit of archaism' that supported the 'nationalistic craze for distinctiveness and cultural self-sufficiency'. While his specific comments had to do with ill-conceived desires to revive 'dead' languages, Toynbee made it clear that these are fuelled by the anachronistic allure of nationalism. This is not only naively romantic, he argued, but nationalism's frequent rejection of modernity is also a great brake on progress. This is certainly a recurring theme of the nationalist ethos, and an interesting example is found in the Irish revival movement of the late nineteenth and early twentieth centuries. The effort here was led in large part by Douglas Hyde (1894), who gave a famous address on the necessity of 'de-anglicising' Ireland. It has since become quite clear that Hyde equated anglicisation with modernisation, and this had the perverse effect of transforming the revival movement from a dynamic to a static entity: what was potentially revolutionary became conservative and reactionary. As we know from similar ethnonational movements elsewhere, this is quite common: once the old injustices and inequities have been taken care of, the motivation for further change ebbs considerably.

9.2.2 Contemporary assessments

In a work that Connor (1978: 356) rightly criticised as 'more exhortatory than academic', similar in tone to the ethnic romanticism that it disdains, Patterson (1977) did assemble some useful and recurring points. He noted, for example, the distressing lack of historical perspective in most approaches to ethnicity and nationalism, and the destructive presence of its opposite: historical selectivity. He expatiated on ethnicity and nationalism as ideologies, as faiths. He drew attention to the negative and distasteful aspects of nationalistic fervour. And, in focussing upon what he saw as a regrettable and retrogressive 'ethnic revival' in the United States, Patterson claimed to detect two main varieties of this fervour. On the one hand, he highlighted a body of work that is frankly pro-ethnic, romantic and anti-modern; Novak (1972/1995) was singled out here, but we could certainly add Fishman to this category. On the other, Patterson pointed to what he saw as more insidious supporters of ethnicity, those who cloak a bias in the guise of social scientific objectivity: Greeley (1974) was taken as an exemplar. Patterson acknowledged that the rejection of modernity which seems to be an important part of the 'reactionary impulse' underpinning national and ethnic manifestations is a theoretically possible option. But he noted that, in practice, most people (and most 'ethnics') want the solace of the past *without* sacrificing the rewards of progress. This is unworkable, Patterson claimed, because those participating in industrialised, technological society have simply altered too much; they cannot go home again, even if this were a worthy objective.

More dispassionate criticism of ethnonationalism, on the grounds that it is regressive and promotes particularism, can be found in the work of John Porter (1972/1980, 1975; see also Vallee, 1981) – a prominent Canadian social scientist, whose early death curtailed his important contributions to our understanding of 'groupness'. Porter was concerned that claims made in respect of *groups* can lead to mistreatment of individuals (see also the discussion in chapter 7). 'It seems to me', he pointed out, 'that making descent groups of such importance because they are the carriers of culture borders on racism with all the confused and emotional reactions that that term brings' (1972/1980: 330, 335). Porter, on reflection, stated:

> Considering as alternatives the ethnic stratification that results from ethnic diversity and the greater possibilities for equality that result from the reduction of ethnicity as a salient feature of modern society, I have chosen an assimilationist position, and between the atavistic responses that can arise from descent group identification and the more liberal view that descent group membership is irrelevant to human interaction, I have chosen the latter.

In a second treatment of the theme, Porter (1975) again argued that ethnonational attachment was a regressive phenomenon, promoted and sustained undesirable social divisions, was historically naive, and ultimately acted against the best interests of individuals. Against what he took to be arguments for the support and continuation of any given culture into the indefinite future, Porter pointed out that 'history is as much the graveyard of cultures as it is of aristocracies' (p. 299). Indeed, how many committed pluralists, I wonder, regret the passing of the British Raj? How many would argue that, because it once existed, it had a right to carry on existing? Porter saw an historical inevitability to movements away from earlier ethnic attachments – particularly in socially heterogeneous societies, particularly where many immigrants rub shoulders – an inevitably that he felt ethnonationalists were unaware of or, more likely, preferred to ignore. He argued against what he saw as 'cultures of the past' that are increasingly less relevant for modern life.

Indeed, a dislike of this world is often the background for arguments on behalf of small, or 'indigenous', or 'authentic', cultures.[5] Standing up for the overdog is not a popular exercise, but is it an advance to counter one species of insensitivity with another? Do the oppressed, as Bertrand Russell (1950) discussed in a famous essay, hold the moral high ground because of oppression itself? Consider Orwell's (1944/1970: 230) observation that 'this business about the moral superiority of the poor is one of the deadliest forms of escapism the ruling class have evolved'. Is it really apposite or accurate for Mühlhäusler (2000) to emphasise a 'holism' that is apparently uniquely associated with the small and the aboriginal, or to cite with approval views of western civilisation as particularly 'artificial' and 'man-made', a world consisting 'almost over-whelmingly of lifeless, inanimate objects'? The disdain here naturally extends to the scientific culture generally, indeed to the generalities and universals that many would see as the pivots of progress. In the same paper in which he finds poetry and deep meaning among those who have not surrendered to the blandishments of capitalism, Fishman (1982: 8) endorses Herder's idea that 'the universal is a fraud, a mask for the self-interest of the dominating over the dominated'. See also the discussion of the 'new' ecology of language, in chapter 10 of this book.

Need it be said that – the crimes, insensitivities and shortcomings of western society notwithstanding – these sorts of arguments are both foolish (sometimes downright nonsensical) and dangerous? Scholars of various stripes have attested to the myopia here. Snow (1959: 27), for instance, argued that 'industrialisation is the only hope of the poor'. Gellner (1968: 405) pointed to the obvious fact that for most ordinary people life has become a great deal better with the rise of the 'scientific-industrial' society; modern liberal democracies offer the best chances – probabilities, not guarantees, of course – for individual freedom and lib-eration. And Steiner (1971: 55) reminded us that modern technological societies are the ones in which discussions about pluralism, relativism and other perspectives on social life have been afforded greatest scope; they are the only ones to engage in meaningful self-criticism, or to adopt postures of 'self-indictment' and 'self-scrutiny' as correctives to ethno-centrism. If these views are thought to be tainted, themselves, with capi-talist bias or modernist insensitivity, consider the non-western assertion of Joseph et al. (1990: 24) that *all* societies are now 'in search of affluence through economic growth'; there is, they continue, 'a universal sub-scription to the Baconian idea that, through science and technology, growth and affluence are attainable'. These are precisely the sentiments of the later Gellner (1995), who based his assessment of the superiority of western scientific culture on its provision of information that virtually everyone in the world is after.

A final and obvious reality check simply involves observing which sorts of societies and lifestyles people leave behind, and which attract them. Of course, 'globalisation' has become the longest four-letter word, and of course the modern 'globalised' economy pushes itself relentlessly into all corners, intent on selling shoes, soft drinks and sex to everyone from Boston to Bhutan – but there is an almost equally powerful 'pull' factor. Globalisation and its ramifications are often welcomed by many who see in them upward physical, social and psychological mobility. Or, reverse the optic, and ask how many of those academic researchers and writers who wax poetic about what is indigenous and small actually alter lifestyles themselves.

In his continuing criticism of unalloyed relativism, Porter (1975: 300) made another point relevant in current debates: 'not all cultures have equal claims on our moral support', he stated, because some endorse values and practices that are generally unacceptable. This is a delicate position, of course. While it should never be forgotten that cultural relativism was a vital corrective, both within and without academia, to earlier ethnocentric insensitivities, Porter yet felt that we have a right to judge cultures, simply because social evolution has shown some aspects of human life to be more 'morally supportable' than others (see also chapter 2 of this book and Musgrove, 1982).[6]

In his thoughtful commentary on multicultural adaptions, on pluralist accommodations in heterogeneous societies, on competing and sometimes conflicting identity claims, Taylor (1992) essentially carried forward Porter's questioning of the moral equivalence of different cultures. He notes that when cultures rub up against one another, and particularly when these cultures are of unequal status in important regards, a struggle for 'recognition' can be expected. Such struggles have come to the fore in a world where the old social hierarchies have collapsed or at least weakened sufficiently to allow subaltern voices to be heard; a politics of equal recognition has been extended further than ever before. Tracing developments through Rousseau and Herder, Taylor outlined the concept of 'authenticity', central to which is the dialogical character of human life; and this dialogue proceeds from, and requires, a sense of group belonging. In the public sphere, this discourse leads to demands for 'equal recognition'. But this, in turn, is now closely tied to a 'politics of difference' in which the uniqueness of individual or group identity has come to be emphasised. It is this that adherents and activists claim is in danger of being ignored or, worse, assimilated to some dominant, overarching majority; and, as Taylor points out, 'this assimilation is the cardinal sin against the ideal of authenticity' (p. 38).

We arrive, then, at an interesting juncture: principles of universal equality are strongly supported, but within them, as it were, is a demand for the recognition of distinctiveness. And, as Taylor notes (1992: 43), competing demands of universal respect and of particularity can lead to problems:

The reproach the first makes to the second is just that it violates the principle of nondiscrimination. The reproach the second makes to the first is that it negates identity by forcing people into a homogeneous mold that is untrue to them.

Taylor gives a specific shape to his points through reference to the recurring tensions between Quebec and the rest of Canada, between a collectivist impulse (to safeguard an allegedly threatened francophone culture) and one that resists any infringement of individual rights and liberties – the latter being, roughly speaking, the western liberal view that society should strive to ensure individual equality but remain neutral on the contents of the 'good life'. Taylor attempts to chart a course between poles, arguing for an 'hospitable' variant of liberalism that should not claim *complete* neutrality. He also touches upon the extended demand that not only should all cultures be given some means of self-defence, their 'equal worth' must also be recognised. Taylor observes here that judgements of equal worth require investigation, but that we might reasonably start from a *presumption* of equality. This seems sensible, whereas the demand that 'as a matter of right . . . we come up with a final concluding judgment' (p. 69) which is favourable is clearly less so. Given Taylor's previous insistence on the 'dialogic' nature of human life, it is unsurprising that he concludes by recommending a continuing search for some social positioning that avoids a cruel homogenisation, on the one hand, and an ethnocentric self-immurement, on the other.

9.2.3 Reculer pour mieux sauter?

The idea that ethnicity is a backward-looking view, that nationalism is ultimately a withdrawal from reality, has been attacked as naïve and unrealistic. Smith (1971: 22, 236) has noted, for example, that nationalism need not be any sort of atavism; on the contrary, it represents 'a vision of the future . . . both traditionalist and modernist'. The idea here is that nationalism looks back, true enough, but only to gather the necessary material to reconstitute and reinvigorate a flagging or moribund sense of group identity. 'Nationalism', Smith goes on to note, 'may be described as the myth of the historical renovation' in the course of which 'a pristine state of true collective individuality' is rediscovered, nurtured and put to work in the service of an identity needed for the present and future (p. 22). Fishman (1972: 9) put the matter similarly: 'nationalism is not so much backward-oriented . . . as much as it seeks to derive unifying and energizing power from widely held images of the past in order to overcome a quite modern kind of fragmentation and loss of identity'.

It is surely the case that some return to the well-springs of the group can be a potent and psychologically useful exercise; this seems particularly likely when the group in question has fallen on hard times. The re-awakened sense of pride and group 'consciousness' that now animates many 'small' communities around the world, from the aboriginal populations of Canada, America and Australia to the 'stateless peoples' of Europe, has many positive attributes. But it is equally true that attempted resuscitation of traditions and practices that are at odds with modern values suggests problems. The baleful consequences of attempting to maintain traditional continuities in North American aboriginal societies have been much in the news of late. A poignant piece by the president of the Innu Nation (Penashue, 2000) described the horrific living conditions of some aboriginal communities. He commented particularly on the infamous cases of Sheshatshiu and Utshimassits (Davis Inlet), and his underlying theme was that official interventions by state and church have led directly to cultural collapse, with all its horrific accompanying statistics (for alcoholism, drug abuse, and so on). On the other hand, we should also remember that official policies of *non*-intervention have been decried, as have those in which large amounts of power and material resources have simply been handed over to aboriginal groups. There are no easy solutions in such matters, and government policies, over a great many years, can be condemned for inconsistency, ill-will, lack of whole-hearted commitment, prejudice and racism. But there is little evidence to suggest that, even where better interventions have been attempted, cultural survival can be assured; see also chapter 8, note 3. Here are two examples of recent efforts to create conditions under which old lifestyles can continue to flourish; they are less tragic than some of the attempted northern resettlements of aboriginal peoples, but no less illustrative of the difficulties.

In May 1999, Makah whalers in northern Washington killed a thirty-ton, ten-metre-long grey whale. Makah culture had historically been built around whaling, and became rich because of it. The decline of the grey whale population led to the abandonment of the hunt in 1926, but by 1994 the now-protected species had returned. It was removed from the endangered list and a renewed Makah hunt was sanctioned for 'cultural purposes'. Given the fierce worldwide debate over whaling, it is not surprising that it then took five years for the new hunt to take place, the beginning of another five-year period during which the Makah would be allowed to take twenty whales. It is also unsurprising that the initial kill was surrounded by heated and acrimonious debate. On the one hand, there was concern for aboriginal rights and cultural continuity, for the maintenance of a particular and at-risk group identity; on the other, there was disgust at an unnecessary slaughter, a reversion to undertakings perhaps once appropriate but now anachronistic and repugnant. As is often the case when age-old practices are dusted off for modern times, the Makah whale hunt was accompanied by the ironic and the bizarre.

The traditional cedar canoe used in the hunt had to be towed into position, and the ceremonial harpoon had to be augmented by .50-calibre armour-piercing weaponry. Makah whalers were photographed standing on the back of the dead or dying animal, wearing modern running-shoes and giving quite non-traditional clenched-fist salutes of victory. A large and modern fishing vessel was needed to land the whale, which, on the way to shore, sank to the bottom; it was retrieved with the use of compressed air. For the 'official' beaching, however, the carcass was lashed to the cedar canoe. Once on shore, the traditional blessings were followed by the butchering (done by an Inuit, as local expertise no longer existed) and, while praising the revitalisation of their culture, many needed a tinned soft drink to wash down the unfamiliar and unpalatable raw blubber (said to taste like a mixture of lamb stew, latex and vaseline). Not all the whale meat was eaten raw, of course: the preparation of traditional whale dishes is now being taught to Makah students with the help of Japanese cookery books.

Most of the reaction to the hunt, however vehement, was unsurprising. Anti-whaling organisations saw it as trophy-hunting; one observer said, 'it used to be about food. Now, it's about fun. I felt total repulsion watching them... doing back flips off the whale' (Watson, 1999). Many politicians condemned the Makah hunt, sensing that the general public's antipathy to whaling was stronger than its support for native traditions. Other aboriginal groups tended to endorse the hunt, however; particularly supportive here were members of the Nuu-Chah-Nulth and other British Columbian bands, some of whom would like to resume whaling themselves. Some commentators not overly enamoured with environmentalism were also supportive, citing both adequate whale stocks and inadequate 'green' reasoning. 'There is no dishonour in what the Makah did this week', observed the *Port Alberni Valley Times*, a Vancouver Island newspaper. Another British Columbian journalist noted that the hunt was 'grotesque, courageous, tragic, defiant, bloody and strangely beautiful... an act carried out against overwhelming odds' (see Glavin, 1999).

But not all responses were quite so predictable. Some environmentalist and animal-rights groups found it difficult to decide between support for traditional aboriginal practices and condemnation of the killing of wildlife. A similar line was taken in some of the subtler editorials. For example, the Vancouver *Province* pointed out that 'we've been teaching our children that whales are almost holy creatures, and . . . to respect native culture. How will our teachers reconcile yesterday's butchery?' Not all native communities were behind the hunt, either. One elder said that 'going back to the old tradition for food, it doesn't add up. In order to get the young kids off drugs . . . it's not necessary to kill a whale'. Another said, 'I don't see the point of it. I don't see no use for the meat . . . They claim to be descendants of the great whalers, but that's long gone' (Lawson, 1999; Claplanhoo, 1999). Still others pointed out that the Makah's case would have been easier to defend had they used purely traditional methods, and put aside their elephant guns and motorboats.[7]

A similar argument was made when, in September 1999, the Mi'kmaq of Nova Scotia were allowed to hunt and fish when no one else was. Their setting of lobster traps particularly incensed local non-native fishermen. Aboriginal practices here were based upon a 1760 treaty; but there were no power boats and modern traps in the eighteenth century. Should such a treaty be good in perpetuity, under conditions unimaginable at the time it was drawn up? Or perhaps those who now wish to benefit from its provisions should be required to use only the old hunting and fishing methods. There are extremely rich grounds for interpretation (and litigation) here. A Supreme Court ruling, for example, held that the original treaty obligations to trade only with the British ought now to be transformed into broader preferential rights. Others argued that this was an unjustified extension of the original wording and intent. Still others noted that even the 'generous' Court interpretation did not suggest completely unregulated activity: catch limits should still be set by the government, within the limits of a 'moderate livelihood' for native fisherman; fishing and hunting rights did not necessarily imply special treatment for aboriginal citizens in (for example) mineral extraction, logging and off-shore gas exploitation; and so on.

Putting aside the more obvious and troubling clashes between past and present, it seems clear enough that a 'return to one's roots' can be a salutary exercise. It must also be recognised, however, that national-ist activity has often been an exercise in power, and that attempts at the revival or rejuvenation of 'groupness' have led to conflict with 'out-group' members. This process is abetted by historical manipulation and selectiveness, indifference to reality, and a strong inclination to racist propaganda. Nationalists, in Orwell's view (1945/1965: 283), believe that their group is the strongest (or ought to be) and the most deserving; and, since 'nationalism is power-hunger tempered by self-deception', they can uphold this belief in the face of overwhelming fact. Nationalist thought, he believed, was characterised by obsession, instability and the belief that the past can be altered (shades here of Renan – but also of Orwell's own *1984*). Orwell was of course prompted to write by the existence of some of the most distasteful modern manifestations of nationalism, but his claim was that the argument applied in principle to all nationalisms. He detected strong tinges of racism in Celtic nationalism, for example: 'the Celt is supposed to be spiritually superior to the Saxon – simple, more creative, less vulgar, less snobbish, etc. – but the usual power-hunger is there under the surface' (p. 294).

What conclusions can we draw here, especially if we acknowledge that the very essence of nationalism is an intangible and subjective quantity, or if we accept Orwell's point that 'all nationalist controversy is at the debating-society level. It is always entirely inconclusive' (p. 293)? Well, it will be apparent from the shape of my argument so far that I believe there is strong evidence for the negative impact of nationalism. Nationalist identity shares with other varieties of groupness the following potential perils: a promotion and maintenance of 'us-and-them' boundaries, a de-emphasis of *individual* rights and interests, and a hardening of group concerns into perceived superiority and racism. Nationalist identity also very often involves romanticised yearnings for a past which, suitably interpreted and restructured, is seen as a bulwark against present inequalities or indignities: in this sense, it can take on ostrich qualities. Nationalism can change quickly from a radical ideology to a reactionary one. It can be static or regressive in the face of unpalatable aspects of modernity.

On the other hand, there is no doubt that – partly *because* of some of these features nationalism has proved a powerful force in the world, one that has endured well beyond the lifespan that many would have predicted. It has had important cultural manifestations. It has been a positive force, particularly in the lives of those who have felt threatened by larger or more influential neighbours. Psychological insight has shown that our group memberships are many and overlapping, and that not all of one's behavioural repertoire need reflect a particular membership: in this regard, it is obvious that many features of nationalism can remain latent for most group members most of the time. A simple affirmation of one's ethnonational identity need go no further than providing a personal point of reference. Translation into action is what may create problems, and this translation may never occur for some group members. Relatedly, there is very often a considerable gulf between the views and behaviour of 'ordinary' group members and those of their activist 'spokesmen': for the former, group identity may be largely a passive attribute, whereas for the latter it can become a galvanic force.

While it is possible to reject nationalism as a force in which bad out-weighs good, this is neither completely accurate nor, more importantly, is it an intellectually appropriate way to deal with a continuingly powerful phenomenon. Social scientists have much interesting work to do in studying the dimensions and degrees of attachment that people have for ethnic, national and other groups. The value judgements that may be made of such groups can be considered independently of careful description and analysis.

National and ethnic identity is simply a continuing fact of social life. Porter and others have argued that such identity is anachronistic, something to be jettisoned and replaced by more rational allegiances; see Edwards (2004b) for a brief comment on so-called 'rational-choice' approaches to group identity. 'Civic' nationalists claim that state and political identities are more rational, less beholden to dubious pasts and more socially inclusive: the attachments of 'blood and belonging' are replaced by altogether cooler assessments of where our best collective interests lie. But blood is still vital to human life and, as we know, it is a thicker liquid than many others. The continuing appeal of ethnonational attachments, particularly at times of uncertainty, upheaval and conflict, rests very much, in fact, upon a solidarity of kinship that mimics that of biological families. And, just as the elective affinities that so powerfully bind us to our relatives are subjective in nature, so the subjective essence of nationalism often proves stronger than the rational and demonstrable markers of civil attachments. As a version of intimate family ties, writ large, the blood of ethnonationalism continues to have greater attractive force than the waters of state. Smith (1995) makes a similar point, devoting a concluding chapter to 'the defence of the nation'. He accepts, as one must, the many dark and terrible aspects of nationalist histories, but he also says that there is really no substitute for ethnonational affiliations, nothing else that can satisfy the continuing human 'needs for cultural fulfilment, rootedness, security and frater-nity' – particularly in a 'globalised' world (p. 159). Providing linkages of 'memory, myth and symbol', these affiliations can still lead people to make the ultimate sacrifice and, in such regards, Smith is surely right to point to the power of nationalism as a 'religious surrogate'. In fact, it would not be an egregious mistake to go further, and to see nationalism as religion *tout court*. One implication of this is that, with declining adherence to traditional religions – belief systems in which the supernatural element is rather more directly acknowledged than it is in most nationalist ones – there is a new one waiting in the wings. This does not contradict the continuingly powerful presence of religion itself in many parts of the world, of course, nor its resurgence in others, nor the obvious ways in which nationalism and religion have combined, both historically and contemporarily, to create even more potent solidarities.

It is clear that, whatever one may feel about ethnic and national attachments, and whatever criticisms may be made of them, they remain vital forces in group identity. For all their essential non-rationality – because of it, in fact – these attachments remain potent. Viewed distastefully by liberals, nationalism has shown a continuing power to recruit intellectual support; see Haugaard's (2006) overview. Scorned by Marxists as outdated sentimentality, it has forced from them a grudging admiration. Both liberalism and Marxism are rationalist philosophies that, naturally enough, have difficulty coming to terms with 'what can only count as irrational attachments' (Ryan, 1984). As Gellner (1994: 34) noted, both have 'under-estimated the political vigour of nationalism'. They have had to admit the weaknesses of their own social frameworks in the face of what seem to be well-nigh universal features of human life. It is easy enough for members of dominant or 'mainstream' groups to be dismissive and fearful of attachments that they often see as only minority-group phenomena; and it is indeed true that the salience of those attachments is generally much greater for 'small' cultures and identities seen to be fragile or under threat (see Sallabank, 2006, for a modern example). But we are all 'ethnics', and ethnonational identity is at least 'passively treasured by nearly all citizens of modern societies, even if they do not know it' (Seton-Watson, 1982: 13). Besides, populations that are currently secure may find themselves in changed circumstances: they may become immigrants, for example, or they may be conquered *in situ* by more powerful neighbours. Under such circumstances, we would predict that latent feelings of solidarity would become more visible. On the other hand, as O'Brien (1973: 50) pointed out, 'we ought not, after all, to idealize minorities, or to forget that today's underdog may be tomorrow's power-crazed bully'.

STUDY QUESTIONS

1. Has nationalism generally been a force for good in the world?
2. Why do minorities within minonorities pose particular challenges for national movements?
3. Discuss the recent history of civic nationalism in Quebec and in France. What are the implications of this for our understanding of nationalism more generally?
4. Is there, in fact, such a thing as civic nationalism?

Further reading

Daniele Conversi's edited book (2002), *Ethnonationalism in the Contemporary World*, as its subtitle reveals, is a *festschrift* for Walker Connor, an eminent scholar of nationalism. It is, however, much more than a collection of adulatory chapters, presenting as it does some powerful contemporary assessments of nationalism in modern times.

John Stuart Mill's (1861/1964) *Considerations on Representative Government* contains some insights on nationalism that no student should overlook.

Ernest Renan's famous Sorbonne address of 1892, 'Qu'est-ce qu'une nation?' (see Renan, 1947, for a printed version) is another classic statement that demands the attention of all serious scholars of nationalism.

In Anthony Smith's (1990) article, 'The supersession of nationalism?', the author turns his attention to an important contemporary debate: are national allegiances fated to disappear under the pressures of globalisation?

10 Language and nationalism

Koestler (1976: 157; see also Safran, 2008) described the descendants of the biblical tribes as 'the classic example of linguistic adaptability', in which a strong and continuing sense of group identity outlived repeated shifts in communicative language:

> first they spoke Hebrew; in the Babylonian exile, Chaldean; at the time of Jesus, Aramaic; in Alexandria, Greek; in Spain, Arabic, but later Ladino – a Spanish-Hebrew mixture written in Hebrew characters, the Sephardi equivalent of Yiddish; and so it goes on. They preserved their religious identity, but changed languages at their convenience.

This is but a striking example of the lack of a necessary connection between the continuation of a particular, traditional or ancestral language and the maintenance of feelings of 'groupness'. But this is not to say that, where such a language has been sustained, it is not an obvious and powerful pillar of identity. And, indeed, it is a commonly held assumption, both without and within academia, that it is the pillar, that its presence may not be sufficient but it is certainly necessary. Here is a brief selection of the sorts of sentiments commonly made by language nationalists (see Edwards, 1995; see also Fishman, 1997):

> Absolutely nothing is so important for a nation's culture as its language. (Wilhelm von Humboldt, 1797)

> Language is the spiritual exhalation of the nation. (Humboldt again)

> Has a nation anything more precious than the language of its fathers? (Johann Gottfried Herder, 1772)

> A people without a language of its own is only half a nation ... to lose your native tongue ... is the worst badge of conquest. (Thomas Davis, 1843)

A nation could lose its wealth, its government, even its territory and still survive, but should it lose its language, not a trace of it would remain. (Firidun Kocharli)

Sluagh gun chanain, sluagh gun anam. (Gaelic: 'a people without its language is a people without its soul').

Hep brezhoneg, breizh ebet. (Breton: 'without Breton there is no Brittany').

Gyn chengey, gyn cheer. (Manx: 'no language, no country').

The care of the national language is at all times a sacred trust. (Friedrich von Schlegel, 1815)

Quand un peuple tombe esclave, tant qu'il tient bien sa langue, c'est comme s'il tenait la clef de sa prison. (Alphonse Daudet, c1873 – drawing upon a contemporary phrase of Frédéric Mistral)

Ireland with its language and without freedom is preferable to Ireland with freedom and without its language. (Eamon de Valera, 1921)

If we accept that it was in the rhetoric surrounding the French Revolution in 1789 that nationalism, national loyalty, the notion of the 'mother country' (or, of course, the 'fatherland') and, above all, the belief in unity and autonomy first found contemporary forceful expression, then it was in the German romanticism of the same period that the notion of a *Volk* and the almost mystical connection between nation and language were expounded so fervently. Thus, O'Brien (1988a) succinctly argued that nationalism was invented by the Germans under French influence. As we have seen in the previous chapters, this is an oversimplification of some magnitude; still, there is little doubt that the linguistic aspects of modern ethnonational affiliations owe a great deal to post-eighteenth-century romanticism. The dialects which were generally disparaged during the Enlightenment, but which had managed to survive, were often idealised by the Romantics, as were the 'smaller' European languages generally. The dilettantism that often accompanies romanticism, however, frequently meant that real linguistic action or recognition in these regards was either of the lip-service variety, or came conveniently late in the day. Sapir pointed out that romantic efforts on behalf of small varieties were merely 'eddies in the more powerful stream of standardization of speech that set in at the close of the medieval period'. National languages themselves, he went on, were 'huge systems of vested interests which sullenly resist critical enquiry' (Mandelbaum, 1963: 88, 118), and few of the nationalists who thundered against them actually abandoned them in their own writings.

These steadily strengthening national languages were, after all, the mediums of sophisticated expression. More rustic varieties might possess romantic salt-of-the-earth connotations, but they were typically seen as less developed forms: the all-dialects-are-valid principle had yet to arrive on the scene. The people who spoke them were sometimes seen as socially backward, or worse. At the time of the revolution, only about one in ten inhabitants of France were monolingual francophones, about a quarter of the population spoke no French at all and another quarter had only a halting command of the language.[1] One of the chapter titles of Robb's (2007) treatment of modern France is 'O Òc Sí Bai Ya Win Oui Oyi Awè Jo Ja Oua' – these being some of the words meaning 'yes' in the many *patois* (defined at the time as 'corrupt and provincial' varieties). The initial reaction to these linguistic realities among the new leaders was reasonably tolerant (see Balibar, 1985; Wardhaugh, 1987; Grillo, 1989). By the mid-1790s, however, l'Abbé Grégoire had analysed the questionnaires he had sent out, and produced the famous report (1794) calling for the promotion of a unifying French competence, and for the 'annihilation' of the *patois*. At the same time, Bertrand Barère – like Grégoire, an important government official – pointed out that superstition spoke Breton, that hatred of the Republic spoke German, that counter-revolution spoke Italian, and that fanaticism spoke Basque (Gershoy, 1962; Wardhaugh, 1987). Robb suggests that this blunt assessment of dubious patriotism did in fact reflect something of the truth, mirrored as it was by southern contempt for the ruling northerners. Little wonder, then, that a decree appeared in the same year, 1794, proscribing the official use of all varieties other than French: the beginnings of a linguistically centralist posture that remained largely unchanged until the mid-twentieth century and which arguably retains much of its force to this day.

Before the Romantic era, local languages and dialects may not have been well thought of, much less idealised or glorified, but there were few systematic attempts to impose the language of the dominant upon subordinate or conquered populations. The Greeks and Romans, for instance, coupled a disdain for subaltern groups with the certainty that social pressure would ensure movement away from local varieties and towards their own powerful languages. Thus, the Romans felt no need to impose Latin and, indeed, considered its acquisition 'a privilege to be sought, like citizenship' (Lewis, 1976: 180). Neither the Ottoman nor the Austro-Hungarian rulers cared a great deal about the many languages spoken under their banners. Under the *ancien régime* in pre-revolutionary France there was considerable tolerance as well; political harmony and regular payment of taxes were far more important than any concern with the languages of the peasants. Generally, as George Clark observed, 'when a country was governed by a limited ruling class, it did not matter much what language the masses spoke, as long as they kept their place' (cited in Spencer, 1985:389; see also Sahlins, 1989; Safran, 2008). Gellner (1983:127) put it more colourfully. He described a 'typical burgher in an agrarian society' who hears one morning that

> the local Pasha had been overthrown and replaced by an altogether new one. If, at that point, his wife dared ask the burgher what language the new Pasha spoke in the intimacy of his home life – was it Arabic, Turkish, Persian, French or English? – the hapless burgher would give her a sharp look, and wonder how he would cope with all the new difficulties when, at the same time, his wife had gone quite mad.

A common practice, then, from quite remote to fairly recent times, was a benign linguistic neglect on the part of rulers, coupled with a belief that their own language was, in any event, superior and would naturally be adopted by anyone of sense. Indeed, as Haugen (1985) remarked, a *laissez-faire* policy *was* often sufficient insurance for the continuation of language shift. There were exceptions to this but, given linguistically diverse empires, peace and fiscal reliability were the major links between rulers and ruled. This was the situation that changed, once a romanticised link between language and nation became strongly forged. Now, language became a rallying-point, something to galvanise the downtrodden, to rally supporters, and to alarm the rulers.

In 1772, Johann Gottfried Herder published his first major philosophical work, *Über den Ursprung der Sprache*, which had been the prize essay at the Berlin Academy of Sciences two years earlier. Arguing against both the divine origin of language and its origin in human invention, Herder stressed that human beings were innately endowed with the capacity for reason and speech. The diversity of languages was seen to be rooted in the variety of social environments such that, over time, a group would naturally come to share a common language. Further, Herder suggested, these speech communities will survive as discrete entities only as long as they preserve their language as a 'collective inheritance'. A nation's self-respect hinges upon its ability and willingness to defend itself, but its very existence is inconceivable without its own language (see Barnard, 1965, 1969). Herder's observations are worth citing here because he proceeds from a discussion of language origins to a philosophy of linguistic nationalism, in which ancestral language and national continuity are intertwined. The 'new humanism' that Herder reflected and sustained was an important part of the romantic reaction to Enlightenment rationalism and to classical themes in art and literature. Much of this feeling in Germany was summarised in anti-French sentiment; like many subsequent nationalist movements, the German romantic variety found it easier to maintain a coherent position when there existed a convenient 'out-group'.

Of course, the Germans were not the only xenophobes here. French culture thought highly of itself and, as well, had many friends in high places outside the country. When Voltaire visited the court in Berlin he felt very much at home; he reported that French was spoken extensively, and exclusively by those of any status: German was only for soldiers and horses (Hertz, 1944; Waterman, 1966). There also existed the feeling that foreigners were constitutionally incapable of appreciating French, the only language of culture.[2] The French were culturally dominant in eighteenth-century Europe, and they endorsed neo-classicism. The burgeoning German consciousness rejected and resented this dominance and, as for neo-classical impulses, why should there not be a powerful *German* neo-classicism? Thus, Fichte (see below) argued that appropriate comparisons here were between the Greeks and the Germans: the former were the torch-bearers of classical antiquity and the latter were the obvious inheritors in any post-classical Europe. The French efforts could then only be 'spurious neo-classicism' (Kedourie, 1960; Shafer, 1955).

None of this anti-French sentiment is necessarily implied in Herder's statement (cited above) about the precious worth of the ancestral language. Nor is it evident in these words from his prize essay:

> what a treasure language is when kinship groups grow into tribes and nations. Even the smallest of nations . . . cherishes in and through its language the history, the poetry and songs about the great deeds of its forefathers. The language is its collective treasure. (Barnard, 1969: 165)

Indeed, Isaiah Berlin (1976; see also Berlin, 2000) concluded that Herder was nationalistic, but neither chauvinistic nor superior. He argued that Herder did not claim that one's own was best but simply that it was, after all, one's own, and that 'to brag of one's country is the stupidest form of boastfulness . . . aggressive nationalism . . . is detestable' (p. 157). In short, Berlin felt that Herder did not fall prey to either the excesses of nationalism generally or to Gallophobia in particular. However, although Herder was certainly less strident than some of his followers, I have already noted (in chapter 7) that he was able to write a poem in which French was characterised as 'the ugly slime of the Seine', something that German speakers were told to 'spew out' (Kedourie, 1960). He also stated that 'a so-called education in French must by necessity deform and misguide German minds' (Fishman, 1972: 53). In short, while Herder is often portrayed as the more or less neutral first proponent of the language–nation link in the modern age, he was, like his disciples, prone to chauvinism and anti-French feelings, prone to revelations of the dark side of nation-alism.

Johann Gottlieb Fichte translated many of Herder's ideas into broader sociopolitical positions. In his *Addresses to the German Nation* (1807/1968), he praised the German language and deprecated others, as part of an ingenious extrapolation from Herder's contention that loss of language entailed loss of identity. Fichte's basic argument was quite simple. Of all the 'Teutonic' peoples (Europeans, including the French), only the Germans remained in their original location and had retained and developed their original language. Fichte dismissed the first difference as unimportant, but the language shift of others was the central pillar in his argument. He pointed out that it was not German *per se* that was superior to (say) French; rather, it was superior because it was the original, and French was inferior because it represented an adoption of foreign elements (i.e. Latin). Given that the original German was superior to the bastardised French (and other 'neo-Latin' varieties), it followed that the German *nation* was superior. There is more than a little Whorfianism in Fichte's claim that the important feature was not

> the previous ancestry of those who continued to speak an original language; on the contrary, the importance lies solely in the fact that this language continues to be spoken, *for men are formed by language far more than language is formed by men.* (p. 48; my italics, J.E.)

Fichte believed that the adoption of foreign elements seriously weakened a society's speech and, given enough time, would essentially kill it. While Germans speak a language that has retained its vitality ever since it 'first issued from the force of nature', the other Teutonic communities have come to speak a language that 'has movement on the surface only but is dead at the root' (pp. 58–9). It hardly needs pointing out that linguistic evidence for these assumptions is not thick on the ground. Anyone can point to *differences* among languages but, as we have already seen, difference does not imply deficiency. For Fichte, however, the infiltration of 'Teutonic' languages by Latin had consequences far beyond the linguistic, and its baleful influence produced a 'lack of seriousness about social relations, the idea of self-abandonment, and the idea of heartless laxity' (p. 57). He believed that no valid comparisons could be made between German and neo-Latin languages: 'if the intrinsic value of the German language is to be discussed . . . a language of equal rank, a language equally primitive, as, for example, Greek, must enter the lists' (p. 59).

Overall, it seemed obvious to Fichte that, because of historical circumstances, the German language was superior to other varieties and,

because of the power of language itself, the German nation was superior
to others. A measure of this dominance is that the German who learns
Latin will also acquire a good grasp of the neo-Latin derivatives. In fact,
Fichte argued, he will be able to learn Latin *better* than will others; he will
consequently understand the neo-Latin varieties more intimately than
will speakers of these forms themselves! In a statement clearly designed
to encourage international understanding and harmony, he pointed out
that the German:

> can always be superior to the foreigner and understand him fully,
> even better than the foreigner understands himself... On the other
> hand, the foreigner can never understand the true German without a
> thorough and extremely laborious study of the German language, and
> there is no doubt that he will leave what is genuinely German
> untranslated. (p. 60)

While it would be incorrect to assume that the linguistic nationalism of the time was purely a German production, it is certainly fair
to observe the powerful and systematic German influence here, an influence that was enthusiastically received elsewhere – in eastern Europe,
to cite one important example (Magocsi, 1982). The sentiments of the
German nationalists have remained important ever since, particularly
in those contexts in which 'small' languages and cultures have been
defended (Vossler, 1932). In chapter 7, I cited Smith's (1971) argument
about Herder's influence on linguistic nationalism; he has also reminded
us (pp. 149–50) that romanticised emphases upon language typically
follow the growth of nationalistic fervour; they do not create it; for
nationalists,

> linguistic studies, like historical, become an often unselfconscious
> means of justifying their prior nationalist conviction – to themselves as
> well as others... nationalist movements, therefore, even in Europe, are
> not linguistic movements – any more than they are historical or ethnic
> or religious or territorial movements. All these attempts to 'reduce'
> nationalism to some kind of more readily intelligible variable end up
> by defeating themselves on empirical grounds – or become tautologies.

Given the thrust of his attempts to link ethnicity with nationalism, we
may find Smith's inclusion of 'ethnic' a little odd here, but his basic
point – that nationalism reflects, at root, a complex sense of groupness
that defies attempts at solely objective labelling – is a good one. Language
is important, but the possession, promotion and continuation of the
'original' or ancestral variety is not a necessary pillar of ethnonationalist
sentiment.

10.2 LANGUAGE PURISM AND PRESCRIPTIVISM

I shall turn, in the next chapter, to language planning *per se*. Here, I want to carry on the discussion of the language–nationalism linkage by attending to one particular aspect of that broader topic. The rationale is that once a strong relationship has been accepted and/or established between a particular language and a particular group affiliation, the 'protection' of the language often becomes paramount. This typically takes the form of purist and prescriptivist impulses and actions. It is important to remember at the outset that linguistic activity here is essentially in the service of *identity* protection.

The work of Thomas (1991) constitutes one of the rare attempts to impose some descriptive or theoretical order here. 'It is clearly premature', he stated, 'to attempt a comparative history of purism' (p. 195), but he does present a very useful categorisation, the chief elements of which I summarise here:

(a) purism and prescriptivism are universal characteristics of standardised (and standardising) languages;
(b) their presence reflects responses to specific problems in specific language settings;
(c) the puristic attitudes and practices in one setting may be transferred to another (as seen, for instance, in the similarities among language academies, councils and other regulatory bodies);
(d) purist and prescriptivist actions are often directed at unwanted external influences, but 'internal' prescriptivism (selecting among dialects, for instance) is also common;
(e) most actions are concerned with elements of the lexico-semantic system, but grammatical purism is often also important, particularly 'internally', of course;
(f) languages vary in terms of their stance on the adoption of 'foreign' elements. Varieties of long national standing are often less prone to 'xenophobic purism' than are those more recently 'emancipated' from the domination of other languages. (Contemporary reactions towards the global dominance of English, however, remind us that linguistic and cultural anxieties can easily re-emerge.)

We may not yet have a comprehensive theoretical understanding of the 'social and psychological impulses which affect language use, language attitudes and language planning' (Thomas, 1991: 8), but it is quite clear that these impulses are centrally about *identity* – and we should commend Thomas for reminding us that purist and pre-scriptivist attitudes and practices are at the very heart of things here.[3] We should always remember, too, that language practices and planning exist in a circular relationship with the desires that motivate them: if our cultural 'impulses' have linguistic consequences, then these, in turn, will influence our thoughts on social identity and social categorisation.

10.2.1 Opinion and need

The clearest examples of language protection are found in the existence and the works of academies. The best-known of these is the *Académie française*. Here, Cardinal Richelieu's forty 'immortals' were given 'absolute power . . . over literature and language' (Hall, 1974: 180). As we shall see below, the efforts of the French academy and other similar institutions have not always been very successful, either in their grammatical and lexicographical productions or, more specifically, in their attempts to intervene in the dynamics of language use. But this hardly detracts from their importance as manifestations of will and intent, nor does it vitiate their symbolic role (see Eastman, 1983). In fact, lack of success may indirectly tell us much about the power of the 'natural tide of language' (as Thomas put it) to resist direction. The establishment of language academies and councils, and their continued existence despite a poor track record, tell us much about the importance of language as a marker of national identity. Thomas noted that 'it has become fashionable to lampoon language academies for their stuffiness, their smugness and their otherworldliness' (p. 111), but he was quite aware of their powerful symbolism. Their pronouncements continue to mark linguistic and nationalistic anxieties which, whatever the logic of the matter, obviously persist in the popular imagination. We may be sure that, when the *Times Higher Education Supplement* (14 May 1993) reported that Maurice Druon – a former Minister of Culture and the *secrétaire perpétuel* of the *Académie française* – called for language watchdogs to guard against poor French on television, many readers (even the perfidious English) nodded in agreement.

Indeed, the letters pages of newspapers everywhere regularly print feverish responses to linguistic barbarisms and bastardisations. A recent, and insightful, illustration is provided by Russell Smith (2007), a Canadian journalist. He had earlier noted that American pronunciations, like 'nooz' for *news*, or 'zee' for *zed* are variants, and not necessarily inferior to British versions or, touching an interesting regional vein, to Canadian usage.[4] His observations prompted a flurry of response from readers who generally made stout assertions that pronunciations like 'nooz' reveal laziness, or perhaps too much exposure to American television; as one writer told Smith, 'it is sad to see our language deteriorate to almost slang'. The 'logic' card was played, too: we spell *pews* like *news* and nobody, not even those Americans, pronounce the former as 'pooze', nor do they say 'pook' for *puke*. Smith points out that this sort of 'logic' just doesn't work in language, particularly in a notoriously irregular medium like English. Finally, he tells us that the woman who essentially equated American usage with slang and deterioration went on to cite Churchill's famous wartime speeches as 'well spoken':

> I am guessing [Smith wrote] she means not only elegantly written but spoken in a British [*sic*] accent. The implication, I think, is that this accent saved us from nazism and that this accent is therefore the language of valour and virtue, and one we should all emulate. This is what I mean about the conflation of usage and morality.

Smith's newspaper piece is interesting in two main ways. First, it points to the interesting Canadian positioning – in language and other things – somewhere between Britain and America; this has always had implications for the much-discussed Canadian identity. Second, Smith is undoubtedly correct to suggest that lurking behind anguished complaints about falling standards and linguistic decay, there are usually deeper worries about moral and social decline, about unwanted foreign influences and, therefore, about group identity.

There have always been influential columnists who write about usage and abusage, and books about the decline of the language and what ought to be done to stem it are both frequent and popular. There has never been a shortage of 'amateur do-gooding missionaries' in this perennially interesting topic (Quirk, 1982: 99; see also my reference to Bloomfield in chapter 4). All such missionary zeal can be easily derided, and, indeed, there is often a dark side arising from prejudice and ignorance. Some of the criticism, however, is more reasoned, particularly that which deals with deliberate or ignorant misuse of existing words, propaganda, jargon and unnecessary neologism. Here we often find literary critics – not linguists, perhaps, but not rank amateurs either – adding their voices to the debate. One thinks immediately, I suppose, of Orwell, but there are many other thoughtful treatments here (e.g. the several works of George Steiner: 1967, 1972, 1978). Running through all such efforts, whether thoughtful or ill-conceived, is a concern for language, and it is not always an ignoble one. In modern times, prescriptivism has not been very popular among linguists, who have typically held that it is neither desirable nor feasible to attempt to intervene in the social life of language. A deliberate renunciation of prescriptivism, of course, is more like atheism than agnosticism: a conscious non-belief is, itself, a belief and, as Hohenhaus (2005) has observed, a refusal to intervene is a sort of 'reverse purism' (see also Crystal, 2006). In any event, it is arguable that, in their rush away from prescriptivism, linguists may have abdicated a useful role as arbiters, and may have left much of the field open to those less well-informed.[5] Bolinger (1980) was one of the few contemporary linguists willing to participate in debates about the 'public life' of language: he rightly criticised the obvious crank elements, but he also understood the desire for standards, the frustration with perceived 'decay' and 'incorrectness', the onslaught of weasel words and jargon. In my view, there remains a need for much more illumination of that persistent no-man's-land between academic linguistics and public language.

We should remember, too, that formal prescriptivist institutions often arose to deal with problems of language regularisation created by advances in printing, increasing literacy and conceptions of national 'groupness'. These issues did not simply arise in the minds of some nationalist élite aiming to forge or strengthen group solidarity. Consider Caxton, having to make a selection from varying English dialects because of the imperatives of printing; consider Samuel Johnson, who was at once contemptuous of any attempt at linguistic 'embalming' and hopeful that his dictionary might somehow 'fix' an English that he saw as degenerating. The tension between a prescriptivism arising from narrow and often unfair conceptions of social inclusion and exclusion, and desires and needs for at least *some* standardisation is surely important in any consideration of the work of all 'language planners'. It is a tension we can observe in virtually all contexts in which a standard variety is struggling to emerge.

Prescriptivist attitudes towards language have always been with us, and complaints about decline and decay, about foreign infiltration, and about the inadequacy of certain varieties are as perennial as misgivings about the younger generation. Within the scholarly community, there is a long tradition of studying language attitudes, supplemented more recently by a revived interest in 'folk linguistics' and 'perceptual dialectology'. This sort of attention has traditionally coincided with arguments against prescriptivist intervention, on the grounds that it is neither appropriate nor feasible to attempt to direct vernacular usage. Historically, of course, matters were rather different in intellectual and policy circles and, indeed, prescriptivist intervention remains common: decisions have to be made when national languages 'emerge' and when some print standardisation is found necessary: debates about identity choice and maintenance are often argued in linguistic arenas; language-planning exercises involve some degree of control; and contemporary debate about what (if anything) ought to be done on behalf of 'endangered' varieties also implies a prescriptivist attitude. The terms themselves are often loaded here, since what is seen as purism when directed against 'foreign' elements may be tagged as standardisation when the focus is inward.

As I noted at the beginning here, a strong connection between nationalism and language leads very naturally to desires to 'protect' and 'purify' that language. Of course, the notion of keeping a language 'pure' and free from foreign taint reveals a profound misunderstanding of the dynamics of all natural languages – but it also reveals a great deal about psychological and social perceptions. It is simply a fact that 'protagonists of national languages tend to involve themselves with questions of linguistic purity' (Quirk, 1982: 59). In fact, as my reference to Caxton and Johnson reveals, interest in linguistic protection and preservation predates the modern wave of nationalism by at least a century or so. This in turn reflects an earlier historical wave, one in which the power of Latin waned and that of the major European languages began to wax: as the latter began to flex their muscles, they naturally felt the need for standardisation of various sorts. And there were identity functions to be served from the beginning, too, even if they were initially more focussed upon the unification of the literate than upon a broader nationalistic 'groupness'. It is certainly possible, however, to see the early efforts as providing an important base for the nationalist impulses that were to come.

10.2.2 Academies

The beginning of 'institutionalised' purism came with the establishment of the *Accademia della Crusca* in Florence in 1582.[6] It was, however, the *Académie française* (founded 1635) that set the pattern for many of the similarly inclined institutions that were to follow in Europe and beyond. In the beginning, the *Académie* addressed quite a small number of people, many of whom saw other languages as at least equal to French for cultured discourse. Its major aim was to reinforce its conceptions of linguistic clarity, simplicity and good taste, to encourage all that was 'noble, polished and reasonable' (Hall, 1974: 177). Most academicians were initially drawn from the church, the nobility or the top echelons of the army, the bodies that would naturally have been considered the inheritors of the best French and the obvious arbiters of good linguistic taste. From the beginning, professional linguists have rarely been members. Since the notion of language purity is a fiction anyway, there is in fact no pressing requirement for 'experts': intelligent, educated individuals from the professions, the literary world and politics are all reasonable people to have as members. However, since dictionary-making and the production of grammars *do* require specialist skills, it will come as no surprise to learn that the academy's first effort here (in 1694) was the inferior piece of work that might be expected from a group of dilettantes.

In modern times, the *Académie française* has become best known for its attempts to keep French free of foreign borrowings and to create where necessary French terms for the products and processes of science and technology. It has thus acquired a modernising function to supplement the original 'purifying' objective. The special aim of keeping English influence at bay began in the nineteenth century and has strengthened since then. Purification plus gate-keeping: these are obvious undertakings on behalf of the maintenance of group boundaries and identity. There is a French-Canadian version here: the *Académie des lettres du Québec*, founded by a group of writers in 1944 as the *Académie canadienne-française* (Barbeau, 1960; Royer, 1995). Although its goal was originally to defend the French language and culture in Canada, it is essentially a literary body, celebrating important francophone writers (including Gabrielle Roy, Germaine Guèvremont and Gilles Vigneault). A more recent establishment was the *Office québécois de la langue française*, also largely devoted to combatting English influence. An outside observer might think that this is an undertaking more relevant in Quebec than in France; after all, there are only about seven million Quebec francophones in a North America populated by fifty times as many anglophones. But if the *Québécois* face a situation much more obvious and immediate, francophones in l'hexagone have been sensitive for a very long time now about the steady retreat of their language and their cultural influence in a world made increasingly safe for English speakers. Such erosion may be harder to contemplate for those whose language once dominated global educated intercourse than it is for some of the other varieties now feeling anglophone pressures.

Similar in intent to the French academy, and much influenced by it, was the *Real Academia Española*, founded in 1713 by the Bourbon king Philip V. Its royal motto – '*Limpia, fija y da esplendor*' – emphasises again the desire to clarify, purify and glorify the language. A dictionary was produced in 1730, and a grammar in 1771. Much of the importance of the academy consists in the way in which it spread its influence to the Spanish New World, spawning associated academies in Colombia (in 1871), Mexico and Ecuador (1875), El Salvador (1880), Venezuela (1881),

Chile (1886), Peru (1887) and Guatemala (1888). In the twentieth century, further institutions were established in Bolivia, Costa Rica, Cuba,
Honduras, Panama, Paraguay, Puerto Rico and the Dominican Republic
(Guitarte and Torres-Quintero, 1974). Today, there exists a formal association of Spanish academies: its brief is to work for the unity of Spanish
and to enshrine historically based standards. It is important to realise
that these are not merely the aspirations of language 'dilettantes' or popular commentators; rather, they reflect the views of Spanish linguists. As
Quirk (1982) pointed out, there is an interesting difference in national
atttitudes between these hispanic professionals and their counterparts
in the English-speaking world, where national academies have not been
generally supported (see below).

Academies charged with maintaining linguistic standards exist far
beyond the Romance area. Arabic academies were established in Syria,
Iraq and Egypt (see Altoma, 1974); Jordan and Ethiopia also have language bodies. A German academy came into being in 1700, with Leibniz
as its first president; in 1743, it was reorganised, and renamed – as
l'Académie royale des sciences et belles-lettres (the French title is of course
significant). The Swedish academy was founded in 1786 by Gustav III, a
Hungarian body in 1830. A Committee for the Hebrew Language was founded
in 1890; in 1953 it became the Hebrew Language Academy (Nahir, 1977).
The Russian academy, like the Spanish, was modelled on the Académie
française, and produced both a dictionary and a grammar towards the
end of the eighteenth century (Anderson, 1991). Even in countries having no formal academy, other prescriptive bodies typically exist – in
Africa, for instance, where the academic task of language purification
has often been preceded by one of language selection. Jomo Kenyatta, acting as a one-man academy, proclaimed in 1974 that Swahili would be
the national language of Kenya: this was followed by the establishment
of the National Cultural Council. In Tanzania, the National Swahili Council
and the affiliated Institute for Swahili Research have acted in an 'academic'
capacity (see Eastman, 1983). Overall, as Mackey (1991: 55) has noted,
'there is hardly any country in the world that does not have some sort
of public or private language planning body'.

Conspicuous by its absence here is any English-language academy.
Quirk (1982: 68) has suggested that there is a longstanding Anglo-Saxon
aversion to 'linguistic engineering' and, indeed, a 'superior scorn' in attitudes to academies, bodies whose goals are seen to be 'fundamentally
alien' to anglophone conceptions of language. Referring, for example,
to the work of the various Spanish academies, Quirk believed that, while
their intention to maintain the unity of Spanish would not be questioned
in an English context – although it would not be copied, either – the

related aim of maintaining linguistic traditions 'would be totally unacceptable, if not incomprehensible'. Perhaps Quirk's perspective here is not entirely correct, however, or perhaps it reflects only a modern position emanating from the global power and strength of English.

There have, after all, been many proponents of an English academy. Richard Verstegan, who argued for the protection and encouragement of the language in his *Restitution of Decayed Intelligence* (1605), issued an early call of sorts for such a body. Later in the seventeenth century, several leading literary lights hoped to see one, and Thomas Sprat (1667) endorsed the hope in his (the first) history of the Royal Society. Baugh (1959: 318) reproduces part of a resolution adopted by the Society in 1664; it noted that, since

> there were persons of the Society whose genius was very proper and inclined to improve the English tongue, particularly for philosophic purposes, it was voted that there should be a committee for improving the English language.

A committee was in fact struck: its twenty-two members included Dryden, Evelyn and Waller. Nothing of substance, however, came of this committee, which might have become the cornerstone of a language academy; those members with intrinsic scientific interests became more and more absorbed in the explosion of natural science that was occurring at the time, and those who were more closely concerned with the intersection of language, identity and nationalism were left without a firm scholarly base (see Ayto, 1983).

A little later, Daniel Defoe proposed that England should follow the example of the French; a body should be established, he said, to

> encourage Polite Learning, to polish and refine the English Tongue, and advance the so much neglected Faculty of Correct Language, to establish Purity and Propriety of Stile, and to purge it from all the Irregular Additions that Ignorance and Affectation have introduc'd. (McArthur, 1992: 8; see also Baugh, 1959)

In a letter to the Lord Treasurer in 1712, Jonathan Swift also proposed the establishment of an academy dedicated to the 'correcting' and 'ascertaining' (i.e. 'fixing') of English (see Vallins, 1954). Swift felt that 'an Infusion of Enthusiastick Jargon' had come to infect English, and that the 'licentiousness' of the Restoration had corrupted the language. The chaos of spelling, the 'barbarous custom of abbreviating words' (like 'rebuk'd' for 'rebuked', or 'mob' for *mobile vulgus*), and the adoption of 'modish speech without regard to its propriety' all offended Swift. Overall, he complained that English was extremely imperfect; that its daily Improvements are by no Means in proportion to its daily Corruptions; that the Pretenders to polish and refine it have chiefly multiplied Abuses and Absurdities; and that in many Instances it offends against every Part of Grammar. (Crowley, 1991: 31)

Building as it did upon sentiments that were quite widely shared, Swift's proposal was initially well received in official quarters. His prescriptivist impulses, however, were allied to strong Tory principles, and when the Tories lost power in 1714, Swift's support evaporated. So, it would appear, did all serious hope of an English language academy.

10.2.3 Dictionaries

In both Britain and the United States, the production of dictionaries by individuals took the place of the institutional prescriptivist approach commonly found elsewhere. From the middle of the seventeenth century, English lexicographers knew all about the work of the French and Italian academies. Samuel Johnson, who published his famous *Dictionary of the English Language* in 1755 – often seen, not least by himself, as the English equivalent of the committee efforts of the continental academies – acknowledged them quite specifically. He held somewhat conflicting ideas of the function of his work. In his *Plan of a Dictionary* (1747), he supported the 'purity' function and, in the preface to the dictionary proper, he hoped that a work based upon the 'undefiled' English of prominent authors might stabilise the language and check its degeneration. At the same time, Johnson opposed an academy, which seemed to him contrary to the 'spirit of English liberty', rejected linguistic 'embalming' and implied that academies could not, in any case, prevent linguistic change (Heath, 1977). He did not agree with the sentiments of the Earl of Chesterfield, his rather tepid patron, who hoped that the lexicographer would be an 'absolute dictator of standards'. Dr Johnson seems to represent very well the general English ambivalence: on the one hand, the idea of some élite body imposing their will on the language was distasteful; on the other, the need for some guidelines was perfectly obvious, in an era when spelling and usage were fluid, and when language was seen as a potential servant in the cause of identity. Hence the one-man approach.

This approach also characterised the production of the next great English dictionary, the one that remains the standard: the *Oxford English Dictionary*. Work began on the 12-volume *OED* in 1857 and was only completed in 1928 (with a thirteenth, supplementary volume appearing in 1933; there have, of course, been further developments since then). The moving force here was James Murray, who, like Johnson before him, knew that dictionaries could only restrain change, not halt it: 'the pen must at length comply with the tongue; illiterate writers will...rise into renown, who, not knowing the original import of words, will use them with colloquial licentiousness, confound distinction, and forget propriety' (as Johnson wrote in his preface).

The lack of an English academy meant that, unlike France or Spain, England could not exert the same sort of uniform linguistic influence on its new-world colonies; it also suggests, of course, greater diffidence in exerting that sort of influence. There was in fact a less overt zeal for the proselytism which often acted in close association with the officialdom of the Latin counterparts. But this is certainly not to imply any general lack of confidence in the obvious merits of English civilisation and the English language; rather, like the Romans before them, these new imperialists felt that the superiority of their way of life hardly needed to be advertised: it was self-evident. There was, of course, the occasional reminder. When Thomas Macaulay became involved in a debate over the medium of instruction in British India, he produced his famous 'Minute on Education' of 1835, cited in Sharp (1920). While he was not, apparently, wholly disposed against the vernacular languages *per se*, he felt obliged to note:

> The claims of our own language it is hardly necessary to recapitulate. It stands preeminent even among the languages of the west...It may safely be said that the literature now extant in that language is of greater value than all the literature which three hundred years ago was extant in all the languages of the world together...The question now before us is simply whether, when it is in our power to teach this language, we shall teach languages in which, by universal confession, there are no books on any subject which deserve to be compared with our own (Sharp, 1920: 110)

As Anderson (1991: 86) has pointed out, Macaulay's hope was for the production of 'a class of persons, Indian in blood and colour, but English in taste, in opinion, in morals and in intellect'. Although somewhat more articulate, Macaulay's view was shared by many of the far-flung Victorian servants of empire. In some parts of the world, of course, English settlers, merchants and administrators did not come into contact with such 'developed' societies: in the Americas, in Africa and in the Antipodes, fewer attempts were made to co-opt the indigenous populations into the establishment.

When the United States became independent in 1776, it naturally inherited the British linguistic tradition. In considering language policy, then, it had no academy to consult directly and, as Heath (1977) points out, the Spanish and French models lacked appeal because of their association with 'crowned heads and royal courts'. While the American founding fathers often pointed to the advantages of multilingualism, they were nevertheless certain of the continuing dominance of English. This *de facto* status made official recognition unnecessary – there is still no official language in the United States – and an academy was not seen to be essential. The security of the language meant that settlements of non-English speakers were not seen as threats and, indeed, other languages were supported. For instance, Benjamin Rush proposed the establishment of a German college. His underlying rationale was an interesting one, however, and one that we have met before here: Rush felt that such an institution would make Germans appreciate the importance and utility of *English*, and might prove an expeditious, while democratic, way of spreading English competence among them (Heath, 1977).

Some Americans did favour the idea of an academy, the most prominent here being John Adams. Like Samuel Johnson before him, Adams felt that such a body could check the 'natural tendency' languages had to 'degenerate'. He also believed that, since England had no academy, there was an opportunity here for the United States to put *its* official stamp on linguistic purity and preservation. But Adams, often suspected of monarchist sympathies, had no success in moving Congress. There were societies, too, whose interests included language, most notably the *American Philosophical Society* (founded by Franklin in 1743) and the *American Academy of Arts and Sciences* (1780). The most directly relevant organisation, however, was the short-lived *American Academy of Language and Belles Lettres*. Like the *Académie française*, it was chiefly interested in standardisation and purity and, also like its French ancestor, it had an élitist membership largely without linguistic expertise. The founders were well aware of republican objections to a national language academy, but proceeded anyway. An example of the institution's determination and sense of rightness in the face of adversity can be seen in its statement that 'happily for us, our forefathers came chiefly from that part of England where their language was most correctly spoken' (Heath, 1977: 30). The members had no more success than had Adams in securing any official sponsorship, and their publications were characterised by 'hyperbole and empty rhetoric'. Generally, their endeavours reflected a common colonial tension between the desire to promote indigenous linguistic and literary models and a continued reliance upon those of the mother country.

In the United States, as in England, such language standardisation as occurred was essentially the result of one man's work, the American Johnson being, of course, Noah Webster. While acknowledging the need for some uniformities, Webster shared both Johnson's pragmatic perspective on linguistic change, and his modesty about the work of the lexicographer. Unlike Johnson, however, Webster had a more overtly political interest: he felt the need to contribute to the linguistic independence of the United States, a need that culminated in his *American Dictionary of the English Language,* published in 1828. He thought that Great Britain and the United States would become more and more linguistically separate, and that entirely different languages would eventually result. He was not at all opposed to this, for it reinforced his nationalistic feelings, and he was no doubt glad to be able to observe that, already, the American people spoke the purest English (see Drake, 1977). Earlier, in his *Dissertations on the English Language* (1789), Webster had urged spelling changes, and these were to signal the chief differences between American and British English (differences that persist today). His view was one that we have seen before: 'a national language is a bond of national union', it 'belongs' to the people, and its maintenance is their responsibility (Quirk, 1982: 65). Still, enamoured as he was of a new 'people's language', Webster (1783: 7) also saw part of his task as the removal of 'improprieties and vulgarisms ... and ... those odious distinctions of provincial dialects'. Old ideas die hard.

STUDY QUESTIONS

1. Why has language always been considered a central pillar – perhaps *the* central pillar – of nationalism?
2. What does the existence of prescriptivist academies, language councils and other similar institutions tell us about the language–identity relationship?
3. Is there such a thing as 'language decay'?
4. Can a case be made – at some time, perhaps, or in some circumstances – for linguistic prescriptivism?

Further reading

In John Edwards's (1995) *Multilingualism,* as part of a comprehensive review of multilingualism and its many ramifications, considerable attention is given to the language–nationalism relationship, and to the agencies committed to preserving and protecting the linkages between language and group identity.

Ralph Grillo's (1989) *Dominant Languages* provides some historical background to the dynamics of languages – and, therefore, identities – in contact.

Nils Langer and Winifred Davies's (2005) edited book, *Linguistic Purism in the Germanic Languages*, is a useful collection on the puristic impulses that so often arise from the language–nationalism linkage; the particular focus on Germanic languages does not detract from the more broadly generalisable value here.

George Thomas's (1991) *Linguistic Purism* is the single best monograph on the subject.

11　Language planning and language ecology

11.1 LANGUAGE PLANNING

As the previous discussion has shown, there are strong prescriptivist impulses underpinning the relationship between language and nationalism. But *all* forms of language planning are necessarily prescriptivist to some degree, since all planning presupposes intentions and desired outcomes. Consequently, all planning – not simply the puristic impulses we have just looked at – touches upon notions of identity. This psychosocial aspect is often part of a larger enterprise fuelled more directly and transparently by practical imperatives. For instance, the standardisation of the emerging national languages of Europe was a necessary development, particularly given the new requirements brought about by the growth of literacy and innovations in printing technology. Standardisation is not the only type of regulatory activity, however. In some societies, choices among different languages may be necessary, to select forms that will receive some legal imprimatur in education and officialdom (for example). Orthographies may have to be developed (or invented), lexicons may need to be modernised, and so on. When these matters demand attention, it is entirely reasonable that linguists – despite the general scholarly reluctance to prescribe, despite their sense that language change is a constant and natural process, despite their view that broad usage is the ultimate criterion of 'correctness' – would bring their skills to bear. Some have argued, indeed, that this is a duty, if for no other reason than that it can act to forestall other, less disinterested action.

Over the last few decades, language planning has become a formal topic within the sociology of language and applied linguistics; it is now an area with its own journals, books and conferences. The single most comprehensive overview remains that of Kaplan and Baldauf (1997), who are also the editors of the important journal, *Current Issues in Language Planning*. A more venerable publication is *Language Problems and Language Planning*, established in 1977, and many other journals publish articles having to do with language planning. It is, after all, a very broad area indeed, encompassing many topics: all facets of language-in-education can be considered under this rubric, as can language contact, conflict, survival, maintenance, spread, shift, revival and death.

The main features of language planning as an academic exercise were outlined by Haugen (1966) in a model having four aspects: norm selection, norm codification, functional implementation and functional elaboration. Here, selection and implementation (often called 'status planning') are extra-linguistic features, social in nature; codification and elaboration ('corpus planning'), on the other hand, deal directly with language itself. The operation of language planning along these lines is theoretically quite straightforward. A linguistic issue arises, such that a choice has to be made between or among varieties. Following this, standardisation can provide a written form, or regularise grammar, orthography and lexicon. Implementation involves spreading the variety through official pronouncements, education, the media, and so on. Various evaluation procedures are often employed at this stage to monitor the degree of acceptance of the chosen form. Finally, elaboration means keeping the language viable in a changing world; obvious necessities here include lexical modernisation and expansion. Haugen's classification overlaps to some degree with Nahir's (1977) discussion of the several aspects of language planning: purification, revival, reform, standardisation and modernisation. Haugen's model tends to stress the planning process *per se*, while Nahir focusses more upon applications.

In practice, language planning is far from straightforward. To begin with, the divisions drawn by Haugen and Nahir are neater on the page than they are in the field; see Edwards (1994b) and Williams (1986). As well, the purely linguistic aspects (codification and elaboration) of planning are less broadly important than the social ones (selection and implementation). In this sense, language planners essentially engage in technical activities *after* important decisions have been taken by others; these decisions are often politically motivated and may owe little or nothing to linguistics, history or, indeed, cultural equity. Matters of codification and elaboration certainly require a great deal of skill, but language planners should not delude themselves into thinking that they are prime movers. In fact, in some ears at least, language planning has an altogether too grandiose ring about it. While those involved usually realise that their work does not occur in isolation, they seem not always to appreciate the radical difference in magnitude between their contributions and those of the *real* planners – politicians, administrators, captains and kings.

Language planning, especially selection and implementation, is a heavily value-laden exercise. Any disinterested theorising becomes compromised in practice, and language planning is usually concerned with applications in highly controversial settings: the maintenance or revival of 'small' or endangered languages, the establishment of a lingua franca, the navigation of acceptable channels among large areas of linguistic diversity, and so on. Planning is inevitably coloured by ideological imperatives and what appears as progress to some may be persecution to others. If not from the beginning, then certainly at the point of application, language planning is subservient to the demands of non-academic interests with social and political agendas. As implied above, planners are often called in after the fact to work out the technical details for the implementation of policies desired by those in power. It is not language planners themselves, nor the results of academic argument, that typically sway the real policy makers. As in other areas of public life, 'experts' are called as needed, and their recommendations are either implemented or gather dust according to how well they support or justify desired positions. The language planner has been likened to the 'management scientist' who rarely makes real decisions but is, rather, employed to organise and analyse data. The real policy makers, those with the requisite political clout, may then balance this work with other important information. In the world of language planning, this other information usually encompasses far more than language alone.

All these points are familiar of course, even though there have been occasional scholarly attempts to defend a more 'scientific' status for language planning, at least at the level of theory (e.g. Cobarrubias, 1983a). But theorising can only remain value-free at the most abstract levels: its application immediately involves opinion and preference. Cobarrubias himself (1983b) felt obliged to admit that working for language change is not a neutral exercise, and planning is 'ultimately contingent upon' the ideological positions of those in power. Many leading lights have agreed. Haugen (1983) pointed out, for instance, that any theory of language planning was forced to 'take a stand' on values, and Neustupný (1983: 27) said that it was 'unrealistic to maintain that language planning theory could or should be a value-free politically neutral discipline . . . [it] has always been governed by socioeconomic value judgements'. Even Fishman (1983: 383), whose breathless endorsement of threatened languages often suggests some stand-alone possibilities for linguistic intervention, has pointed out that planning is secondary to more basic social currents, 'often but the plaything of larger forces'. Williams (1981: 221) bluntly argued that language planning is undertaken by those who have the power to do so, and that it is therefore 'designed to serve and protect their interests'. He was really only echoing the more general observation of Elie Kedourie (1960: 125), in a comment about the rationalisation of language borders:

> It is absurd to think that professors of linguistics and collectors of folklore can do the work of statesmen and soldiers. What does happen is that academic enquiries are used by conflicting interests to bolster up their claims, and their results prevail only to the extent that somebody has the power to make them prevail.

None of this means that professional linguistic assistance is trivial, and one certainly hopes that relevant expertise is drawn upon before important decisions are taken. But language planning is a species of social engineering and, as such, is commissioned and implemented by those in power. To succeed, of course, language planning does not solely depend upon the imprimatur of the powerful; it also requires acceptance from those whose linguistic habits are to be affected. Even the most dictatorial policies may result in social upheavals if they are repressive and/or unpopular enough. More benign policies, on the other hand, may languish due to misreading of the social context. There is in some sense, then, a natural check on the implementation of 'top–down' planning that fails to engage the sympathies of its intended recipients. Unfortunately, this may come too late to avoid distress or social disturbance, especially where the actions of policy makers are unfeeling, inadequate or otherwise deficient.

Although language planning has now 'come of age', in the sense that it has established itself as a category within the larger sociology of language literature, theory has tended to lag behind practices (see Jahr, 1992) – and these practices have, after all, been going on for a very long time. When Haugen (1983) reviewed his initial formulation, he found no compelling reason to substantially alter it. In 1983, Neustupný outlined a language planning 'paradigm', the key features of which emphasised 'problems' to be solved and methods of 'correction'. He also noted that theoretical advances would most probably reside in some typological approach. If this is the case, then we remain largely in a pre-theoretical phase, since most work is still of the case-study variety: the area awaits its Linnaeus. Edwards (2007b) has provided a summary of typological efforts in the area. This is not to say, of course, that careful descriptive work should be downgraded; indeed, one could argue that there has often been a premature social-scientific rush to immature and undoubtedly ephemeral theorising. Neustupný's summary points are apposite here: language planning is not a free-standing enterprise, to be understood only through attention to language itself; relatedly, it cannot be a value-free or sociopolitically neutral exercise or discipline.

In their useful overview, Kaplan and Baldauf (1997: 302) suggest that 'language planners' are caught somewhere between linguistic description and prescriptivism. On the one hand, they are now largely drawn from the scholarly ranks, and this implies a disinterested and dispassionate stance. On the other, their work 'contains a kernel of prescriptivism by definition'. As I have implied – as I will further illustrate – there is usually much more than a kernel here. Kaplan and Baldauf try to make the case that language planning is descriptive in its data-gathering mode but, beyond that, becomes prescriptive. This, I think, is already an admission of the heavy prescriptive weighting overall, since the activities that come after fact-finding (recommendations for action, selection of policies, implementation, review, and so on) consume much the greatest amounts of time and energy. Even the initial survey work, however, even the assembling of the necessary data, is initiated for reasons that are rarely dispassionate or apolitical. Kaplan and Baldauf recognise this themselves, for, shortly after saying that data-assembly is 'essentially descriptive', they point out that, even when most 'objective and disinterested, the language planner is not a pure descriptivist' (p. 303).

Language planning as a field is in fact so broad as to encompass virtually all aspects of the social life of language, as Kaplan and Baldauf's very long roster of topics and sub-topics indicates. *Any* application of *any* combination of linguistic and sociological matters can be placed under the heading. This is a useful reflection of reality, chaotic in tooth and claw, but it does pose serious difficulties for any tight definitions, for any meaningful or substantive theoretical statements. Furthermore, much of the wide and traditional language-planning perspective has now been translated and shrunk into the now trendy 'ecology of language'. Kaplan and Baldauf capture this translation very well in a diagrammatic representation of 'forces at work in a linguistic eco-system' (p. 311). This simply shows how existing concerns (for language death, change, revival, and so on) as expressed by various agencies (including government, education, community institutions) can easily be seen as facets of an ecological model. This comes at the beginning of a section entitled 'Towards a model for language planning', but the many details presented, as well as one or two further diagrams, only go to show the sprawling nature of any such 'model'.

11.2 THE ECOLOGY OF LANGUAGE

While I cannot go into all the detail that the area really deserves (for which see Edwards, 2002a, 2008), the prominence of the 'new ecology of language' demands at least some brief consideration here. Indeed, even a cursory look at the framework, the assumptions and the scope of this apparently new perspective will illuminate some of the more important features of the contemporary sociology of language, and will bear directly upon our language-and-identity theme. This section also allows me some brief scope to touch upon some important specifics: contact and conflict between 'large' and 'small' languages, minority-language dynamics, endangered varieties and language 'rights' among them. I call the perspective only 'apparently new', by the way, because nuanced investigations of the social life of language have always been ecologically minded, found under a number of related headings: applied linguistics, the sociology of language, geolinguistics, anthropological linguistics, and so on.

As a term and a focus of study, *ecology* is a mid nineteenth-century coinage of Ernst Haeckel and, as its Greek root (*οίκος* = 'home') implies, the emphasis is upon the holistic study of environments within which lives are lived and intertwined. Haeckel, Darwin's 'German bulldog', was concerned with the struggle for existence within the 'web of life', a struggle that includes both the beneficial and inimical inter-relationships among plants, animals and, indeed, inorganic surroundings: 'the totality of relations of organisms with the external world', as Haeckel put it (Hayward, 1995: 26). Ecology is about adaptations whose necessity arises from inevitable linkages. The most salient feature, then, of an ecological perspective is a concern for a 'big picture' that stresses connections and avoids narrow isolationism. Hayward (1995) compared 'ecological thinking' with 'enlightenment thinking', with the implication that what has worked so powerfully in contemporary physical science rests upon an analytical reductionism that may be inappropriate in other spheres. A familiar argument, for instance, holds that the imitation of natural-science methods in (say) the social sciences is a process driven more by envy than by utility. By contrast, the *gestalt* nature of ecology – dynamic, 'situated', interactive – with its commitment to 'complex wholes and systems', might prove more valuable in the arena of human behaviour (Garner, 2004: 37). It is certainly true that an 'atomistic materialistic ontology', as Hayward (1995: 29) so felicitously put it, has produced results more risible than reasonable in fields like social psychology. But it is an error of some magnitude to assume that an ecological perspective *per se* means some phenomenological rejection of an empirical mindset. After all, 'classical' science works with exactly the same sense of interconnectedness as any ecology; indeed, what could possibly be more ecological than the physicists' continuing search for a unified field theory, a 'theory of everything'? As well, even the most ecologically minded investigations have to engage in reductionism, if only for practical reasons. Informed holistic argument is well aware of this, and tries to establish a meaningful difference between the sort of anti-intellectual atomism that will never produce anything other than great piles of isolated 'findings' and the reasoned investigation that, while examining 'x', never loses sight of 'y' and 'z'. But this degree of nuance is largely lost on the 'new' ecologists, whose writings suggest only a very naive phenomenology.

The term 'ecology of language' is particularly associated with Einar Haugen (1972). His intent was to emphasise the linkages among languages and their environments, with particular regard to status and function. He produced a list of contextualising questions about who uses the language, its domains, varieties, written traditions and family relationships, degree and type of support it enjoys, and so on; for more details, and a typological expansion, see Edwards (1992). In themselves, these questions are neutral in tone. However, Haugen (1987: 11) went on to refer to a 'problem of *social ecology*: keeping alive the variety and fascination of our country, diverting the trend toward steamrollering everything and everyone into a single, flat uniformity'. Haugen did not mean to imply that 'social ecology' was essentially devoted to the promotion of diversity, simply that any such promotion would fall within its remit. As we shall see, however, the maintenance of diversity has come to be virtually synonymous with the new ecology of language.

The breadth of the ecology-of-language view, a breadth that would logically follow from its parent discipline, has been progressively reduced and the label of ecology increasingly co-opted.[1] To go back no further than Haeckel's formulation, ecology involves adaptation and struggle within an extremely broad range of relationships. While earlier 'non-interventionist' linguistic views often acknowledged a Darwinian sort of linguistic struggle, and while there are some contemporary researchers who would claim an ecological perspective that reflects a range of possibilities (from linguistic health all the way to extinction, perhaps), the field now generally argues for more pacific interaction. As Mühlhäusler (2000: 308) noted in a review article:

> functioning ecologies are nowadays characterized by predominantly mutually beneficial links and only to a small degree by competitive relationships ... metaphors of struggle of life and survival of the fittest

should be replaced by the appreciation of natural kinds and their ability to coexist and cooperate.

This is an inappropriate and unwarranted limitation; more reasonable, surely, is Mackey's (1980:35) earlier observation that linguistic environments (like all others) can be 'friendly, hostile or indifferent'. With the new ecology, then, we are given a view of a world in which there is room for all languages, where the goodness of diversity is a given, where 'the wolf also shall dwell with the lamb'. This is certainly a kinder and gentler picture, but surely the key word here is 'should', surely the key question is whether the desire is also the reality. We might remember Woody Allen's reworking of that passage from Isaiah: 'the lion and the calf shall lie down together, but the calf won't get much sleep'.

11.2.1 Language and biology

When Haugen began to popularise the term 'ecology' in the 1970s, the biological model that it brought to mind was not very popular among linguists. Haugen himself reminded his readers that its value was only metaphorical: it suggested some analogies between languages and organisms, it was a useful fiction with some possible heuristic value, but it ought not to be 'pushed too far' (Haugen, 1972: 58). Even Mühlhäusler (see below) has acknowledged that the ecological metaphor is not something to be understood 'in terms of truth conditions – a language is no more an ecology than a mental organ or a calculus' (see Fill and Mühlhäusler, 2001: 3). Nonetheless, unlike Garner (2004: 33), who wrote that an ecological metaphor for language is 'too limited and inconsistent to become a really useful tool', Mühlhäusler has argued that the metaphor helps 'in advancing a knowledge of human language . . . its potential is far from exhausted' (p. 3). I think, however, that this is a mistaken view, that the 'new' ecology of language provides no further insights, and represents in fact a limitation upon earlier and fuller understandings. Mühlhäusler was more accurate than he no doubt meant to imply when he suggested that metaphors are 'searchlights that selectively illuminate the terrain and leave others in the dark' (p. 3). Just so.

   The most basic problem with the biological approach to language is, quite simply, that language is not organic. Languages themselves obey no natural imperatives, they have no intrinsic qualities that bear upon any sort of linguistic survival of the fittest, they possess no 'inner principle of life'. As I pointed out in chapter 3, however, the biological metaphor has long been an appealing one, and its rejuvenation under the banner of the new ecology suggests that Aitchison's (2000) dismissal of the beans-and-chrysanthemums notion was a touch too hasty; see also Kibbee (2003) for further pointed criticism of the organic metaphor. A linkage between nature and culture, between what is provided and what is constructed, can be a valuable one in a world increasingly aware of environmental issues. The advantages of adding anxieties about language decline to concerns with pollution, loss of plant and animal habitats and industrial depredation seem obvious. While not without its difficulties, diversity can make the world richer and more interesting. If we intervene to save the whales, or to clean up oil spills, or to keep historic buildings from the wrecker's ball, or to repair and preserve rare books and manuscripts, then why should we not also stem language decline, ensure a future for all varieties, prevent larger languages from swallowing smaller ones, and so on? These are the sorts of useful questions that a biological metaphor can prompt.

Recent ecological arguments, however, have attempted to make the link between linguistic and other types of diversity much more than metaphoric. For instance, Harmon (1996) and others feel that there may be more than analogy between linguistic and biological diversity, that areas in the world rich in one are also extensive in the other, that the two diversities are 'mutually supportive, perhaps even coevolved' (Maffi, 2000a: 175). More pointedly still, Maffi (2000b: 17) suggested that 'the persistence of vigorous, thriving linguistic diversity around the world may afford us our best chance of countering biodiversity loss and keeping the planet alive and healthy'. Readers interested in these dubious, not to say bizarre, assertions can reflect on the relationships among 'endemic' languages, flora and fauna, as outlined in Skutnabb-Kangas (2002). Setting aside difficulties of measurement and interpretation, we should be reminded here of the classic principle that correlation need not imply causation.

Dubious argument apart, there is in any event a practical problem that purported linkages between animals and languages cannot overcome: it is much more difficult to maintain the latter than it is to preserve the former. I don't mean to say, of course, that saving rare species is easy. But, when we have been able to muster sufficient resources and to garner enough support, we *have* intervened with some success in the lives of snails and whales. We have passed regulations forbidding some sorts of hunting and fishing, and allowing stocks to recover. We have banned the importation of materials whose removal damages or impoverishes the environment elsewhere. We have outlawed clear-cutting and prescribed reforestation. It is clear enough that we haven't always done very well, that the environment continues to be harmed in important ways, and so on. But we have a potential level of control here that is impossible with human societies and their languages, unless we were willing to act in the dictatorial ways that are open to us with plants and animals.

Pennycook (2004) provides some careful notes on the difficulties associated with the preservation of languages, stressing particularly the problem of reconciling preservation with the dynamic nature of language and the undesirable levels of regulation that may be required to effect maintenance. (I recall here Weir's remark about the Irish *Gaeltacht* – Irish-speaking area – coming to resemble 'wild west reservations for the native Irish'; 1973: 91.) Pennycook makes a third point of interest too, one that has to do with the definition of just *what* is to be preserved. He cites Ammon's (2000) argument that 'inner-circle' English speakers should become more tolerant of non-native variation, and Phillipson's (2002: 169) apparent rejection of the point. In his review of an anthology (by Ammon himself), Phillipson observes that 'several of the articles by people for whom English is not the mother tongue contain language errors that affect comprehension'. This is a reasonable enough comment, it seems to me, but he goes on to add ' . . . as well as countless German-influenced forms that disrupt, without perhaps impeding, comprehensibility'. This is rather less reasonable, particularly in a world in which various 'localised' or 'indigenised' Englishes are increasingly accepted and, more particularly still, in the light of the 'new' ecology's vaunted respect and tolerance for linguistic diversity; see the recent treatments of 'Euro-English' by Mollin (2006) and Modiano (2007).

11.2.2 Human interference

A common ecological assumption is that it is human interference which necessitates ecological management and planning; 'healthy ecologies', we are told, are both 'self-organizing' and 'self-perpetuating', but 'human actions [can] upset the original balance' (Mühlhäusler, 2000: 310). Well, in what sphere of life have human actions *not* altered things? Indeed, what social spheres could there possibly be *without* such actions? This seems like lamenting the fact that we have two ears. We also note here the curiously static quality of much ecological thinking: the implication often seems to be that – once some balance is achieved, some wrong righted, some redress made – the new arrangements will, because of their improved moral basis, be 'self-perpetuating'. But history is the graveyard of cultures. It is naively selective to pay attention to some and not to others; see also my reference to the British Raj in chapter 8.

11.2.3 Literacy and education

Part of the ideological underpinning of the new ecology is a distrust of literacy and education, on the grounds that they often undercut the preservation of linguistic diversity. Indeed, it is sometimes argued that literacy promotion actually works against 'linguistic vitality'. Literacy is often seen as a sort of bully, then, in the same way that large languages are the villains, and small ones the victims: written varieties can push oral ones aside, writing is seen as sophisticated and, indeed, more likely to bear the truth, and so on. It is also sometimes seen as a sort of Trojan horse, with speakers of at-risk varieties lulled into a false sense of security once writing arrives. It is certainly reasonable to point out the cruel fallacy that literacy inevitably leads to social or political improvement, or to refer to the single-mindedness of literacy campaigns. It is also true that writing does not automatically augment veracity (do you believe everything you read in the papers?). It would surely be a dangerous instance of isolationism, however, to try and purchase language maintenance at the expense of literacy.

A broader, related point is the suggestion that formal education is not always the ally of enduring diversity and bilingualism, for it often has intrusive qualities, championing literacy over orality, and imposing foreign (i.e. western) values and methods upon small cultures. Again there is the idea of cultural bullying. It is not difficult to sympathise with laments about supposedly intrusive 'foreign' education paradigms but – given that all education worthy of the name is multicultural in nature – the argument may be self-defeating. Formal education necessarily involves broadening the horizons, going beyond what is purely local and 'traditional'. In an unequal world whose disparities create risks for languages, education will perforce become yet another evidence of those disparities. Those concerned with gaining a place in the media for minority languages have learned that the media are double-edged swords: while it is clear that access to them is important, they also facilitate the transmission of those larger influences upon decline. There are similar 'risks' associated with the medium of education.

11.2.4 Linguistic diversity

When we turn to matters under this heading, we turn to the philosophical heart of the new ecology. To speak of language diversity and its maintenance in the modern world is to speak of the power of English, the contemporary linguistic steamroller (to use Haugen's term). The global scope of English is of the greatest importance, and discussions of it are very animated. This is not solely because of the *fact* of the spread and penetration of the language but also because of disagreements over the degree (if any) of intentionality fuelling that spread. In the fevered imaginations of some writers in the area, there has been a virtual conspiracy at work here. Such an understanding fails on a number of counts: first, on the invocation of Occam's razor; second, on any sensitivity to historical precedent; third, on any informed awareness of the interconnectedness of all strands in the sociopolitical fabric.

A preference for diversity, linguistic and otherwise, is one that I share; indeed, I find it difficult to imagine that any educated perspective would vote for monotony over colour, for sameness over variety. But to see the new ecology as largely undergirded by this preference is not only to criticise its rather more grandiose assertions; it is also to suggest that the old difficulties in maintaining endangered languages have not, after all, been lessened through new insights. These difficulties, after all, have been heightened and exacerbated in modern times, as more and more languages and language domains fall under the shadow of English. There are two essential questions here. First, on what basis is linguistic diversity a good and valuable thing? The answer involves that preference for heterogeneous landscapes just noted, an aesthetic appreciation that values multidimensionality. Preference alone, of course, is not the nub of the matter, nor should it be, at least not in scholarly discussion. It is necessary to construct arguments that reinforce and buttress preference and, indeed, go beyond it; and those who associate themselves with the new ecology do indeed attempt such constructions. But, before turning to these, I should like to make a little aside. Could some (much?) of the impetus fuelling preferences for diversity derive from guilt? I am surely not the only one to have noticed how many of the discussions emanate from outside the communities concerned, how many of those arguing for the maintenance of threatened varieties do so from the most secure of personal linguistic bases (sometimes, indeed, finding expression in quite prestigious accents). Orwell, as usual, had something apposite to say in this connection:

> It cannot be altogether an accident that nationalists of the most extreme and romantic kind tend not to belong to the nation they idealize ... not merely the men of action, but even the theorists of nationalism are frequently foreigners. (1944/1970: 208)

Perhaps some of the guilt – if guilt there be – represents a developed-world reflex when confronted with social situations so much less attractive than one's own. This might be seen as a reasonable response, especially since the privileged positions of the few have historically rested upon the less appealing positions of the many. Isn't it rather disingenuous not to acknowledge such motivations, however, and aren't they more likely to persist because of their cathartic value than because of any useful consequences for the intended beneficiaries?[2]

The second question has to do with the conditions necessary for diversity to thrive. More pointedly, how might endangered languages best be supported? One would certainly be more indulgent towards the formal shortcomings of the 'new' ecology if its assumptions and its programmes actually seemed to make a difference on the ground. In fact, however, these shortcomings only serve to highlight difficulties that have been quite well understood for some time. Most of these can be summarised by observing that, unless one is interested only in some archival embalming, the maintenance of languages involves much more than language alone. To put it another way: the conditions under which a variety begins to suffer typically involve a stronger linguistic neighbour and, hence, language endangerment is best understood as a *symptom* of bigger things, a particular sort of fall-out from a larger collision. Acknowledgement of this simple and indisputable statement of affairs must surely suggest the scope of the difficulties commonly encountered.

'Language loss' is something of a misnomer. Although varieties have certainly disappeared, their *speakers* are never at a *loss* and, during the shift from one medium to another, very few individuals actually say nothing. But the idea of some absolute loss typically underpins arguments in support of the maintenance of diversity. It is easy to find expressions that make an oversimplified connection between one – and only one – language and a given environment; for obvious reasons, such expressions often have a romanticised tinge. Here, for example, is Garner (2004: 237–8):

> The huge majority of languages are [sic] spoken by small communities with an intimate relationship to their physical environment, for example in the jungles of South America and the arid lands of Australia. If the language which expresses that relationship dies, so does the understanding of the environment and the knowledge of how to live in harmony with it.

It is sometimes denied that there is any linguistic determinism behind such observations. Garner himself makes the sensible point, for instance, that the Dubliner who speaks no Irish ('Erse', to cite Garner's quaint terminology) can be just as Irish as the inhabitant of the deepest *Gaeltacht*; well, just as Irish ... but different. Still, it is not unreasonable to see a species of Whorfianism animating the sorts of sentiments expressed and implied in the quotation above. And the larger point is this: there is surely an irony in an ecology allegedly sensitive to *dynamic* interconnectivities that so often seems to be resting upon a philosophy of stasis. Mufwene (2002: 176–7) points out the curious tendency to decry the loss of 'ancestral cultures, as if cultures were static systems and the emergence of new ones in response to changing ecologies was necessarily maladaptive'. The determinism that goes hand-in-hand with such a static view reflects the mistaken sense that 'only one language can best mirror or convey a particular culture' (pp. 177–8).

Despite the vaunted accuracy, value and morality of the 'new ecology', it is clear that our understanding of linguistic diversity and, in particular, of linguistic endangerment has not been enhanced. Like Pennycook (2004: 214), I am dubious about the 'bright new dawn of language policy' that contemporary ecology purportedly represents. We are no nearer a strong logical base for the support of diversity, nor are we any closer to effective methods of maintenance, methods that are neither too draconian or undemocratic, nor workable only in highly restricted contexts. And there may be deeper waters here, too. Putting aside the unprecedented strength and scope of English in the current linguistic and cultural climate, for instance, history suggests an ebb and flow in matters of diversity and uniformity. Just as the power of Latin, which must have been seen in some quarters as a linguistic assassin, eventually spawned a renewed heterogeneity, so some contemporary opinion holds that linguistic globalisation stimulates counter-moves in support of local identities: consider the growth of indigenised 'Englishes', for example.

Revenons à nos moutons. The new ecology takes linguistic diversity as an unalloyed good, to be defended wherever it seems to falter. It is a perspective implicit in recent language-rights manifestos, covenants and declarations. These have a chequered provenance, make several sorts of linguistic claims, and have received various degrees of official response. Beyond the legalistic approach of formal proclamations, however, there are several bases upon which a defence of diversity can rest – among these are moral, scientific, economic and aesthetic foundations. Apart from assumptions of inherent language rights (see below), the morality of diversity suggests that language attrition means loss of accumulated experience and knowledge. Secondly, it is argued that multilingual societies reach higher levels of achievement, and that linguistic 'encounters' aid scientific advance. This in turn suggests that language diversity is economically beneficial and that emphasis placed upon lesser-used varieties will prove more worthwhile than simply broadening the base of those who learn 'big' varieties. Finally, an aesthetic appreciation values all diversity, and regrets all loss. The moral argument is the most interesting one here, while the others can be dealt with quite briefly. Scientific arguments that repertoire expansion involves enhanced intellectual capacity, for instance, are not proven; and, as for diversity *per se* aiding discovery, it could just as easily be said that language differences typically constitute a barrier to international exchange. Economic ratio-nales for diversity are even harder to sustain. This is clearly the case at 'macro' levels, but social costs and social responses are, after all, built upon individual coral. And the aesthetic argument, one that holds diver-sity valuable beyond any crass instrumentality? Although educated the-ses (by Matthew Arnold and John Stuart Mill, among others) have been made for the propriety and elegance of uniformity, perhaps it would be churlish to advance any alternatives here; indeed, on logical grounds, it may be pointless. *De gustibus*, and so on.

As with the other arguments, the more interesting moral 'case' is a debatable one. Dixon (1997:144) has suggested that 'once a language dies, a part of human culture is lost forever', and this is of course true if one accepts that the language itself is the part that is lost. The sugges-tion, of course, implies more than that, but there is no evidence for such a point of view, nor, indeed, *could* there be any such evidence. Nonethe-less, Skutnabb-Kangas has written that, while 'traditional' knowledge might 'linger' after language shift, 'the richness and diversity of that knowledge cannot survive even one generation of language loss' (2000: 259). Phillipson (1992: 166) has even asserted that the spread of English entails the 'imposition of new mental structures'. Putting aside the last strange point altogether, we might ask if the insights of the Greeks and the Romans have, in fact, disappeared completely; is their 'world view' gone forever? Of course, theirs was a literate world, one that left records of itself; so, perhaps some might think that fairer examples of language-loss-as-knowledge-loss should refer to 'small' languages with only oral traditions. If, for the sake of argument, we were to accept that when *they* go they do take most of their particular cultural insights with them, wouldn't this be a rationale for the promotion of literacy? Recall at this point, however, the ecological stance on literacy sketched in the preceding section.

Overall, then, the defence of linguistic diversity is not as straightfor-ward as some might imagine. As part of a scholarly exchange, Ladefoged argued that 'statements such as "just as the extinction of any animal species diminishes our world, so does the extinction of any language" are appeals to our emotions, not to our reason' (1992: 810). Does this suggest that the case for diversity has no basis at all? Quite the contrary. But it is important to see on what base it really rests and this, I think, is clear, even if it is not always presented to us clearly or directly. It is a base constructed of perceptions of morality and aesthetic preference. These are the essential animating articles of faith that underpin all 'new' eco-logical expression. The first, which is itself predicated upon arguments about human rights or, sometimes, *ius naturale*, is more debatable than the second, where the non-rational nature of *de gustibus* is in fact its strongest element.

11.2.5 Language rights

Any discussion of the 'moral' foundations of the new ecology quickly brings up the matter of linguistic human rights. Ecological organisations formed expressly for the protection of endangered languages (the American *Terralingua* society, for example, or the *Foundation for Endangered Languages*, based in the UK) typically have a charter or a statement of intent stressing linguistic rights. The former, for instance, observes that 'deciding which language to use, and for what purposes, is a basic human right' (Terralingua, 1999). As well, existing language associations have argued for rights; thus, the *Teachers of English to Speakers of Other Languages* organisation (TESOL) passed a resolution in 2001 asserting that 'all groups of peoples have the right to maintain their native language . . . a right to retain and use [it]'. The other side of the coin, they argue, is that 'the governments and the people of all countries have a special obligation to affirm, respect and support the retention, enhancement and use of indigenous and immigrant heritage languages'. Such specialised manifestos typically model themselves upon charters endorsed by the United Nations, the European Union and other international bodies.

There are many problems associated with language rights. Government resolutions and charters, for example, are often outlined in a manner so general as to be virtually useless. There are often reasons for cynicism, too, for believing that official commitments remain solely at the level of lip-service. As well, while many modern governments are more tolerant of diversity now than they have been in the past, toleration need not imply positive action, and arguments linking linguistic uniformity with efficiency, and about the need for one language to bind disparate groups within state borders, are still frequently encountered. Consequently, supporters of language rights generally report finding existing legislation to be inadequate, and no sort of guarantee of protection.

Beyond official cynicism, or a reluctance to act based upon immediate and mercenary assessments, there are deeper issues. Language rights are usually meant to have an effect at the group level; indeed, their existence is generally motivated by the plight of small groups whose languages and cultures are at risk. This may sit uneasily with traditional liberal-democratic principles that enshrine rights in individuals, not collectivities. This is not the place for fuller discussion, but it should be noted that broader matters of pluralist accommodation in societies that are both democratic and heterogeneous – language rights are obviously a subset of concern here – are now of the greatest importance. They have become part of the province of political philosophy, for instance, which implies a very welcome breadth of approach, a search for cross-society generalities, an escape from narrower and intellectually unsatisfying perspectives (some of which, indeed, have been little more than outbreaks of special pleading); see, for example, Rawls (1999), Dworkin (2000), Taylor (1992, 1994) and Kymlicka (1995a, 1995b). The discussions here, whatever their specifics, and however their strengths and weaknesses may be perceived in different quarters, all suggest that any isolated statement or claim of language rights is simplistic and unprofitable.

There are even more basic issues with which the framers of language-rights manifestos rarely engage: do rights *exist* and, if they do, what sorts of things are they? Perhaps there are no rights; perhaps there are only cultural claims. This is a line of argument taken by Kukathas (1992), for example, and a brief overview by Brumfit (2001) brought the matter squarely to language rights. At the moment, he pointed out, these are typically assertions of things that ought to be, rather than statements which, through general agreement, have become objectified (usually in legal terms). Rights to language, then, are typically not of the same order as, say, those that proclaim freedom from slavery. While legal rights imply moral ones, the reverse does not necessarily hold, although what is merely desirable today may of course become lawfully codified tomorrow. The difficulty for moral claims is to effect this transition. For now, at least, this has generally not occurred, and it is disingenuous to imply that *claims* are sufficient to somehow give language rights the same strength of footing as those rights underpinned by criminal or civil codes.[3] And there is, above all else perhaps, a powerful practical matter to be faced here. While it is possible to legislate rights of language expression, it is rather more difficult to legislate rights to be *understood*; typically, this has occurred only in very limited domains (in selected dealings with civil services, for example), not in the vast unofficial ones where languages really rise or fall.

11.2.6 The romantic perspective

The perspectives on language diversity and its inherent 'rightness' suggest a rejuvenation of those romanticised nationalistic assertions already touched upon. This sense is reinforced when we find that current ecological models tend to identify some types of political villains more readily than others: unrestrained free-market capitalism, unfettered industrialisation, galloping globalisation. And, just as eighteenth-century romanticism was a reaction to more enlightened thought, so it has again become possible to find disparagement of the scientific culture and concern for the 'privileging' of its knowledge over 'folk

wisdom'. There is a special regard for 'small' cultures and local knowl-
edges, and it takes two forms: first, a simple, straightforward and,
indeed, perfectly reasonable desire for the survival of such cultures and
systems; second, the argument that they are in some ways superior to
larger or broader societies and values. This view is generally expressed
in some muted fashion, but occasionally the mask slips:

> without romanticizing or idealizing the indigenous cultures, it is clear
> that they are superior to the mass culture because their members
> retain the capability of living in at least relative harmony with the
> natural environment. (Salminen 1998: 62)

Despite the half-hearted disclaimer, this is romanticism *tout court*. Or
consider this dedicatory line in a recent anthology: 'to the world's indigenous and traditional peoples, who hold the key to the inextricable link
between [*sic*] language, knowledge and the environment' (Maffi, 2001).

A dislike of the contemporary world is often the background, in
fact, for arguments on behalf of 'indigenous' cultures. Polzenhagen
and Dirven (2004: 22) thus discuss the 'pronounced anti-globalisation,
anti-Western and anti-Cartesian' stance of the romanticised ecology-of-
language model. The disdain for modernity naturally extends to the scientific culture generally, indeed to the generalities and 'universals' that
many would see as the pivots of progress. A representative comment,
reminiscent of the views of Fishman that I have already reproduced (see
chapter 8), is provided by Chawla (2001: 118): 'Indians have traditionally treated the inanimate and animate world with awe and concern
in ways that do not indiscriminately damage the natural environment'.
Two points can be made whenever we encounter such sentiments. First,
as briefly outlined in chapter 2, there is a great deal of evidence that
'indigenous' peoples can be as profligate as any contemporary urbanite
when opportunity and circumstance permit. Second, even if aboriginal
societies *were* the sensitive stewards of nature they are so often depicted
to be, this says nothing about the goodness of their languages, nor of any
connection between those varieties and concepts uniquely expressible
in and through them.

The unrealistic and potentially harmful romanticism that lies behind
arguments for 'small' languages and cultures has been analysed in a
recent chapter by Geeraerts (2003). He does overstate his case a little:
his contrast between 'language-as-communication' (central to rational
thinking) and 'language-as-expression-of-identity' (the underpinning of
romanticism) is too neat. It could be argued, after all, that speakers in
many majority-language 'mainstream' settings can have their linguistic
cake and eat it too: the language that carries their culture, traditions

and literature is also the language in which they do their shopping. But Geeraerts's observations on romanticised ecologies are accurate and timely. He discusses the assumptions made about the equivalence of all cultures, about the goodness of diversity and about global English as international oppressor. In this last connection, Polzenhagen and Dirven (2004) have reminded us that the sanction of Standard English in the educational system and in other important social arenas has attracted similar accusations of oppression and social exclusion. Yet, just as one could argue that Standard English actually levels a very bumpy playing field, so the use of English as lingua franca in non-native contexts may permit a desirable unity of action – in movements for national liberation, for instance. Thus, Canagarajah (1999a: 207; see also 1999b) has argued that the linguistic-imperialism model neglects its contribution to 'modifying, mixing, appropriating, and even resisting discourses'.

Geeraerts's most valuable contribution, however, lies in the historical tracing of the romantic and rationalist perspectives. This enables him to place some of the current ecological thinking firmly in a context that includes some matters we have already touched upon here: the linguistic philosophies of Herder and Condillac, the *Dialektik der Aufklärung*, the competing claims of civic and ethnic nationalism (*Staatsnationalismus* and *Volksnationalismus*) and modern tendencies to either globalisation or what Geeraerts refers to as post-modern awareness. Enlarging upon this, Polzenhagen and Dirven (2004: 9) go on to discuss some of the insights of Mufwene (2001, 2002); their characterisation of his sensible position – 'he adopts much of the ecology-of-language view and, to a significant degree, the biological metaphors of language, but incorporates many of the rationalist arguments' – reflects a reasonable and appropriate stance, one that is regrettably rare.

11.2.7 The 'new' ecology in summary

The 'new' ecology of language is not so much a refinement of scientific methodology in the face of new understandings and new challenges as it is a sociopolitical ideology. Phillipson and Skutnabb-Kangas (1996: 429) point out that 'the ecology-of-language paradigm involves building on linguistic diversity worldwide, promoting multilingualism and foreign language learning, and granting linguistic human rights to speakers of all languages'. Mühlhäusler (1996: 2) says that language ecology implies that linguists become 'shop stewards for linguistic diversity'. These sentiments may suggest many things, but they do not imply disinterested scholarship.

It is interesting that an ecology that, by its nature, ought to be multi-faceted, inclusive and, above all, aware of nuanced perspectives, should often see things in simplistic or dichotomous ways, should often construct inflexible and monochromatic outlines. Skutnabb-Kangas (2002; see also Phillipson, 2003), for instance, has provided a table in which ten factors are listed for each of two 'paradigms': a diffusion-of-English model and an ecology-of-language one. Every item noted for the first is negative; every one of the ten 'ecological' factors is positive. The ecological thrust means multilingualism and diversity, communicative equality, economic democratisation, resource redistribution, and so on. The spread of English, on the other hand, is associated with linguistic imperialism and genocide, subtractive bilingualism, cultural homogenisation and capitalism. (Also to be found on this negative side of the ledger, interestingly enough, are 'rationalisation based on science and technology' and 'modernisation and economic efficiency'.) Monolingualism is also found in the negative column. Elsewhere, Skutnabb-Kangas (2000: 248) has discussed 'monolingual stupidity' and has argued, in characteristically temperate manner, that

> like cholera or leprosy, monolingualism ... is a dangerous illness ... its promotion is dangerous for peace in the world. The center of the contaminated area is Europe ... [which] has been particularly successful in contaminating the ex-colonies of European states.

Mühlhäusler (2000) has also given us a couple of lists: a dozen points of contrast between what he terms 'segregational linguistics' (old and bad) and the 'ecological paradigm' (new and good), and ten statements describing the ambit and the underpinnings of the latter. These are interesting because they summarise the ecological enterprise and expose its chief assumptions and concerns. Many of the statements, however, are naive or questionable (e.g. 'the non-cognitive functions of language are primary' or 'ecological language planning encourages permeable boundaries'), while others are unoriginal or truistic (e.g. 'languages are an integral part of larger communication processes' or 'language planning requires attention to the overall physical and cultural ecology'). Such summaries and dichotomies are, in themselves, surely illustrative of underlying thought processes.

My critical remarks here are not directed at ecology *per se*, of course, for who could gainsay its essential elements? But I think that the underlying ideology of the 'new' ecology of language is insufficiently examined and, in fact, builds in various assumptions as if they were unremarkable, and beyond enlightened debate. While some of its underpinnings may be appropriate in some cases, there can be little doubt that a wholesale acceptance of them would be both unwise and counterproductive.

Endangered languages, and the identities with which they are associated, are of obvious interest to linguists, and a number of linguists
now seem more or less committed advocates in the service of language
maintenance. This is a change from earlier hands-off postures that traditionally held it to be neither appropriate nor feasible to intervene in the
social life of language; the work of academies, for example, was regularly
interpreted as psychologically understandable but linguistically naive.
The older view remains, however, more appropriate than many modern commentators would have us believe, and the material presented
in this section surely testifies to that. Beyond the specifics, the most
general flaw in the 'new' ecological stance is the discussion of language
as if it were a free-standing phenomenon that could and would respond
to focussed intervention. This is plainly not the case, particularly since
wholesale social reworking is too revolutionary for modern ecolinguists:
they want only some selected sociopolitical adjustments. This is always
a difficult undertaking, and generally an unworkable one. To intervene
on behalf of a threatened minority language, for instance, while leaving
more or less intact all the other aspects of social evolution that link
the community in desired and desirable ways with the wider world, has
generally resulted in failure.

The 'new' ecology of language is now very much a growth industry,
but it is hard to see that it has done anyone any good – except, of
course, for those scholars who have found ample opportunity for publishing arguments on the side of the angels, and for fostering debate,
if only amongst themselves. The latter outcome is of course a common
one across all sorts of scholarly discourse, but there is surely a special poignancy here, inasmuch as virtually all the writing is presumably
meant to have applied value, intended to make a real contribution to the
lives of those whose 'small' languages and cultures are overshadowed by
large and overbearing ones. While it is an acknowledged duty of intel-
lectuals to avoid over-simplification, to search out explanatory nuance,
to probe with scholarly lancets and not with the blunter instruments
wielded in less sophisticated or disinterested quarters, I am tempted to
say that a great deal of the research effort here has been misguided,
disingenuous, or both.

11.3 THE CONSEQUENCES OF BABEL

I turn here – at the end – to the simple facts that there are many languages in the world, and that this has all sorts of consequences for
'groupness'. Some of these have already been touched upon in these
pages, while others deserve fuller treatments that I cannot provide here

(see Edwards, 2007c). For instance, it would be entirely appropriate here to discuss the methods traditionally employed to bridge language gaps. There is translation, for instance. It is quite obvious that calling upon the services of translators and interpreters makes sense. It is perhaps less obvious that the consequences for group identity may not always be positive. The translator is one whose linguistic competence provides entry to two or more language communities, and we have already noted the worry that important elements of 'groupness' may be taken across the frontier, and shared more widely than members might like. Identity and its components may not always be secret matters, but they are always family matters; see also below.

Other bridges across linguistic chasms involve the several types of lingua franca: pidgin and creole varieties are to be found under this heading, as are 'artificial' or constructed languages like Esperanto. Most important, of course, are the large 'natural' varieties – Greek, Latin, French, Arabic, Italian, English and others – that have historically functioned as 'languages of wider communication'. *All* categories here are relevant to discussions of identity. Pidgins, for instance, typically have only limited and purely instrumental uses. When the settlements that first gave rise to them achieve some permanence, however, and when (particularly) children begin to arrive in pidgin-dominated communities, then the stage is set for pidgins to become more developed, to take on more and more of the attributes of fully fleshed mediums. Pidgins become creoles; nobody's mother tongue becomes somebody's mother tongue. And the circle continues when creoles then come into contact with other languages, and new pidgins are spawned (Edwards, 1985). As to the identity-carrying potential of constructed languages like Esperanto and Ido: this has traditionally been described as absent. Steiner (1992: 494) wrote that such varieties are disqualified from anything but 'trivial or *ad hoc* usage' because they lack any 'natural semantics of remembrance'. But theoretically there is no reason why a beginning could not be made here, why a constructed language could not bear speakers' identity. Indeed, there are some children who are, today, being brought up as native speakers of Esperanto. There is, however, a very large gulf indeed between what is possible and what is likely; see Edwards (in press b).

Central to the theme of this book are two matters arising from cultural and linguistic contact. When 'big' languages threaten smaller ones, and when cultural identities are seen to be at risk of being swamped or assimilated into larger units, a number of entirely predictable linguistic reactions occur – or would, if resources and circumstances permitted. Attempts will be made to preserve and protect a language that has traditionally been the carrier of group identity; resistance will be mounted to the pressures for language shift that follow cultural contact with larger or materially more attractive societies; and, where language shift is underway, efforts will be made to revive or resuscitate the flagging variety. All of this may take place at the level of language, but it is driven by the identity of which that language is considered to be a chief buttress. Hence, the most important features here are symbolic and cultural rather than pragmatic or instrumental: people go to the barricades over ideas, not over tools. It can also be understood that, in language-shift and language-maintenance scenarios, minority groups and their plights – real or imagined, grassroots or manipulated – naturally occupy centre stage.

Indeed, the awareness of language and cultural issues is part of any definition of 'minority group'. At the same time, any consideration of minority groups in isolation from the larger communities in whose shadows they must exist can obviously tell only half the story, at best. To reiterate an earlier point: the conditions under which a language begins to suffer, the conditions under which people begin to think about such things as language shift, maintenance, decline, death and revival, always involve a stronger linguistic neighbour. For general treatments of language spread, decline and revival, see Edwards (1985 and 1995: particularly chapters 3 and 4, respectively); for a more focussed consideration of endangered languages, and language revival, see Edwards (2007b); and, for specific discussions and categorisations of minority groups and their languages, see Edwards (1997b, 2004a). All of these phenomena have implications for identity and attempts to shore it up in the face of danger. While the specificities are many, the important generalities have already been touched upon in earlier sections of this book: they all revolve around the relationship between language and group identity, and they will be thrown into greater and more dramatic relief when social systems of unequal clout come into contact, or conflict. Such heightened salience always involves minority–majority encounters, because points of contact in which one party is stronger than another generally cast things in such frameworks. Mere numbers, of course, typically take a back seat to other manifestations of dominance and subordination.

11.4 BILINGUALISM AND IDENTITY

One of the most obvious consequences of a multiplicity of languages – and one of the most interesting from the point of view of *identity* – involves bilingual (or multilingual) adaptations.

Old ideas that bilingualism meant a splitting of finite cognitive potential or, worse, a diminution of intellectual capacities, have long since
been retired by research. The contemporary wisdom is that bilingualism does not mean loss; indeed, some have argued that increases in
linguistic repertoire correlate with heightened sensitivity, enhanced
cultural awareness, perhaps even greater cognitive flexibility and all-
round *nous*. Studies in language acquisition, particularly those focusing
upon very young children, demonstrate the ease with which varieties
can be added, or learned simultaneously with others. Academic and popular treatments devoted to the production and maintenance of bilingual
children abound; again, there is little suggestion of any cognitive price
to be paid for this in normal circumstances. Simply put, bilingualism
(or multilingualism, of course) is an ability possessed by the majority
of human beings – most of them relatively uneducated, many of them
illiterate – an ability almost effortlessly acquired by the youngest of
them.

There is an extensive literature on bilingualism, and it is largely concerned with the variations among linguistic gears and axles occasioned
by bilingual competence (see Edwards, 1995). These technicalities, however, do not fully explain the topic's interest and appeal. To approach
this, we have to move beyond language itself, beyond developmental
psycholinguistics, beyond experimental studies and educational programmes that illuminate and facilitate repertoire expansion. We have
to go beyond instrumental matters altogether, and consider issues of
psychology and sociology, of symbol and subjectivity. In a word, we
must think about the relationship between language and identity, and
how this relationship may alter when more than one variety is involved.

Speaking a particular language means belonging to a particular
speech community; speaking more than one may (or may not) suggest variations in identity and allegiances. Much of interest here rests
upon arguments about the degree to which bilinguals possess either two
(theoretically) separately identifiable systems of language, from each of
which they can draw as circumstances warrant, or some more intertwined cognitive-linguistic duality. As Hamers and Blanc (2000) point
out, we are far from having compelling empirical data here. Whether
we are interested in verbal communication, its paralinguistic accompaniments or the broader reaches of personality traits generally, we
find very little experimental evidence. It is interesting that, in their
magisterial overview of bilingualism, Baker and Jones (1998) give only
six pages (out of more than 750) to a discussion of personality. But
although the contemporary research literature may not be very enlightening about issues that may be relevant for the construction of bilingual

identities, there *are* some interesting speculations that bear upon the matter.

Consider, for instance, the view that bilinguals must have some sort of split mentality: two individuals in one, as it were. Grosjean (1982) and others have reported that bilinguals themselves sometimes feel that language choice draws out, and draws upon, different personalities. But the evidence is anecdotal at best, and indeed there are obvious logical and rational difficulties which any two-in-one arrangement would create. There is, however, evidence that language choice may implicate different *aspects*, at least, of the personality: bilinguals responding to interviews and questionnaires are liable to give slightly different pictures of themselves, depending upon the language used. They may make different responses to objective or projective probes, responses may be more emotional through one variety (typically, but not inevitably, their maternal language) and, in fact, they may more strongly affirm their sense of ethnic identity in one language than in another (see the several studies discussed and summarised by Hamers and Blanc). The fact that different social settings and variations in language–affect linkages lead to different patterns of self-presentation clearly does not imply separate personalities, although it does suggest an enhanced repertoire of possibility.

Some older speculations, as well as continuingly popular ideas, have been rather more pointed. Leonard Bloomfield, the eminent philologist and structural linguist, described White Thunder, one of his native informants, as lacking an adequate grasp of both of his languages: '[he] speaks less English than Menomini, and that is a strong indictment, for his Menomini is atrocious . . . he may be said to speak no language tolerably' (1927: 437). Most linguists today would deny this 'semilingualism', but Bloomfield's notion is still reflected in contemporary descriptions like *Franglais*, or *Japlish*, or *Tex-Mex*, descriptions that imply that the speakers are just like White Thunder. One may imagine that these are the prejudices of monolinguals, but bilinguals too have been wont to see their 'mixed' linguistic behaviour as embarrassing, lazy or bastardised. However, when they are asked why this behaviour persists, they typically give reasons having to do with choosing some particularly apposite *mot juste*, helping a listener understand more quickly and fully, strengthening feelings of friendship and intimacy, and so on. In other words, their practices, known in the literature under headings like code-mixing, code-switching and borrowing, are entirely reasonable. If a speaker has two or more languages to draw upon, it makes good sense to maximise the usefulness of this happy circumstance. But the old misunderstandings still crop up, sometimes in rather unexpected quarters.

In his amusing account of travels round Britain, Paul Theroux (1984: 163–4) wondered

> whether the Welsh could be explained in terms of being bilingual, which is so often a form of schizophrenia, allowing a person to hold two contradictory opinions in his head at once, because his opinions remain untranslated. The Welsh had that mildly stunned and slap-happy personality that I associated with people for whom speaking two languages was a serious handicap. It made them profligate with language, it made them inexact... a kind of confusion.

This is quite a remarkable display of ignorance: in one short passage, Theroux reveals that he knows very little about language and languages, about mental illness, and about the Welsh. It is interesting, too, that neither this American novelist's French-Canadian ancestry nor his Peace Corps exposure to several African societies seems to have produced the linguistic awareness that might have been expected.

Older views also often saw bilingual 'tensions' as contributors to emotional strains: *anomie* and lowered self-esteem, for example. These were often most remarked upon in immigrant or minority-group situations, a fact that suggests very strongly that any such stresses are not linguistic in origin but, rather, result from broader pressures associated with cultures in contact, with cross-group antagonism and prejudice, with poverty and disadvantage. It is not really *that* long ago that an American study concluded that 'the use of a foreign language in the home is one of the chief factors in producing mental retardation' (Goodenough, 1926: 393). Weinreich, in his classic study of languages in contact (1953), presented a long list of disorders allegedly suffered by bilinguals: moral depravity, stuttering, left-handedness, idleness and excessive materialism among them. Some of these are simply stupid, of course, and reflect anti-'foreign' prejudices of the wildest nature. Where emotional problems have been linked with bilingualism, we generally observe a classic instance of the fallacy that correlation implies causation; among immigrant and minority populations, as Diebold (1968) pointed out, bilingualism is often one of the responses to the same social contact that also produces psychological stresses and strains.

If we put aside the technicalities of bilingualism, and if we (rightly) dismiss claims that having more than one language can be a problem in and of itself, we may turn to matters of attachment and identity. What is the significance of bilingual or multilingual capabilities that link individuals to more than one ethnocultural community? What does it mean, and how does it feel, to have a foot in more than one camp? Of course, a great deal of bilingualism has very little emotional significance: the purely instrumental fluencies needed to conduct simple business transactions do not, after all, represent much of an excursion from one's ethnic base camp. This is probably a rather larger category than is often thought; breadth of multiple fluencies *per se* need not imply any increased psychological depth. On the other hand, it is certainly possible to hold dual (or multiple) allegiances involving different-language groups in the absence of personal bilingualism. The attachment felt by the English-speaking Irish or Welsh to a culture and an ancestry whose language they no longer possess is a psychologically real one, and demonstrates the continuing power of what is intangible and symbolic; see my earlier discussion (chapter 7). Indeed, there often exist continuing attachments to the 'lost' language itself as an important aspect of that ancestry. The fact that such attachments rarely lead to actual linguistic revival is regrettable in the eyes of those who feel that language is *the* pillar of culture, but this is not the place to explore the reasons why passive sympathies do not become active ones: the point is, again, that these attachments, however attenuated or 'residual', have a meaning, and represent a sort of symbolic bilingual connectivity.

I have already made the argument that a continuing sense of ethnic-group identity need not inevitably depend upon the continuing use of the original language in ordinary, communicative dimensions – but it can hardly be denied that linguistic continuity is a powerful cultural support. It is not the only pillar, but it is clearly an important one. This, then, becomes an interesting issue for those many bilinguals whose competence is more deep-seated and whose abilities go beyond a shallow instrumentality; they are the individuals one usually has in mind when considering the relationship between bilingualism and identity. If we are to think about this socio-psychological relationship, it may be useful to consider the manner in which bilingualism arises. Yet again, we are confronted with a topic whose complexity can only be acknowledged in passing. Still, we can note two broad divisions of relevance: the first comprises those bilinguals who have a kinship attachment to each group (we can accept either real or perceived attachments for present purposes); the second is made up of people who have, in a more formal way, acquired another linguistic citizenship, as it were.

The latter division involves what has been referred to as *élite* bilingualism, a variety best exemplified by members of the educated classes whose formal instruction would historically have been seen as incomplete without the acquisition of another language or two. Élite bilingualism typically involves prestigious languages – although the term could reasonably be extended to cover the competence of those whose maternal variety is of lesser-used status, as well as of those lucky, or intelligent,

or industrious enough to have achieved upward mobility through education. Élite bilingualism is usually discussed in comparison with *folk*
bilingualism, where the latter signifies that necessity-induced repertoire
expansion that I have just touched upon. The distinction seems apt, particularly when one considers that the élite variety often had as much to
do with social-status marking as it did with a thirst for knowledge and
cultural boundary crossing. In earlier times, not to have known Latin
or Greek or French in addition to one's vernacular would have been
unthinkable for educated people – but unthinkable, perhaps, in the
same way that it would have been unthinkable not to have had servants.
Among those fortunate élite bilinguals, of course, there were (and are)
many driven by purer scholastic motives. But acknowledging this also
means acknowledging that élite bilingualism need not rule out those
'motives of necessity' more usually associated with the folk variety. It is
just that necessity itself becomes a little more rarefied: one's intellectual
pursuits and desires may demand, for example, the acquisition of other
languages and the acquaintance of other cultures.

It is not difficult to see that the life's work of a sensitive scholar
could depend upon or, at least, produce – as an incidental result of
more specific researches – an extended allegiance or sense of belonging.
Indeed, this scenario also theoretically applies to those whose excursions
across boundaries are motivated by nothing more than interest. After all,
given a threshold of intelligence and sensitivity, the difference between
the scholar and the amateur lies in formality of focus. The general point
here is that we can ally ourselves, by more or less conscious effort, with
another group, and that a formally cultivated bilingualism can act as
the bridge here. It is important, I think, to acknowledge the depth that
can be attained by such effort.

The other broad category here comprises those bilinguals who have
some real or understood blood attachment to more than one language
community. Part of that large literature to which I have already referred
concerns itself with onset and timing, and with the consequences for
fluency to which technicalities of acquisition lead. In terms of identity,
it is surely the case that the deeper the linguistic and cultural burrowing
into another community, the greater the impact upon identity. This in
turn suggests that those whose bilingual competence is nurtured early
will, other things being equal, have a firmer foot in the two (or more)
camps. It will usually be the case, of course, that one camp will have
psychological and emotional primacy: however many hearths we may
visit with ease and comfort, the fires still burn brightest at home.

But there are some cases where home itself is difficult to establish, at
least in any simple unidimensional sense. There are some cases, that is,

where bilingual or multilingual capacities, linked to their several cultural bases, develop so early and so deeply that a primary allegiance is hard to discover. There are generally two ways to consider the situations of those whose bilingualism begins at the parental knee. The first is simply that two or more base camps are home simultaneously; the second is that one primary home indeed exists, but it is constructed from materials taken from the several sources. George Steiner (1992), for example, has claimed early and continuing competence in German, French and English. He also notes that careful self-examination – of which variety emerges spontaneously at times of emergency or emotion, of which language is dreamt in, of which is associated with earliest memories – shows that no one of the three seems dominant. By his own account he is maternally and perfectly trilingual and, furthermore, he suggests that such 'primary' multilingualism is, as I have implied above, an integral state of affairs. There has been virtually no research on the consequences for identity of multilingual tapestries so closely woven, but one imagines that there are subtleties here that go far beyond simple additive relationships. It is of course difficult to define and assess perfectly and fully balanced bilingualism, and it may be that even polyglots like Steiner would fall short under the most rigorous examination. Nonetheless, more attention to deep-seated multiple fluencies is indicated. As we move towards the bilingualism of more ordinary individuals, we move towards the idea of a more unitary identity: woven from several strands, to be sure, but inevitably influenced by one language and culture more than by others. The linguistic capabilities of most bilinguals are shallower than those of the Steiners of the world – broader, sometimes, but rarely as deep.

We rely largely upon inference to support the contention that it is the identity components, the symbols of the tribe, that energise languages beyond their instrumental existences. The obvious example that we have considered in this book is the powerful association between language and nationalism. Since the latter is, among other things, a pronounced and often mobilising sense of groupness, it follows that any language component will be carefully delineated. And so, historically, it is. The language in which you do your shopping, and which – if you thought much about it – is also the variety in which your group's tradition is inscribed, can become a symbol of your oppressed state, a rallying-point, a banner under which to assemble the troops. Would people be so ready to sacrifice for something that was of purely mundane importance? We might regret that circumstances encourage us to put aside a familiar tool, and learn to use another – but, as I have already implied, we go to war over histories, not hammers.

The important associations of a particular language with a particular base camp are made clearer – and here we move from languages in general back to languages in tandem – when we think about translation. This is an exercise driven by obvious necessity and, if language were not invested with emotion and association, its operation would be unremarkable. While employing them, we might applaud those whose expertise allows them the access denied the rest of us, but we would rarely be suspicious. And yet the old proverb says *traduttori, traditori*. We would hardly equate translation with treason unless we feared that 'hoarded dreams, patents of life are being taken across the frontier' (Steiner, 1992: 244). And what are 'patents of life', if not the psychological collections of past and present that we feel to be unique to ourselves? An informal Whorfianism tells us that every language interprets and presents the world in a somewhat different way, that the unique wellsprings of group consciousness, traditions, beliefs and values are intimately entwined with a given variety. Translation may mean the revealing of deep matters to others, and cannot be taken lightly. The translator, the one whose multilingual facility permits the straddling of boundaries, is a necessary quisling. But necessity is not invariably associated with comfort, and not even their employers care very much for spies and traitors. The tenor here is one of psychological privacy and coherence, one which – while not inevitably secretive – nonetheless wraps its hoarded dreams in a particular linguistic package.[4] The point of general interest here is that group identity is based on important narratives *and* the language in which they are told. Small wonder, then, that translation can be virtually blasphemous, and that multiple linguistic capabilities may be suspect. Such potentials need not worry bilinguals themselves, of course, but they clearly reinforce – from a negative perspective, in this case – the idea that the psychological heart of bilingualism is identity.

As we have seen throughout this book, language and identity are powerfully and complexly intertwined, and contexts of bilingualism and multilingualism only reinforce this point. This leads me to a final matter of relevance. For monolingual majority-group speakers in their own 'mainstream' settings, the instrumentality and the symbolism of language are not split and, for most such individuals, the language–identity linkage is not problematic: indeed, it is seldom considered. Minority-group speakers, however, rarely have this luxury. For them, matters of language and culture are often more immediate. Now, while it is true that no simple equation exists between bilingualism and minority-group membership, it is also true that many bilinguals are found in the ranks of 'smaller' or threatened societies. An implication is that a link will often exist between bilingualism and a heightened awareness of, and concern for, identity. Specific linguistic manifestations include some that I have already touched upon: attempts at language maintenance or revival, the use of language in ethnic or nationalist struggles, the efforts to sustain at least some domains in the face of external influence, and so on. A more general consequence is that the position and the responses of minority groups focus attention on the possibility and, in many instances, the inevitability of a split between the communicative and the symbolic functions of language. You may have to live and work in a new language, a medium that is not the carrier of your culture, or the medium of your ancestry, or the vehicle of your literature. Such settings provide an extended relevance to the study of bilingualism and identity. First, the attitudes and actions of bilinguals in situations of risk and transition have a special poignancy and visibility: identities, like every-thing else, are thrown into sharper relief when threats are perceived. Second, these same attitudes and actions can galvanise others, and can remind a larger and often unreflective society that matters of language and identity are not relevant for 'ethnics' and 'minorities' alone.

The contribution of bilingualism in our story is, then, of both intrin-sic and generalisable value. We need to know more about it, not only because it is an important issue in its own right, but also because it may illuminate wider patches of ground. More specifically, I have tried to argue here that the importance of being bilingual is, above all, social and psychological rather than linguistic. Beyond types, categories, meth-ods and processes is the essential animating tension of identity. Beyond utilitarian and unemotional instrumentality, the heart of bilingualism is belonging.

STUDY QUESTIONS

1. Can language planning be a free-standing or independent activity?
2. Discuss how modern treatments of language ecology have imposed quite narrow limitations on what should be a very broad perspective.
3. Discuss the romanticism that often seems to surround treatments of endangered languages.
4. What are the implications of bilingual and multilingual compe-tences for individual and social identities?

Further reading
John Edwards's (2003) article, 'Contextualizing language rights', is a critical appraisal of some modern conceptions of language 'rights'.

John Edwards's (2008) article, 'The ecology of language: Insight and illusion',
   is another critical appraisal, this time of the 'new' ecology of language
   (in which considerations of language 'rights' often figure prominently).
Robert Kaplan and Richard Baldauf's (1997) *Language Planning: From Practice
   to Theory* is the best modern monograph on the subject of language
   planning, in all its many facets.
Salikoko Mufwene's (2008) book, *Language Evolution: Contact, Competition
   and Change*, is a powerful and dispassionate treatment of language
   dynamics.

Glossary

The terms here are described only in the senses they possess within the language-and-identity ambit

academies – learned institutions, found in most countries or national regions, charged particularly with the definition, the protection, the purity and the enhancement of the national language; see also **prescriptivism** and **purism**.

accent – a particular variety of pronunciation – not to be confused with **dialect**, a broader language division of which accent is only one part.

accommodation – the process by which speech and language patterns and usages are adjusted according to perceptions of context and circumstance.

attitude – a psychological posture that has cognitive, affective and behavioural components. One's knowledge of, or belief in, something – coupled with an emotional reaction to it – should logically underlie particular courses of action; see also **belief**.

belief – the cognitive component of attitude; thus, many 'attitude' question-naires and surveys are in reality assessments of belief only.

bilingualism – some degree of competence in each of two languages. There are several important dimensions – of degree, scope, balance, and so on – that cut across the four basic linguistic capacities (speaking, listening, reading and writing); see also **multilingualism**.

constructed language – a consciously created variety, typically meant to act as a neutral and/or global **lingua franca**. The best-known example is Esperanto, invented by Ludwig Zamenhof in the late nineteenth century.

cosmopolitanism – a multicultural allegiance – perhaps to 'humanity' writ large – often seen to supersede narrower and darker national attach-ments. It is sometimes associated with pan- or, indeed, post-ethnicity.

covert prestige – reflects the perceived attractiveness of nonstandard speech varieties, a quality arising from the 'toughness', directness and mas-culinity associated with working-class usage.

creole – the variety that – usually, but perhaps not always – results when a **pidgin** becomes a mother tongue, when a lean and simplified **lingua franca** grows in linguistic complexity and nuance.

cultural relativism – the view that yardsticks for making cross-cultural com-parisons do not exist, and that values and practices can only be understood – and evaluated – in their own social contexts. In this, it has proved a necessary and useful counterbalance to the narrow absolutism of **ethnocentrism** – but not, of course, without creating a new set of interpretational difficulties.

dialect – within a language, a variety associated with a particular group or region. Dialects differ from one another, to greater or lesser degree, in terms of vocabulary, grammar and pronunciation (**accent**).

Ebonics – the dialect of English also known as Black English, or African American Vernacular English.

endangered language – a variety, often that of a **minority** group, that is threatened – in terms of scope, status and usage – by a 'larger' or more dominant language.

ethnicity – the group identity or allegiance that rests upon shared ancestry, whether real or perceived. It is typically sustained by such cultural bonds as language and religion, but it can be sustained by more subjective or symbolic contributions to a sense of 'groupness'; see also **nationalism**.

ethnocentrism – a sense of the rightness or superiority of a particular culture – usually one's own – and the consequent tendency to measure all others against it; see also **cultural relativism**.

gender – a social-cultural identity along the femininity–masculinity dimension, superimposed upon sex differences – where the latter form purely biological distinctions.

glossolalia – the religious 'language' – essentially meaningless but comprising fluent word- and sentence-like utterances – also known as 'speaking in tongues'.

identity – self-definition by groups or individuals. It can draw upon many attributes (class, region, ethnicity, nation, religion, gender, language, and so on), either singly or in combination.

language – beyond its familiar and obvious instrumental importance, language can also be a powerful emblem of groupness, an emotionally charged symbol, a central pillar of individual and social identity, and a pivotal rallying-point for ethnonational movements.

language death – the termination of the regular use of a language, most frequently due to **language shift**; see also **language decline, maintenance, revival** and **shift**.

language decline – the process by which a language loses ground in the face of strong external competition.

language ecology – the reality and the study of language in context, taking into account all the many intertwinings between language and other aspects of social life. In a broad sense, it is a fully fleshed sociology of language; in a narrower sense, it has come to represent a concern for language diversity and the protection of 'small' or **endangered** varieties.

language maintenance – the process of protecting and enhancing a language, most typically relevant in situations where **language shift** is looming.

language planning – deliberate action – reflecting official or unofficial policies or ideologies – to influence the course of a language. It includes such activities as formulating and promulgating a **standard** variety, intervening on behalf of **endangered** languages, creating or refining orthographies, and so on.

language revival – the process by which a flagging or moribund variety is reinvigorated.

language rights – a term reflecting the opinion that individuals and groups – particularly, of course, those whose cultures and languages are seen to be at risk or **endangered** – have the right to have these protected and maintained.

language shift – the process undergone by speech and language communities who move from one language to another – typically because the usefulness of their original variety has weakened in the face of powerful external linguistic and cultural pressures.

lingua franca – any variety that allows communication among speakers of different languages. Typically and historically, lingua francas have been 'big' languages (like Latin) that have achieved dominance either regionally or globally, but **constructed** languages and **pidgins** have also served as 'link' languages.

minority-language group – a speech community whose numerical status – or, more importantly, whose social and political weakness – means that its language and culture are threatened by powerful neighbours.

multilingualism – linguistic capacity that extends across more than two languages. As with **bilingualism**, the interest here is often upon social rather than individual manifestations.

nationalism – essentially **ethnicity** writ large, ethnicity with an added political awareness that typically calls for either partial or full self-government.

nonstandard dialect – if one variety within a language achieves **standard** status, it follows that others must be nonstandard. In the mouths of linguists, at least, the term is purely descriptive and has no pejorative overtones.

pidgin – a lexically and grammatically simplified **lingua franca** that links different language communities for purely instrumental purposes.

prescriptivism – the doctrine that one particular dialect – or manner of speaking – is 'proper', and that its use should therefore be prescribed, while others are proscribed. Prescriptivism often embodies narrow and authoritarian impulses on behalf of a **standard** thought to be uniquely correct; see also **purism**.

purism – the desire to protect a language or dialect from unwanted outside influence, foreign borrowings, neologisms, jargon, and so on. A strongly conservative impulse, purism tends to see all change as decay and deterioration; see also **prescriptivism**.

Sapir–Whorf hypothesis – the idea that particular languages imply particular cognitive interpretations of the world (linguistic determinism), that distinctions available in one language may not be in another (linguistic relativism). This 'strong' linkage between language and thought is generally rejected, but a 'weaker' Whorfianism – one that argues for connections between particular languages and *habitual* ways of organising experience – is probably accurate.

standard dialect – that variety of a language that has achieved social dominance – as reflected in its use in print, by educated people, in official capacities, and so on. Such dominance reflects social and historical forces, and does not imply any inherent linguistic superiority; see also **nonstandard** and **substandard**.

stereotypes – overly generalised descriptions or classifications of individuals and groups, often built upon faulty or inadequate bases, and often feeding prejudice. In the popular mind, stereotypes are typically understood as false and hostile in tone, but it is important to remember that their continuing strength reflects a need to make sense – however inaccurately – of a complicated social world.

substandard dialect – within the academic grove, a non-existent entity (see **standard** and **nonstandard**); commonly thought to exist, however, by those who believe that the standard, and only the standard, is correct.

voice appropriation – the process by which outsiders take it upon themselves to speak for group members, to describe and evaluate their cultural narratives, and so on. Where the outsiders are majority-group members and the 'insiders' belong to subaltern communities, voice appropriation is often seen as a sort of neo-colonialism.

Notes

Notes to chapter 2

1 As part of an evolving niche within sociolinguistics and the sociology of language, there is an increasing number of studies of various aspects of 'language in the media' – see the recent collections edited by David *et al.* (2006) and by Johnson and Ensslin (2007). There is a much wider literature, of course, upon the power and scope of the popular media generally. All of this documents the fact that the media do much more than represent or reflect society: they also exert powerful formative pressures. None of this work has really been mined, however, for its specific influences upon personal and group identity. Within the more focussed field of minority cultures and languages, however, considerable attention has been given to the role of the media in bolstering and encouraging identities seen to be 'at risk' (see Cormack and Hourigan, 2007, for example).

Perhaps the most vibrant of the current approaches linking media studies to cultural and political allegiances is that which stresses the discursive contexts in which identities are presented and debated. Much of the work here looks at the public media – newspapers, magazines and other popular cultural records – and draws upon the pioneering work of Lakoff and Johnson (1980) on metaphor. Thus, Musolff (2000, 2004), Charteris-Black (2005) and Manz *et al.* (2004) have recently investigated European 'discourses of identity'. We have only to think for a moment of the powerful associations conjured up by phrases like 'Eastern Europe' or 'The Balkans', or to consider the interesting tensions that arise in attitudinal contexts involving national cross-perceptions, to realise what interesting and revealing information there is to be mined here.

The media's frequent use of metaphor, metonymy and synecdoche – all of which reflect some sort of allusive shorthand, often in stereotypic fashion – suggests obvious avenues of approach here.

2 The essence of the 'Sokal affair' is that the physicist Alan Sokal wrote a jargon-ridden pastiche purporting to show that scientific findings – dealing, in this case, with the law of gravity – were reflections of social and linguistic interpretation. Sokal's hoax was eminently successful, since *Social Text*, a journal of post-modern perspective, was happy to publish it in 1996. Scientists were generally delighted to see this confirmation that the emperor had no clothes; as for the benighted journal editors, they actually tried to claim that, even though a parody, Sokal's article was worth publishing as an attempt to link post-modernism with science. Full coverage of all the relevant details can be found in Sokal (2008).

3 Ernest Gellner's observation that 'the production of obscurity in Paris compares to the production of motor cars in Detroit' is a little unkind to the motor trade; see Edwards (2003).

It is another concern that discourse analysis, particularly in its 'critical' guise, is – in its vehement assertion of the impossibility of objectivity or neutrality – one of the most ideologically driven of modern undertakings (see Wardhaugh, 2006; and, again, Edwards, in press a).

A recent commentator in the *Times Literary Supplement* (J.C., 2007: 32) gave a representative sample of post-modern horror, as well as a comment that will gladden the hearts of all aspirants to clear thinking. He cites a book that deals with terrorism and homosexuality (Puar, 2007):

> Displacing queerness as an identity or modality that is visibly, audibly, legibly or tangibly evident – the seemingly queer body in a 'cultural freeze-frame' of sorts – assemblages allow us to attune to movements, intensities, emotions, energies, affectivities, and textures as they inhabit events, spaciality, and corporealities.

The *TLS* critic then notes how difficult it is to 'unscramble the language of academic theory', refers to Puar's whole book as a 'semantic riot', and observes that 'it may be a characteristic of people who speak in a private language that, once they get going, there is no stopping them, even though no one can understand'.

Notes to chapter 3

1 It must be understood, of course, that conceptions of beauty and attractiveness can vary considerably – across cultures, and within cultures across time. The connotations of fatness, for example – as depicted by Orwell in *Burmese Days* – were powerfully positive among the indigenous population, but not for their European administrators. The full-figured beauties painted by Rubens seem unattractively obese by modern standards. Similarly, while we are accustomed to read of prejudice against black people and, sometimes, of the corollary that this leads to an overestimation of all things white, it is equally true that in many parts of the world – in Asia, in Africa, in the Americas – darker-skinned groups have traditionally found whiteness distinctively unappealing.

2 Stewart's use of words like 'tribal' and 'primitive' is now dated, and increasingly politically incorrect. A recent statement by the Association of Social Anthropologists (2007) specifically discouraged the use of 'primitive' – this, in support of a campaign undertaken by Survival International, a British-based charity that describes itself as 'the movement for tribal peoples' – and the ASA is not very comfortable with the word 'tribal', either (see Blackman, 2007).

3 Some have suggested that the Sioux–snake association is the result of inaccurate or folk etymology. Nonetheless, there is no doubt that the word 'Sioux' has taken on negative connotations within the population itself. Similarly, the Inuit case is not altered by the recent suggestion that 'Eskimo' may derive from an Amerindian word having to do with snowshoes.

   Names for places often reflect the same sort of social influences that account for names for groups. Monmonier (2006) makes an intriguing study of the dyanamic history of toponyms that come to be seen as offensive or derogatory. As he blandly, but very accurately, notes at the end of his book: 'What's in a name? More than most of us realize' (p. 149). See also Baldauf and Kaplan (2007) for an overview of naming practices and policies.

   Where the name for a people is also the name of their language, we often find that the denigration involved in naming the former extends also to the latter. In some instances there was essentially a blanket condemnation: the Portuguese referred to all Bantu varieties as the languages of dogs, for instance. In an analogous racial slur, the Belgians and the French sometimes referred to their black subjects as *macaques* (see Kitoko-Nsiku, 2007). The term (sometimes in variant spellings) continues to be used offensively in Europe. And, indeed, not just in Europe: in 2006, George Allen, an American senator twice referred to a cameraman of Indian background as a *macaca*. This is of course an unusual epithet in an American mouth, but Allen's mother grew up a francophone in Tunisia, and commentators suggested that he had heard her use the term.

4 There are obvious links here with the traditional suspicions of translators, those necessary quislings who straddle linguistic and cultural borders; see also chapter 10.

5 The 'noble savage' generally brings Rousseau to mind, but in fact he never spoke of such a being (see Ellington, 2001). It was the woman generally considered to be the first 'professional' female writer, Aphra Behn, who popularised the idea for an English audience with her *Oroonoko* (subtitled *The Royal Slave*), which was published in 1688. But she, in turn, was preceded by John Dryden. His play, *The Conquest of Granada*, was produced in late 1670 or early 1671 and, in it, Almanzor says 'I am as free as Nature first made man / 'Ere the base Laws of Servitude began / When wild in woods the noble Savage ran' (Part 1, Act 1, Scene 1, lines 207–9).

The question for Rousseau was not, in any event, one of some sort of 'return to nature', something seen to be an unworkable option. Rather, it involved making the best adaptation possible, of making society 'legitimate'; if Rousseau had been writing today, he might perhaps have used that noxious word, 'authentic'.

6 This contradicts the assertion by Ahmed (1995), who reports that – in a BBC discussion about the *Satanic Verses* controversy – Gellner stated that 'one society cannot be judged by the yardstick of another'. This sounds very un-Gellnerish to me.

Notes to chapter 4

1 Groups that have shifted, in communicative terms, from their ancestral variety to another may retain a distinctiveness at the level of accent or dialect. Such 'marking' – as in the case, say, of the English-speaking Irish, Welsh or Scots, of Portuguese-speaking Brazilians, of Spanish-speaking Peruvians, or of German-speaking Austrians – can obviously come to be a very powerful agent of identity indeed.

2 Weinreich (1945) pointed out that he was not the author of the phrase. He reported hearing it from an audience member who came up to him after a lecture in early 1944. There have been occasional suggestions, as well, that it originated earlier in the twentieth century, coined perhaps by a linguist (Antoine Meillet), perhaps by a colonial administrator (Louis-Hubert Lyautey).

Notes to chapter 5

1 Standard English, at least in informal usage, *does* allow copula-verb deletion: it is permissible to say things like 'That your car?' or 'You leaving now?'

2 Much of the work in this section deals with either class or ethnic variation – and often both in combination. Some of the studies may appear dated. This is largely because points of focus have moved elsewhere. In social science, unlike its 'harder' companion disciplines, such mobility need imply very little about the solution of existing problems and the natural progression on to the next. There are, instead, fashions at work here. Current investigations involving language and class are more likely to concern themselves with fine-grained discourse-analytic approaches, and less likely to assess attitudes (at least in any more or less direct manner). Jenkins (2007) also correctly points to another problem, hardly unique in the annals of social science: studies of language attitudes and of sociolinguistics have not intertwined to the extent that they logically should. I have already expressed

some reservations about discourse-analytic approaches; here I need only add that – for my purposes – the sorts of attitude studies that I cite here provide the best available pertinent insights.

A recent succinct overview of language attitudes can be found in Giles and Edwards (in press); see also Jenkins (2007), Giles and Billings (2004), Garrett *et al.* (2003) and Kristiansen *et al.* (2005). On the basis of a large-scale survey of reactions to some three dozen accents of English, Coupland and Bishop (2007) report that earlier findings about perceived prestige and social attractiveness have remained broadly intact; they do note, however, some nuances associated with the age and gender of informants.

Notes to chapter 6

1 Glossolalia, best documented by Goodman (1972) and Samarin (1972), is not solely a western Pentecostal phenomenon; Sawyer (2001) reminds us of examples found among Australian and North American aboriginal groups.
2 This is a debatable claim, but here is not the place to go into the details of language revival *per se.*
3 Titley (2000: 79) suggests that, while 'the penal laws were not as severe in practice as they were in intent' – a dilution that hardly lets the English off the hook – they did remove the indigenous Catholic clergy from their traditional leadership positions; see also O'Brien (1989) on the force of legal injunctions, or the lack of it, by the end of the eighteenth century. It should of course be remembered that anti-Catholic legislation was not unique to Ireland: Catholics in England suffered under the same strictures – and, at the same time, they were actively persecuting Protestants on the Continent.

For an interesting commentary on the Irish, the English, and Catholicism in the mid nineteenth century, see the recent archival study by McNicholas (2007).
4 There is an irony here, in that Douglas Hyde and many of the other leaders in the Irish literary and language revival were, in fact, Protestant, members of the Anglo-Irish ascendancy (see Pritchard, 2004; Tanner, 2004; Edwards, 2007a). Risteárd Ó Glaisne (1967, 1981, 2000) provides useful historical details – as well as strong personal convictions – on the relationship between Protestantism and Irish.
5 Sad to relate that, despite the Commission's recommendation, the prevailing antipathy within and without the Education Department meant that prior to 1918 the only official developments were 'cosmetic concessions in 1886, 1904 and 1906' (Devine, 1999: 401). And, indeed, the Education Act of 1918 hardly proved to be a momentous turning-point for Gaelic at school. But all that is another story.

Notes to chapter 7

1 Largely, but by no means entirely. There has never been any shortage of women who, for reasons ranging all the way from complete cowardice to utter conviction, have endorsed the general superiority of men. A recent much-discussed example is the statement, attributed to Camille Paglia, that 'if women ran the world, we'd still be living in grass huts'.
2 Cameron's title (*The Myth of Mars and Venus*) is a reworking of the title of John Gray's best-selling book, *Men are from Mars, Women are from Venus* (1992), the general argument of which was that men *do* while women *talk*. Am I the only one, by the way, who finds Gray's title unnecessarily clumsy? Why didn't he call his book *Men are from Mars, Women from Venus* – wouldn't that have been better? And why is it, anyway, that so many writers on language matters, both 'popular' and academic, seem to have such a poor command of language themselves?

3 The survey was conducted in 2003 by the Hay Group, and involved 45 women in senior corporate roles; for comparative purposes, less successful women were also studied, as were groups of more and less successful male executives. It is interesting that the subtitle to Immen's (2008b) newspaper article is 'For women, the best of both gender worlds' – it could be argued, after all, that their successful 'blending' of traditional male and female styles and postures is an accommodation that men never have to make.

Re the Clintons, language and power: a new study by Suleiman and O'Connell (2008) reveals that Bill and Hillary speak and are spoken to differently in media interviews. The authors note (p. 45) that 'even though Hillary Clinton is a politician herself, she still follows, to some extent, the historic designation of women's language as the language of the non-powerful' – this, on the basis of her use of intensifiers, hedges and other 'female' speech markers.

4 If time and space were available, this would be an appropriate place for a brief digression on *jargon*, the language practices associated with particular groups (occupational, criminal, class, club, and so on). From the larger perspectives of self-definition and identity, there are obvious matters of importance here. From the narrower ones of gender and language, any medium that is restricted in some way or another is likely to have something to say about relationships between men and women. On the larger issue, a good introduction is provided by Burke and Porter (1995), within which the specific contribution by Roberts is recommended.

5 Good general overviews of language and gender are provided by Sunderland (2006), Eckert and McConnell-Ginet (2003), Romaine (1999), Gibbon (1999), Crawford (1995), Coates (1996, 2003, 2004), Holmes (1995), Mills (2003) and Cameron (1995).

Notes to chapter 8

1 There is considerable debate about the possible reconciliation of group rights with liberal principles, the latter having traditionally emphasised the individual. Like many other issues touched upon in this book, I cannot provide fuller treatment here. Two things are worth noting, however. First, current global uncertainties have made things more and more difficult for multicultural philosophies and practices; second, the depth and subtlety of many of the arguments underpinning support for multiculturalism, for cultural pluralism and group 'recognition', have convinced some that they are positions hardly tenable outside the academic cloisters.

2 Once again, this is not the place for further attention to a compelling issue: governmental and organisational apologies, with or without tangible accompaniments, for past wrongs done to certain groups of people. There is a growing literature on the subject and, of course, a great deal of heated debate. There is now, too, a very useful website which provides commentary and an extensive archive of related documents, speeches, and so on: see http://political-apologies.wlu.ca (see also Beauchamp's [2007] general overview; and chapter 2).

3 There are many, many ramifications of aboriginal–mainstream relations in Canada, and elsewhere. One vitally important issue concerning the protection of the weakest involves the integration (or not) of minority groups into majority settings, and one recent extension of *this* is the adoption or fostering (or not) of impoverished aboriginal children by white adults. Arguments have been made – and often accepted, sometimes with the most tragic of results – that such children should only be placed in aboriginal homes, for the sake of 'cultural continuity'. Wente (2007) cites the case of an infant who was removed from a safe foster home (white) so that he could be brought up in a more 'appropriate' (aboriginal) one,

where he soon died from neglect. This is not to say, of course, that arguments at the cultural level are always misplaced, nor to assume that white homes are invariably more caring than aboriginal ones. But children's needs should surely be placed before anything else, especially given the horror stories that often come to light about the status of some aboriginal communities. Consider this:

> Ninety-eight per cent of the adults in Pauingassi [an aboriginal 'first nation' in northern Manitoba] are alcoholics. Eighty per cent of the adolescents are addicted to solvents. Fifty per cent of the kids under 18 are wards of the child-protection system, and 20 per cent are thought to suffer from varying degrees of fetal alcohol syndrome. (Wente, 2007)

Putting aside all considerations of causes, effects and blame – and while we await social solutions, remedial action, compensatory policies, and so on – would it be better to remove a neglected baby from such a setting, or not? And if it proved impossible to find aboriginal fosterage, what then? Should we leave children in squalor, but in 'their culture'? The title of Wente's newspaper piece really says it all: 'White guilt, dead children – in the name of political correctness'.

A final note here: could anything be more bizarrely trivial, in these contexts, than worrying about the preservation of language? A similar point was made by Spolsky (2004: x):

> Should we be wondering about the official use of French and the role of the vernaculars in a country with excess mortality [due to AIDS]? Or about the prospects for Bosnian when so many of its speakers were recently massacred?

Yet scholars have argued for – and continue to spend considerable amounts of time and money on – language-maintenance programmes in places like Pauingassi. There are some contexts in which priorities ought to be readjusted, I think.

See also the brief discussion of North American aboriginal groups in the following chapter.

4 Marx made these observations in the paper entitled 'Der achtzehnte Brumaire des Louis Napoleon' – so called because on that date (9 November 1799) Bonaparte established his French dictatorship. Engels, like many others since, called Marx's historical essay 'a work of genius'. Be that as it may, it opens with these famous and oft-cited words: 'Hegel remarks somewhere that all facts and personages of great importance in world history occur, as it were, twice. He forgot to add: the first time as tragedy, the second as farce.'

5 The Hungarian prime minister, Pál Teleki, who committed suicide when he realised that his signature on the 1940 Berlin Pact (an extension of the Italo-German axis of 1936) committed his country to invade Yugoslavia, related an interesting anecdote about a disputed border district: Cieszyn (Polish) / Těšín (Czech) – formerly under Habsburg rule (as Teschen). Asking how many Poles lived in the area, Teleki was told that the number varied between 40,000 and 100,000. His informant explained that many villagers changed their stated nationality, almost on a weekly basis, according to individual and community interests. (I have expanded here upon an anecdote reported by Kedourie [1960].) Border communities are particularly likely, of course, to reveal such identity dynamics; for contemporary illustrations, see Llamas (2006, 2007), as well as the very useful work of Wilson and Donnan (1998) and Donnan and Wilson (1999).

6 Hobsbawm's view of national *languages* is much less contentious, and it illustrates once again the difference between what nationalists say (and perhaps believe) and what seem to be the real facts of the case. Thus, while activists whose job it

is to galvanise and then organise ethnonationalist sentiments typically make a 'primordialist' claim for their variety (see also below), national languages usually have to be more or less consciously summoned into life as standardised forms of existing dialects. All the 'losing' idioms can then be 'downgraded to dialects' (1990: 51).

As we have seen, the existence of a standard dialect logically implies that all others are nonstandard – a description that reflects nothing of intrinsic linguistic inferiority. Standards achieve their status through social processes that create a *primus inter pares*. But Hobsbawm is quite right to use the word 'downgraded', because social prejudices can easily conjure deficiency out of difference. The perfectly acceptable and non-pejorative 'nonstandard' can easily become 'substandard'. Max Weinreich famously noted that a language was a dialect that had an army and a navy: in the same way, some dialects are more strongly armed than others.

7 A brief but revealing exchange of views can be found in the twin articles of Gellner (1996) – his last public word on nationalism before his death on Guy Fawkes day, 1995 – and his pupil, Smith (1996). In his final published interview, Gellner told Targett (1995) that 'nationalism is an expression of an industrial society which romanticises pre-industrial society'; and, he went, on, 'there is no relationship whatsoever between what nationalism says about itself and what is really the case'. Typically forthright comments. Joseph (2004: 231–2) wins the prize for the best brief description of Gellner's ideas: in two short paragraphs he provides a concise and accurate summary.

8 In April 2004, the Association for the Study of Nationalism held its annual conference at the London School of Economics. In honour of the retirement and the research focus of Anthony Smith, and picking up its title from an important article by Connor (1990), the theme was 'When is the Nation?', and a stellar cast was assembled including Anthony Smith, Eric Hobsbawm, John Breuilly, Walker Connor, Pierre van den Berghe, Steven Grosby and Krishan Kumar – to debate questions about the age and origins of nationalism. I was fortunate enough to attend this meeting, and now I have in front of me the books that emerged from it (Ichijo and Uzelac, 2005; Young et al., 2007). The first, with ten chapters and the edited transcripts of the question-and-answer sessions that punctuated the conference sessions, is an exceptionally useful collection to have under one roof; the second is strong on illustrative case studies.

Notes to chapter 9

1 Safran (2008) suggests that the French Revolution changed nationalism: from being a sort of 'secular religion', it became further secularised as a 'civic' phenomenon. As the solidarity function of a state language came into prominence, the old sense of *cuius regio eius religio* evolved into *cuius natio eius lingua* (see Lapierre, 1988).

2 Benn's dismissal is not to be equated with Gellner's observation (1983: 124) that nationalism's 'precise doctrines are hardly worth analysing', since the latter meant to imply that, while the phenomenon itself was clearly of great interest, the ideas with which nationalists galvanised their cause were often dubious, or unworthy, or worse. Even so, Gellner still did us a disservice in suggesting that the content of nationalist discourse is simply something to be disdained. At the very least, we should remember that ignoring bizarre conceits can be a recipe for future trouble.

3 The attractions offered by closed circles of belief are obvious: in the religious world, answers are provided to life's deepest questions; in the terrestrial one, we are given the materials to better understand our group's history, its triumphs, its repression

and its future. The essence, in all cases, has to do with feelings of psychological control and understanding.

This is surely what animates other and more clearly fictional closed worlds – Tolkien's Middle-Earth, for instance, or Freud's psychoanalytic universe, or science-fiction confections. A sense of control that stems from feelings of comprehension is also the basis of the attraction exerted by clubs and societies, and I suspect that it is present, too, in many hobbies and pastimes. Think of the grown-up man (it's always a man – interestingly enough) who builds and operates elaborate model railways. It may be difficult to take seriously a continuum that is anchored at one end by religion and at the other by toy trains; nevertheless, there are some connecting threads here.

4 Given the obvious similarities between nationalism and religion – or, indeed, considering nationalism as a religion itself – it is not surprising that defenders of the former will often try and explain away its bleaker and more destructive aspects by claiming, as the religious are wont to do, that while the 'faith' itself is pure and good it is all too often warped in the hands of the unworthy.

5 I put 'indigenous' and 'authentic' in inverted commas because they have been co-opted, and have taken on quite specific resonances in some circles. The rejection of modernity is often a type of west-bashing, a practice reminiscent of a familiar posture, commented upon by nineteenth-century statesmen like Canning and Disraeli, but given most notable form in *The Mikado*: 'The idiot who praises, with enthusiastic tone / All centuries but this, and every country but his own.' Disraeli was a little kinder than Gilbert: for 'idiot' he gave us 'cosmopolitan critic'.

6 Any hint of 'moral absolutism' constitutes the cardinal sin for relativists. Consequently, they often find themselves in difficult straits nowadays, when fundamentalist sabre-rattling and debates about 'the clash of civilisations' can tend to steamroll over cultural nuance and sensitivity. Gertrude Himmelfarb (1999) has suggested that thoroughgoing relativists will feel that their stance obliges them to admit that even questions about 'the force and the meaning' of the Jewish holocaust depend upon one's 'perspective'. However, the university students whose views Himmelfarb draws upon, and whose endorsement of cultural relativism means that they cannot be wholly unsympathetic to (say) Aztec sacrificial practices, or scalping, or slavery, *will* still object to killing whales, the depletion of the rain forest, medical experimentation on animals and female circumcision (and also to some selected vices: smoking, for instance). It seems that there are, after all, some 'absolutes' still acceptable within a largely relativist academia. Outside the cloisters, of course, things are somewhat different. In a journalistic comment about the intellectual pleasures of disagreement and controversy, Fernández-Armesto (2007) recently noted that in the current American climate – in what he calls the 'land of over-developed sensitivities – to feel 'offended' has become the moral equivalent to saying 'you feel raped, starved or strangled'. Consequently, students and others are now to be 'protected' from the cut-and-thrust dangers of scholarly debate; the former president of Harvard is 'uninvited' to speak because petitioners claim to be 'offended' by his views; and so on.

7 A few years later, a very similar case arose among the Inuit whalers of Alaska. The Associated Press reported that the hunters were beginning to use penthrite, a 'humane explosive', in place of the black-powder bomb that was 'traditionally' attached to harpoons (see Pagano, 2005). More than a few newspaper readers noted that it was strange enough to think that Eskimo hunters would go after bowhead whales with grenades, and stranger still that this could be considered a traditional or ancestral method (see Gardiner, 2005).

Notes to chapter 10

1 In fact, as Robb (2007) points out, it took a long time for French to approach universality within l'*hexagone*. A quarter of new recruits still spoke only *patois* in the army of the 1860s, and by the end of the century three-quarters of the population were still less than completely fluent in French.

See also the relevant coverage in the recent popular treatment by Nadeau and Barlow (2007).

2 Two centuries after Voltaire, Maurras said that no Jew could ever apprehend the beauty of Racine's line, 'Dans l'Orient désert quel devint mon ennui' (Kedourie, 1960: 72). André Gide, an exact contemporary, suggested that Jews might come to grips with French-as-instrument, but never with the 'soul' of the language. And Heinrich von Treitschke – the nineteenth-century historian, politician and anti-semite – repeated the sentiment: German-speaking Jews were oriental wanderers for whom language had no 'inner meaning' (Safran, 2008; von Treitschke, 1916; Weinberg, 1995).

3 The collections edited by Jernudd and Shapiro (1989) and Langer and Davies (2005), along with Wexler's (1974) earlier treatment of linguistic purism in Ukraine, can also be usefully consulted, although the emphasis in these volumes is on specific cases rather than descriptive or theoretical generalities. See also Burke (2004) for an interesting chapter on language 'purification' in renaissance Europe.

4 As many scholars and more casual observers have noted, Canadian English reflects both American and British influences. Chambers (1998: 263) thus refers to a 'double standard in many matters of spelling and pronunciation'. There are variations (by age and region, for instance), such that Ontarians are more likely to write *colour* and Albertans *color*. There are historical reasons, of course, having to do with waves of immigration but there are also important attitudinal factors:

> Canadians came to regard British standards as superior, whether or not they were the ones we ourselves practised ... at many points in our history, being patriotically Canadian has defined itself as being anti-American. (p. 264)

5 See Edwards (1994c, 2006; also Bruthiaux, 1992) for some further notes on the role that linguists ought to play. It can be an exciting one, even tragic. Heap (2007) and Moller (2007) discuss the activities of Aníbal Otero, whose linguistic work in Galicia and Portugal brought him to the attention of the fascists in 1936. His death sentence was commmuted to one of life imprisonment, and he ended up spending five years in jail for the 'crime' of language study. Something to point out to aspiring linguistic field-workers, perhaps.

6 Some have set this date a bit earlier (see Bowen, 1970; Hall, 1974). There is room for debate, since various unofficial bodies and town academies in Italy date from the middle of the fifteenth century.

Notes to chapter 11

1 There are some few exceptions. Calvet's (1999) treatment, for instance, does not make a simplistic equation between language ecology and the defence of threatened varieties.

2 I note that Joseph (2007: 538) has made exactly the same point. Even though the idea of 'linguistic imperialism' is clearly 'ideologically overdetermined and counterproductive', its adherents still benefit from its continuing appeal, 'not so much for the exploited third world it seeks to defend as for middle-class western scholars who suffer from acute ... postcolonial guilt syndrome'; see also Brutt-Griffler (2006).

3 A *Universal Declaration of Linguistic Rights* was approved in Barcelona in June 1996. It makes the usual assertions and jejune statements. Its Article 25, for example, states that 'all language communities are entitled to have at their disposal all the human and material resources necessary to ensure that their language is present to the extent they desire at all levels of education within their territory: properly trained teachers, appropriate teaching methods, text books, finance, buildings and equipment, traditional and innovative technology'. Despite its title, the UDLR is essentially the child of some interested parties: elements of PEN International, some NGOs, language 'experts', and so on. See www.linguistic-declaration.org.

4 The earlier discussion, about the use of language to conceal rather than to communicate, and about the highly charged matter of 'voice appropriation', is of course relevant here.

References

Abd-el-Jawad, Hassan 2006. Why do minority languages persist? The case of Circassian in Jordan. *International Journal of Bilingual Education and Bilingualism* 9: 51–74.

Abley, Mark 2000. Whose voice it is . . .? *Times Literary Supplement*, 5 May.

Abrams, Dominic and Michael Hogg (eds.) 1990. *Social Identity Theory*. London: Harvester Wheatsheaf.

Acton, John (Lord) 1862. Nationality. *Home and Foreign Review* 1: 1–25.

Ahmed, Akbar 1995. Complete teacher in a divided world. *Times Higher Education Supplement*, 17 March.

Aitchison, Jean 2000. *Language Change: Progress or Decay?* 3rd edn. Cambridge: Cambridge University Press.

Allcock, John 1994. Heart of the matter. *Times Higher Education Supplement*, 25 March.

Allport, Gordon 1961. *Pattern and Growth in Personality*. New York: Holt, Rinehart & Winston.

Altoma, Salih 1974. Language education in Arab countries and the role of the academies. In Joshua Fishman (ed.), *Advances in Language Planning*. The Hague: Mouton.

American Speech-Language-Hearing Association 1997. *Omnibus Survey*. Rockville, Maryland: ASHA.

Ammon, Ulrich 2000. Towards more fairness in international English: Linguistic rights of non-native speakers? In Robert Phillipson (ed.), *Rights to Language*. Mahwah, NJ: Erlbaum.

Ammon, Ulrich, Klaus Mattheier and Peter Nelde (eds.) 1995. *Europäische Identität und Sprachenvielfalt*. Tübingen: Niemeyer. [= *Sociolinguistica* 9]

Anderson, Benedict 1991. *Imagined Communities: Reflections on the Origin and Spread of Nationalism*. London: Verso.

Anderson, Christopher 1818. *A Brief Sketch of Various Attempts which have been made to Diffuse a Knowledge of the Holy Scripture through the Medium of the Irish Language*. Dublin: Graisberry & Campbell.

Anderson, Perry 1992. *A Zone of Engagement*. London: Verso.

Anderssen, Erin 1999. Aboriginal women file suit against Ottawa. *Globe & Mail* [Toronto], 16 June.

271

Andreä, Johann 1619. *Reipublicae Christianopolitanae descriptio.* Argentorum [Strasbourg]: Zetzner.

d'Anglejan, Alison and G. Richard Tucker 1973. Sociolinguistic correlates of speech style in Quebec. In Roger Shuy and Ralph Fasold (eds.), *Language Attitudes: Current Trends and Prospects.* Washington: Georgetown University Press.

Anthias, Floya and Nira Yuval-Davis 1992. *Racialized Boundaries.* London: Routledge.

Appiah, Kwame Anthony 2005. *The Ethics of Identity.* Princeton, NJ: Princeton University Press.

 2006. *Cosmopolitanism.* New York: Norton.

Armstrong, John 1982. *Nations Before Nationalism.* Chapel Hill, NC: University of North Carolina Press.

Association of Social Anthropologists 2007. ASA statement on the use of 'primitive' as a descriptor of contemporary human groups. www.theasa.org.

Aubin, Benoît 1996. The battle of the language ayatollahs. *Globe & Mail* [Toronto], 23 November.

Ayto, John 1983. English: Failures of language reform. In Istán Fodor and Claude Hagège (eds.), *Language Reform / La réforme des langues / Sprachreforme* (volume 1). Hamburg: Helmut Buske.

Bacon, Francis 1620. *Instauratio magna* . . . London: Bill & Norton. [The *Novum Organum* appears as the second part here.]

 1626. *Sylva Sylvarum, or, a Naturall History in Ten Centuries.* London: Lee. [The *New Atlantis*, subtitled *A Worke Unfinished*, appears with its own pagination here.]

Baker, Colin and Sylvia Prys Jones 1998. *Encyclopedia of Bilingualism and Bilingual Education.* Clevedon: Multilingual Matters.

Bakhtin, Mikhail 1981. *The Dialogic Imagination.* Austin, TX: University of Texas Press. [A collection of essays written, in Russian, in the 1930s.]

Baldauf, Richard and Robert Kaplan (eds.) 2007. *Language Planning and Naming.* Clevedon: Multilingual Matters [= *Current Issues in Language Planning* 8(3)].

Balibar, Renée 1985. *L'institution du français.* Paris: Presses Universitaires de France.

Balthazar, Louis 1995. Within the black box: Reflections from a French Quebec vantage point. *American Review of Canadian Studies* 25: 519–41.

Banks, Russell 2000. Who will tell the people? *Harper's Magazine* (June), 83–8.

Barbeau, Victor 1960. *L'Académie canadienne-française.* Montreal: Des Marais.

Barker, Ernest 1927. *National Character and the Factors in its Formation.* London: Methuen.

Barnard, Frederick 1965. *Herder's Social and Political Thought.* Oxford: Clarendon.

 (ed.) 1969. *J. G. Herder on Social and Political Culture.* Cambridge: Cambridge University Press.

Barnes, Sandra 2003. The Ebonics enigma: An analysis of attitudes on an urban college campus. *Race, Ethnicity and Education* 6: 247–63.

Barros, Maria 1994. Educaçao bilíngüe, lingüística e missionários. *Em Aberto* 14(63): 18–37.

Barth, Fredrik (ed.) 1969. *Ethnic Groups and Boundaries*. Boston: Little, Brown.

Baugh, Albert 1959. *A History of the English Language*. 2nd edn. London: Routledge & Kegan Paul.

Baugh, John 2000. *Beyond Ebonics: Linguistic Pride and Racial Prejudice*. New York: Oxford University Press.

  2002. Linguistics, education, and the Ebonics firestorm. In James Alatis, Heidi Hamilton and Ai-Hui Tan (eds.), *Linguistics, Language, and the Professions*. Washington: Georgetown University Press.

  2004. Ebonics and its controversy. In Edward Finegan and John Rickford (eds.), *Language in the USA: Themes for the Twenty-first Century*. Cambridge: Cambridge University Press.

  2006. Linguistic considerations pertaining to *Brown v. Board*: Exposing racial fallacies in the new millennium. In Arnetha Ball (ed.), *With More Deliberate Speed: Achieving Equity and Excellence in Education*. Oxford: Blackwell [= *Yearbook of the National Society for the Study of Education*, vol. 105:2].

Bauman, Zygmunt 2001. *Community: Seeking Safety in an Insecure World*. Cambridge: Polity.

Baycroft, Timothy 2004. European identity. In Gary Taylor and Steve Spencer (eds.), *Social Identities: Multidisciplinary Approaches*. London: Routledge.

Beauchamp, Gordon 2007. Apologies all around. *American Scholar* 76(4): 83–93.

Beck, Cave 1657. *The Universal Character, by Which All the Nations in the World may Understand One Another's Conceptions, Reading out of One Common Writing their Own Mother Tongues*. London: Weekley.

Beiner, Ronald 1999. Nationalism's challenge to political philosophy. In Ronald Beiner (ed.), *Theorizing Nationalism*. Albany, NY: State University of New York Press.

du Bellay, Joachim 1b49/1939. *The Defence and Illustration of the French Language*. London: Dent.

Bendor-Samuel, John 1999. Summer Institute of Linguistics. In Bernard Spolsky (ed.), *Concise Encyclopedia of Educational Linguistics*. Amsterdam: Elsevier. [Reprinted in John Sawyer and J. M. Y. Simpson (eds.), 2001. *Concise Encyclopedia of Language and Religion*. Amsterdam: Elsevier.]

Benn, Stanley 1967. Nationalism. In Paul Edwards (ed.), *Encyclopedia of Philosophy*, vol. 5. New York: Macmillan & The Free Press.

Benthall, Jonathan 1995. Missionaries and human rights. *Anthropology Today* 11(1): 1–3.

Berdichevsky, Norman 2003. Hebrew vs Yiddish: The worldwide rivalry. In Arthur Kurzweil (ed.), *Best Jewish Writing, 2003*. San Francisco: Jossey-Bass.

Berger, David 2007. Missing Milton Himmelfarb. *Commentary* 123(4): 54–8.

Berger, Peter, Brigitte Berger and Hansfried Kellner 1973. *The Homeless Mind*. New York: Random House.

Berger, Peter and Richard Neuhaus 1977. *To Empower People: The Role of Mediating Structures in Public Policy*. Washington, DC: American Enterprise Institute. [A second, updated version appeared in 1996, edited by Michael Novak, with material from other contributors, and with a new subtitle: *From State to Civil Society*.]

Berlin, Isaiah 1976. *Vico and Herder: Two Studies in the History of Ideas*. London: Hogarth.

   2000. *Three Critics of the Enlightenment: Vico, Hamann, Herder*. Princeton, NJ: Princeton University Press.

Best, Deborah, John Williams, Jonathan Cloud, Stephen Davis, Linda Robertson, John Edwards, Howard Giles and Jacqueline Fowles 1977. Development of sex-trait stereotypes among young children in the United States, England and Ireland. *Child Development* 48: 1375–84.

Billig, Michael 1995. *Banal Nationalism*. Thousand Oaks, CA: Sage.

Blackman, Stuart 2007. Drive to ban 'primitive' names sparks debate. *Times Higher Education Supplement*, 30 March.

Blake, Norman 1981. *Non-Standard Language in English Literature*. London: André Deutsch.

Block, David 2006. Identity in applied linguistics. In Tope Omoniyi and Goodith White (eds.), *The Sociolinguistics of Identity*. London: Continuum.

Bloomfield, Leonard 1927. Literate and illiterate speech. *American Speech* 2: 432–9.

   1944. Secondary and tertiary responses to language. *Language* 20(2): 45–55.

Boberg, Charles 1999. The attitudinal component of variation in American English foreign <a> nativization. *Journal of Language and Social Psychology* 18: 49–61.

Bochart, Samuel 1646. *Geographiæ Sacræ* . . . Cadomi [Caen]: Cardonelli.

Bodine, Ann 1975. Sex differences in language. In Barrie Thorne and Nancy Henley (eds.), *Language and Sex: Difference and Dominance*. Rowley, MA: Newbury House.

Bolinger, Dwight 1980. *Language – The Loaded Weapon*. London: Longman.

Borel, Pierre 1655. *Tresor de recherches et antiquitez gauloises et françoises* . . . Paris: Courbé.

Boswell, James 1791/1958. *Life of Samuel Johnson*. London: Oxford University Press.

Bourdieu, Pierre 1990a. *The Logic of Practice*. Cambridge: Polity.

   1990b. *In Other Words: Essays Towards a Reflexive Sociology*. Cambridge: Polity.

   1991. *Language and Symbolic Power*. Cambridge: Polity.

Bourdon, Marie-Claude 2000. L'anti Grey Owl. *L'Actualité* 25(4): 20–3.

Bourke, Ulick 1875. *The Aryan Origin of the Gaelic Race and Language*. London: Longmans, Green.

Bowen, Jean Donald 1970. The structure of language. In Albert Marckwardt (ed.), *Linguistics in School Programs*. Chicago: University of Chicago Press.

Bragg, Melvyn and Stanley Ellis 1976. *Word of Mouth*. London: BBC Television.
Breakwell, Glynis (ed.) 1992. *Social Psychology of Identity and the Self Concept*. London: Surrey University Press.
Breakwell, Glynis and Evanthia Lyons (eds.) 1996. *Changing European Identities*. Oxford: Butterworth-Heinemann.
Brehm, Sharon, Saul Kassin and Steven Fein 1999. *Social Psychology*. Boston: Houghton Mifflin.
Breton, Raymond 1964. Institutional completeness of ethnic communities and the personal relations of immigrants. *American Journal of Sociology* 70: 193–205.
    1988. From ethnic to civic nationalism: English Canada and Quebec. *Ethnic and Racial Studies* 11: 85–102.
Breuilly, John 1993. *Nationalism and the State*. 2nd edn. Manchester: Manchester University Press.
    2001. The state. In Alexander Motyl (ed.), *Encyclopedia of Nationalism*. London and New York: Academic Press.
Bringhurst, Robert 1999. *A Story as Sharp as a Knife: The Classical Haida Mythtellers and their World*. Vancouver: Douglas & McIntyre.
Brown, David 2000. *Contemporary Nationalism*. London: Routledge.
Brown, Penelope and Stephen Levinson 1987. *Politeness: Some Universals in Language Use*. Cambridge: Cambridge University Press.
Brubaker, Rogers 1996. *Nationalism Reframed*. Cambridge: Cambridge University Press.
    1999. The Manichean myth: Rethinking the distinction between civic and ethnic nationalism. In Hanspeter Kriesi, Klaus Armingeon, Hannes Siegrist and Andreas Wimmer (eds.), *Nation and National Identity*. Chur, Switzerland: Rügger.
    2004. *Ethnicity Without Groups*. Cambridge, MA: Harvard University Press.
Brubaker, Rogers and Frederick Cooper 2000. Beyond 'identity'. *Theory and Society* 29: 1–47. [Reprinted in Brubaker's *Ethnicity Without Groups*.]
Brumfit, Christopher 2001. *Individual Freedom in Language Teaching*. Oxford: Oxford University Press.
Bruthiaux, Paul 1992. Language description, language prescription and language planning. *Language Problems and Language Planning* 16: 221–4.
Brutt-Griffler, Janina 2006. Language endangerment, the construction of indigenous languages and world English. In Martin Pütz, Joshua Fishman and JoAnne Neff-van Aertselaer (eds.), *'Along the Routes to Power': Explorations of Empowerment Through Language*. Berlin: Mouton de Gruyter.
Bucholtz, Mary 1999. You da man: Narrating the racial other in the linguistic production of white masculinity. *Journal of Sociolinguistics* 3: 443–60.
Bull, Tove and Toril Swan (eds.) 1992. *Language, Sex and Society*. Berlin: Mouton de Gruyter [= *International Journal of the Sociology of Language* 94].
Bulwer, John 1644. *Chirologia, or the Naturall Language of the Hand . . . 2 vols*. London: Twyford.

Bumsted, Jack 1982. *The People's Clearance: Highland Emigration to British North America, 1770–1815*. Edinburgh: Edinburgh University Press.

Burke, Peter 2004. *Languages and Communities in Early Modern Europe*. Cambridge: Cambridge University Press.

Burke, Peter and Roy Porter (eds.) 1995. *Languages and Jargons: Contributions to a Social History of Language*. Cambridge: Polity.

Buss, Allan 1976. Galton and sex differences: An historical note. *Journal of the History of the Behavioral Sciences* 12: 283–5.

Butler, Mary 1901. *Irishwomen and the Home Language*. Dublin: Gaelic League.

Butler, Samuel 1663. *Hudibras*. London: Marriot. [The first part only; the second part appeared in 1664, while the third and final section was published only in 1678.]

Cabantous, Alain 1998. *Histoire du blasphème en Occident*. Paris: Albin Michel.

Cahen, Michel 1994. *Ethnicité politique*. Paris: L'Harmattan.

Cahill, Edward 1930. *Ireland's Peril*. Dublin: Gill & Son.

Calhoun, Craig 1994. *Social Theory and the Politics of Identity*. Oxford: Blackwell.
   2005. Introduction (to the Transaction edition). In Hans Kohn (ed.), *The Idea of Nationalism: A Study in its Origins and Background*. New Brunswick, NJ: Transaction. [A new edition of Kohn's 1944 classic.]

Calvet, Louis-Jean 1999. *Pour une écologie des langues du monde*. Paris: Plon.

Cameron, Deborah (ed.) 1990. *The Feminist Critique of Language*. London: Routledge.
   1992a. 'Not gender difference, but the difference gender makes' – explanation in research on sex and language. *International Journal of the Sociology of Language* 94: 13–26.
   1992b. *Feminism and Linguistic Theory*. 2nd edn. London: Macmillan.
   1995. *Verbal Hygiene*. London: Routledge.
   2006. *On Language and Sexual Politics*. London: Routledge.
   2007. *The Myth of Mars and Venus: Do Men and Women Really Speak Different Languages?* Oxford: Oxford University Press.

Cameron, Deborah, Elizabeth Frazer, Penelope Harvey, Ben Rampton and Kay Richardson 1992. *Researching Language: Issues of Power and Method*. London: Routledge.

Campanella, Tommaso 1602/1623. *Realis philosophiae epilogisticae partes quatuor...* Frankfurt: Tambach. [The 1623 volume contains the *Civitas solis*, written two decades earlier.]

Campbell, Douglas and Ray MacLean 1974. *Beyond the Atlantic Roar: A Study of the Nova Scotia Scots*. Toronto: McClelland & Stewart.

Canagarajah, A. Suresh 1999a. On EFL teachers, awareness and agency. *ELT Journal* 53: 207–14.
   1999b. *Resisting Linguistic Imperialism in English Language Teaching*. Oxford: Oxford University Press.

Carew, Richard 1614. The excellencie of the English tongue. In William Camden (ed.), *Remaines Concerning Britaine: But Especially Englande, and the Inhabitants Thereof*. London: Leggatt.

Carr, Jo and Anne Pauwels 2006. *Boys and Foreign Language Learning: Real Boys Don't Do Languages*. Basingstoke: Palgrave Macmillan.

Carranza, Miguel and Ellen Bouchard Ryan 1975. Evaluative reactions of bilingual Anglo and Mexican American adolescents toward speakers of English and Spanish. *International Journal of the Sociology of Language* 6: 83–104.

Carroll, John 1972. *Language, Thought and Reality: Selected Writings of Benjamin Lee Whorf*. Cambridge, MA: MIT Press.

Castoriadis, Cornelius 1997. *World in Fragments*. Stanford: Stanford University Press.

Chambers, Jack 1998. English: Canadian varieties. In John Edwards (ed.), *Language in Canada*. Cambridge: Cambridge University Press.

Chapman, R. W. (Robert William) 1932. Oxford English. *Society for Pure English* 4(37).

Charteris-Black, Jonathan 2005. *Politicians and Rhetoric: The Persuasive Power of Metaphor*. Basingstoke: Palgrave.

Chawla, Saroj 2001. Linguistics and genes, people and languages. In Alwin Fill and Peter Mühlhäusler (eds.), *The Ecolinguistics Reader*. London: Continuum.

Cheyne, William 1970. Stereotyped reactions to speakers with Scottish and English regional accents. *British Journal of Social and Clinical Psychology* 9: 77–9.

Choy, Stephen and David Dodd 1976. Standard-English-speaking and non-standard Hawaiian English-speaking children: Comprehension of both dialects and teachers' evaluations. *Journal of Educational Psychology* 68: 184–93.

Cinnirella, Marco 1997. Towards a European identity? *British Journal of Social Psychology* 36: 19–31.

Claplanhoo, Charlie 1999. Untitled. *Globe & Mail* [Toronto], 20 May.

Clery, N. 1927. Five miles from anywhere. *Catholic Bulletin* 17: 875–7.

Clunie, Barnaby 2005. A revolutionary failure resurrected: Dialogical appropriation in Rudy Wiebe's *The Scorched-Wood People*. *University of Toronto Quarterly* 74: 845–65.

Coates, Jennifer 1996. *Women Talk*. Oxford: Blackwell.

2003. *Men Talk*. Oxford: Blackwell.

2004. *Women, Men and Language*. London: Longman.

Cobarrubias, Juan 1983a. Language planning: The state of the art. In Juan Cobarrubias and Joshua Fishman (eds.), *Progress in Language Planning*. Berlin: Mouton.

1983b. Ethical issues in status planning. In Juan Cobarrubias and Joshua Fishman (eds.), *Progress in Language Planning*. Berlin: Mouton.

Coe, Michael 1992. *Breaking the Maya Code*. London: Thames & Hudson.

Cohen, Joshua, Matthew Howard and Martha Nussbaum (eds.) 1999. *Is Multiculturalism Bad for Women?* Princeton, NJ: Princeton University Press.

Colby, Gerard and Charlotte Dennett 1995. *Thy Will Be Done: The Conquest of the Amazon: Nelson Rockefeller and Evangelism in the Age of Oil*. New York: HarperCollins.

Colley, Ann 2005. Review of *Language and Woman's Place: Text and Commentaries* [Robin Lakoff]. *Journal of Language and Social Psychology* 24: 421–8.

Comenius, Johann (Jan Komenský) 1668/1938. *Via lucis vestigata et vestiganda*... Amsterdam: Conrad. [The direct quotations are from Ernest Campagnac's translation, published by Liverpool University Press in 1938.]

Committee on Irish Language Attitudes Research 1975. *Report, as submitted to the Minister for the Gaeltacht*. Dublin: Government Stationery Office.

Condry, John and Sandra Condry 1976. Sex differences: A study of the eye of the beholder. *Child Development* 47: 812–19.

Condry, Sandra, John Condry and Lee Pogatshnik 1983. Sex differences: A study of the ear of the beholder. *Sex Roles* 9: 697–704.

Connor, James 2007. *The Sociology of Loyalty*. New York: Springer.

Connor, Walker 1978. A nation is a nation, is a state, is an ethnic group, is a... *Ethnic and Racial Studies* 1: 377–400.

1990. When is a nation? *Ethnic and Racial Studies* 13: 92–103.

1994. *Ethnonationalism: The Quest for Understanding*. Princeton, NJ: Princeton University Press.

1997. Foreword. In Joshua Fishman, *In Praise of the Beloved Language*. Berlin: Mouton de Gruyter.

Conversi, Daniele 2001. Cosmopolitanism and nationalism. In Athena Leoussi (ed.), *Encyclopaedia of Nationalism*. New Brunswick, NJ: Transaction.

2002. Conceptualizing nationalism: An introduction to Walker Connor's work. In Daniele Conversi (ed.), *Ethnonationalism in the Contemporary World: Walker Connor and the Study of Nationalism*. London: Routledge.

2007. Mapping the field: Theories of nationalism and the ethnosymbolic approach. In Athena Leoussi and Steven Grosby (eds.), *Nationalism and Ethnosymbolism: History, Culture and Ethnicity in the Formation of Nations*. Edinburgh: Edinburgh University Press.

Cooper, Robert (ed.) 1982. *Language Spread: Studies in Diffusion and Social Change*. Bloomington: Indiana University Press.

1989. *Language Planning and Social Change*. Cambridge: Cambridge University Press.

Cormack, Mike and Niamh Hourigan (eds.) 2007. *Minority Language Media*. Clevedon: Multilingual Matters.

Cornelius, Paul 1965. *Languages in Seventeenth- and Early Eighteenth-Century Imaginary Voyages*. Geneva: Droz.

Cosby, William 1997. Elements of igno-ebonics style. *The Wall Street Journal*, 10 January.

Coupland, Nikolas and Hywel Bishop 2007. Ideologised values for British accents. *Journal of Sociolinguistics* 11: 74–93.

Couture, Jocelyne, Kai Nielsen and Michel Seymour (eds.) 1998. *Rethinking Nationalism*. Calgary: University of Calgary Press.

Craig, Gordon 1990. Herder: The legacy. In Kurt Müller-Vollmer (ed.), *Herder Today*. Berlin: Mouton de Gruyter.

Crawford, Mary 1995. *Talking Difference: On Gender and Language*. London: Sage.

Crowley, Terry 1989. Language issues and national development in Vanuatu. In István Fodor and Claude Hagège (eds.), *Language Reform / La réforme des langues / Sprachreforme*, vol. 4. Hamburg: Helmut Buske.

Crowley, Tony 1991. *Proper English? Readings in Language, History and Cultural Identity*. London: Routledge.

Crystal, David 2006. *Language and the Internet*. 2nd edn. Cambridge: Cambridge University Press.

Dalgarno, George 1661. *Ars signorum, vulgo character universalis et lingua philosophica*. London: Hayes.

Dally, Ann 1991. *Women Under the Knife: A History of Surgery*. London: Hutchinson.

David, Maya, Hafriza Burhanudeen and Ain Nadzimah Abdullah (eds.) 2006. *The Power of Language and the Media*. Frankfurt: Peter Lang.

Delanty, Gerard 2006. Nationalism and cosmopolitanism: The paradox of modernity. In Gerard Delanty and Krishan Kumar (eds.), *The Sage Handbook of Nations and Nationalism*. Thousand Oaks, CA: Sage.

Devine, Thomas 1974. *Clanship to Crofters' War*. Manchester: Manchester University Press.

  1999. *The Scottish Nation, 1700–2000*. London: Penguin.

Dewar, Daniel 1812. *Observations on the Character, Customs and Superstitions of the Irish: and on Some of the Causes which have Retarded the Moral and Political Improvement of Ireland*. London: Gale & Curtis.

Diamond, Sara 1989. *Spiritual Warfare: The Politics of the Christian Right*. London: Pluto Press. [My citations are from the 1990 edition, published by Black Rose, Montreal.]

Dickson, Lovat 1939. *Half-Breed: The Story of Grey Owl*. London: Peter Davies.

Dickson, Lovat 1973. *Wilderness Man: The Strange Story of Grey Owl*. Toronto: Macmillan.

Diebold, A. Richard 1968. The consequences of early bilingualism in cognitive and personality information. In Edward Norbeck, Douglass Price-Williams and William McCord (eds.), *The Study of Personality: An Interdisciplinary Appraisal*. New York: Holt, Rinehart & Winston.

Dieckhoff, Alain 2005. Beyond conventional wisdom: Cultural and political nationalism revisited. In Alain Dieckhoff and Christophe Jaffrelot (eds.), *Revisiting Nationalism*. London: Hurst.

Dieckhoff, Alain and Christophe Jaffrelot (eds.) 2005. *Revisiting Nationalism*. London: Hurst.

Dixon, Robert 1997. *The Rise and Fall of Languages*. Cambridge: Cambridge University Press.

Dobrin, Lise and Jeff Good 2007. Endangered language linguistics: Whose mission? Paper presented at the *Linguistic Society of America* conference, Anaheim, January 2007.

Donnan, Hastings and Thomas Wilson 1999. *Borders: Frontiers of Identity, Nation and State*. Oxford: Berg.

Drake, Glendon 1977. *The Role of Prescriptivism in American Linguistics, 1820–1870*. Amsterdam: John Benjamins.

Dworkin, Ronald 2000. *Sovereign Virtue: The Theory and Practice of Equality*. Cambridge, MA: Harvard University Press.

Eastman, Carol 1983. *Language Planning*. San Francisco: Chandler & Sharp.

   1984. Language, ethnic identity and change. In John Edwards (ed.), *Linguistic Minorities, Policies and Pluralism*. London: Academic Press.

Eastman, Carol and Thomas Reese 1981. Associated language: How language and ethnic identity are related. *General Linguistics* 21: 109–16.

Eckert, Penelope and Sally McConnell-Ginet 2003. *Language and Gender*. Cambridge: Cambridge University Press.

Eco, Umberto 1992. Preface. In Roberto Pellerey, *Le lingue perfette nel secolo dell'utopia*. Rome: Laterza.

   1993. *Ricerca della lingua perfetta nella cultura europea*. Rome: Laterza. [Eco's English publishers (in 1995) are Blackwell, and it is from this edition that I have taken my direct quotations.]

Edgerton, Robert 1992. *Sick Societies: Challenging the Myth of Primitive Harmony*. New York: The Free Press.

Edwards, John 1977. Ethnic identity and bilingual education. In Howard Giles (ed.), *Language, Ethnicity and Intergroup Relations*. London: Academic Press.

   1979a. Social class differences and the identification of sex in children's speech. *Journal of Child Language* 6: 121–7.

   1979b. Review of *After Babel* [George Steiner]. *Language Problems and Language Planning* 3: 51–4.

   1979c. Judgements and confidence in reactions to disadvantaged speech. In Howard Giles and Robert St Clair (eds.), *Language and Social Psychology*. Oxford: Blackwell.

   1983a. *The Irish Language*. New York: Garland.

   1983b. Review of *The Language Trap* [John Honey]. *Journal of Language and Social Psychology* 2: 67–76.

   1984a. Irish and English in Ireland. In Peter Trudgill (ed.), *Language in the British Isles*. Cambridge: Cambridge University Press.

   1984b. Introduction. In John Edwards (ed.), *Linguistic Minorities, Policies and Pluralism*. London: Academic Press.

   1985. *Language, Society and Identity*. Oxford: Blackwell.

   1989. *Language and Disadvantage*. 2nd edn. London: Cole & Whurr.

   1992. Sociopolitical aspects of language maintenance and loss: Towards a typology of minority language situations. In Willem Fase, Koen

Jaspaert and Sjaak Kroon (eds.), *Maintenance and Loss of Minority Languages*. Amsterdam: Benjamins.

1994a. Ethnolinguistic pluralism and its discontents. *International Journal of the Sociology of Language* 110: 5–85.

1994b. Language planning and education in Singapore and Malaysia. In Abdullah Hassan (ed.), *Language Planning in Southeast Asia*. Kuala Lumpur: Dewan dan Pustaka.

1994c. What can (or should) linguists do in the face of language decline? In Margaret Harry (ed.), *Papers from the Seventeenth Annual Meeting of the Atlantic Provinces Linguistic Association*. Halifax: Saint Mary's University.

1994d. Review of *Researching Language* [Deborah Cameron, Elizabeth Frazer, Penelope Harvey, Ben Rampton and Kay Richardson]. *Ecumene* 1: 402–5. [*Ecumene* became *Cultural Geographies* in 2002.]

1995. *Multilingualism*. London: Penguin.

1997a. *Is Past a Prologue? Language and Identity at Century's End*. Toronto: Robert F. Harney Professorship, University of Toronto.

1997b. Language minorities and language maintenance. *Annual Review of Applied Linguistics* 17: 30–42.

1998. *Language in Canada*. Cambridge: Cambridge University Press.

1999a. Reactions to three types of speech sample from rural black and white children. In Lilian Falk and Margaret Harry (eds.), *The English Language in Nova Scotia*. Lockeport, Nova Scotia: Roseway.

1999b. Linguistic and cultural reminiscences. *Journal of Multilingual and Multicultural Development* 20: 83–6.

1999c. Refining our understanding of language attitudes. *Journal of Language and Social Psychology* 18: 101–10.

2002a. Old wine in new bottles: Critical remarks on language ecology. In Annette Boudreau, Lise Dubois, Jacques Maurais and Grant McConnell (eds.), *L'écologie des langues: mélanges William Mackey*. Paris: l'Harmattan.

2002b. Sovereignty or separation? Contemporary political discourse in Canada. In Daniele Conversi (ed.), *Ethnonationalism in the Contemporary World: Walker Connor and the Study of Nationalism*. London: Routledge.

2003. Contextualizing language rights. *Journal of Human Rights* 2: 551–71.

2004a. Language minorities. In Alan Davies and Catherine Elder (eds.), *The Handbook of Applied Linguistics*. Oxford: Blackwell.

2004b. Rational nationalism? *Journal of Ethnic and Migration Studies* 30: 837–40.

2006. Players and power in minority-group settings. *Journal of Multilingual and Multicultural Development* 27: 4–21.

2007a. The intellectual presence in nationalist revival efforts. Unpublished paper.

2007b. Back from the brink: The revival of endangered languages. In Marlis Hellinger and Anne Pauwels (eds.), *Handbook of Language and Communication: Diversity and Change*. Berlin: Mouton de Gruyter.

2007c. Societal multilingualism: Reality, recognition and response. In Peter Auer and Li Wei (eds.), *Handbook of Multilingualism and Multilingual Communication*. Berlin: Mouton de Gruyter.

2008. The ecology of language: Insight and illusion. In Angela Creese, Peter Martin and Nancy Hornberger (eds.), *Encyclopedia of Language and Education: Ecology of Language*. New York: Springer. [This is volume 9 of the 10-volume second edition of this encyclopedia.]

in press a. *What Every Teacher Should Know about Language*. Clevedon: Multilingual Matters.

in press b. *The Social Life of Language*. Amsterdam: John Benjamins.

Edwards, John and Maryanne Jacobsen 1987. Standard and regional standard speech: Distinctions and similarities. *Language in Society* 16: 369–80.

Edwards, John and John Williams 1980. Sex-trait stereotypes among young children and young adults: Canadian findings and cross-national comparisons. *Canadian Journal of Behavioural Science* 12: 210–20.

Ehrlich, Susan and Ruth King 1994. Feminist meanings and the (de)politicization of the lexicon. *Language in Society* 23: 59–76.

Ekka, Francis 1972. Men's and women's speech in Kūrux. *Linguistics* 81: 21–31.

Ellington, Ter 2001. *The Myth of the Noble Savage*. Berkeley: University of California Press.

El Yamani, M., Danielle Juteau and Marie McAndrew 1993. Towards a redefinition of ethnic boundaries in Quebec: 'Us' and 'them' in the media discourse on the *affaire Parizeau*. Paper presented at the conference of the Canadian Ethnic Studies Association, Vancouver.

Epps, Patience 2007. Linguists and missionaries: An Amazonian perspective. Paper presented at the *Linguistic Society of America* conference, Anaheim, January 2007.

Epps, Patience and Herb Ladley 2007. Syntax, souls or speakers? On SIL and community language development. Unpublished paper.

Eriksen, Thomas Hylland 2002. *Ethnicity and Nationalism*. London: Pluto Press.

Erikson, Erik 1968. *Identity, Youth and Crisis*. New York: Norton.

Errington, Joseph 2001. Colonial linguistics. *Annual Review of Anthropology* 30: 19–39.

2008. *Linguistics in a Colonial World: A Story of Language, Meaning and Power*. Oxford: Blackwell.

Fellman, Jack 1973a. *The Revival of a Classical Tongue: Eliezer Ben-Yehuda and the Modern Hebrew Language*. The Hague: Mouton.

1973b. Concerning the 'revival' of the Hebrew language. *Anthropological Linguistics* 15: 250–7.

1976. On the revival of the Hebrew language. *Language Sciences* 43(17).

1997. Eliezer Ben-Yehuda: A language reborn. *Ariel: Israel Review of Arts and Letters* 104.

Ferguson, Charles 1982. Religious factors in language spread. In Robert Cooper (ed.), *Language Spread: Studies in Diffusion and Social Change*. Bloomington: Indiana University Press.

1987. Literacy in a hunting-gathering society: The case of the Diyari. *Journal of Anthropological Research* 43: 223–37.

Fernández-Armesto, Felipe 2007. In the U.S.... *Times Higher Education Supplement*, 5 October.

Fichte, Johann Gottlieb 1807/1968. *Addresses to the German Nation*. New York: Harper & Row.

Fidell, Linda 1975. Empirical verification of sex discrimination in hiring practices in psychology. In Rhoda Unger and Florence Denmark (eds.), *Woman: Dependent or Independent Variable?* New York: Psychological Dimensions.

Fill, Alwin and Peter Mühlhäusler 2001. Introduction. In Alwin Fill and Peter Mühlhäusler (eds.), *The Ecolinguistics Reader*. London: Continuum.

Fischer, John 1958. Social influences on the choice of a linguistic variant. *Word* 14: 47–56.

Fishman, Joshua (ed.) 1966. *Language Loyalty in the United States*. The Hague: Mouton.

1972. *Language and Nationalism*. Rowley, MA: Newbury House.

1977. Language and ethnicity. In Howard Giles (ed.), *Language, Ethnicity and Intergroup Relations*. London: Academic Press.

1982. Whorfianism of the third kind. *Language in Society* 11: 1–14.

1983. Progress in language planning: A few concluding sentiments. In Juan Cobarrubias and Joshua Fishman (eds.), *Progress in Language Planning*. Berlin: Mouton.

1989. *Language and Ethnicity in Minority Sociolinguistic Perspective*. Clevedon: Multilingual Matters.

1993. In praise of my language. *Working Papers in Educational Linguistics* (University of Pennsylvania) 9(2): 1–11.

1997. *In Praise of the Beloved Language: A Comparative View of Positive Ethnolinguistic Consciousness*. Berlin: Mouton de Gruyter.

2006. A decalogue of basic theoretical perspectives for a sociology of language and religion. In Tope Omoniyi and Joshua Fishman (eds.), *Explorations in the Sociology of Language and Religion*, Amsterdam: Benjamins.

Florack, Arnd and Ursula Piontkowski 2000. Acculturation attitudes of the Dutch and the Germans towards the European Union: The importance of national and European identification. *Journal of Multilingual and Multicultural Development* 21: 1–13.

Flores, Nancy and Robert Hopper 1975. Mexican Americans' evaluations of spoken Spanish and English. *Speech Monographs* 42: 91–8.

Forde, Patrick 1901. *The Irish Language Movement: Its Philosophy*. Dublin: Gaelic League.

Fordham, Signithia 1999. Dissin' 'the standard': Ebonics as guerrilla warfare at Capital High. *Anthropology & Education Quarterly* 30: 272–93.

Fox, Annie, Danuta Bukatko, Mark Hallahan and Mary Crawford 2007. The medium makes a difference: Gender similarities and differences in instant messaging. *Journal of Language and Social Psychology* 26: 389–97.

Frank, Francine and Frank Anshen 1983. *Language and the Sexes*. Albany: State University of New York Press.

Frankfurt, Harry 2005. *On Bullshit*. Princeton, NJ: Princeton University Press.

Franklin, Karl (ed.) 1987. *Current Concerns of Anthropologists and Missionaries*. Dallas: International Museum of Cultures. [Proceedings of an SIL conference.]

Freeman, Derek 1983. *Margaret Mead and Samoa: The Making and Unmaking of an Anthropological Myth*. Cambridge, MA: Harvard University Press.

Fullerton, Robert 1916. *The Prudence of St Patrick's Irish Policy*. Dublin: O'Brien & Ards.

Gagnon, André and Richard Bourhis 1996. Discrimination in the minimal group paradigm. *Personality and Social Psychology Bulletin* 22: 1289–1301.

Gagnon, Lysiane 1994. How the word 'nationalism' changed its meaning in the Quebec lexicon. *Globe & Mail* [Toronto], 23 April.

    1997a. Two arguments a federalist must never make. *Globe & Mail* [Toronto], 24 August.

    1997b. How Quebec's sovereigntists have appropriated the province's key symbols. *Globe & Mail* [Toronto], 30 August.

Galton, Francis 1883. *Inquiries into Human Faculty and its Development*. London: Macmillan.

Gans, Herbert 1979. Symbolic ethnicity: The future of ethnic groups and cultures in America. *Ethnic and Racial Studies* 2: 1–20.

    1985. Review of *The Varieties of Ethnic Experience* [Micaela DiLeonardo]. *Contemporary Sociology* 14: 302–4.

Gardiner, Scott 2005. A little kaboom of irony. *Globe & Mail* [Toronto], 12 November.

Garner, Marc 2004. *Language: An Ecological View*. Bern: Peter Lang.

Garrett, Peter, Nikolas Coupland and Angie Williams 2003. *Investigating Language Attitudes*. Cardiff: University of Wales Press.

Geeraerts, Dirk 2003. Cultural models of linguistic standardization. In René Dirven, Roslyn Frank and Martin Pütz (eds.), *Cognitive Models in Language and Thought: Ideologies, Metaphors and Meanings*. Berlin: Mouton de Gruyter.

Gellner, Ernest 1964. *Thought and Change*. London: Weidenfeld & Nicolson.

    1968. The new idealism: Cause and meaning in the social sciences. In Imre Lakatos and Alan Musgrave (eds.), *Problems in the Philosophy of Science*. Amsterdam: North-Holland.

    1983. *Nations and Nationalism*. Oxford: Blackwell.

    1994. *Encounters with Nationalism*. Oxford: Blackwell.

    1995. *Anthropology and Politics*. Oxford: Blackwell.

    1996. Do nations have navels? *Nations and Nationalism* 2: 366–70.

Gera, Deborah 2003. *Ancient Greek Ideas on Speech, Language and Civilization*. Oxford: Oxford University Press.

Gershoy, Leo 1962. *Bertrand Barère: A Reluctant Terrorist*. Princeton, NJ: Princeton University Press.

Gibbon, Margaret 1999. *Feminist Perspectives on Language*. London: Longman.

Giddens, Anthony 1985. *The Nation-State and Violence*. Cambridge: Polity.

Giles, Howard and Andrew Billings 2004. Assessing language attitudes. In Alan Davies and Catherine Elder (eds.), *The Handbook of Applied Linguistics*. Oxford: Blackwell.

Giles, Howard and Richard Bourhis 1975. Black speakers with white speech: A real problem? Paper presented at the Fourth International Congress of Applied Linguistics, Stuttgart.

Giles, Howard, Richard Bourhis and Ann Davies 1979. Prestige speech styles: The imposed norm and inherent value hypotheses. In William McCormack and Stephen Wurm (eds.), *Language and Society*. The Hague: Mouton.

Giles, Howard, Richard Bourhis and Donald Taylor 1977. Towards a theory of language in ethnic group relations. In Howard Giles (ed.), *Language, Ethnicity and Intergroup Relations*. London: Academic Press.

Giles, Howard, Richard Bourhis, Peter Trudgill and Alan Lewis 1974. The imposed norm hypothesis: A validation. *Quarterly Journal of Speech* 60: 405–10.

Giles, Howard and Nikolas Coupland 1991. *Language: Contexts and Consequences*. Milton Keynes: Open University Press.

Giles, Howard and John Edwards, in press. Attitudes to language: Past, present and future. In Kirsten Malmkjær (ed.), *The Linguistics Encyclopedia*. 3rd edn. London: Routledge.

Giles, Howard and Peter Powesland 1975. *Speech Style and Social Evaluation*. London: Academic Press.

Giles, Howard and Ellen Bouchard Ryan 1982. Prolegomena for developing a social psychological theory of language attitudes. In Ellen Bouchard Ryan and Howard Giles (eds.), *Attitudes Towards Language Variation*. London: Edward Arnold.

Giles, Howard and Philip Smith 1979. Accommodation theory. In Howard Giles and Robert St Clair (eds.), *Language and Social Psychology*. Oxford: Blackwell.

Githens-Mazer, Jonathan 2008. Locating agency in collective political behaviour: Nationalism, social movements and individual mobilisation. *Politics* 28: 41–9.

Glavin, Terry 1999. Untitled. *Globe & Mail* [Toronto], 20 May.

Gleason, Philip 1983. Identifying identity: A semantic history. *Journal of American History* 69: 910–31.

Gleitman, Lila and Henry Gleitman 1970. *Phrase and Paraphrase*. New York: Norton.

Globe & Mail [Toronto] (1992–2007) Leaders. 24 November 1992; 1 March 1995; 1 November 1995; 30 January 1996; 1 December 1997; 20 October 2007; 24 October 2007; 3 November 2007.

Goffman, Erving 1959. *The Presentation of Self in Everyday Life*. Garden City, NY: Doubleday.

1961. *Encounters*. Indianapolis: Bobbs-Merrill.

1963. *Stigma.* Englewood Cliffs, NJ: Prentice-Hall.

1976. Gender advertisements. *Studies in the Anthropology of Visual Communication* 3: 65–154. [Published as a book by Harper & Row, 1979.]

1981. *Forms of Talk.* Oxford: Blackwell.

Goodenough, Florence 1926. Racial differences in the intelligence of school children. *Journal of Experimental Psychology* 9: 388–97.

Goodman, Felicitas 1972. *Speaking in Tongues.* Chicago: University of Chicago Press.

Gordon, Raymond (ed.) 2005. *Ethnologue: Languages of the World.* 15th edn. Dallas: Summer Institute of Linguistics.

Goropius Becanus, Joannus (Jan van Gorp) 1569. *Origines Antwerpianae...* Antwerp: Plantin.

Gramsci, Antonio 1978. *Selections from Political Writings.* London: Lawrence & Wishart.

1985. *Selections from Cultural Writings.* London: Lawrence & Wishart.

Graves, Robert 1927/1972. *Lars Porsena, or, The Future of Swearing and Improper Language.* London: Kegan, Paul, Trench, Trubner & Co. [Later edition published by Martin Brian & O'Keeffe.]

1929/1960. *Goodbye to All That.* London: Cassell. [My citation is from a Penguin edition.]

Gray, John 1992. *Men are from Mars, Women are from Venus.* New York: Harper-Collins.

1996. Parizeau's year of disgrace taught him nothing. *Globe & Mail* [Toronto], 2 November.

Greeley, Andrew 1974. *Ethnicity in the United States.* New York: Wiley.

Green, Jonathon 1996. *Words Apart: The Language of Prejudice.* London: Kyle Cathie.

Green, Lorraine 2004. Gender. In Gary Taylor and Steve Spencer (eds.), *Social Identities: Multidisciplinary Approaches.* London: Routledge.

Greenfeld, Liah 1992. *Nationalism: Five Roads to Modernity.* Cambridge, MA: Harvard University Press.

2006. Modernity and nationalism. In Gerard Delanty and Krishan Kumar (eds.), *The Sage Handbook of Nations and Nationalism.* Thousand Oaks, CA: Sage.

Grégoire, Henri (Abbé) 1794. *Rapport sur la nécessité et les moyens d'anéantir les patois et d'universaliser l'usage de la langue française.* Paris: Imprimerie nationale.

Grenoble, Lenore and Lindsay Whaley 2006. *Saving Languages: An Introduction to Language Revitalization.* Cambridge: Cambridge University Press.

Grillo, Ralph 1989. *Dominant Languages.* Cambridge: Cambridge University Press.

Groebner, Valentin 2004. *Der Schein der Person: Steckbrief, Ausweis und Kontrolle im Europa des Mittelalters.* Munich: Beck.

Grosby, Steven 1991. Review of *Nations and Nationalism Since 1780* [Eric Hobsbawm]. *Ethnic and Racial Studies* 14: 418–20.

Grosby, Steven 2001. Hobsbawm's theory of nationalism. In Athena Leoussi (ed.), *Encyclopaedia of Nationalism*. New Brunswick, NJ: Transaction.

Grosby, Steven 2005. *Nationalism: A Very Short Introduction*. Oxford: Oxford University Press.

Grosjean, François 1982. *Life With Two Languages*. Cambridge, MA: Harvard University Press.

Grove, Richard 2001. Atavistic mistakes. *Times Higher Education Supplement*, 22 June.

Guibernau, Montsarrat 2001. Globalization and the nation-state. In Montsarrat Guibernau and John Hutchinson (eds.), *Understanding Nationalism*. Cambridge: Polity.

Guitarte, Guillermo and Rafael Torres-Quintero 1974. Linguistic correctness and the role of the academies in Latin America. In Joshua Fishman (ed.), *Advances in Language Planning*. The Hague: Mouton.

Gumperz, John (ed.) 1982. *Language and Social Identity*. Cambridge: Cambridge University Press.

Ha Tu Thanh and Rhéal Séguin 1998. Ethnic voters should not get 'veto', Landry says. *Globe & Mail* [Toronto], 1 September.

Haas, Mary 1944. Men's and women's speech in Koasati. *Language* 20: 142–49.

Hale, Thomas 1998. *Griots and Griottes*. Bloomington: Indiana University Press.

Hall, Robert 1974. *External History of the Romance Languages*. New York: Elsevier.

Hall, Stuart 1996. Introduction: Who needs identity? In Stuart Hall and Paul du Gay (eds.), *Questions of Cultural Identity*. London: Sage.

Hall, Stuart and Paul du Gay (eds.) 1996. *Questions of Cultural Identity*. London: Sage.

Halliday, Michael 1968. The users and uses of language. In Joshua Fishman (ed.), *Readings in the Sociology of Language*. The Hague: Mouton.

Hamers, Josiane and Michel Blanc 2000. *Bilinguality and Bilingualism*. 2nd edn. Cambridge: Cambridge University Press.

Hannah, Annette and Tamar Murachver 2007. Gender preferential responses to speech. *Journal of Language and Social Psychology* 26: 274–90.

Harmon, David 1996. Losing species, losing languages: Connections between biological and linguistic diversity. *Southwest Journal of Linguistics* 15: 89–108.

Hassig, Ross 1992. *War and Society in Ancient Mesoamerica*. Berkeley: University of California Press.

Haugaard, Mark 2006. Nationalism and liberalism. In Gerard Delanty and Krishan Kumar (eds.), *The Sage Handbook of Nations and Nationalism*. Thousand Oaks, CA: Sage.

Haugen, Einar 1966. Dialect, language, nation. *American Anthropologist* 68: 922–35.

1972. The ecology of language. In Anwar Dil (ed.), *The Ecology of Language: Essays by Einar Haugen*. Stanford: Stanford University Press.

1983. The implementation of corpus planning. In Juan Cobarrubias and Joshua Fishman (eds.), *Progress in Language Planning*. Berlin: de Gruyter.

1985. The language of imperialism. In Nessa Wolfson and Joan Manes (eds.), *Language of Inequality*. The Hague: Mouton.

1987. *Blessings of Babel: Bilingualism and Language Planning*. Berlin: Mouton de Gruyter.

Hayward, Tim 1995. *Ecological Thought: An Introduction*. Cambridge: Polity.

Headland, Thomas 1996. Missionaries and social justice: Are they part of the problem or part of the solution? *Missiology* 24: 167–78.

Heap, David 2007. The *Linguistic Atlas of the Iberian Peninsula* (*ALPI*): A geolinguistic treasure 'lost' and found. *Toronto Working Papers in Linguistics* 27: 83–92.

Heath, Shirley Brice 1977. A national language academy? Debate in the new nation. *International Journal of the Sociology of Language* 11: 9–43.

Heine, Bernd 1979. *Sprache, Gesellschaft und Kommunikation in Afrika*. Munich: Weltforum.

Hellinger, Marlis and Anne Pauwels 2007. Language and sexism. In Marlis Hellinger and Anne Pauwels (eds.), *Handbook of Language and Communication: Diversity and Change*. Berlin: Mouton de Gruyter.

Henze, Rosemary and Kathryn Davis 1999. *Authenticity and Identity: Lessons from Indigenous Language Education*. Arlington, VA: American Anthropological Association [= *Anthropology & Education Quarterly* 30(1)].

Herder, Johann Gottfried 1772. *Abhandlung über den Ursprung der Sprache*. Berlin: Voss.

Herman, Simon 1961. Explorations in the social psychology of language choice. *Human Relations* 14: 149–64.

Hertz, Friedrich 1944. *Nationality in History and Politics*. London: Routledge & Kegan Paul.

Himmelfarb, Gertrude 1999. *One Nation, Two Cultures*. New York: Knopf.

Hirst, Julia 2004. Sexuality. In Gary Taylor and Steve Spencer (eds.), *Social Identities: Multidisciplinary Approaches*. London: Routledge.

Hobbes, Thomas 1651. *Leviathan, or, The Matter, Forme, and Power of a Common Wealth, Ecclesiasticall and Civil*. London: Crooke. [My citation is from Dent's *Everyman* edition, 1973.]

Hobsbawm, Eric 1990. *Nations and Nationalism Since 1780*. Cambridge: Cambridge University Press.

Hobsbawm, Eric and Terence Ranger (eds.) 1983. *The Invention of Tradition*. Cambridge: Cambridge University Press.

Hogg, Michael and Dominic Abrams 1988. *Social Identification*. London: Routledge.

Hohenhaus, Peter 2005. Elements of traditional and 'reverse' purism in relation to computer-mediated communication. In Nils Langer and Winifred Davies (eds.), *Linguistic Purism in the Germanic Languages*. Berlin: Walter de Gruyter.

Hollinger, David 1995. *Post-Ethnic America: Beyond Multiculturalism*. New York: Basic Books.

2006. *Cosmopolitanism and Solidarity*. Madison: University of Wisconsin Press.

Holmes, Janet 1992. *Introduction to Sociolinguistics*. London: Longman.

1995. *Women, Men and Politeness*. London: Longman.

Honey, John 1983. *The Language Trap*. Kenton, Middlesex: National Council for Educational Standards.

Hook, Sidney 1989. Is teaching 'Western Culture' racist or sexist? *Encounter* 73(3): 14–19.

Hooson, David 1994. *Geography and National Identity*. Oxford: Blackwell.

Hughes, Geoffrey 2006. *An Encyclopedia of Swearing*. Armonk, NY: Sharpe.

Hughes, Susan 2002. Expletives of lower working-class women. *Language in Society* 21: 291–303.

Hurka, Thomas 1989. Should whites write about minorities? *Globe & Mail* [Toronto], 19 December.

Hutchinson, John 1994. *Modern Nationalism*. London: Fontana.

Hvalkof, Søren and Peter Aaby (eds.) 1981. *Is God an American? An Anthropological Perspective on the Missionary Work of the Summer Institute of Linguistics*. London: Survival International / Copenhagen: International Work Group for Indigenous Affairs.

Hyde, Douglas 1894. The necessity for de-anglicising Ireland. In Charles Duffy, George Sigerson and Douglas Hyde (eds.), *The Revival of Irish Literature*. London: Unwin.

Ichijo, Atsuko and Gordana Uzelac (eds.) 2005. *When is the Nation?* London: Routledge.

Igartua, José 2006. *The Other Quiet Revolution: National Identities in English Canada, 1945–71*. Vancouver: University of British Columbia Press.

Ignatieff, Michael 1993. *Blood and Belonging: Journeys into the New Nationalism*. Toronto: Viking / Penguin.

Immen, Wallace 2008a. Women in top positions on the decline. *Globe & Mail* [Toronto], 16 January.

2008b. I am woman: Should I roar like man? *Globe & Mail* [Toronto], 25 January.

Isajiw, Wsevolod 1980. Definitions of ethnicity. In Jay Goldstein and Rita Bienvenue (eds.), *Ethnicity and Ethnic Relations in Canada*. Toronto: Butterworth.

1990. Ethnic identity retention. In Raymond Breton, Wsevolod Isajiw, Warren Kalbach and Jeffrey Reitz, *Ethnic Identity and Equality*. Toronto: University of Toronto Press.

Isenberg, Andrew 2000. *The Destruction of the Bison*. Cambridge: Cambridge University Press.

J. C. 2007. Turban terrorist. *Times Literary Supplement*, 7 December.

Jahr, Ernst Håkon 1992. Sociolinguistics: Language planning. In William Bright (ed.), *International Encyclopedia of Linguistics*, vol. 4. Oxford: Oxford University Press.

Jay, Timothy 1992. *Cursing in America*. Amsterdam: Benjamins.

2000. *Why We Curse*. Amsterdam: Benjamins.

Jenkins, Jennifer 2007. *English as a Lingua Franca: Attitude and Identity*. Oxford: Oxford University Press.

Jenkins, Richard 1997. *Rethinking Ethnicity*. Thousand Oaks, CA: Sage.

2004. *Social Identity*. 2nd edn. London: Routledge.

Jernudd, Björn and Michael Shapiro (eds.) 1989. *The Politics of Language Purism*. Berlin: Mouton de Gruyter.

Jespersen, Otto 1922. *Language: Its Nature, Development and Origin*. London: Allen & Unwin.

1946. *Mankind, Nation and Individual*. London: Allen & Unwin.

Johnson, Sally and Astrid Ensslin (eds.) 2007. *Language in the Media*. London: Continuum.

Johnson, Sally and Ulrike Meinhof (eds.) 1997. *Language and Masculinity*. Oxford: Blackwell.

Johnson, Samuel 1747. *The Plan of a Dictionary of the English Language*. London: Knapton.

1755. *A Dictionary of the English Language*. London: Knapton.

Jones, Katherine 2001. *Accent on Privilege: English Identities and Anglophilia in the United States*. Philadelphia: Temple University Press.

Jones, Thomas 1688/1972. *The British Language in its Lustre, or, A Copious Dictionary of Welsh and English . . .* London: Baskerville & Marsh.

Jones, William 1798. The third anniversary discourse, delivered 2nd February, 1786: On the Hindus. *Asiatick Researches* 1: 415–31.

Jonson, Ben 1612. *The Alchemist*. London: Burre & Stepneth. [The play was first produced two years earlier.]

Joos, Martin 1967. *The Five Clocks*. New York: Harcourt, Brace & World. [First published by the Indiana University Research Center in Anthropology, Folklore and Linguistics, Bloomington, 1962.]

Joseph, George, Vasu Reddy and Mary Searle-Chatterjee 1990. Eurocentrism in the social sciences. *Race and Class* 31(4): 1–26.

Joseph, John 2004. *Language and Identity: National, Ethnic, Religious*. Basingstoke: Palgrave Macmillan.

2007. Review of *Along the Routes to Power* [Martin Pütz, Joshua Fishman and JoAnne Neff-van Aertselaer]. *Journal of Multilingual and Multicultural Development* 28: 537–9.

Kaplan, Robert and Richard Baldauf 1997. *Language Planning: From Practice to Theory*. Clevedon: Multilingual Matters.

Katz, David 1981. The language of Adam in seventeenth-century England. In Hugh Lloyd-Jones, Valerie Pearl and Blair Worden (eds.), *History and Imagination: Essays in Honour of H. R. Trevor-Roper*. London: Duckworth.

Katz, Welwyn 1987. *False Face*. Vancouver: Douglas & McIntyre.

1989. My own story, plain and coloured. *Canadian Children's Literature* 54: 31–6.

Keating, Michael 2001. *Nations Against the State*. Basingstoke: Palgrave.

Kedourie, Elie 1960. *Nationalism*. London: Hutchinson. [My citations are from the 1961 Praeger paperback edition.]

Keeshig-Tobias, Lenore 1990. Stop stealing native stories. *Globe & Mail* [Toronto], 26 January.

Kempe, Anders 1688. *Die Sprachen des Paradises...* Hamburg: Kopman. [Albrecht Kopman is in fact the translator of Kempe's pamphlet – although the Swedish original is now lost; this German version, at least, appeared under the pseudonym 'Simon Simplex'.]

Kennedy, Michael 1999. 'Lochaber no more': A critical examination of Highland emigration mythology. In Marjory Harper and Michael Vance (eds.), *Myth, Migration and the Making of Memory: Scotia and Nova Scotia, c1700–1900*. Halifax: Fernwood.

Kibbee, Douglas 2003. Language policy and linguistic theory. In Jacques Maurais and Michael Morris (eds.), *Languages in a Globalising World*. Cambridge: Cambridge University Press.

Kiesling, Scott 2007. Men, masculinities and language. *Language and Linguistics Compass* 1: 653–73.

Kindell, Gloria 1997. Summer Institute of Linguistics: What does SIL have to do with sociolinguistics? In Christina Bratt Paulston and G. Richard Tucker (eds.), *The Early Days of Sociolinguistics*. Dallas: Summer Institute of Linguistics.

Kinsella, W. P. (William) 1977. *Dance Me Outside*. Ottawa: Oberon.

Kissau, Scott 2006. Gender differences in motivation to learn French. *Canadian Modern Language Review* 62: 401–22.

Kister, Meir 1993. Adam: A study of some legends of Tafsīr and Hadīth literature. *Israel Oriental Studies* 13: 113–74.

Kitoko-Nsiku, Edouard 2007. Dogs' languages or people's languages? The return of Bantu languages to primary schools in Mozambique. *Current Issues in Language Planning* 8: 258–82.

Knox, Dilwyn 1990. Ideas on gesture and universal languages, c1550–1650. In John Henry and Sarah Hutton (eds.), *New Perspectives on Renaissance Thought: Essays in the History of Science, Education and Philosophy*. London: Duckworth.

Kockel, Ullrich and Máiréad Nic Craith (eds.) 2007. *Cultural Heritages as Reflexive Traditions*. Basingstoke: Palgrave Macmillan.

Koestler, Arthur 1976. *The Thirteenth Tribe*. London: Hutchinson. [My citation is from the 1980 Picador paperback.]

Kohn, Hans 1944/2005. *The Idea of Nationalism: A Study in its Origins and Background*. New York: Macmillan / New Brunswick, NJ: Transaction.
    1967. *Prelude to Nation-States*. Princeton, NJ: Van Nostrand.

Kramarae, Cheris 1981. *Women and Men Speaking*. Rowley, MA: Newbury House.

Krech, Shepard 1999. *The Ecological Indian: Myth and History*. New York: Norton.

Kretzschmar, William 1998. *Ebonics*. [Special Issue of the *Journal of English Linguistics* 26:2.]

Kristiansen, Tore, Peter Garrett and Nikolas Coupland 2005. *Subjective Processes in Language Variation and Change*. Copenhagen: Reitzel [= *Acta Linguistica Hafniensa* 37].

Kroskrity, Paul 1993. *Language, History and Identity*. Tucson: University of Arizona Press.

Kukathas, Chandran 1992. Are there any cultural rights? *Political Theory* 20: 105–39.

Kymlicka, Will 1989. *Liberalism, Community and Culture*. Oxford: Clarendon.

  1995a. *Multicultural Citizenship: A Liberal Theory of Minority Rights*. Oxford: Clarendon.

  (ed.) 1995b. *The Rights of Minority Cultures*. Oxford: Oxford University Press.

  1999. Misunderstanding nationalism. In Ronald Beiner (ed.), *Theorizing Nationalism*. Albany: State University of New York Press.

  2000. Modernity and national identity. In Shlomo Ben-Ami, Yoav Peled and Alberto Spektorowski (eds.), *Ethnic Challenges to the Modern Nation State*. London: Macmillan.

  2007. *Multicultural Odysseys: Navigating the New International Politics of Diversity*. Oxford: Oxford University Press.

le Laboureur, Louis 1667. *Les avantages de la langue françoise sur la langue latine*. Paris: de Luyne.

Labov, William 1966. *The Social Stratification of English in New York City*. Washington: Center for Applied Linguistics.

  1976. *Language in the Inner City*. Philadelphia: University of Pennsylvania Press.

  1977. *Sociolinguistic Patterns*. Philadelphia: University of Pennsylvania Press.

  1982. Objectivity and commitment in linguistic science: The case of the Black English trial in Ann Arbor. *Language in Society* 11: 165–201.

  1994. *Principles of Linguistic Change*. Vol. 1: *Internal Factors*; Vol. 2: *Social Factors*. Oxford: Blackwell.

Ladefoged, Peter 1992. Another view of endangered languages. *Language* 68: 809–11.

Lakoff, George and Mark Johnson 1980. *Metaphors We Live By*. Chicago: University of Chicago Press.

Lakoff, Robin 1973. Language and woman's place. *Language in Society* 2: 45–79.

  1975. *Language and Woman's Place*. New York: Harper & Row.

  1990. *Talking Power*. New York: Basic Books.

  2004. *Language and Woman's Place: Text and Commentaries*. New York: Oxford University Press. [This revised and expanded edition of the 1975 book includes two dozen commentaries, under the editorship of Mary Bucholtz.]

Lambert, Wallace, Robert Hodgson, Robert Gardner and Steven Fillenbaum 1960. Evaluational reactions to spoken languages. *Journal of Abnormal and Social Psychology* 60: 44–51.

Langer, Nils and Winifred Davies (eds.) 2005. *Linguistic Purism in the Germanic Languages*. Berlin: Walter de Gruyter.

LaPiere, Robert 1934. Attitudes versus actions. *Social Forces* 13: 230–7.

Lapierre, Jean-William 1988. *Le pouvoir politique et les langues: Babel et Léviathan.* Paris: Presses Universitaires de France.

Laver, John and Peter Trudgill 1979. Phonetic and linguistic markers in speech. In Klaus Scherer and Howard Giles (eds.), *Social Markers in Speech.* Cambridge: Cambridge University Press.

Lawson, Steven 1999. Untitled. *Globe & Mail* [Toronto], 20 May.

Leaper, Campbell and Melanie Ayres 2007. A meta-analytic review of gender variations in adults' language use. *Personality and Social Psychology Review* 11: 328–63.

Leet-Pellegrini, Helena 1980. Conversational dominance as a function of gender and expertise. In Howard Giles, Peter Robinson and Philip Smith (eds.), *Language: Social Psychological Perspectives.* Oxford: Pergamon.

Leibniz, Gottfried 1717. *Collectanea etymologica, illustrationi linguarum, veteris Celticæ, Germanicæ, Gallicæ, aliarumque inservientia.* Hanover: Förster.

1838–1840. *Deutsche Schriften.* Berlin: Veit [edited by Gottschalk Guhrauer, in two volumes].

Lenin, Vladimir Ilyich 1951. *Critical Remarks on the National Question.* Moscow: Progress.

Lenneberg, Eric 1967. *Biological Foundations of Language.* New York: Wiley.

Leoussi, Athena (ed.) 2001. *Encyclopaedia of Nationalism.* New Brunswick, NJ: Transaction.

Leoussi, Athena and Steven Grosby (eds.) 2007. *Nationalism and Ethnosymbolism: History, Culture and Ethnicity in the Formation of Nations.* Edinburgh: Edinburgh University Press.

Le Page, Robert and Andrée Tabouret-Keller 1985. *Acts of Identity.* Cambridge: Cambridge University Press.

Lessnoff, Michael 2002. *Ernest Gellner and Modernity.* Cardiff: University of Wales Press.

Levy, Leonard 1993. *Blasphemy.* Chapel Hill: University of North Carolina Press.

Lewis, E. Glyn 1976. Bilingualism and bilingual education: The ancient world to the Renaissance. In Joshua Fishman (ed.), *Bilingual Education.* Rowley, MA: Newbury House.

Lewis, Norman 1988. *The Missionaries.* London: Secker & Warburg.

Lewis, Paul 2001. Missionaries and language. In Rajend Mesthrie (ed.), *Concise Encyclopedia of Sociolinguistics.* Amsterdam: Elsevier.

Lippi-Green, Rosina 1997. *English with an Accent: Language, Ideology and Discrimination in the United States.* London: Routledge.

Llamas, Carmen 2006. Shifting identities and orientations in a border town. In Tope Omoniyi and Goodith White (eds.), *The Sociolinguistics of Identity.* London: Continuum.

2007. 'A place between places': Language and identities in a border town. *Language in Society* 36: 579–604.

McArthur, Roshan 1996. Taboo words in print. *English Today* 47: 50–8.

294 References

McArthur, Tom 1992. Academy. In Tom McArthur (ed.), *Oxford Companion to the English Language*. Oxford: Oxford University Press.

McCrone, David 1998. *The Sociology of Nationalism*. London: Routledge.

Mac Dhonuill, Alastair 1751. *Ais-eiridh na Sean Chánoin Albannaich; no, An nuadh Oranaiche Gaidhealach*. Duneidiunn [Edinburgh]: Go feim an Ughdair [i.e. published by the author]. [The title translates as *The Resurrection of the Old Scottish Language; or, The New Gaelic Songbook*.]

MacEachern, Donna 1988. The influence of first names on school marks. Unpublished B.A. (Hons) thesis, St Francis Xavier University.

McGarry, John 2001. Northern Ireland, civic nationalism, and the Good Friday agreement. In John McGarry (ed.), *Northern Ireland and the Divided World*. Oxford: Oxford University Press.

MacInnes, John 1992. The Scottish Gaelic language. In Glanville Price (ed.), *The Celtic Connection*. Gerrard's Cross: Colin Smythe.

MacKenzie, Alexander 1883. *The History of the Highland Clearances; Containing a Reprint of Donald MacLeod's 'Gloomy Memories of the Highlands'; Isle of Skye in 1882; and a Verbatim Report of the Trial of the Braes Crofters*. Inverness: MacKenzie.

Mackey, William 1980. The ecology of language shift. In Peter Nelde (ed.), *Languages in Contact and Conflict*. Wiesbaden: Steiner.

  1991. Language diversity, language policy and the sovereign state. *History of European Ideas* 13: 51–61.

McKerl, Mandy 2007. Multiculturalism, gender and violence: Multiculturalism – is it bad for women? *Culture and Religion* 8: 187–217.

M'Leod (Macleod), Donald 1841. *History of the Destitution in Sutherlandshire*. Edinburgh: M'Leod. [A collection of letters published in the *Weekly Chronicle*, Edinburgh, in 1840 and 1841 – later appearances under the title *Gloomy Memories of the Highlands*. The 1857 Canadian edition I cite here was self-published (printed by Thomson) in Toronto.]

McNicholas, Anthony 2007. *Politics, Religion and the Press: Irish Journalism in Mid-Victorian England*. Frankfurt: Peter Lang.

Maffi, Luisa 2000a. Language preservation vs. language maintenance and revitalization: Assessing concepts, approaches and implications for the language sciences. *International Journal of the Sociology of Language* 142: 175–90.

  2000b. Linguistic and biological diversity: The inextricable link. In Robert Phillipson (ed.), *Rights to Language*. Mahwah, NJ: Erlbaum.

  (ed.) 2001. *On Biocultural Diversity: Linking Language, Knowledge and the Environment*. Washington: Smithsonian Institute Press.

Magocsi, Paul 1982. The language question as a factor in the national movement. In Andrei Markovits and Frank Sysyn (eds.), *Nationbuilding and the Politics of Nationalism*. Cambridge, MA: Harvard University Press.

Makoni, Busi, Sinfree Makoni and Pedzisai Mashiri 2007. Naming practices and language planning in Zimbabwe. *Current Issues in Language Planning* 8: 437–67.

Makoni, Sinfree and Ulrike Meinhof 2004. Western perspectives in applied linguistics in Africa. *AILA Review* 17: 77–104.

Makoni, Sinfree and Alastair Pennycook 2007. Disinventing and reconstituting languages. In Sinfree Makoni and Alastair Pennycook (eds.), *Disinventing and Reconstituting Languages*. Clevedon: Multilingual Matters.

Malešević, Siniša 2002. Identity: Conceptual, operational and historical critique. In Siniša Malešević and Mark Haugaard (eds.), *Making Sense of Collectivity: Ethnicity, Nationalism and Globalization*. London: Pluto Press.

2004. *The Sociology of Ethnicity*. Thousand Oaks, CA: Sage.

Mandela, Nelson 1994. *A Long Walk to Freedom*. Johannesburg: Macdonald Purnell.

Mandelbaum, David 1963. *Selected Writings of Edward Sapir*. Berkeley: University of California Press.

Manz, Stefan, Andreas Musolff, Jonathan Long and Ljiljana Šarić (eds.) 2004. *Discourses of Intercultural Identity in Britain, Germany and Eastern Europe*. Clevedon: Multilingual Matters [= *Journal of Multilingual and Multicultural Development* 25(5/6)].

Marsh, Joss 1998. *Word Crimes*. Chicago: University of Chicago Press.

Martí, Fèlix, Paul Ortega, Itziar Idiazabal, Andoni Barreña, Patxi Juaristi, Carme Junyent, Belen Uranga and Estibaliz Amorrortu 2005. *Words and Worlds: World Languages Review*. Clevedon: Multilingual Matters.

Martin, David 1990. *Tongues of Fire: The Explosion of Protestantism in Latin America*. Oxford: Blackwell.

Marx, Karl 1852/1963. Der achtzehnte Brumaire des Louis Napoleon. *Die Revolution*, 1 May. [Later versions replace 'Napoleon' with 'Bonaparte'; my citation is from the 1963 publication by International Publishers, New York.]

Maturi, Walter 1962. D'Azeglio. In Alberto Ghisalberti (ed.), *Dizionario Biografico degli Italiani*, vol. 4. Rome: Istituto della Enciclopedia Italiana.

Maurud, Oivind 1976. Reciprocal comprehension of neighbour languages in Scandinavia. *Scandinavian Journal of Educational Research* 20(2): 49–72.

May, Stephen 2001. *Language and Minority Rights: Ethnicity, Nationalism and the Politics of Language*. London: Longman.

Meek, Donald 2000. God and Gaelic: The Highland churches and Gaelic cultural identity. In Gordon McCoy and Maolcholaim Scott (eds.), *Aithne na nGael – Gaelic Identities*. Belfast: Queen's University, Institute of Irish Studies.

Menezes de Souza, Lynn 2007. Entering a culture quietly: Writing and cultural survival in indigenous education in Brazil. In Sinfree Makoni and Alastair Pennycook (eds.), *Disinventing and Reconstituting Languages*. Clevedon: Multilingual Matters.

Mill, John Stuart 1861/1964. *Considerations on Representative Government*. London: Dent.

Mills, Jean 2006. Talking about silence. *International Journal of Bilingualism* 10: 1–16.

Mills, Sara 2003. *Gender and Politeness*. Cambridge: Cambridge University Press.

Milroy, Lesley and Dennis Preston 1999. *Attitudes, Perceptions, and Linguistic Features*. Thousand Oaks, CA: Sage [= *Journal of Language and Social Psychology* 18:1].

Minogue, Kenneth 2001. Gellner's theory of nationalism: A critical assessment. In Athena Leoussi (ed.), *Encyclopaedia of Nationalism*. New Brunswick, NJ: Transaction.

Modiano, Marko 2007. Euro-English from a 'deficit linguistics' perspective? *World Englishes* 26: 525–33.

Moller, Heather 2007. Valuable work of imprisoned linguist recovered. *Alumni Gazette* [University of Western Ontario], Summer: 30.

Mollin, Sandra 2006. *Euro-English: Assessing Variety Status*. Tübingen: Gunter Narr. [This book derives from the author's Freiburg dissertation, The Institutionalization of Euro-English? Form and Function of an Emerging Non-native Variety of English in Europe.]

Monck Mason, Henry 1846. *History of the Origin and Progress of the Irish Society, Established for Promoting the Education of the Native Irish, through the Medium of their own Language*. Dublin: Goodwin, Son & Nethercott.

Monmonier, Mark 2006. *From Squaw Tit to Whorehouse Meadow: How Maps Name, Claim and Inflame*. Chicago: University of Chicago Press.

Montagu, Ashley 2001. *The Anatomy of Swearing*. Philadelphia: University of Pennsylvania Press. [First published by Macmillan, 1967.]

Montagu, Mary Wortley (Lady) 1709/1965. *The Complete Letters of Lady Mary Wortley Montagu*. Oxford: Clarendon. [In 3 illustrated volumes, edited by Robert Halsband, the letters here date from 1708 to 1762, the year of Lady Montagu's death.]

Moody, Roger (ed.) 1988. *The Indigenous Voice*. 2 vols. London: Zed Books.

Moran, Joseph 2001. Jesuit missionaries to sixteenth century Japan. In John Sawyer and J. M. Y. Simpson (eds.), *Concise Encyclopedia of Language and Religion*. Amsterdam: Elsevier.

Morgan, Prys 1983. From a death to a view: The hunt for the Welsh past in the romantic period. In Eric Hobsbawm and Terence Ranger (eds.), *The Invention of Tradition*. Cambridge: Cambridge University Press.

Morris, Charles 1946. *Signs, Language and Behavior*. Englewood Cliffs, NJ: Prentice-Hall.

Mount, Ferdinand 1995. Ruling passions. *Times Literary Supplement*, 17 February.

Mufwene, Salikoko 2001. *The Ecology of Language Evolution*. Cambridge: Cambridge University Press.

　2002. Colonisation, globalisation and the future of languages in the twenty-first century. *International Journal on Multicultural Societies* 4: 162–93.

　2008. *Language Evolution: Contact, Competition and Change*. London: Continuum.

Mugglestone, Lynda 1995. *'Talking Proper': The Rise of Accent as Social Symbol.* Oxford: Clarendon.

Mühleisen, Susanne 2007. Language and religion. In Marlis Hellinger and Anne Pauwels (eds.), *Handbook of Language and Communication: Diversity and Change.* Berlin: Mouton de Gruyter.

Mühlhäusler, Peter 1996. *Linguistic Ecology.* London: Routledge.

2000. Language planning and language ecology. *Current Issues in Language Planning* 1: 306–67.

Müller, Max 1862. *Lectures on the Science of Language.* London: Longman, Green, Longman & Roberts.

Müller-Hill, Benno 1988. *Murderous Science.* Oxford: Oxford University Press.

Musgrove, Frank 1982. *Education and Anthropology.* Chichester: Wiley.

Musolff, Andreas 2000. *Mirror Images of Europe: Metaphors in the Public Debate about Europe in Britain and Germany.* Munich: Iudicium.

2004. *Metaphor and Political Discourse.* Basingstoke: Palgrave.

Nadeau, Jean-Benoît and Julie Barlow 2007. *The Story of French.* Toronto: Vintage.

Nahir, Moshe 1977. The five aspects of language planning. *Language Problems and Language Planning* 1: 107–23.

Nairn, Tom 1977. *The Break-up of Britain: Crisis and Neo-nationalism.* London: New Left Books.

1997. *Faces of Nationalism.* London: Verso.

2003. It's not the economy, stupid. *Times Literary Supplement*, 9 May.

Napier Commission (Royal Commission of Inquiry into the Conditions of the Crofters and Cottars in the Highlands and Islands of Scotland) 1884. *Report, with Appendices.* Edinburgh: Her Majesty's Stationery Office.

Nash, Ronald 1995. Review of *We Were Not the Savages* [Daniel Paul]. *Journal of Multilingual and Multicultural Development* 16: 331–3.

Nelson, Leif and Joseph Simmons 2007. Moniker maladies: When names sabotage success. *Psychological Science* 18: 1106–12.

Neustupný, Jirí 1983. Towards a paradigm for language planning. *Language Planning Newsletter*, 9(4).

Niedzielski, Nancy 2005. Linguistic purism from several perspectives: Views from the 'secure' and 'insecure'. In Nils Langer and Winifred Davies (eds.), *Linguistic Purism in the Germanic Languages.* Berlin: Walter de Gruyter.

Nielsen, Kai 1996. Cultural nationalism: Neither ethnic nor civic. In Ronald Beiner (ed.), *Theorizing Nationalism.* Albany: State University of New York Press.

Novak, Michael 1972 / 1995. *The Rise of the Unmeltable Ethnics.* New York: Macmillan. [The updated edition was published in 1995 by Transaction, New Brunswick, NJ.]

O'Brien, Conor Cruise 1973. On the rights of minorities. *Commentary* 55(6): 46–50.

O'Brien, Conor Cruise 1988a. *Passion and Cunning*. London: Weidenfeld & Nicolson.

O'Brien, Conor Cruise 1988b. *Godland*. Cambridge, MA: Harvard University Press.

O'Brien, Gerard 1989. The strange death of the Irish language, 1780–1800. In Gerard O'Brien (ed.), *Parliaments, Politics and People: Essays in Eighteenth-Century Irish History*. Dublin: Irish Academic Press.

Ó Conaire, Breandán 1973. Flann O'Brien, *An Béal Bocht* and other Irish matters. *Irish University Review* 3: 121–40.

O'Donoghue, Daniel 1947. Nationality and language. In Columban League (ed.), *Irish Man – Irish Nation*. Cork: Mercier.

O'Faolain, Sean 1951. The death of nationalism. *The Bell* 17(2): 44–53.

Ogbu, John 1999. Beyond language: Ebonics, proper English and identity in a Black-American speech community. *American Educational Research Journal* 36: 147–84.

Ó Glaisne, Risteárd 1967. *The Irish Language: A Protestant Speaks to his Co-Religionists*. Longford: Nua-Éire.

1981. Irish and the Protestant tradition. *The Crane Bag* 5(2): 33–44.

2000. *De Bhunadh Protastúnach nó Rian Chonnradh na Gaeilge*. Dublin: Carbad.

O'Leary, Philip 1994. *The Prose Literature of the Gaelic Revival, 1881–1921: Ideology and Innovation*. University Park, PA: Pennsylvania State University Press.

Olender, Maurice 1989. *Les langues du paradis*. Paris: Gallimard – Le Seuil.

1994. Europe, or how to escape Babel. *History and Theory* 33(4): 5–25.

Olson, Kenneth 2007. SIL International: An insider's view. Paper presented at the *Linguistic Society of America* conference, Anaheim, January 2007.

Omoniyi, Tope 2006a. Hierarchy of identities. In Tope Omoniyi and Goodith White (eds.), *The Sociolinguistics of Identity*. London: Continuum.

2006b. Societal multilingualism and multifaithism [sic]: A sociology of language and religion perspective. In Tope Omoniyi and Joshua Fishman (eds.), *Explorations in the Sociology of Language and Religion*. Amsterdam: Benjamins.

Omoniyi, Tope and Joshua Fishman (eds.) 2006. *Explorations in the Sociology of Language and Religion*. Amsterdam: Benjamins.

Orridge, Andrew 1981. Varieties of nationalism. In Leonard Tivey (ed.), *The Nation State: The Formation of Modern Politics*. Oxford: Martin Robertson.

Ortner, Sherry 1996. *Making Gender*. Boston: Beacon.

Orwell, George 1941 / 1964. England your England. In *Inside the Whale and Other Essays*. Harmondsworth: Penguin. [First published by Secker & Warburg in 1941 in the three-part collection, *The Lion and the Unicorn*.]

1944/1970. As I please. *Tribune*, 30 June and 28 July, 1944. [These and other 'As I please' articles – Orwell's regular weekly contribution to *Tribune*, between December 1943 and February 1945 – are presented in *The Collected Essays, Journalism and Letters of George Orwell*, edited in four volumes by Sonia Orwell and Ian Angus. Harmondsworth, Middlesex:

Penguin. The citations here are found on pp. 208 and 230 of the third volume.]

1945/1965. Notes on nationalism. In *Decline of the English Murder and Other Essays*. Harmondsworth: Penguin. [First published in *Polemic* 1, October 1945.]

Özkırımlı, Umut 2000. *Theories of Nationalism: A Critical Introduction*. New York: St Martin's Press.

2005. *Contemporary Debates on Nationalism: A Critical Engagement*. Basingstoke: Palgrave.

Özkırımlı, Umut and Steven Grosby 2007. Nationalism theory debate: The antiquity of nations. *Nations and Nationalism* 13: 523–37.

Pagano, Rosanne 2005. Eskimos try new explosive in whale kill. *Associated Press*, 10 November.

Pandey, Anjali 2000. *Symposium on the Ebonics Debate and African American Language* [special section of *World Englishes* 19:1].

Paré, Ambroise 1564. *Dix livres de la chirurgie*. Paris: Le Royer.

Paton, David 2006. *The Clergy and the Clearances: The Church and the Highland Crisis, 1790–1850*. Edinburgh: John Donald.

Patterson, Orlando 1977. *Ethnic Chauvinism: The Reactionary Impulse*. New York: Stein & Day.

Pečujlić, Miroslav, Gregory Blue and Anouar Abdel-Malek (eds.) 1982. *Science and Technology in the Transformation of the World*. London: Macmillan.

Pearse, Padraic 1916. *The Murder Machine*. Dublin: Whelan.

Pelham, Brett, Mauricio Carvallo and John Jones 2005. Implicit egotism. *Current Directions in Psychological Science* 14: 106–10.

Penashue, Peter 2000. Untitled. *Globe & Mail* [Toronto], 7 December.

Penny, Laura 2005. *Your Call is Important to Us: The Truth About Bullshit*. Toronto: McClelland & Stewart.

Pennycook, Alastair 2004. Language policy and the ecological turn. *Language Policy* 3: 213–39.

Pennycook, Alastair and Sophie Coutand-Marin 2003. Teaching English as a missionary language. *Discourse: Studies in the Cultural Politics of Education* 24: 337–53.

Pennycook, Alastair and Sinfree Makoni 2005. The modern mission: The language effects of Christianity. *Journal of Language, Identity and Education* 4: 137–55.

Peritz, Ingrid 2007. Protest letter's signatories warn against growing xenophobia in Quebec. *Globe & Mail* [Toronto], 2 November.

Perkins, John 2004. *Confessions of an Economic Hit Man*. New York: Plume.

Petyt, K. Malcolm 1980. *The Study of Dialect*. London: André Deutsch.

Phillips, Anne 2007. *Multiculturalism Without Culture*. Princeton, NJ: Princeton University Press.

Phillips, Patrick 2007. *The Challenge of Relativism*. London: Continuum.

Phillipson, Robert 1992. *Linguistic Imperialism*. Oxford: Oxford University Press.

2002. Review of *The Dominance of English as a Language of Science* [Ulrich Ammon]. *Journal of Language, Identity and Education* 1: 163–9.

2003. *English-Only Europe? Challenging Language Policy*. London: Routledge.

Phillipson, Robert and Tove Skutnabb-Kangas 1996. English only worldwide, or language ecology. *TESOL Quarterly* 30: 429–52.

Picard, André 1994. *Québécois* voices. *Globe & Mail* [Toronto], 3 March.

1998. Quebec group would deny vote to non-French speakers. *Globe & Mail* [Toronto], 3 April.

Pickering, William (ed.) 1992. *Anthropology and Missionaries: Some Case Studies*. Oxford: Oxford University Anthropological Society [= *JASO (Journal of the Anthropological Society of Oxford)* 22(2)].

Pike, Kenneth 1962. *With Heart and Mind: A Personal Synthesis of Scholarship and Devotion*. Grand Rapids, Michigan: Eerdmans.

Polzenhagen, Frank and René Dirven 2004. Rationalist or romantic model in language policy and globalisation. Paper presented at the LAUD (Linguistic Agency, University of Duisburg) conference, Landau.

Pompa, Cristina 2003. *Religião como tradução: missionários, Tupi e 'Tapuia' no Brasil colonial*. Bauru: Editora da Universidade do Sagrade Coração.

Poole, Ross 1999. *Nation and Identity*. London: Routledge.

Porter, John 1972/1980. Dilemmas and contradictions of a multi-ethnic society. In Jay Goldstein and Rita Bienvenue (eds.), *Ethnicity and Ethnic Relations in Canada*. Toronto: Butterworth. [The second edition appeared in 1980.]

1975. Ethnic pluralism in Canadian perspective. In Nathan Glazer and Daniel Moynihan (eds.), *Ethnicity: Theory and Experience*. Cambridge, MA: Harvard University Press.

Poser, William 2006. The names of the First Nations languages of British Columbia. Unpublished paper.

Pritchard, Rosalind 2004. Protestants and the Irish language: Historical heritage and current attitudes in Northern Ireland. *Journal of Multilingual and Multicultural Development* 25: 62–82.

Provine, Robert, Robert Spencer and Darcy Mandell 2007. Emotional expression online. *Journal of Language and Social Psychology* 26: 299–307.

Puar, Jasbir 2007. *Terrorist Assemblages*. Durham, NC: Duke University Press.

Pullum, Geoffrey 1991. *The Great Eskimo Vocabulary Hoax, and Other Irreverent Essays on the Study of Language*. Chicago: University of Chicago Press.

Purchas, Samuel 1613. *Purchas his Pilgrimage, or Relations of the World and the Religions observed in All Ages and Places Discouered, from the Creation unto this Present*... London: Fetherstone.

Quirk, Randolph 1982. *Style and Communication in the English Language*. London: Edward Arnold.

Ramirez, J. David, Terrence Wiley, Gerde de Klerk, Enid Lee and Wayne Wright (eds.) 2005. *Ebonics: The Urban Education Debate*. 2nd edn. Clevedon: Multilingual Matters.

Rampton, Ben 2007. Neo-Hymesian linguistic ethnography in the United Kingdom. *Journal of Sociolinguistics* 11: 584–607.

Rampton, Ben, Karin Tusting, Janet Maybin, Richard Barwell, Angela Creese and Vally Lytra 2004. U.K. linguistic ethnography: A discussion paper. (www.ling-ethnog.org.uk)

Rampton, Ben, Janet Maybin and Karin Tusting (eds.) 2007. *Linguistic Ethnography: Links, Problems and Possibilities.* Oxford: Blackwell [= *Journal of Sociolinguistics* 11(5)].

Rappaport, Joanne 1984. Las misiones protestantes y la resistencia indígena en el sur de Colombia. *América Indígena* 44: 111–27.

Ratzinger, Joseph 2005a. Cardinal Ratzinger on Europe's crisis of culture. (www.zenit.org/article-13705?l=english). [Ratzinger's lecture was given in Subiaco, on 1 April, the day before the death of John Paul II.]

2005b. *L'Europa di Benedetto nella crisi delle culture.* Siena: Cantagalli.

Rawls, John 1999. *The Law of Peoples.* Cambridge, MA: Harvard University Press.

Read, E. 1980. Hercules or Hydra? Similarities and differences amongst evangelical missions. *Survival International* 4: 9–16.

Renan, Ernest 1882/1947. Qu'est-ce qu'une nation? In Henriette Psichari (ed.), *Oeuvres complètes de Ernest Renan.* Paris: Calmann-Lévy. [The essay first appeared in 1882.]

Resnick, Philip 2005. Cosmopolitanism and nationalism. In Alain Dieckhoff and Christophe Jaffrelot (eds.), *Revisiting Nationalism.* London: Hurst.

Rich, F. 1997. The Ebonic plague. *Globe & Mail* [Toronto], 9 January.

Richards, Eric 1973. How tame were the Highlanders during the Clearances? *Scottish Studies* 17(1): 35–50.

1982. *A History of the Highland Clearances*, Vol. 1: *Agrarian Transformation and the Evictions, 1746–1886.* London: Croom Helm.

Rickford, John 2002. Linguistics, education and the Ebonics firestorm. In James Alatis, Heidi Hamilton and Ai-Hui Tan (eds.), *Georgetown University Round Table on Languages and Linguistics 2000: Linguistics, Language and the Professions: Education, Journalism, Law, Medicine and Technology.*

de Rivarol, Antoine 1784. *De l'universalité de la langue francaise.* Berlin: Bailly & Dessenne.

Robb, Graham 2007. *The Discovery of France.* London: Picador.

Roberts, Marie 1995. Masonics, metaphor and misogyny. In Peter Burke and Roy Porter (eds.), *Languages and Jargons: Contributions to a Social History of Language.* Cambridge: Polity.

Robinson, W. Peter (ed.) 1996. *Social Groups and Identities.* Oxford: Butterworth-Heinemann.

Robinson, W. Peter and Howard Giles (eds.) 2001. *The New Handbook of Language and Social Psychology.* New York: Wiley.

Romaine, Suzanne 1997. Review of *Verbal Hygiene* [Deborah Cameron]. *Language in Society* 26: 423–6.

1999. *Communicating Gender.* Mahwah, NJ: Erlbaum.

Rosenzweig & Co. 2008. *The Annual Rosenzweig Report on Women at the Top Levels of Corporate Canada*. Toronto: Rosenzweig.

Roshwald, Aviel 2006. *The Endurance of Nationalism: Ancient Roots and Modern Dilemmas*. Cambridge: Cambridge University Press.

Rosie, Anthony 2004. Cyber identity. In Gary Taylor and Steve Spencer (eds.), *Social Identities: Multidisciplinary Approaches*. London: Routledge.

Royce, Anya 1982. *Ethnic Identity*. Bloomington: Indiana University Press.

Royer, Jean 1995. *Chronique d'une académie, 1944–1994: de l'Académie canadienne-française à l'Académie des lettres du Québec*. Montreal: l'Hexagone.

Rubin, Milka 1998. The language of creation or the primordial language: A case of cultural polemics in antiquity. *Journal of Jewish Studies* 49: 306–33.

Russell, Bertrand 1950. *Unpopular Essays*. London: Allen & Unwin.

Ryan, Alan 1984. More country matters. *Sunday Times*, 4 March.

Ryan, Ellen Bouchard 1979. Why do low-prestige varieties persist? In Howard Giles and Robert St Clair (eds.), *Language and Social Psychology*. Oxford: Blackwell.

Ryan, Ellen Bouchard and Miguel Carranza 1975. Evaluative reactions of adolescents toward speakers of Standard English and Mexican American accented English. *Journal of Personality and Social Psychology* 31: 855–63.

Ryan, Ellen Bouchard, Miguel Carranza and Robert Moffie 1977. Reactions towards varying degrees of accentedness in the speech of Spanish-English bilinguals. *Language and Speech* 20: 267–73.

Safran, William 2005. Language and nation-building in Israel: Hebrew and its rivals. *Nations and Nationalism* 11: 43–63.

2008. Language, ethnicity and religion: A complex and persistent linkage. *Nations and Nationalism* 14: 171–90.

Sahlins, Peter 1989. *Boundaries: The Making of France and Spain in the Pyrenees*. Berkeley: University of California Press.

Salkie, Raphael 2004. Blair's lessons in ethics of respect. *Times Higher Education Supplement*, 8 October.

Sallabank, Julia 2006. Guernsey French, identity and language endangerment. In Tope Omoniyi and Goodith White (eds.), *The Sociolinguistics of Identity*. London: Continuum.

Salminen, Tapani 1998. Minority languages in a society in turmoil: The case of the northern languages of the Russian Federation. In Nicholas Ostler (ed.), *Endangered Languages*. Bath: Foundation for Endangered Languages.

Samarin, William 1972. *Tongues of Men and Angels*. New York: Macmillan.

Samuels, David 2006. Bible translation and medecine man talk: Missionaries, indexicality, and the 'language expert' on the San Carlos Apache Reservation. *Language in Society* 35: 529–57.

Sapir, Edward 1921. *Language*. New York: Harcourt Brace.

Sattel, Jack 1983. Men, inexpressiveness and power. In Barrie Thorne, Cheris Kramarae and Nancy Henley (eds.), *Language, Gender and Society*. Rowley, MA: Newbury House.

Sawyer, John 2001. Religion and language. In Rajend Mesthrie (ed.), *Concise Encyclopedia of Sociolinguistics*. Amsterdam: Elsevier.

Sawyer, John and J. M. Y. Simpson (eds.) 2001. *Concise Encyclopedia of Language and Religion*. Amsterdam: Elsevier.

Scherer, Klaus and Howard Giles (eds.) 1979. *Social Markers in Speech*. Cambridge: Cambridge University Press.

Schiffman, Harold 1996. *Linguistic Culture and Language Policy*. London: Routledge.

Schnapper, Dominique 1994. *Communauté des cityoyens: sur l'idée moderne de nation*. Paris: Gallimard.

van Schrieck, Adriaen 1614. *Van t'beghin der eerster Volcken van Europen, in sonderheyt van den Oorspronck ende saecken der Neder-Landren...* Ypre: Bellet.

Schulz, Muriel 1990. The semantic derogation of woman. In Deborah Cameron (ed.), *The Feminist Critique of Language: A Reader*. London: Routledge.

Schumacher, Ernst 1973. *Small is Beautiful: A Study of Economics as if People Mattered*. London: Blond & Briggs. [My citation is from the 1974 Sphere paperback.]

Scott-Moncrieff, George 1932. Balmorality. In David Thomson (ed.), *Scotland in Quest of her Youth*. Edinburgh: Oliver & Boyd.

Séguin, Rhéal 2000. Bouchard given mandate to set his own agenda. *Globe & Mail* [Toronto], 8 May.

  2007a. PQ would require that immigrants learn French. *Globe & Mail* [Toronto], 19 October.

  2007b. Quebec unveils plan to attract more immigrants. *Globe & Mail* [Toronto], 2 November.

Semmel, Bernard 1984. *John Stuart Mill and the Pursuit of Virtue*. New Haven, CT: Yale University Press.

Seton-Watson, Hugh 1982. The history of nations. *Times Higher Education Supplement*, 27 August.

Shafer, Boyd 1955. *Nationalism. Myth and Reality*. New York: Harcourt Brace.

Sharp, Henry 1920. *Selections from Educational Records, Part 1: 1781–1839*. Calcutta: Superintendent of Government Printing.

Shibutani, Tamotsu and Kian Kwan 1965. *Ethnic Stratification*. New York: Macmillan.

Simon, Richard 1678. *Histoire critique du Vieux Testament*. Paris: Billaine.

Skene-Melvin, David 1989. Advocating bigotry. *Globe & Mail* [Toronto], 30 December.

Skutnabb-Kangas, Tove 1986. Who wants to change what and why. In Bernard Spolsky (ed.), *Language and Education in Multilingual Settings*. Clevedon: Multilingual Matters.

  2000. *Linguistic Genocide in Education or Worldwide Diversity and Human Rights*. Mahwah, NJ: Erlbaum.

2002. Some philosophical and ethical aspects of ecologically based language planning. In Annette Boudreau, Lise Dubois, Jacques Maurais and Grant McConnell (eds.), *L'écologie des langues*. Paris: L'Harmattan.

Smith, Anthony 1971. *Theories of Nationalism*. London: Duckworth.

1986. *The Ethnic Origins of Nations*. Oxford: Blackwell.

1990. The supersession of nationalism? *International Journal of Comparative Sociology* 31: 1–31.

1991. *National Identity*. London: Penguin.

1992. National identity and the idea of European unity. *International Affairs* 68: 55–76.

1995. *Nations and Nationalism in a Global Era*. Cambridge: Polity.

1996. Nations and their pasts. *Nations and Nationalism* 2: 358–65.

1998. *Nationalism and Modernism*. London: Routledge.

1999. *Myths and Memories of the Nation*. Oxford: Oxford University Press.

2001a. State and nation. In Athena Leoussi (ed.), *Encyclopaedia of Nationalism*. New Brunswick, NJ: Transaction.

2001b. Ethno-symbolism. In Athena Leoussi (ed.), *Encyclopaedia of Nationalism*. New Brunswick, NJ: Transaction.

2001c. *Nationalism: Theory, Ideology, History*. Cambridge: Polity.

2007. The power of ethnic traditions in the modern world. In Athena Leoussi and Steven Grosby (eds.), *Nationalism and Ethnosymbolism: History, Culture and Ethnicity in the Formation of Nations*. Edinburgh: Edinburgh University Press.

Smith, Donald 1990. *From the Land of Shadows: The Making of Grey Owl*. Saskatoon: Prairie Books.

Smith, Philip 1985. *Language, the Sexes and Society*. Oxford: Blackwell.

Smith, Russell 2007. Who knew 'nooz' was about morality? *Globe & Mail* [Toronto], 20 December.

Smitherman, Geneva (ed.) 1981a. *Black English and the Education of Black Children and Youth: Proceedings of the National Invitational Symposium on the King Decision*. Detroit: Center for Black Studies, Wayne State University.

1981b. What go round come round: *King* in perspective. *Harvard Educational Review* 51: 40–56.

2006. *Word From the Mother: Language and African Americans*. London: Routledge.

Snow, C. P. 1959. *The Two Cultures and the Scientific Revolution*. Cambridge: Cambridge University Press.

Snyder, Louis 1968. *The New Nationalism*. Ithaca, NY: Cornell University Press.

Sokal, Alan 2008. *Beyond the Hoax*. Oxford: Oxford University Press.

Sokal, Alan and Jean Bricmont 1997. *Impostures intellectuelles*. Paris: Jacob.

Sommers, Christina Hoff 2000. *The War Against Boys: How Misguided Feminism is Harming our Young Men*. New York: Simon & Schuster.

Spencer, John 1985. Language and development in Africa. In Nessa Wolfson and Joan Manes (eds.), *Language of Inequality*. The Hague: Mouton.

Spender, Dale 1980. *Man Made Language*. London: Routledge & Kegan Paul.

Spolsky, Bernard 1989. Remarks made at Fourth International Conference on Minority Languages, Ljouwert.

2003. Religion as a site of language contact. *Annual Review of Applied Linguistics* 23: 81–94.

2004. *Language Policy*. Cambridge: Cambridge University Press.

Sprat, Thomas 1667. *The History of the Royal-Society of London, for the Improving of Natural Knowledge*. London: Martyn & Allestry.

Stam, James 1976. *Inquiries into the Origin of Language*. New York: Harper & Row.

Staples, Brent 1997. The last train from Oakland. *The New York Times*, 24 January.

Stark, Andrew 1995. Vive le Québec anglophone! *Times Literary Supplement*, 21 September.

Steigerwald, David 2004. *Culture's Vanities: The Paradox of Cultural Diversity in a Globalized World*. Lanham, MD: Rowman & Littlefield.

Steinberg, Stephen 2001. *The Ethnic Myth*. Boston: Beacon.

Steiner, George 1967. *Language and Silence*. London: Faber & Faber.

1971. *In Bluebeard's Castle*. London: Faber & Faber.

1972. *Extraterritorial*. London: Faber & Faber.

1978. *On Difficulty*. Oxford: Oxford University Press.

1992. *After Babel: Aspects of Language and Translation*. 2nd edn. Oxford: Oxford University Press.

Stevenson, James 1997. Parizeau reinforces ethnic remarks. *Globe & Mail* [Toronto], 26 November.

Stewart, George 1975. *Names on the Globe*. New York: Oxford University Press.

Stoll, David 1982. *Fishers of Men or Founders of Empire? The Wycliffe Bible Translators in Latin America*. London: Zed Books.

1984. ¿Con que derecho adoctrinan a nuestros indígenas? La polémica en torno al Instituto Lingüístico de Verano. *América Indígena* 44: 9–24.

1990. *Is Latin America Turning Protestant? The Politics of Evangelical Growth*. Berkeley: University of California Press.

Street, Richard and Howard Giles 1982. Speech accommodation theory. In Michael Roloff and Charles Berger (eds.), *Social Cognition and Communication*. London: Sage.

Suleiman, Camelia and Daniel O'Connell 2008. Gender differences in the media interviews of Bill and Hillary Clinton. *Journal of Psycholinguistic Research* 37: 33–48.

Sunderland, Jane 2006. *Language and Gender: An Advanced Resource Book*. London: Routledge.

Tajfel, Henri (ed.) 1978. *Differentiation Between Social Groups*. London: Academic Press.

(ed.) 1982. *Social Identity and Intergroup Relations*. Cambridge: Cambridge University Press.

Tannen, Deborah 1986. *That's Not What I Meant!* New York: Morrow.

1990. *You Just Don't Understand: Women and Men in Conversation.* New York: Morrow.

(ed.) 1993. *Gender and Conversational Interaction.* New York: Oxford University Press.

1994. *Gender and Discourse.* New York: Oxford University Press.

Tannen, Deborah, Shari Kendall and Cynthia Gordon (eds.) 2007. *Family Talk* New York: Oxford University Press.

Tanner, Marcus 2004. *The Last of the Celts.* New Haven, CT: Yale University Press.

Targett, Simon 1995. Final frontiers. *Times Higher Education Supplement,* 10 November.

Taylor, Charles 1992. *Multiculturalism and 'The Politics of Recognition'.* Princeton, NJ: Princeton University Press.

1994. *Multiculturalism: Examining the Politics of Recognition.* Princeton, NJ: Princeton University Press. [An expanded version of Taylor, 1992.]

Taylor, Gary and Steve Spencer (eds.) 2004. *Social Identities: Multidisciplinary Approaches.* London: Routledge.

Terralingua 1999. *Statement of Purpose.* Hancock, MI: Terralingua.

TESOL 2000. *TESOL Board of Directors Reaffirms Position on Language Rights.* Alexandria, VA: TESOL.

Thériault, Lise 2005. *La pleine participation à la société québécoise des communautés noires.* Québec: Ministère de l'Immigration et des Communautés Culturelles.

Theroux, Paul 1984. *The Kingdom by the Sea.* Harmondsworth: Penguin.

Thomas, George 1991. *Linguistic Purism.* London: Longman.

Titley, Alan 2000. *A Pocket History of Gaelic Culture.* Dublin: O'Brien.

Todd, Loreto 1997. Ebonics: An evaluation. *English Today* 13(3): 13–17.

Touraine, Alain 1997. *Pourrons-nous vivre ensemble?* Paris: Fayard.

Toynbee, Arnold 1956. *A Study of History.* Oxford: Oxford University Press. [A 2-volume abridgement by David Somervell.]

von Treitschke, Heinrich 1916. *Politics.* London: Constable.

Trevelyan, George Macaulay 1949–1952. *Illustrated English Social History,* 4 vols. London: Longmans, Green.

Trevor-Roper, Hugh and George Urban 1989. Aftermaths of empire. *Encounter* 73(5): 3–16.

Trudgill, Peter 1972. Sex, covert prestige and linguistic change in the urban British English of Norwich. *Language in Society* 1: 179–95.

1975. *Accent, Dialect and the School.* London: Edward Arnold.

1983. *On Dialect.* Oxford: Blackwell.

2000. *Sociolinguistics: An Introduction to Language and Society.* 4th edn. London: Penguin.

Tucker, G. Richard and Wallace Lambert 1969. White and Negro listeners' reactions to various American-English dialects. *Social Forces* 47: 463–8.

Turner, John 1991. *Social Influence.* Milton Keynes: Open University Press.

Turner, John and Howard Giles (eds.) 1981. *Intergroup Behaviour*. Oxford: Blackwell.

Tusting, Karin and Janet Maybin 2007. Linguistic ethnography and interdisciplinarity. *Journal of Sociolinguistics* 11: 575–83.

Uzelac, Gordana 2002. The morphogenesis of nation. In Siniša Malešević and Mark Haugaard (eds.), *Making Sense of Collectivity: Ethnicity, Nationalism and Globalization*. London: Pluto Press.

Vallancey, Charles 1772. *An Essay on the Antiquity of the Irish Language . . . with a Preface Proving Ireland to be Thule of the Ancients*. Dublin: Powell.

Vallee, Frank 1981. The sociology of John Porter: Ethnicity as anachronism. *Canadian Review of Sociology and Anthropology* 18: 639–50.

Vallins, George 1954. *Spelling*. London: André Deutsch.

Vandenbussche, Wim, Roland Willemyns, Jetje de Groof and Eline Vanhecke 2005. Taming thistles and weeds amidst the wheat: Language gardening in nineteenth-century Flanders. In Nils Langer and Winifred Davies (eds.), *Linguistic Purism in the Germanic Languages*. Berlin: de Gruyter.

Van Der Myl, Abraham 1612. *Lingva Belgica . . .* Lugdvni Batavorvm [Leiden]: Commelin.

Venezky, Richard 1981. Non-standard language and reading: Ten years later. In John Edwards (ed.), *The Social Psychology of Reading*. Silver Spring, MD: Institute of Modern Languages.

Verstegan, Richard [Richard Rowlands] 1605. *A Restitution of Decayed Intelligence, in Antiquities: concerning the most Noble and Renowned English Nation . . .* London: Norton & Bill. [The book was printed, by Verstegan himself, in Antwerp.]

Vico, Giambattista 1725. *Principj* [sic] *di una scienza nuova . . .* Naples: Mosca.

Viroli, Maurizio 1995. *For Love of Country: An Essay on Patriotism and Nationalism*. Oxford: Clarendon.

Vossler, Karl 1932. *The Spirit of Language in Civilization*. London: Routledge.

Waddington, Dave 2004. Music. In Gary Taylor and Steve Spencer (eds.), *Social Identities: Multidisciplinary Approaches*. London: Routledge.

Walker, Daniel 1972. Leibniz and language. *Journal of the Warburg and Courtauld Institutes* 35: 294–307.

Walvin, James 2002. Should we pay for the sins of our fathers? *Times Higher Education Supplement*, 9 August.

Wardhaugh, Ronald 1987. *Languages in Competition*. Oxford: Blackwell.
  2006. *An Introduction to Sociolinguistics*. 5th edn. Oxford: Blackwell.

Waterman, John 1966. *A History of the German Language*. Seattle: University of Washington Press.

Watson, Paul 1999. Untitled. *Globe & Mail* [Toronto], 20 May.

Webb, Nick 2005. *The Dictionary of Bullshit*. London: Robson.

Weber, Max 1910/1961. *From Max Weber: Essays in Sociology*, translated and edited by Hans Gerth and Charles Wright Mills. London: Routledge & Kegan Paul.

1922/1968. *Economy and Society*, translated by Ephraim Fischoff; edited by Günther Roth and Claus Wittich. New York: Bedminster. [Originally *Wirtschaft und Gesellschaft*, 1922.]

Webster, Noah 1783. *Grammatical Institutes, Part 1*. Hartford, CT: Hudson & Goodwin.

1789. *Dissertations on the English Language*. Boston: Thomas.

1828. *An American Dictionary of the English Language*. New York: Converse.

Weinberg, Henry 1995. National character, 'Jewish writing' and linguistic determinism. *Nineteenth Century French Studies* 23: 488–94.

Weiner, Brian 2005. *Sins of the Parents: The Politics of National Apologies in the United States*. Philadelphia: Temple University Press.

Weinreich, Max 1945. Der YIVO un di problemen fun undzer tsayt. *YIVO-Bleter* 25(1): 3–18.

Weinreich, Uriel 1953. *Languages in Contact*. The Hague: Mouton.

Weir, Anthony 1973. Irish newspeak. In Robert Bell, Gerald Fowler and Ken Little (eds.), *Education in Great Britain and Ireland: A Source Book*. London: Routledge & Kegan Paul.

Wente, Margaret 2007. White guilt, dead children . . . *Globe & Mail* [Toronto], 13 October.

Wetherell, Margaret 2007. A step too far: Discursive psychology, linguistic ethnography and questions of identity. *Journal of Sociolinguistics* 11: 661–81.

Wexler, Paul 1974. *Purism and Language*. Bloomington: Indiana University Research Center for the Language Sciences.

Widen, Sherri and James Russell 2002. Gender and preschoolers' perception of emotion. *Merrill-Palmer Quarterly* 48: 248–62.

Wiebe, Rudy 1977. *The Scorched-Wood People*. Toronto: McClelland & Stewart.

Wilkie, William 1757. *The Epigoniad*. Edinburgh: Kincaid & Bell.

Wilkins, John 1668. *An Essay Towards a Real Character, and a Universal Language*. London: Gellibrand.

Williams, Frederick 1974. The identification of linguistic attitudes. *Linguistics* 136: 21–32.

1976. *Explorations of the Linguistic Attitudes of Teachers*. Rowley, MA: Newbury House.

Williams, Glyn 1981. The problematic in the sociology of language. *Journal of Multilingual and Multicultural Development* 2: 219–25.

1986. Language planning or language expropriation? *Journal of Multilingual and Multicultural Development* 7: 509–18.

Williams, John, Susan Bennett and Deborah Best 1975. Awareness and expression of sex stereotypes in young children. *Developmental Psychology* 11: 635–42.

Williams, John and Deborah Best 1982. *Measuring Sex Stereotypes: A Thirty-Nation Study*. Beverly Hills, CA: Sage.

1990. *Sex and Psyche: Gender and Self Viewed Cross-Culturally*. Newbury Park, CA: Sage.

Williams, John, Howard Giles and John Edwards 1977. Comparative analyses of sex-trait stereotypes in the United States, England and Ireland. In Ype Poortinga (ed.), *Basic Problems in Cross-Cultural Psychology*. Amsterdam: Swets & Zeitlinger.

Williams, Melissa 1998. *Voice, Trust and Memory: Marginalized Groups and the Failure of Liberal Representation*. Princeton, NJ: Princeton University Press.

Williams, Robert (ed.) 1975. *Ebonics: The True Language of Black Folks*. St Louis: Institute of Black Studies.

Wilson, James 1998. *The Earth Shall Weep: A History of Native America*. New York: Grove.

Wilson, Thomas and Hastings Donnan (eds.) 1998. *Border Identities: Nation and State at International Frontiers*. Cambridge: Cambridge University Press.

Wojtas, Olga 1990. Shrugging off the guru's mantle. *Times Higher Education Supplement*, 26 January.

Wolff, Hans 1959. Intelligibility and inter-ethnic attitudes. *Anthropological Linguistics* 1: 34–41.

Wolfram, Walt 1998. Language ideology and dialect: Understanding the Oakland Ebonics controversy. *Journal of English Linguistics* 26: 108–21.

2005. Ebonics and linguistic science: Clarifying the issues. In J. David Ramirez, Terrence Wiley, Gerda de Klerk, Enid Lee and Wayne Wright (eds.), *Ebonics: The Urban Education Debate*. 2nd edn. Clevedon: Multilingual Matters.

Worm, Ole (Olaus [Olins] Wormius) 1636. *Rúnir, seu Danica literatura antiqvissima* . . . Hafnia [Copenhagen]: Martzan. [*Rúnir*, or *Runer*, means 'in the Runic characters'.]

Wright, Wayne 2005. Scholarly references and news titles. In J. David Ramirez, Terrence Wiley, Gerda de Klerk, Enid Lee and Wayne Wright (eds.), *Ebonics: The Urban Education Debate*. 2nd edn. Clevedon: Multilingual Matters.

Wyld, Henry 1934. *The Best English*. Oxford: Clarendon.

Yack, Bernard 1999a. The myth of the civic nation. In Ronald Beiner (ed.), *Theorizing Nationalism*. Albany: State University of New York Press.

1999b. Review of *Community of Citizens* [Dominique Schnapper]. *American Journal of Sociology* 104: 1581–3.

Yakabuski, Konrad 2007. Young, diverse Quebec is curiously attracted to its ancestors. *Globe & Mail* [Toronto], 3 November.

Young, Mitchell, Eric Zuelow and Andreas Sturm (eds.) 2007. *Nationalism in a Global Era: The Persistence of Nations*. London: Routledge.

Yuval-Davis, Nira 2001. Gender relations and the nation. In Alexander Motyl (ed.), *Encyclopedia of Nationalism*. London & New York: Academic Press.

Ziff, Bruce and Pratima Rao (eds.) 1997. *Borrowed Power: Essays on Cultural Appropriation*. New Brunswick, NJ: Rutgers University Press.

Zorn, Jeffrey 1982. Black English and the *King* decision. *College English* 44: 314–20.

Index

(Although there is some overlap, this index generally omits entries for material clearly to be found under a heading shown in the table of contents. Space constraints have meant that not all personal names have been listed here.)

academies   213–23
  Académie française   213, 216–17
  Académie royale des sciences et belles-lettres   218
  Accademia della Crusca   216
  Real Academia Española   217
accent   67, 74–5
accommodation theory   31–2
de Acosta, José   120
Acton, John (Lord)   171, 189, 191–2
Adams, John   222
Allen, Woody   232
Allport, Gordon   18
American Academy of Language and Belles Lettres   222
Anderson, Benedict   165, 170, 171, 192, 218, 221
Andreä, Johann   176, 268n6
Angelou, Maya   81
Arabic   104–5
Aramaic   104
Arnold, Matthew   239
associated language   56–7
attitude   6, 83–97
  confidence ratings   84–7
  'latitude of acceptance'   86
d'Azeglio, Massimo   172

Babel   106–7, 109
Bacon, Francis   176
Bakhtin, Mikhail   41
Baldauf, Richard   225, 229, 256
Barère, Bertrand   207
Barnes, Sandra   82

Barth, Fredrik   9, 25, 32, 157
Baugh, John   77, 79–81, 98
Bauman, Zygmunt   16
Beck, Cave   121
Belaney, Archie: *see* Grey Owl
belief   6, 84
du Bellay, Joachim   58, 62
Benedict XVI (Pope)   102
Ben-Yehuda, Eliezer   111–12
berdache   127
Berger, Peter   23
Berlin, Isaiah   209
bilingual education   79–80
Black English; *see also* Ebonics   6, 73–6, 82, 93–4, 97
Bloc Québécois   181, 183
Block, David   15
Bloomfield, Leonard   83, 214, 249
Boberg, Charles   69
Bolinger, Dwight   215
Bopp, Franz   62
Bouchard, Lucien   183
Bourdieu, Pierre   24–5
Bowdler, Thomas   144
Brown v. *Board of Education*   77
Brubaker, Rogers   15, 23, 151–2, 155, 266n4
Brumfit, Christopher   241
Bulwer, John   121

Calhoun, Craig   15, 178–9
Cameron, Deborah   51, 137–9, 141–2, 147, 149, 150
Campanella, Tommaso   176, 268n5

Carew, Richard   57
Carib Indians   132–3
Catholicism (in Ireland)   112–15
Caxton, William   215, 216
Charles V of Spain (Holy Roman
    Emperor)   57, 121
Chomsky, Noam   43, 187
clearances (Scottish)   115–18
Clinton, Hillary   140
Coates, Jennifer   139–40, 143–4, 147
code-switching   30
Comenius, Johann   121–2
Condry, John   132
Condry, Sandra   132
Connor, Walker   44, 153–4, 156, 163,
    164, 169–74, 179, 204, 267n6
Constantine I (Roman Emperor)   101
copula deletion   74
Cosby, Bill   81–2
covert prestige   68–71, 83–97
Crystal, David   215
cuius regio, eius religio   101, 124

Dalgarno, George   121
Darwin, Charles   230–1
Daudet, Alphonse   206
Davis, Thomas   205
Defoe, Daniel   219
dialect   5–6
    aesthetic quality   66–8
    attitude   83–97
    continua   63
    covert prestige   68–71, 83–97
    mutual intelligibility   63–5
    standard and nonstandard   62,
        65–71, 142–6
    'substandard'   65, 73
Dickens, Charles   21–2
dictionaries   220–3
discourse analysis   24–5
Donne, John   20
Dostoevski, Fyodor   41, 146

Eastman, Carol   56
Ebonics; see also Black English   6,
    75–6
Eco, Umberto   107–9, 124–5
Edenic language   103–10
Edwards, John passim
élite bilingualism   251

Elizabeth I of England   113
Eriksen, Thomas Hylland   155, 163,
    174
Erikson, Erik   15, 19, 261n3
Errington, Joseph   108, 119, 124–5
ethnocentrism   4, 48–51

Fichte, Johann   164, 170, 209–11
Fischer, John   133–4
Fishman, Joshua   43–4, 100, 123, 161,
    163, 192–3, 195, 197, 205, 209,
    227, 242, 269n2
folk bilingualism   252
Franklin, Benjamin   144, 222
French Revolution   168, 206–7
Freud, Sigmund   128, 149

Gaelic (Scottish)   115–18
Gaeltacht   114
Galton, Francis   128
Gans, Herbert   45, 160
Gates, Henry Louis   81
Geeraerts, Dirk   242–3
Gellner, Ernest   10, 49–50, 52, 165–6,
    170–1, 188, 195, 203, 208
gender   8–9, 71, 127–32, 150
Giles, Howard   26, 31–2, 66–7, 83, 88,
    94, 98, 134
Gladstone, William   28
Gleason, Philip   15, 261n2
glossolalia   105, 121
Goffman, Erving   18, 30, 130
Gramsci, Antonio   188
Graves, Robert   28, 148
Greenfeld, Liah   167
Grégoire, Henri (Abbé)   207
Grey Owl (Archie Belaney)   42
Groebner, Valentin   16
Grosby, Steven   21–2, 164
Grose, Francis   144
Gumperz, John   15
Gustav III of Sweden   218

Haeckel, Ernst   230–1
Hall, Stuart   16
Halliday, Michael   95
Haugen, Einar   208, 226–9, 231–2
Hebrew   103–12
    language academy   218
Henry VIII of England   113–14

Herder, Johann   163–4, 195, 205,
     208–10, 211, 233, 243
Herman, Simon   30
hijara   127
Himmelfarb, Milton   99, 123
Hobsbawm, Eric   45, 52, 164, 166
Holmes, Janet   133, 137, 144, 146–7,
     149
Hook, Sidney   43
Hooson, David   15
Hughes, Geoffrey   143
Hughes, Susan   143
von Humboldt, Wilhelm   205
Hutchinson, John   157, 163
Hyde, Douglas   193
hypercorrection   69

identity   2–3, 13–14
idiolect   21–2
Ignatieff, Michael   176–7
Innu   198
Institute for Swahili Research
     218
Irish   112–15
Isajiw, Wsevolod   156, 159, 161

Jackson, Jesse   81
Jakobson, Roman   43
Jeffery, Pamela   140
Jenkins, Jennifer   89
Jenkins, Richard   18–19, 26, 154–5,
     157, 159, 163, 165
Jespersen, Otto   54, 62, 149
Johnson, Samuel   38, 117, 128, 215–16,
     220–1
Jones, Thomas   61
Jones, William   109
Joos, Martin   29–30
Joseph, John   15, 20, 33

Kaplan, Robert   225, 229, 256
Kedourie, Elie   112, 163, 167–70, 174,
     191–2, 209, 228
Kierkegaard, Søren   54
'King Decision'   77–9
Kohn, Hans   11, 167–9, 170, 174,
     178
Komenský, Jan: *see* Comenius, Johann
Koestler, Arthur   205, 269n2
Kramarae, Cheris   147–8

Krech, Shepard   47–8
Kroskrity, Paul   15
Kymlicka, Will   152, 266n5

Labov, William   6, 69, 71–5, 78–9, 88,
     93, 98
Ladefoged, Peter   239
Lakoff, Robin   127–32, 135–7, 150
Lambert, Wallace   89–91
Landry, Bernard   181, 183
language
     attitude   83–97
     and biology   232–4
     change   61–3
     communicative   4–5, 55–7
     constructed   246
     creole   246
     and culture   55–7
     definition   53–5
     diversity   235–40
     ecology   12–13
     first ('Edenic')   103–10
     and gender   71, 138–9
     'goodness'   57–61
     literacy   235
     miscommunication   139–40
     oral history   40
     'pathology'   75–6
     pidgin   246
     planning   12
     politeness   142–6
     popular opinion   213–16
     relativism   60–1
     rights   240–1
     romanticism   241–3
     and silence   138–9
     social markers   88–9
     style   29–30
     swearing   142–6
     symbolic   4–5, 55–7
     verbosity   138–9
LaPiere, Robert   83
Lawrence, T. E. (of Arabia)   28
Leibniz, Gottfried   108, 218
Lenneberg, Eric   59
Leoussi, Athena   21–2
Le Page, Robert   15, 27
Liebowitz, Annie   140
Lincoln, Abraham   16, 138
lingua humana: *see* Edenic language

literacy: *see* language
logos 102–3, 110

Macaulay, Thomas 221
Mackey, William 218, 232
Macleod (M'Leod), Donald 115–17
Maffi, Luisa 233, 242–3
Makah 198–200
Makoni, Sinfree 36, 119
Malešević, Siniša 15
Mandela, Rolihlahla (Nelson) 36
Marx, Karl (and Marxism) 154–5, 165, 192, 203
matched-guise technique 89–93
May, Stephen 24, 164
Maybin, Janet 17
McArthur, Roshan 144
Mead, Margaret 43
mediating structures 23
Memphite Theology 102, 124
Mi'kmaq 200
Milgram, Stanley 84
Mill, John Stuart 171, 189–90, 204, 239
minimal groups 25–7, 35, 120, 263n5
Minogue, Kenneth 166
'minority-group reaction' 90–3
'Minute on Education' 221
missionaries 7–8, 118–25
Mistral, Frédéric 206
modernity 164–71
Montagu, Ashley 145
Montagu, Mary Wortley (Lady) 126
de Montaigne, Michel 20
Mount, Ferdinand 23, 166
Mühlhäusler, Peter 99, 120, 231–2, 234, 243–4
Müller, Max 107–8, 119
Murray, James 220

Nairn, Tom 165, 170
naming 3–4, 140–2
  pejorative 36–8, 39, 40, 263n6
Napier Commission 117
nationalism 9–12
  backward-looking 197–203
  civic 11, 175–80
  contemporary assessments 193–7
  general perspectives 189–93
  and modernity 164–71
  terminology 153–4, 171–4, 267n6

nation-state 172, 175, 267n1
'noble savage' 46–8

'Oakland Resolutions' 79–80
O'Brian, Patrick 36–8, 263n6
O'Brien, Conor Cruise 163, 203, 206
O'Brien, Flann 62
O'Faolain, Sean 191
Office québécois de la langue française 217
Ogbu, John 93–4
Omoniyi, Tope 17, 100, 123
Orwell, George 19, 25, 71, 187, 194, 200–1, 214, 236
Oxford English Dictionary 220

Paré, Ambroise 126, 264n1
Parizeau, Jacques 180–4
Parti Québécois 180–4
Patterson, Orlando 159, 172, 193
Pearse, Padraic 62, 65–71
Pennycook, Alastair 234, 238
Pentecost 105
Petyt, Malcolm 63
Philip V of Spain 217
Phillips, Anne 151–2, 265n2
Phillipson, Robert 234, 239, 243–4
Pike, Kenneth 102, 124
Popper, Karl 54
Porter, John 159, 194, 196
prescriptivism 12
Protestantism (in Scotland) 115–18
Pullum, Geoffrey 60
purism 12

Quebec
  aboriginal groups 152–3, 266n5
  nationalism 11, 180–5
  nationalist terminology 38–9
Quirk, Randolph 214, 216, 218, 223

Rampton, Ben 17, 51
Ratzinger, Joseph: *see* Benedict XVI
Received Pronunciation 67
relativism 4, 48–51
religion 6–8, 35–6, 40, 263n5
Renan, Ernest 154, 171, 190–1, 201, 204, 267n7
Rickford, John 77, 98
de Rivarol, Antoine 57
Romaine, Suzanne 139, 141

romanticism 206–7, 241–3
Rosten, Leo 21–2
Royal Society 219
Rubin, Milka 103–5, 125
Rush, Benjamin 222
Russell, Bertrand 194
Ryan, Ellen Bouchard 90–1, 96

Safran, William 6, 100, 111, 125, 205, 208, 264n4, 269n2
Sapir, Edward 53, 59–61, 206
Sapir–Whorf hypothesis: *see* Whorf
Schnapper, Dominique 179–80
Schumacher, Ernst 178
Skutnabb-Kangas, Tove 233, 239, 243–4
Smith, Anthony 21–2, 33, 157, 163, 166–70, 172, 174–6, 178, 187, 191–2, 197, 202, 204, 211, 267n2
Smith, Russell 213–14
Smitherman, Geneva 78, 94
Snow, C. P. 195
Sokal, Alan 24
Spencer, Steve 17–18
Spolsky, Bernard 1, 13, 43, 100, 102
Steiner, George 43, 49, 54–5, 100, 103, 123, 187, 195, 214, 246, 253–4, 263n2
stereotypes 34–5, 127–32, 150, 262n1
Stewart, George 36
Summer Institute of Linguistics 7–8, 120–1, 123–5
Swift, Jonathan 99, 219, 264n1
symbolic ethnicity 160–1

Tabouret-Keller, Andrée 15, 27
Tajfel, Henri 25–7, 32, 35, 120, 263n5

Talleyrand, Charles-Maurice 54
Tannen, Deborah 139, 148
Taylor, Charles 185, 196–7
Taylor, Gary 17–18
Terence (Publius Terentius) 20
Theroux, Paul 250
Thomas, George 212–13, 223
Townsend, William 101, 124
Toynbee, Arnold 193
Trevelyan, George Macaulay 144
Trudgill, Peter 65, 67–72, 88, 132–4
Tusting, Karin 17

de Valera, Eamon 206
Verstegan, Richard 219
Vico, Giambattista 107
Virchow, Rudolf 128
voice appropriation 3, 39–42
Voltaire (François-Marie Arouet) 209

Weber, Max 156, 159, 171, 187
Webster, Noah 222
Weinreich, Max 64
Weinreich, Uriel 250
Wetherell, Margaret 17
Whorf, Benjamin Lee (and Whorfianism) 60–1, 115
Wilkie, William 126, 265n3
Wilkins, John 105
William III of England 113
Williams, Frederick 85–6
Wittgenstein, Ludwig 54
Wolfram, Walt 80
Wycliffe Bible Translators 123–4
Wyld, Henry 65–7, 89

Zimbardo, Philip 84